BREAD AND STONES

BREAD AND STONES

Leadership
and the Struggle to
Reform the United Nations
World Food Programme

James Ingram

Library of Congress Control Number: 2006906013

Published by BookSurge, LLC
Charleston, South Carolina, USA

For sales please contact:
www.booksurge.com

ISBN 1–4196–4470–X (Paper)
ISBN 1-4196-2595-0 (Cloth)

Book and cover design, Tony Silver & Associates
Front cover photograph: WFP Executive Board, WFP/Rein Skullerud

FOR
ODETTE

What man is there of you,
whom if his son ask bread,
will he give him a stone?

Saint Matthew, chapter 7, verse 9

It must be considered
that there is nothing more difficult to carry out,
nor more doubtful of success,
nor more dangerous to handle,
than to initiate a new order of things.
For the reformer has enemies in all those
who profit by the old order and
only lukewarm defenders
in all those who would profit by the new.

Machiavelli: The Prince

CONTENTS

Illustrations:

FOREWORD

Gareth Evans*

The World Food Programme (WFP) is now not only the world's biggest humanitarian agency, but one of its most respected and effective. That it became so is very much the legacy of Jim Ingram, the organisation's Executive Director from 1982 to 1992, and the author of this intriguing case study.

The story he tells–about how the WFP emerged from being a demoralised dependency of the Food and Agriculture Organization (FAO) to become a fully fledged international agency in its own right–is much more than a tale of a bureaucratic dog-fight. But as such it is a classic: the FAO Director-General, Edouard Saouma, was a larger-than-life character determined to concede not an ounce of his hitherto absolute authority to anyone, whatever the rational merits of the case might be. And he was certainly not prepared to give in to an Australian diplomat, who had ideas of his own about how a global humanitarian mission should be run, and whose tenacity Saouma grossly underestimated.

The blow-by-blow account of the legal, financial, administrative, procedural–and always political–manoeuvres by which Saouma's campaign was conducted makes absorbing reading, although one's enjoyment of the spectacle, in all its excruciating pettiness, is tempered by remembering how high the stakes were for the hundreds of thousands of men, women and children who depended each year of the battle on the WFP's effective performance.

Ingram's side of the argument–presented here with as much academic detachment as one could reasonably expect from one of the antagonists–has unquestionably prevailed in the judgement both of his contemporaries and of history. That it did so is testament to his competence, leadership abilities and perseverance. It is also testament to another factor all too rare in public life: Ingram's willingness to take his personal interests out of the equation, and announce that he would seek no further public office when his reform task was done. Would that many more followed that lead.

For those with a less than boundless fascination for the specifics of the FAO/WFP relationship, the larger interest of this book lies in what it tells us about the UN system and international organisations generally, what they are uniquely capable of doing in the interests of global peace, development and human rights, but what they so often fall short of delivering.

We can see very starkly the dangers for effective management of North-South antagonism becoming endemic, as is now, unhappily, becoming apparent again after a period of some optimism that those days might have been behind us. We can see even more sharply the risks that flow from an absence of a spirit of collegiality between the component programs and agencies of the UN system all too apparent still. We see the paralysis or worse that all too often sets in when a Secretary-General or his Deputy lack any kind of directive power to get the fiefdoms marching to the same drummer. And we see how the politics of the system continually work to inhibit the Secretary-General exercising even the persuasive power that the office undoubtedly has.

The crucial ingredient is leadership–at the top of the system as a whole, and in each of its component parts. Chief executives, as Ingram puts it, must be the drivers of reform: competent and brave enough to break through, as the needs of effective delivery require, the culture of circumspection, mutual accommodation and tolerance of poor performance that prevails throughout the disfunctional UN family–and wise enough, if they do acquire real power within some part of the system, to exercise it well.

A better system of selection or election, institution by institution, is a necessary condition for better leadership: some important agencies–UNDP and UNHCR–have now introduced much more competitive and transparent processes, but there is a long way to go before this becomes routine. Having clearly defined term limits–in the case of the UN Secretary-Generalship itself, preferably a single seven-year term–is an important additional ingredient.

But in the end any system is only as good as those in ultimate control of it, and the member states of the UN system have more to answer for than any of the bureaucratic players for what continues to go wrong. Too often the oversight of the system and its components by member states, through the various governing bodies and budgetary or other supervisory committees, is wrongly focused or simply incompetent, producing, as Ingram acutely puts it, 'a vicious circle, by which government interest in the UN system declines because of the ineffectualness of the system and ineffectualness grows with the decline of good government oversight'.

My own strong view is that the failure of the 2005 World Summit to embrace more than a small handful of the many reform proposals before it—careful in conception, long in preparation and readily implementable as most of them were—was more than anything else a reflection of the failure of heads of government to take the process seriously, and work to persuade their peers. When there was that engagement, as in the case of the Canadian Prime Minister's highly focused efforts to win support for the 'responsibility to protect' principle, the results were very positive.

The further problem, nicely brought out in this volume, is that when governments do closely engage, at the highest level, in the working of the UN system, all too often it is to advance or protect national interests narrowly conceived, rather than to do what is best for the international community as a whole. And leadership posts are, unhappily, the primary currency in which national ambitions tend to be articulated and national achievement measured. Although there are occasional idiosyncratic exceptions to this rule—Ingram's own experience being a case in point, having to rely as he did for national support on an unusually non-chauvinist minister—too many governments too much of the time seem unembarrassed about playing within the UN system a brand of politics they would be embarrassed to be caught out playing at home.

There are no easy solutions for any of these problems. But what books like this can do—and what this one does with great clarity and force—is spell out what those problems are, and just how debilitating for so many people around the world is the failure to resolve them. The UN was founded, in the opening words of its Charter, 'to save succeeding generations from the scourge of war...to reaffirm faith in the dignity and worth of the human person...and to promote social progress and better standards of life in larger freedom'. For those men and women of goodwill and commitment throughout the international community who remain determined to make the UN system live up to these great ideals, Jim Ingram's book is both a handbook and an inspiration.

Brussels, 25 May 2006

*Gareth Evans is President and CEO of the International Crisis Group. He was Australian Foreign Minister (1988-96), Co-Chair of the International Commission on Intervention and State Sovereignty (2000-2001) and a Member of the Secretary-General's High Level Panel on Threats, Challenges and Change (2004)

ACKNOWLEDGMENTS

My ten years with the World Food Programme (WFP) were the most satisfying of my career. As the late Rick Throssell once said to me, 'You have the best job in the world: succoring the hungry and strengthening the United Nations'. That I could do something to further those goals owed everything to the support, idealism and integrity of the international civil servants who staffed the Programme. I cannot name them all or even the many who impressed me or to whom I am grateful. However, I do wish to express my thanks to those closest to me, namely Christine Mussapi, Salahuddin Ahmed, Tekle Tomlinson, William Barnsdale, Paul Kelloway, Mohammed Zejjari and Tun Myat. I was not easy to work for, I know, but their commitment to our goals never wavered.

When I left WFP, I was urged by many to write an anecdotal memoir but that had no immediate appeal, even though I did want to leave a permanent record of my WFP experience as a way of acknowledging my admiration of, and indebtedness to, my colleagues. However, ten years later I was ready to think again about the past. Reading for the first time through the diaries I kept of my service with WFP I felt they could provide the basis for an account of the process that led to the reforms we achieved, reforms that continue to be relevant. However, I no longer had access to secretarial or other assistance and found the prospect of writing a well documented historical memoir daunting. That I persevered owes a great deal to the encouragement of many, including my family, especially Odette, Catherine and Philippe. However, it was due to the persuasion of Dominic Kelly, and the practical help of his wife Sarah, that got me to make a serious beginning.

I am indebted to those who took the time to read through my first drafts. Their comments and suggestions gave me the confidence to persist with, and to improve upon, my manuscript. I am particularly indebted to Richard Jolly, William Maley, Raymond Hopkins, John Shaw, John Powell, Thomas

Weiss, Jens Schulthes, Amanda O'Connell, Paul Kelloway, Justin Stanwix, Sandy Ross, Gareth Evans and my children for their inputs. I am also grateful for the devotion and expertise of my editor Francesca Beddie. I hasten to add that they in no way bear any responsibility for the deficiencies my readers may find with *Bread and Stones*.

James Ingram
Canberra
June 2006

NOTES ON THE TEXT

1. All monetary values are in United States (US) dollars ($) expressed in contemporary values.
2. All quantities are given in metric tons, unless otherwise specified.
3. One billion equals 1,000 million.
4. To 1967, WFP was written in the American/Australian spelling. Thereafter it has been written in the English spelling 'World Food Programme'.
5. Names of persons are given in full when first refered to: thereafter by their last name only.
6. My diaries usually refered to my closest colleagues by their first names. However for consistency, diary extracts have been edited to show only their last names.
7 Extracts from the diary are italicised.

LIST OF ABBREVIATIONS

ACC	Advisory Committee on Coordination
ACIAR	Australian Centre for International Agricultural Research
ADAA	Australian Development Assistance Agency
ADAB	Australian Development Assistance Bureau
AusAID	Australian Agency for International Development
AFP	Additional Financial Procedures
CFA	Committee on Food Aid Policies and Programmes
CGIAR	Consultative Group on International Agricultural Research
ECOSOC	Economic and Social Council
ECA	Economic Commission for Africa
EC	European Commission
EA	External Auditor
EPLF	Eritrean People's Liberation Front
EU	European Union
FAC	Food Aid Convention
FAO	United Nations Food and Agriculture Organization
FRG	Federal Republic of Germany (West Germany)
GIEWS	Global Information and Early Warning System
G77	Group of Developing Countries
OECD	Organisation of Economic Cooperation and Development
ICRC	International Committee of the Red Cross
IEFR	International Emergency Food Reserve
IFAD	International Fund for Agricultural Development
IFPRI	International Food Policy Research Institute
INTERFAIS	WFP's computerised information system
ILO	International Labor Organization
JIU	Joint Inspection Unit
PNG	Papua New Guinea
PRO	Protracted Refugee Operation

PRRO	Protracted Relief and Recovery Operation
PWA	Price Waterhouse Associates
RHC	Relief and Rehabilitation Committee
SCG	Sub-Committee on Governance of the CFA
SCP	Projects Sub-Committee of the CFA
SLPA	Sudan People's Liberation Army
UN	United Nations
UNBRO	United Nations Border Relief Operation
UNCTAD	United Nations Conference on Trade and Development
UNDP	United Nations Development Programme
UNDRO	United Nations Disaster Relief Office
UNESCO	United Nations Educational, Scientific and Cultural Organization
UNFPA	United Nations Fund for Population Activities
UNHCR	United Nations High Commissioner for Refugees
UNICEF	United Nations Children's Fund
UPU	Universal Postal Union
USAID	United States Agency for International Development
USSR	Union of Soviet Socialist Republics
WFC	World Food Council
WFP	World Food Programme
WHO	World Health Organization

INTRODUCTION

This book tells the story of a political struggle for United Nations (UN) reform. I launched the battle in 1982 when I became the chief executive or Executive Director of the World Food Programme (WFP). It lasted nearly ten years and ended by freeing the WFP from its situation as a brow-beaten dependency of the UN Food and Agriculture Organization (FAO). The stakes were high. If my supporters and I had not been successful more lives may have been lost and human suffering been greater. Today, WFP is the world's largest humanitarian agency and acknowledged as a great UN success story. In 2003 it provided food to 104 million people and delivered over four million tons of food to victims of conflict and natural disaster that year, some two thirds of global emergency food aid. It is widely applauded for its efficient discharge of this task year after year.

In a sense this is a depressing tale because it shows how disfunctional the UN system of related agencies, created by governments and overseen by them, can become. On the other hand it is a harbinger of hope. Reform is possible.

This account suggests that the key ingredients for successful reform are: strong, disinterested leadership from executive heads; willingness by governments to recognise that an improved international order cannot be secured without genuine commitment to common goals; and the preparedness to act. Unfortunately, governments are inclined to assess interests at their lowest common denominator and with insufficient attention to building the strong international order they claim to want. In this regard, the United States of America emerges in my story as especially disappointing even though it had a proprietorial attitude to the WFP and was its biggest contributor.

There are few frank accounts by the former heads of UN functional agencies dealing with the detail of the political processes which bring about significant change. The result is an incomplete understanding in

1

government, academia and the media about how this segment of the UN system[1] actually works. Moreover, most studies are directed to issues of peace and security per se, despite the fact that most of the career staff in the system and most expenditure are directed to other goals of the UN Charter.

Although this book is not about overall reform of the system, the case study of WFP reform illuminates obstacles to reform which are system wide. It aims to contribute to a better understanding in government and academia of those obstacles. Among them are procedures for the selection of agency executive heads. I therefore go into some detail about my appointment and re-appointment. These accounts throw light on the flawed system of senior appointments throughout the UN system and the need to further improve it.

The heads of UN agencies such as WFP combine the political and managerial responsibilities of minister and permanent departmental head in national governments. On top of that, they must satisfy a political oversight body to which they are responsible. To be fully effective they therefore need both political and managerial skills. Talking in the abstract about leadership is not enough. We need to understand how secretariat leadership works in the United Nations by seeing it in action and dealing with concrete problems. My narrative gives one account of how the leader must function in the international system if he wishes to achieve serious reform. It also underlines the point that to achieve a better functioning international system requires appropriate leadership by agency heads in the fields of economic development and humanitarian intervention, and not only in relation to war and peace.

There are critical flaws in UN modes of operation. Having given much of my working life to the United Nations and continuing to see it as an essential agent in the better management of globalisation I do not want to give comfort to its enemies. However, I am convinced that the tacit 'cover up' characteristic of UN culture is a serious impediment to meaningful reform. That is my justification for writing candidly, even bluntly, at times. History is made by individuals and their interactions with other individuals, at least as much as by impersonal forces. The story I tell, though a contribution to history and a case study of leadership and reform, is also a story of political and personal competition, with no certainty about outcomes, until the end.

The struggle for reform in WFP was a human drama whose outcome ultimately had a touch of Shakespearean inevitability, although at the time that was never evident to me and my colleagues. The changes we wrought were fought tooth and nail by the Director-General of FAO, Edouard Saouma. Had the personalities been different, so too would have been the reform process.

Inevitably our struggle was represented by some as no more than a clash of personalities. In fact it was never so simple, though of course our personalities influenced the style and tactics each of us used. Despite times of bitter division, I was always drawn to Saouma's personality and respected his commitment to the interests of FAO as he saw them.

The official documentation and the archives of the UN, FAO and WFP, as well as academic analyses, tell some of the story of WFP's transformation but little about how and why it happened.[2] It was a highly political, at times dramatic, process. A full understanding of that process is historically important and provides lessons relevant to the continuing attempts to reform the UN system.

When I speak of reform what precisely do I have in mind? The changes I sought were essential to enable WFP to fulfil its mandate and become more effective and efficient and so better serve the interests of all. Nevertheless, they were represented by my opponents as intended to enhance my personal power. Member states did gradually come to understand that the issue at stake was governance and that they must confront the question of whether ultimate responsibility for WFP rested with them in reality or in name only. My narrative tells the story of their slowness both to answer that question affirmatively and then to act decisively to assert their authority. It is also an account of a failure of governance at all levels up to and including the General Assembly of the United Nations.

My diary is a primary source for this account. I began the diary because, by the end of 1983, I felt that the events I was involved in were extraordinary, going beyond the usual norms of bureaucratic conflict. They deserved to be recorded. It was only a few years ago that I looked at them again and realised the unique insight they give to the inner workings of an agency of the UN system and of the central role played by chief executives. That reading impelled me to write this account which takes a more personal approach than have my previous writings on the UN.[3] I have included extracts from my diary to give a sense of immediacy and verisimilitude about the events described and to display the role of leadership and relationships in shaping outcomes in the United Nations. The pervasive power of today's media over-emphasises personalities in national politics. In UN agencies their importance is under-estimated.

By giving a candid description of the struggle for constitutional reform in WFP from my vantage point as its chief executive officer, I hope to cast light on the complex functions of leadership and top management. I believe understanding of these functions is enhanced by the telling of stories of leaders and managers. In this respect I find Howard Gardner's approach convincing. His ground-breaking anatomy of leadership, *Leading Minds* (1995), is based on the biographies of outstanding world leaders in a diversity of fields. Equally, the advice given by Peters and Austin (1985, p.420) in their acclaimed book, *A Passion for Excellence: The Leadership Difference*, is relevant. They urge the 'would-be effective leader to become a reader of biographies', even though good biographies of managers are rare.

This account is as accurate as possible. It is written with the benefit of official documents, records of conversations and other documentation, as well as from my diary. However, it is an incomplete history. A full account would require access to the archives of governments, the UN and FAO and the stories of other protagonists. The novelist Joyce Carol Oates recently wrote:

> The technique of memoir resembles that of fiction: selection, distillation, dramatisation. Inevitably much is omitted. Inevitably, much is distorted. Memoirs are notoriously unreliable, particularly in individuals prone to mythmaking and the settling of old scores, which may well be all of us.[4]

All that I think is true. However, being aware of these risks and deliberately writing so long after the events themselves, I have felt no inclination to settle scores or otherwise write a self-serving account. How successful I have been is for others to judge.

This book is mainly about my political leadership and does not say as much about my managerial role as Executive Director of WFP. That is not because I did not see management as important; on the contrary, I saw it as my primary function and spent most of my time on it. However, as countless texts on management make clear, there is incomplete agreement on what precisely the manager does because his task embraces many functions and their interrelationships, the whole process guided consciously or unconsciously by an underlying intellectual framework.

As manager my overall task was to ensure that WFP carried out its work as effectively as possible: simple to say but very hard to implement. To oversee successfully an organisation responsible for mobilising, purchasing and delivering several million tons of food each year to help feed around 100 million hungry people spread throughout the developing world is a challenge.

WFP personnel have a wide range of technical skills and specialised knowledge, including in logistics, global food markets, development theory, assessment of food needs. They also have to understand the political and developmental goals of recipient governments and of the developed countries donating the food and money used to overcome hunger and promote development. Managing this diverse multi-talented, multi-national, multi-lingual staff was a much more taxing job than any similar assignment in the Australian civil service.

Furthermore, it was my officers–and not I–whose lives were sometimes at risk when working to ensure that victims of armed conflict received their WFP rations. They are WFP's heroes. They tell exciting stories of their endeavours as perusal of most editions of *Pipeline*, WFP's monthly staff magazine, shows. I have few adventures to relate. Difficult and tense as my negotiations over access to famine victims were with dictatorial leaders in Afghanistan, Sudan and Eritrea,[5] my life was never seriously at risk. I endured no hardships even in remote areas of the poorest countries. I always got VIP treatment.

Nor was it my job to design our projects using food to promote economic and social development. That was a specialised skill, well developed in WFP. Instead, I had to make sure we found and retained sufficient staff with appropriate qualifications; and to organise them in the most effective way so that used our resources wisely. This was not a simple management task. The questions of which countries should benefit and their respective shares were often intensely political questions in which my involvement was critical.[6] Moreover, there is a substantial political dimension to the relationships between organisations of the UN system in, for example, the coordination of their activities, which can be time consuming.

The executive director should be a key player in policy development. Giving food to poor people sounds pretty simple. In fact ensuring it helps more than harms is complex. Accordingly, I found the development of appropriate policies for the use of food aid by WFP intellectually challenging.[7]

It was also my responsibility to raise the food and money we needed for our task. (All donations to WFP are voluntary.) To do so, it was essential that I retain the confidence of governments. That meant I had to travel a great deal to donor and developing countries to ensure that my goals for WFP, unfiltered through their Rome representatives, were well understood by governments; and to encourage them to increase their contributions.

In short, although this book is not about problems of management, or a text on the uses and abuses of food aid, or about the circumstances of humanitarian intervention, it does touch on these subjects. Thus the reader may be encouraged to look more deeply into them, as well as into the central theme of UN reform.

Finally, a word about the structure of this book. The full significance of the reform saga cannot be grasped by those unfamiliar with WFP and the United Nations. Accordingly, I begin by describing the UN system and WFP's place in it. I then briefly outline what WFP does and the significance of its work for the international community. Although under-appreciated, except by the poor and hungry who benefited, WFP was already an important developmental and humanitarian agency in 1982.

Because the story I tell was a process extending over nine years, with a beginning and an end which was never certain, I tell it chronologically. To help the reader retain the thread I give a brief summary of each chapter at its head. Mid-way, I include an 'interlude' to broaden understanding of what WFP was doing in 1987, the year I began my second term. The book concludes with a chapter drawing out lessons for reform of the UN system.

---

1   An explanation of the UN system, and the place of functional organisations such as WFP and FAO within it, is given in the following chapter.

2   The bare bones of what happened have been set out in at least two scholarly works (Charlton 1992; Shaw 2001 pp. 205-224).

3   For details see under 'Ingram' in the list of References.

4   *New York Review of Books*, Vol L. Number 16, p. 23.

5   See chapters 9 and 13.

6   See especially chapter 3.

7   This is attested to by the substantial and still growing academic literature on food aid (OECD 2006).

1

THE UN SYSTEM AND WFP

On the distinction between the United Nations and the United Nations system, together with the place of WFP within the system and a brief survey of the genesis of food aid and of WFP followed by an outline of the work of WFP.

THE UN AND THE UN SYSTEM

There is a good deal of confusion in the term 'United Nations' loosely used to refer to a number of distinct things. The principal association is with the United Nations as a supposed embodiment of 'world government', signified by the handsome building on the East River in New York. It is there that the General Assembly of all member countries meets. The General Assembly is the supreme decision-making body and may consider any issue within the scope of the United Nations Charter. The Security Council is the United Nations organ responsible for peace and security; it also meets at United Nations Headquarters. Its relationship to the General Assembly is defined in the Charter.

The Secretary-General is the head of the secretariat or international civil service that provides administrative support, principally to the General Assembly, Security Council and their numerous standing and ad hoc subsidiary bodies.

A substantial part of the output of the United Nations is a vast flow of resolutions which embody 'decisions' taken by governments. These decisions can be about any issue which finds a place on the international agenda. Because the United Nations and its subsidiary bodies generally do not have power to enforce their decisions–the Security Council is the

7

principal exception—most of these resolutions are not much more than cosmetic. The result is that the United Nations is sometimes condemned as an expensive 'talking shop'. There is some substance in the charge. However, there is much more to the institution than that.

Beyond this, the United Nations moves from being a single, if already very complex, entity into a kind of confederation, in many ways incoherent, of essentially autonomous intergovernmental organisations, the whole known as the United Nations system. Within this confederation there are several categories of organisations all of which have links with the Economic and Social Council (ECOSOC), itself an organ established under the United Nations Charter and reporting to the General Assembly. (See Appendix III)

In law, though not always in terms of practical impact, the most important are the 'specialised agencies' established by formal intergovernmental treaty in the same way as the United Nations itself. They each have separate headquarters and staffs and are headed by chief executives elected by member nations. There are about 20 of these agencies. FAO is one of the most important. Other prominent ones are the World Health Organization (WHO), the United Nations Educational, Scientific and Cultural Organization (UNESCO) and the International Labour Organization (ILO). Some pre-date the establishment of the United Nations proper, for example the Universal Postal Union (UPU).

The specialised agencies deal with discrete areas of international cooperation, for example civil aviation, telecommunications, shipping, food and agriculture, labour standards, meteorology, intellectual property. Though formally included among them, the International Monetary Fund (IMF) and World Bank stand apart. Their constitutions give effective power to the rich developed countries, and their staffs are not part of the 'common system' of the UN civil service, which adheres to uniform standards for grades, salaries and conditions of service. There are five levels of professional posts (P1 to P5) to which appointments and promotions are supposedly, but in reality far from universally, made on merit alone. Immediately above, in ascending order of rank are Directors D1 and D2, Assistant Secretary-General and Under Secretary-General. In the specialised agencies the equivalent top level posts are Assistant Director-General and Deputy Director-General. The Executive Director of WFP is at the Under Secretary-General/Deputy Director-General level.

The specialised agencies are linked to the United Nations through individual agreements with ECOSOC, which is entrusted with limited powers of supervision. It also coordinates their activities as well as those of scores of other entities dealing with economic or social questions that are subsidiary to the Council. These include various specialised commissions, such as the Population Commission, and the Regional Economic Commissions, for example the Economic Commission for Africa (ECA), and a miscellany of committees, boards and institutes.

THE OPERATIONAL PROGRAMS AND FUNDS

In terms of practical impact in developing countries, an important category of organisations carries out what are called the 'operational' activities of the United Nations. The principal operational agencies or programs are the United Nations Development Programme (UNDP), the United Nations Children Fund (UNICEF) and WFP. These organisations primarily exist to extend aid to developing countries. The United Nations High Commissioner for Refugees (UNHCR) also comes within this category but has additional responsibilities for the legal protection of refugees.

Unlike the specialised agencies the operational programs were established by resolutions adopted by, for example, the United Nations General Assembly. Each has its own intergovernmental committee setting policy and overseeing operations and expenditure and their own distinct staffs under the authority of their own chief executives. Some, including WFP, have much bigger budgets than any of the specialised agencies and are better known to the world public. They are wholly or partly funded by voluntary contributions, mainly from governments, whereas the United Nations and the specialised agencies are financed through compulsory levies on member states. However, unlike the plenary bodies of the specialised agencies the operational programs lack certain powers, for example to amend their own constitutions.

Moreover, the executive heads of these programs are not chosen by election. Most are simply appointed by the Secretary-General of the United Nations, although governments may be consulted. In one or two instances, the person chosen by the Secretary-General is confirmed by the General Assembly of the United Nations. Their status is therefore lower than the heads of the specialised agencies.

By custom, though not by right, the heads of the operational programs were members, while it existed, of the Administrative Committee on Co-ordination (ACC) made up of the heads of the specialised agencies meeting under the Chairmanship of the UN Secretary-General. The ACC met several times a year supposedly to ensure that the activities of the various members were well coordinated. The ACC has been succeeded by the Chief Executive Board with similar functions and membership.

There is no centralised administrative hierarchy within the UN system. The UN Secretary-General cannot give directions to the heads of the specialised agencies, who are legally answerable only to their own plenary bodies. In the ACC he was no more than first among equals. For the operational programs, it is rare indeed for the Secretary-General to make more than suggestions and in my experience he makes almost none. The intergovernmental bodies charged with oversight and coordination of the economic and social work of the UN system, in particular ECOSOC, perform poorly. It could scarcely be otherwise given the extraordinary mishmash of organisations governments have created.

The media use the term 'United Nations' indiscriminately to refer either to the United Nations political bodies in New York or the system of entities described above, or some part of the latter. The work of legally autonomous specialised agencies may also be loosely described as the work of the United Nations, as in the 'United Nations announced', when it was, say, the FAO that made the announcement. Nor do the media usually distinguish between those who govern and those who administer the system. Loose phraseology, for example to the effect that the United Nations 'failed' when the failure lies with a Security Council member vetoing action, can create the misleading impression that there is something wrong with the institution as such. For those knowledgeable about the United Nations none of this matters. They can tell from the context what is meant. However, this imprecision does not help the general public understand what the United Nations is, what it can or cannot do, its strengths and weaknesses. This confusion is sometimes used by governments as a way of blurring blame for their own failures.

Accordingly, when I refer to the United Nations (UN) I mean the institution in New York, serviced by the UN Secretary-General. Where I refer to the UN system I mean the whole family of organisations.

Component organisations are referred to by their individual names. Similarly, I distinguish between the secretariats of UN system organisation and their intergovernmental governing bodies, unless the context makes this unnecessary.

GENESIS OF WFP

When I arrived in Rome in 1982, WFP was already a major UN system operational agency, having been established in 1961 as the dedicated food aid arm of the system. Until then, food delivered through United Nations agencies had been provided ad hoc to deal with specific food emergencies or in small feeding programs. By 1960 the use of food to promote economic development was well established in bilateral aid programs but there was no counterpart United Nations effort as there was for technical assistance delivered through UNDP and specialised agencies like FAO, or capital aid through the World Bank.

The United States of America (United States) had led the way in using food as a resource to promote economic development, as distinct from the alleviation of hunger. Thus food was a critical component of assistance under the 1948 Marshall Plan for the rehabilitation of European economies. Commodities were supplied to individual governments which sold them through market channels, the proceeds supporting their reconstruction budgets. The method proved extraordinarily successful and provided the model for the provision of food aid by the United States to developing countries. Through the 1950s surplus farm commodities constituted from 30 to 50 per cent of American foreign economic assistance[8]. At that time the United States was overwhelmingly the major donor of aid to developing countries.

However, 'program food aid', as food aid used as budgetary support became known, was a controversial form of aid from its inception, criticised for its potential disincentive effects on local food production, its creation or reinforcement of consumer preference for imported foods, for example wheat instead of sorghum, and for facilitating fiscal irresponsibility on the part of recipient governments. Countries that depended on wheat export earnings were highly critical of this kind of food aid. Australia's Sir John Crawford summed up their argument: 'In a very real sense, commercial wheat exporters, in this case principally Australia, have contributed to Indian development through loss of market' (Wit, 1964 p.61). During the

1950s FAO brought about international agreement on the principles that should govern the disposal of agricultural surpluses to minimise their potentially disruptive impact on commercial markets (FAO, 1954).

I learned this as a young diplomat in the Australian Embassy in Washington in the mid-1950s. I accompanied Crawford and his Minister, the redoubtable Sir John 'Blackjack' McEwen, on a call on the US Secretary of Agriculture, Ezra Taft Benson. The purpose was to persuade Benson that the adverse impact on Australia's cereal exports would be diminished if the USA bought some Australian wheat to use in its Public Law 480 programs of food aid. After a moment of reflection, the quietly spoken Benson said gravely, 'Mr. Minister, the United States has a surplus of food not a surplus of money.' That was the end of the matter, McEwen falling silent.

By 1960 the United States had come to favour the creation of a multilateral food aid agency in order to spread the burden to other rich countries of meeting the food needs of developing countries, while providing a new outlet for surplus food production which was increasing rapidly in Europe—in other words to protect its markets.

The UN General Assembly adopted a resolution in 1960 inviting FAO to establish procedures by which, 'with the assistance of the United Nations system, the largest practicable amounts of surplus food could be used against hunger'. The Director-General of FAO, B R Sen, set up a high level group under the chairmanship of the distinguished development economist, H W Singer (FAO, 1961). Its report emphasised that the surplus problem could best be dealt with by expanding demand for food in developing countries. The group's thinking was influenced by the FAO's pioneering studies on using food to speed up economic development. These became the model for WFP's subsequent food-for-work development projects (for some examples see below) in India and elsewhere (FAO, 1985). The group considered that food aid used this way could expand demand without harmful economic consequences, such as inflation. The group described the rationale for their approach as follows:

> If sufficient food stuffs could not be supplied in a country to meet the increased demand from the additionally employed workers on construction or other investments, then either more resources (circulating capital) would have to be spent for (food) imports, or the amount of additional investment would have to be reduced (Shaw, 2001, p.23).

In addition employed workers would have to be fed during the period of construction and if sufficient extra food was not available from internal production or imports then food prices would rise, worsening the circumstances of the poor.

The experts favoured the creation of social development programs, specifically land reform, school feeding, support for poor secondary school students, and relief and welfare for the old, handicapped and destitute. These would be delivered through a series of projects with defined goals linked to consumption by targeted beneficiaries of specified quantities of foods nutritionally appropriate for each project.

They also advocated the creation of national food reserves in developing countries and of an international emergency reserve to meet the relief needs of victims of famine and other disasters.

Over a five-year period they estimated that about $12.5 billion worth of agricultural commodities could not be sold through normal market channels and would therefore be available for food aid programs through the United Nations or from individual donor countries.

Sen submitted proposals reflecting the tenor of the group's report but the entity that eventually emerged, due in large measure to George McGovern, then head of President Kennedy's Food for Peace office and subsequent Senator and Democrat candidate for the presidency, was modest and tentative. In late 1961 the United Nations General Assembly and the Conference of FAO passed identical resolutions establishing WFP as a joint UN/FAO program in Rome. However, it was set up as a three-year experiment with a pledging target for food and cash of $100 million over that period. In effect this was a pilot scheme to test whether the theory behind project aid could be realised in practice. Denied the opportunity to give program aid as provided by the United States and other bilateral donors, WFP was the channel for only two per cent of global food aid during the pilot phase.

The experiment was judged successful and parallel resolutions were again adopted by the General Assembly and FAO Conference in December 1965 which extended the World Food Programme 'on a continuing basis for as long as multilateral food aid is found feasible and desirable, on the understanding that the Programme will be regularly reviewed before each Pledging Conference'.

WFP went from strength to strength. By the end of its first decade it had committed $1.2 billion to 540 development projects in 94 developing countries benefiting some 24 million people. In the next decade the pace quickened. Assistance to the value of $5.3 billion was committed to over 1,100 projects directly helping 94 million people. By 1982, the year of my arrival, operations extended to 114 countries.

WFP was now the principal grant funding program of the UN system with its assistance targeted on the poorest populations of low-income food deficit countries. By 1982 WFP was handling no less than 20 per cent of global food aid, a measure of the esteem in which donors held it. By comparison for other grant aid categories, e.g. technical assistance, the UN system share was under five per cent.[9]

WHAT DOES WFP DO?

WFP does more than feed people; it is also a valuable means for helping poor people improve their lot. Thus nutritional benefit is only one of several sought by the Programme. Let me give some examples drawn from my personal experience of WFP's imaginative use of food in support of economic and social development.[10]

During my first year I visited our aid projects in Thailand, Bangladesh and Pakistan, among others, in order to acquire first hand a sense of what in practice was involved in the use of food aid for development, and in support of humanitarian disaster victims. As an intergovernmental agency WFP assistance is directed to beneficiaries through their governments, though occasionally partner government delegate implementation to a non-government organisation (NGO).

Food-for-Work

The visit in December 1982 to Bangladesh, the largest recipient of our development assistance, was especially important. After a meeting with the Prime Minister[11] and other ministers, we were whisked off by helicopter. Flying across the delta revealed a dense network of canals and villages, but few roads. During the dry season, the time of our visit, rural labourers had few opportunities for gainful employment even though the agricultural infrastructure of canals and roads, most of which run on top of canal embankments, needed to be extended or repaired. However, funds to pay labourers were either unavailable or insufficient. That was why each dry season WFP provided wheat as a wage to hundreds of thousands of unskilled workers. This was a classic food-for-work project, ideally suited to a densely populated, impoverished country, which utilised human powered earth moving on a large scale. While critics argued that payment of wheat to rice eaters would develop an inappropriate change of diet, subsequent expert studies supported the Bangladeshi government's view that this change of taste had overall been beneficial because it had established the necessary market for the burgeoning new wheat-growing industry in Bangladesh.[12]

That visit convinced me of the worth of this kind of WFP development activity which brought with it a strong welfare component. It also showed me how, following Bangladesh's frequent calamitous floods and cyclones, the food-for-work program could easily be expanded to provide relief to those affected in conjunction with the rehabilitation of damaged infrastructure.[13]

The project distributed around 200,000 tons of wheat each year. Forty million workdays were generated. Work for 1.8 million persons was created. They were paid in kind on a piece-work basis.

There can be pitfalls in large-scale food-for-work programs. They require sophisticated planning and organisation, as well as the resources to finance necessary infrastructure such as, in the case of Bangladesh, concrete culverts and other permanent built structures. If these are not supplied, the same work may have to be done again in the following dry season. The relative dearth of the necessary associated financial resources handicapped the success of many of our food-for-work projects, including in Bangladesh. Attempts to overcome the problem are touched upon in chapter 9.

Corruption at various levels of government can mean some leakage of food away from a project into commercial channels. However, because of the visibility of commodities and their bulkiness, the scale of corruption and its deleterious effects is usually less than it would be if the works were financed with cash. Data on misappropriation of commodities for all WFP projects continues to be systematically collected. Overall commodity losses for all projects were less than five per cent during my time.

WFP undertakes many variations on the food-for-work theme. Another that impressed me in my early days was its use for the payment of wages to workers engaged in construction of the Rajasthan irrigation canal in India. Here the workers in a remote desert area, far from towns, were paid with cash but WFP food was sold to them at heavily subsidised prices, the proceeds being invested by government in the project. It was very exciting to see a constant stream of camel-drawn carts removing sand dislodged by dragline excavators as part of the construction of an immense piece of infrastructure that would enable a big increase in irrigated food production. It was an excellent example of an appropriate mix of quite low technology joined with an abundant source of cheap labour.

WFP supported massive food-for-work projects in Ethiopia intended to improve agricultural productivity through the construction of terraces over an extended area, the impact of which could easily be seen when flying overhead. Here, as in Bangladesh, food was the sole emolument. Research studies found that most participants preferred a food wage, especially during the Ethiopian famine of 1985-86 and in areas where markets were poor (Shaw, p. 94).

In my first year I also visited an interesting project in Pakistan, where food constituted a part wage for afforestation of a water catchment. This was in the valley above the giant Mangla dam, whose opening by President Ayub Khan I had witnessed while accompanying the Australian Minister of Foreign Affairs on an official visit nearly twenty years before. Tree planting is also labour intensive and well suited to food-for-work. Clearly, this was a well run development project which really reached the rural poor. One of the great advantages of food-for-work is that it is self targeting on the very poor, because it is only they who are willing to work for food. Even in 1982, it was a cliché that the target of development assistance was the poor. However, WFP was the only UN system aid agency to reach large numbers of the poorest of the poor, and on a scale rarely if ever matched by NGO assistance.

Many food-for-work projects I visited in more sparsely populated countries in Africa had novel elements that served social rather than economic goals. For example, in Tunisia WFP was assisting a project intended to slow the movement of marginal farmers to the cities. Supply of food was used as an inducement to introduce water harvesting measures in very low rainfall areas, thus enabling the planting of olive trees. In this and village access road schemes, I was often brought face to face with the way a little outside interest can galvanise poor peasants to take action to improve their lot. The food became secondary to the encouragement to community action it stimulated. The outside world, not least the local government, was seen to care. Often women were the driving force. From Peru to Guatemala, Cameroon to Lesotho, from Egypt to Syria and Bangladesh to China, I was impressed by the dynamism unleashed by our projects. The enthusiasm and pride of the poor in their accomplishments was humbling. The hand-out mentality was entirely absent.

Dairy Development

An important category among our development projects was the use of surplus, mainly European, milk powder and butter oil to promote dairy development (Shaw, p.123-127). The successful model—'Operation Flood'—had been developed in India. In brief, WFP milk products were used to re-constitute milk and blend it with fresh whole milk. The proceeds generated by the sale of the product were invested in the local dairy industry, especially in farms, cattle breeding and milk processing factories.

Cuba was one country where our dairy projects were of great importance. The milk from state dairy farms was blended with imported milk powder supplied by WFP and was the foundation of the Cuban government's ability to provide significant amounts of milk-based products to its people. Given the austerity of daily life these were one of the few 'luxuries' available. A similar situation prevailed in Nicaragua.

Social Welfare

The projects so far described were intended to promote mainly economic development though, as indicated, they often had useful social benefits also. A second category of projects was designed primarily to advance social goals. Possibly the most important was the provision of food to primary schools which, in addition to the nutritional benefit, provided an incentive to parents in poor areas to send their children, especially daughters, to school. It is now conventional wisdom that good nutrition is important for brain development and assists school learning. However, like food-for-work projects these could not realise anything like their full potential unless strongly backed, financially and administratively, by the relevant authorities. Broadly speaking they worked best in better off countries like Brazil. However, I was always impressed by the enthusiasm of teachers and pupils and the imagination they displayed in preparing nutritional meals based on cereals and vegetable oil and quite often some local produce from school gardens. I ate many such dishes in remote areas of poor African countries. They were always tasty.

Another category of social welfare projects was support for mother and child health care. Their goal was to encourage attendance at health and family planning clinics by providing take home food as an incentive. Time after time, I was uplifted by the enthusiastic appreciation of poor women for the valuable income supplement our assistance provided.

My visit to a social welfare project in Bangladesh left a particularly vivid impression. In that country Moslem custom, I was told, allows a husband to banish his wife and to deny her any further support. There were several million women in this category. Our project fed them and their children and, to the extent that resources permitted, taught them skills that might help them gain an income.

Of course all the visits I made were choreographed, which meant they were of little value in terms of a definitive assessment of the true worth of the projects I saw. This was the responsibility of our professional Evaluation Service. Nevertheless, quite often I learned a great deal, not least through gaining a concrete impression of activities otherwise described in the dry jargon of development and UN bureaucracy.

On one visit there was a heart-rending departure from the host government's script. We were brought to a village to witness food distribution to the indigent women living in the area. The ceremony was dramatically interrupted when several very distressed women, some with babies or toddlers, burst in and pleaded for food. The situation was explained to me by one of our officers. Although the project embraced hundreds of thousands of women there were still many who could not be included because of insufficient resources. Doubtless there was favouritism by local officials in determining who to include, with the result that not all the most deserving always benefited. Nevertheless, everyone who was helped was in desperate need. Where there is so much extreme poverty to insist on incontrovertible needs assessment to identify the most deserving would be 'to make the best the enemy of the good'.

Humanitarian Emergency Assistance

By the time I came to WFP, the Programme had begun to shift its emphasis away from development to meeting emergency needs. During its first decade it spent less than 10 per cent of its resources on emergencies. In 1977, new emergency commitments were 19.7 per cent of the total. By 1982 the proportion had grown to 23.6 per cent. That shift has continued until the present day. In 2004 almost 84 per cent of WFP food deliveries were for relief.[14]

Within the relief category a significant shift has also occurred. WFP classifies emergencies in three categories: sudden natural disasters, crop failure due to drought and man-made disasters. From 1977 to 1982 responses to man-made disasters rose from 18.8 per cent of emergency assistance to 63.6 per cent. It was in those years that WFP became the major source of food for Cambodian refugees living on the border with Thailand, having fled the Pol Pot regime, and Afghan refugees on the Pakistan border displaced following the Soviet Union's invasion of their country. Throughout my two terms and subsequently WFP became more and more the principal supplier and coordinator of food assistance to the victims of armed conflict.

My visits to war-torn places were memorable experiences. On my way to take up my appointment I stopped in Bangkok to visit the border Cambodians (or Kampucheans as they were then called). At the beginning of 1982 WFP had assumed managerial oversight of the United Nations Border Relief Operation (UNBRO). WFP Rome saw this as the coming of age of WFP: it was now playing a central humanitarian role as a UN system organisation. I wanted to see what that role meant in practice. As it turned out, I felt not a great deal. The WFP official responsible for day-to-day management of UNBRO operated under the overall supervision of the UNDP Resident Representative who was, as everywhere that WFP operated, also designated to be the WFP country representative. Some UNDP representatives took seriously their responsibility to the WFP Executive Director for the work of the Programme and some did not, as I found on this occasion. To complicate matters further, political direction was exercised by a Special Representative of the UN Secretary-General who also maintained an office in Bangkok. This complex relationship proved increasingly unsatisfactory as explained in Chapter 9.

It quickly became evident that UNBRO was serving Thai national interests. I was flown to the border in a Thai army helicopter which was an indication of the intimacy of the relationship between UNBRO and the Thais. While it was pleasing to see the Khmer well housed, fed and healthy, it was also evident that the camps provided a haven for armed dissidents operating within Kampuchea against the Pol Pot regime. In retrospect it turned out to be the beginning of a learning experience that UN agencies are sometimes a poor instrument for achieving their professed humanitarian aims. I will have more to say about this important matter in a later chapter.

The main purpose of the journey to Pakistan was to visit some of the hundreds of thousands of refugees encamped on the border with Afghanistan. WFP was the provider of food to sustain the refugees but the overall operation was under the leadership of UNHCR. In the company of the minister responsible we travelled from Peshawar to the border.

My first impression was the harshness of the conditions in which the refugees were supported, as compared with the border Kampucheans. Almost all were accommodated in tents. Camps were essentially self-run. Thus the only education appeared to be traditionally Islamic, based on study of the Koran under religious teachers. It was one of many 'steps back in time' I would make while in WFP. On this occasion I was reminded of medieval illustrations of Jewish students of the Talmud.

The focus of this excursion was a meeting with an assembled group of some thousand Afghan men at which the minister was to introduce me and the Afghan leader was to thank WFP for its succour. As translated, the speech was appropriate enough but the leader concluded, seemingly with an unscripted question, passionately spoken and with no trace of irony: 'Food is well and good and we are very appreciative, but where are the guns?' Even more clearly than on the Thai/Cambodian border, while our assistance served a laudable humanitarian goal it was also sustaining combatants of one side in an ongoing war.

Project Design and Logistics

Each WFP operation is a separate project usually designed following an expert mission to the country seeking assistance. Project designs specify goals to be achieved, the target beneficiaries, the rations to be supplied to them, and the obligations of the recipient or partner government. Project performance is monitored periodically by WFP resident staff. Formal evaluations of completed projects are comprehensive and carried out by a dedicated unit at headquarters independent of project design and management. Overall, however, in my time the resources devoted to project appraisal and design fell short of those applied to projects with similar goals funded by the international development banks. To some extent we were able to address this problem by developing some valuable joint projects with these institutions, particularly the International Fund for Agricultural Development (IFAD) and the World Bank.

Once projects are approved the specified foods have to be obtained from donors or purchased in commercial markets and then shipped to the countries concerned. The big range of donated commodities complicates project design and logistics. There are sometimes insufficient pledges of basic foods such as cereals and vegetable oil, and instead too many which were difficult to use, even exotic, and relatively expensive. To some extent the foods provided to beneficiaries are influenced by WFP's need to make use of the commodities pledged by governments. I was sometimes personally confronted by the problems created by such donations.

Thus in 1983 I visited Saudi Arabia to persuade it to reduce the proportion of dates in its contribution. The Saudis had recently changed their donation from cash only to two thirds dates and one third cash, proportions laid down in the WFP Basic Documents described in a following chapter. While dates were part of the diet in the Middle East and North Africa, they were usually eaten as a delicacy for special occasions, for example during the fasting month of Ramadan. In Saudi Arabia they had even been a staple but had ceased to be so as the country became wealthier. Dates were not, however, likely to be a normal part of the diet of potential WFP food recipients.

The Saudis were impervious to any arguments about dietary preference: 'Dates were good enough for our forefathers; if they are hungry they will eat dates', went the refrain. I soon saw why when I was taken to a brand new factory filled with the latest Californian machinery for processing and packing dates. Clearly, the Saudis were lifting a leaf out of the practice book of some of the other donors—they wanted to use the Programme to help establish new markets for surplus foods. Even more daunting was to see 4,000 tons of dates stacked in cartons, requiring about 150 large semi-trailer trucks to move them, and with a shelf life of only a few months. 'There is our gift to WFP', said the Minister, with more than a touch of pride. Somehow our staff was able to utilise this gift, which was maintained year after year. Uneasy though I felt about this, I also considered that the overall balance of advantage for the Programme lay in accepting the Saudi contribution. I was also uncomfortable about Italy's insistence on supplying increasing quantities of high-value freeze-dried products, well in excess of what WFP could appropriately use. Over time it became apparent that Italy was doing so in order to assist a politically influential Sicilian firm over-invested in their production. Again, we found ways to use the donation. There were other instances where donors insisted on inappropriate donations but few required my personal intervention to the extent that these did.

To foster good donor relations WFP does its best to use pledged commodities in countries and for projects preferred, or sometimes stipulated, by donors. That most pledged resources are donations in kind, title to which does not pass to the Programme when pledged, complicates management and has the potential to politically skew the distribution of resources. Sometimes the promised commodities are not in fact available when requested. The United States reserves the right not to supply commodities to projects or countries of which it disapproves even when the Programme's governing body has formally endorsed the project. Further, uniquely among donors, the US insists that its food be transported in American ships.

To some extent therefore WFP is somewhat less than a fully multilateral international organisation. I first became aware of this situation while still head of the Australian overseas aid agency when my predecessor at WFP called on me in Canberra. Rather naively, I was taken aback when quite flatly he said that WFP would be willing to ship our Australian contribution to our preferred beneficiary countries. That prospect was held out as the carrot to induce us to increase our contribution.

When commodities arrive in-country they have to be transported to the project region, often over long distances on poor roads. In the poorest countries WFP subsidises internal transport costs.

Assembling a broad range of foodstuffs, ensuring their delivery to hundreds of projects in more than one hundred countries with millions of individual beneficiaries is a formidable logistical task. In 1982, the Programme shipped almost two million tons of food, 35 per cent more than the previous year. Forty-five different commodities were distributed of which 86 per cent were cereals or cereal based, six per cent milk products, five per cent fats and oils and three per cent miscellaneous products including canned meat and fish and the aforementioned dates.

WFP is acknowledged as an accomplished logistical performer. That is an important reason why donors put a higher proportion of their total food aid through the Programme as compared with other categories of aid disbursed through UN system organisations.

In the distribution of food to famine victims in remote districts of Africa during the major droughts that periodically afflict that continent, WFP is increasingly active in supporting the professionalisation of government emergency planning and food distribution agencies; and in the upgrading of ports, railways and road transport. Increasingly it has become involved in aerial distribution and in 2002 was officially designated as the logistics agency of the UN system.

WFP and FAO

When I assumed my post, WFP was alone among UN system operational agencies in being a joint Programme of the UN and of a specialised agency, namely FAO. The powers of each were defined in the WFP Basic Documents, especially its General Regulations (see Chapter 4) which gave FAO the more important role. WFP's location in Rome reinforced FAO dominance. There had been logic in the placement of WFP under FAO, given both were concerned with feeding the world. The latter's constitution states that it shall 'collect, analyse, interpret and disseminate information relating to nutrition, food and agriculture', agriculture also encompassing fishing and forestry. To that end, it was to promote national and international action with respect to research, education, conservation and processing, marketing and agricultural credit and commodities policies. The main instruments at its disposal were intergovernmental conferences and the provision of technical assistance to member states. As an organisation of agricultural professionals its bias was very much the promotion of agricultural production.

As a consequence, FAO saw WFP assistance as most appropriate when it was directed towards increasing agricultural production. Social goals were seen as subsidiary. From its establishment, until I left the Programme in 1992, WFP development projects broadly within FAO's field of expertise averaged around 65 per cent of total commitments each year. However, over time it became apparent that the nutritional and income transfer effects of food aid, as for example in Bangladesh food-for-work or school feeding generally, was usually the primary benefit, best achieved when the social benefit was explicitly recognised in project design. Use of WFP resources for promoting food production and infrastructure was disappointing because the necessary associated financial assistance was almost always not available. Even the technical assistance needed to help the implementing government make a success of the project was rarely provided by FAO or others. This was so even though UNDP was charged with coordination of technical assistance and its representatives in developing countries were also WFP's chief representatives.

That WFP was not set up exclusively as an FAO offshoot but as a joint UN/FAO program was precisely because food aid was envisaged at the time of its creation as a broadly useful resource for the promotion of overall development. As such, WFP would have been a better fit with the soft loan window of the World Bank. This was proposed by UN Secretary-General Dag Hammarskjöld in 1960 but was rejected by the President of the Bank (Shaw, pp.27-28), presumably because he disliked food aid as much as he did soft loans. Though established much later, a better fit than FAO would have been with IFAD, also in Rome, with which we built close relations.

In short, although a close connection with FAO initially made sense, as time went by the relationship became more problematic. In the light of experience of the best uses of development food aid FAO technical strengths in agriculture became less relevant. With the shift to emergency food aid, in particular the substantial increase in assistance to the victims of conflict, FAO had little useful expertise. More importantly, the cultures of the two organisations were different. WFP was wholly action oriented, whereas FAO's culture was bureaucratic. It was skilled in agricultural problem analysis, statistics and conference management. For many governments its most important achievement was its role in the on-going creation of international food standards to protect consumers and ensure fair practices in international food trade. It administered a corps of experts charged with skill transfer to developing countries, but their work had little in common with that of WFP's field staff. By the time I came to Rome it had long been clear in WFP that food aid would be used more effectively by a stand-alone operational agency like UNICEF. The extraordinary achievements of WFP since the constitutional reforms achieved in 1991 are testimony to that.

8   For a succinct overview of the history of food aid, including the creation of WFP, see: Singer (1987). For a recent comprehensive history of the establishment of WFP and an analytical account of its work see: Shaw (2001).

9   Technical assistance to developing countries has been defined as 'a transfer of knowledge and skills...to permit them to make effective use both of their own meagre supplies of capital and of whatever capital is made available from abroad' (Millikan and Rostow, 1957). Food aid is usually seen as a third category of development assistance.

10   For an overview of contemporary academic analysis of global food aid and a comprehensive bibliography see: OECD, 2006.

11   On almost all of my official visits to developing countries I was received by the head-of-state/government.

12   For a comprehensive review of food-for-work in Bangladesh, see: Mahabub Hossain and M. Mokaddem Akhash (1993).

13   The British colonial government in India had made considerable use of food-for-work beginning in the nineteenth century. It was well established in the three successor states.

14   For further information see: Appendix II: Statistical Tables.

2

MY PATH TO ROME

How I came to cap my diplomatic career with a high post at the United Nations and the intense political process by which I became head of WFP.

The course of our lives is set by contingencies and choices. One morning in the spring of 1945 my mother drew my attention to an advertisement in the Melbourne *Age*. It invited candidates to sit a competitive examination, success in which was a first step in selection as a trainee for the fledgling Australian diplomatic service. She persuaded me to do the exam. If she had not, my life would have turned out very differently. I would not have become an Australian Ambassador, nor the only Australian to head a United Nations program, nor met the woman who married me and bore our three children.

In our circumstances it was a surprising recommendation. My father, the seventh of nine children, lost his father when he was eight and, as a consequence, left school at age twelve. Mum lost her mother when she was seven and her father at seventeen. However, she did have a secondary education. Our family was not affluent. I remember well my father being out of work during the Great Depression but by the time the Second World War broke out he had become a successful salesman of Austin motor cars. Because of an accident as a teenager that had crippled a leg he was rejected for service in both world wars. The disruption of war saw the end of the sales business and our financial circumstances deteriorated sharply, especially with three children to support of whom I was the eldest. My father took a low-level clerical post in a government agency concerned with war production.

27

As Catholics my parents did not wish me to attend a state high school. Fortunately at this time the Victorian government introduced a scholarship scheme which met a substantial part of the fees at approved Catholic secondary schools. I won one of those scholarships. The experience at De la Salle College has left mixed emotions. Like the nuns at primary school the brothers were mostly caring people who lived well the high ideals of their Christian faith. In those days primary school had eight grades to be completed at the school leaving age of 14. I had finished the curriculum at age 11. For my secondary schooling I was therefore on average two years younger than my contemporaries. Moreover, I was slow to mature physically, so that in a culture that valued sporting success I was at a further disadvantage, indeed seen by some as a bit of a misfit. I am grateful to the brothers for the sensitivity they showed me.

Nor was I a star scholastic achiever. I was competent at all subjects but did not excel in any. I preferred to spend my free time pursuing other interests rather than in study. Our school was focused on encouraging vocations to the religious life and in assisting the upward mobility of Catholics. Students were mainly being prepared for the civil service. Otherwise, law and medicine were seen as the best options in the face of widespread discrimination against Catholics in that era. The curriculum therefore focussed on mathematics, physics, chemistry, English, French and Latin, the latter being a pre-requisite for training for the priesthood. With only two exceptions none of my teachers aroused my interest in their specialties. However, the headmaster had a passion for science, which he communicated to me. Such ambition as I had was to make a career in chemistry. There was no counselling to help in making a future work choice, the brothers' own narrow experience not helping. Parental guidance was the most important factor.

With their fears that the Depression would return, my parents wanted me to obtain a secure civil service post. Mum's preference was for teaching. I finished school in 1944 and considered taking up a teacher's training scholarship but in the end declined because I was expected to take a science degree and, despite my interest in the natural sciences, which I still maintain, the prospect of the associated laboratory work did not attract me. I was much more focussed on the likelihood that, in little over a year, I would be joining the Australian Air Force. To mark time I took a clerical post with the Victorian State Rivers and Water Supply Commission and began a part-time degree in economics at Melbourne University.

When the war ended, years earlier than we expected, my mother worried I might be stuck with being a clerk. She knew how wide my interests were, especially in issues of public policy and the history of international relations leading to the war. Reading the advertisement's description of the attributes sought for Australia's diplomats she thought I was well suited. As I pondered the possibilities of a diplomat's life, I began to hope I would be accepted. That I was successful owed much more to my self-education and mum's confidence in me than to my formal schooling.

A DIPLOMATIC CAREER

The Australian diplomatic service had begun just before the Second World War. The wartime Labor Government realised it was no longer appropriate to leave the pursuit of Australian national interests in many countries of importance to Australia to the embassies and diplomats of the United Kingdom. It therefore moved to expand the nascent Australian diplomatic service as quickly as feasible and to ensure the service was genuinely open to talent, unlike its European counterparts, historically drawn from the aristocracy and comfortably off upper middle class. I was a beneficiary of that enlightened policy. A principal tool was the creation of a cadetship system with trainee diplomats being selected on the basis of a competitive examination. University degrees were not a prior requirement in order that the many defence force personnel, whose studies had been interrupted by war service, would not be disadvantaged. Accordingly, all cadets underwent a specifically designed course at the then Canberra University College, in our case lasting only eighteen, intensive, months. In large measure we learned the craft of diplomacy on the job. It was a well conceived system, suited to the times.

My first overseas assignment was as Third Secretary to Tel Aviv in 1950, four years after beginning my apprenticeship. Two days before our departure I married my Parisian wife, Odette, who until our engagement had been working in the French Legation in Canberra. We had had only three weeks' notice but I wanted her to be with me from the beginning of this exciting new life. Then, as ever afterwards, she put my interests ahead of her own.

In Tel Aviv I had first-hand contact with the early peacekeeping work of the United Nations, which chaired Mixed Armistice Commissions designed to supervise the truce agreements between Israel and each of its neighbours. At the time there were many clandestine incursions by Palestinians into Israel so the work of the Commissions was important in ensuring that hostilities between Israel and the Arab states did not resume. I was left with the impression that, under the right conditions, the United Nations could make a practical contribution to peace and security.

I left Israel critical of the Arab states' policy of using Palestine refugees as a pawn in their aim to destroy Israel. I began to form the conviction that some way must be found for the international community to ensure refugees were treated with genuine humanitarianism, a conviction strongly reinforced after I joined WFP.

After a short posting in Canberra, to my delight I was posted to Washington, far and away our most important post, in 1956. That posting was the defining point in my professional life. At one time or another during my assignment in Washington I reported on virtually every significant international issue of concern to Australia, including being privy to clandestine operations of the CIA against Indonesia's President Sukarno and attending a top secret meeting between the New Zealand Prime Minister and Australian Minister for External Affairs with the Secretary of State, John Foster Dulles, who gave a brilliant *tour d'horizon* covering all the issues of concern to the United States at the time. I was enormously impressed by the capabilities of the State Department and by its commitment to excellence, a characteristic of the country and its institutions. I loved the vitality of America and the civility of its people.

My interest in the United Nations was sharpened by my assignment to our UN mission for the extended 1956-57 session of the General Assembly, which dealt with the Soviet invasion of Hungary, the Suez crisis and the ensuing Anglo/French/Israeli attack on Egypt. Australia was on the Security Council at this time. The stakes were probably higher and the debates among world leaders more exciting than ever before or since at the United Nations. For a young diplomat it was a time of accelerated learning of the craft of multilateral diplomacy. My Middle East expertise was put to good use, for example in the debates about the future of Palestinian refugees. While this experience at the General Assembly did not lead me to think of a career with the United Nations, it reinforced my view that, important as Australia's alliance with America was, it should always be complemented by vigorous support for the United Nations. Just because we had a small population and isolated geographical situation we should not put all our eggs in the American basket.

For the next five years I had no involvement with the United Nations; instead working in Brussels, Canberra and Jakarta. I opened our mission to the European Community which provided insight into the working of a major intergovernmental organisation not part of the United Nations. In the Indonesia of 1962-1964 I witnessed as extreme poverty as I was ever to see anywhere, even in Africa. President Sukarno was at the height of his power but his policies had brought about virtual economic collapse. I became convinced that Australia's long-term security depended on building a prosperous, eventually democratic, Southeast Asia. With my economics background and pragmatic approach to problem solving, I concluded that a well judged Australian aid program was the most important among the few tools available to us to encourage such progress. We provided modest development assistance at the time, which was useful for keeping open a substantive relationship with a broader range of Indonesians than our tense political relationship would otherwise have allowed. However, I was convinced that, as soon as Sukarno departed office, the aid program should be expanded to the point of making a serious impact on the economic development of Indonesia. In fact that happened but never on the scale I thought necessary, neither in Indonesia nor in the rest of Southeast Asia.

The only sustainable route for raising living standards is through economic development. Trickle down does work though it works better and faster with good governance. However, Australia has always thought small in the aid area, with the exceptions of Papua New Guinea and the island nations of the South Pacific. Essentially, our focus has been on aid simply as a means to build good will towards, and better understanding of, Australia. Though useful in itself, our aid is marginal in the promotion of economic and social development.

After my Jakarta tour of duty ended, I went back to the United States in 1964, this time to New York as Counsellor in our Mission to the United Nations. I was assigned to handle trade and development issues.

The sixties were a time of great ferment and creativity in the United Nations. The effective end of colonisation brought an explosion in membership with a resulting heavy emphasis on development issues. The Soviets formed a *de facto* alliance with many of the new members of the United Nations who were determined to set the future agenda for the UN system. My posting coincided with the creation of the United Nations Conference on Trade and Development (UNCTAD) which, in the political circumstances of the time, was taken seriously by both developed and developing countries. However, led by their top trade officials, the developed countries resisted every effort to change the international trade and financial systems, then as now detrimental to developing countries. One morning we found written on the blackboard in the caucus room of developed countries the following: Technical assistance, YES; Capital aid, MAYBE; Trade liberalisation, NEVER! Possibly one of our number, incensed by the general negativity of the rich countries, had chosen to show us up to ourselves. The sequence showed accurately our preference for aiding developing countries in ways least costly to ourselves—a preference which continues.

The WFP had been established shortly before I arrived in New York. UNICEF and UNDP were at the height of their prestige, embodying the practical idealism which attracted outstanding people to work within the United Nations system. Many of the founders of these organisations were still active in them. It was very satisfying to play my part in building better relations between developed and developing countries, a difficult task with many African delegates still smarting from their personal experiences of colonialism and racial discrimination.

At my first stint at the UN in 1956-57 I had been an adviser behind the scenes. Now, as a representative, I had many occasions to speak on behalf of Australia in different boards and committees, including from the podium of the General Assembly in plenary session. There were also endless meetings of delegations of the 'Western European and Others' group to which Australia belonged. The creation of UNCTAD had resulted in the formation of caucuses of developed, developing and Soviet bloc countries to negotiate the texts of substantive agreements, a methodology carried over into the UN system as a whole. The caucus of developing countries, known as the G77, was still operative in Rome when I came there nearly twenty years later. I learned a lot about the workings of the various secretariats, developed my parliamentary skills and built friendly relationships with many delegates. All this was to prove immensely valuable when I came to head WFP.

Becoming an Australian Ambassador represented the summit of my ambition at this time. Only when I was sounded out about a possible appointment by the joint heads of the newly created UNDP, Paul Hoffman and David Owen, did it enter my mind that heading the right UN system agency one day would make a very good cap to any diplomat's career. From New York I returned to Canberra where I was Assistant Secretary responsible for Asia (other than Southeast Asia), the South Pacific and the Americas. I was not involved in UN or aid issues.

I was appointed Ambassador to the Philippines in 1970. It was quickly evident to me that, relative to elsewhere in Southeast Asia, Australia had neglected opportunities to build substantive relationships with the Philippines. I fought hard and succeeded in introducing a bigger aid program as a way of rectifying this.

Some three years later I went to Ottawa. I was simultaneously Australia's first High Commissioner to the Caribbean states of Jamaica, Guyana, Trinidad and Tobago and the Bahamas. We had a special interest in Jamaica and Guyana, which had taken the lead to establish an association of bauxite producers. Australia, as the world's largest producer, was included. Inspired by the success of OPEC, the developing countries wanted to create a bauxite cartel.

A CHANGE OF DIRECTION

By the early 1970s most other OECD countries, but not Australia, had created a department of government dedicated to the provision of aid to developing countries, entirely separate from the foreign ministry. When it came into office in 1972, the Whitlam Labor government established the Australian Development Assistance Agency (ADAA) as a statutory body whose head was directly answerable to the Minister for Foreign Affairs. ADAA's establishment was resisted and resented by the Department of Foreign Affairs, which feared loss of control over Australia's foreign aid program.

The agency had been in operation for about a year when Foreign Affairs, knowing my interest in foreign aid, cut short my posting in Ottawa and assigned me to head ADAA's Bilateral Division. I took up the post in January 1975.

I was delighted to join ADAA. I believed the aid program was an integral tool of Australian foreign policy, even potentially its most important, if it was used as a serious instrument for economic development. Economic growth could only be realised over the long term which meant that aid should be managed from a similar perspective, though there would of course always be an element of political 'short-termism'.

Foreign Affairs' dislike of ADAA was shared by the regulatory departments of Treasury and the Public Service Board. The former was contemptuous of all aid, except that extended by the World Bank, an institution in which Treasury had a vested interest. With these opponents, it was not surprising, therefore, that a new Liberal government decided to abolish ADAA and subsume it within the Department of Foreign Affairs. The Australian Development Assistance Bureau (ADAB) was born in June 1976. The former Director-General of ADAA was given a diplomatic post and in due course I was appointed Director, that is chief executive, of the new organisation, which had the same functions as its predecessor, though with an end to full autonomy.

The new government also implemented staff cutbacks. ADAB was a principal victim. Through the whole of my tenure there was a permanent staff squeeze, making it impossible to recruit the expertise required to fully modernise administration or bring in up-to-date knowledge of aid best practice. Instead, too many of the most competent officers were lost to departments of greater opportunity; and the proportion of less capable officers increased. Altogether, much of my time was taken up in daunting battles over money and staff but I left satisfied that, without my efforts, ADAB would have ceased to exist and Australia's aid program been gravely weakened.

Moreover, we still managed to introduce important policy initiatives: a vastly expanded program of assistance to the island states of the South Pacific; the creation of a program to assist countries of the Indian Ocean; the commencement of a technical assistance program to Communist China, which made Australia one of the first OECD countries to do so; the active involvement of the Australian scientific establishment in broad aspects of the program, especially agriculture and health. For the first time the full resources of the tertiary education sector were brought to bear in a systematic way on training in Australia and on support for developing countries' educational institutions. Relations with the NGOs providing overseas assistance were strengthened.

Support for international agricultural research had begun under ADAA. An enduring achievement of my tenure was the creation of a new statutory body, the Australian Centre for International Agricultural Research (ACIAR), which has flourished and brought great kudos to Australia worldwide.

My one policy disappointment was my inability to convince the Government that untied budget support aid to PNG should be progressively reduced and a program of aid directed to specific development projects gradually implemented. This would ensure, I argued, greater discipline in directing resources to serious investment goals and diminish PNG governments' temptation to maintain popularity through excessive expenditure on current consumption. However, I was up against too formidable a group of influential Australians including my mentor, the late Sir John Crawford, who were convinced, mistakenly as it turned out, that Australia had left behind a model administration which would not be another example of failed colonisation as in much of Africa.

I left ADAB in 1982 after more than seven years. Throughout, I had been sustained and encouraged by the full support of my ADAB colleagues. I was proud of our policy achievements and of the esteem in which we were held within much of the Australian civil service, among the aid NGOs and our peer counterparts in the other developed countries. I was made an Officer in the Order of Australia in 1984 in recognition of my service.

INTERNATIONAL CIVIL SERVANT

Toward the end of my time with ADAB, I decided to look for new opportunities. I was not attracted to a senior ambassadorial post. I loved my career as a professional diplomat but the time had come to find a new challenge.

My diplomatic experience had tempered belief in the concepts of 'balance of power' and 'national interest' as sufficient over the long term to secure the peace and security of Australia, distant from the sources of Western power. Australian interests would ultimately be better served by a world of strong institutions of global governance. Meanwhile, the United Nations system remained the basis for the growth in law-based functional regimes that I favoured.

During the Cold War the peace and security work of the UN became largely moribund. It was the various functional agencies (even if some of the more prominent of these, for example UNESCO and FAO, were seen as relative failures) which underpinned what importance the system as a whole retained. With my background in development and humanitarian assistance

I believed I could make a contribution to sustaining and improving the UN system's relevance in this critical area.

The evolution in my thinking probably owed something to my personal background. The Australia in which I grew up was overwhelmingly populated by persons originating in the British Isles. During the nineteen thirties and early forties the culture was still heavily influenced by English Protestantism, commitment to the British monarchy and nostalgia for Britain as 'home'. The bitter divisions during the First World War between those who saw Australia as an integral part of the British Empire, and therefore supported conscription, and those who opposed it still endured. Irish Catholics and Australian nationalists generally were in the latter camp. My parents were mainly of English extraction but, due to two strong-minded Irish great grandmothers, were Catholic. I probably absorbed the sense of coming from the 'underdogs' in society. That may have led me to sympathise with the underdogs of the Third World. More importantly perhaps, on both maternal and paternal sides, I was a fourth-generation descendant of English-born pioneer settlers of the Western District of Victoria. I was brought up on an ethic of personal self-reliance. My father was a lifelong Australian nationalist and supporter of the Labor Party, itself strongly imbued with Australian national consciousness. I therefore entered upon my diplomatic career regarding the still strong commitment in Australian society and politics to the link with Britain as anachronistic. At the time, though I regarded our alliance with the United States as very much in the national interest, I also felt that Australia alone must take responsibility for its national security. In the end no alliance could be the permanent foundation of our security. I was idealistic but not sentimental. The world must be made a better place, which for a diplomat meant support for multilateralism and international law. Furthermore a just, and therefore peaceful, world order required lifting the Third World out of oppression and poverty.

On Becoming a Candidate

Sir John Crawford suggested that I move to the World Bank, where I had become respected for my efforts to improve Australia's support for agriculture within our aid program. However, in practice the presidency of the Bank was open only to American citizens. Though less prestigious, heading a UN system agency proper might be just as satisfying. I was a professional diplomat not a professional economist. The right United Nations organisation would enable me to do something concrete to improve global governance and assist developing countries. But how to get such a post? Executive heads were selected through a process of political competition between countries. No Australian had ever headed a UN system operational agency. Australia was not a major contributor to voluntary funded agencies and overall our foreign policy gave little weight to support for the United Nations, notwithstanding the creative role played by Australia in the formation of the UN system. As an Australian I was not well placed to realise my ambition.

I knew my chances would be much improved if I was personally well known in international development circles. As head of ADAB I had made a point of representing Australia at meetings of the governing bodies of some of the multilateral development agencies, including the World Bank. WFP was not among them. My staff spoke very well of it but at the time I shared the conventional prejudice against food aid. Nevertheless, it was through my participation in an entirely different multilateral organisation, not connected with the United Nations, that I became a candidate for the post of chief executive of the World Food Programme.

In the spring of 1981 I attended in Paris a meeting of the Consultative Group on International Agricultural Research (CGIAR) in whose work I had taken a keen interest. The CGIAR oversaw the work of the various international agricultural research institutes established around the globe over the previous 20 or 30 years and whose work had led to the 'green revolution'. Australia funded these institutes from its aid budget.

FAO was a sponsor of the CGIAR. The responsible FAO official was Assistant Director-General, Professor Dieter Bommer, whom I got to know well at CGIAR meetings. Bommer told me the Canadian Executive Director of WFP, Mr Gerry Vogel, had died suddenly and it would now be necessary to choose a new Executive Director.

The method of appointment of the WFP Executive Director was uniquely complex, involving both the Secretary-General of the United Nations and the Director-General of FAO. In coming to their decision, they were enjoined to consult with the members of WFP's governing body, the Committee on Food Aid Policies and Programmes (CFA)—some thirty in all with a small majority from developing countries. In practice, therefore, the appointment was a quasi election since neither the Secretary-General nor the Director-General would feel free to appoint someone who did not have a substantial measure of governmental support.

WFP was wholly funded by voluntary contributions from governments. In recognition of this, developing countries had come to accept that its head should be drawn from among the donors. Indeed, with only one exception, previous Executive Directors had been from donor countries. Although Australia was not a major donor, Bommer thought an Australian could be appointed. He suggested I might like therefore to be a candidate and that, if I wished, he would arrange for me to meet his Director-General, Edouard Saouma.

I was sceptical. From time to time Australians had stood as candidates for UN system organisations but without success. Australia simply lacked the political weight and strength of will to get its nominees home. However, I agreed to the meeting with Saouma, which took place a few weeks later after the finish of my business in Europe.

Meeting Edouard Saouma

It was the first time I had visited the FAO headquarters. These had been provided by the Italian Government, the core building having housed the pre-war ministry responsible for Italy's colonies. The Director-General's

Edouard Saouma and the author, 1991

office was located on the fourth floor of a newer building. It looked out on the Circus Maximus behind which was the Palatine Hill covered with ruined palaces going back to the time of the Roman Emperors. Beyond the ruins was a beautiful skyline of pines, spires and towers built over many centuries. This superb, virtually unparalleled, view never failed to raise my spirits. Over the years, that was some compensation for the many frustrating visits I made to that office.

The Director-General's rooms were accessed by a lift dedicated to that purpose, a luxury I rarely encountered in other agencies, and certainly not one enjoyed by the Secretary-General. A guard was always on duty to reserve its use for the Director-General and his visitors. When I exited the lift I found myself in a long corridor. Another uniformed guard directed me to proceed up the corridor where I was met by yet another who pointed me to the Director-General's waiting room. I was not surprised to learn subsequently that Saouma was obsessed with his personal security and that security in FAO was tighter than in any other UN agency.

Saouma was a Lebanese Christian whose community's dominance of Lebanese political institutions was threatened by the Muslim majority. Not surprisingly, Saouma was unsympathetic to the Palestinian cause. He once spoke to me of his admiration for Israeli Prime Minister Menachem Begin. Saouma had won good marks from the United States for keeping the Palestine issue off FAO's agenda, something most of his peers in other specialised agencies had not been able to do. His task was made easier in that the Soviet Union was not a member of FAO.

I was apprehensive about the meeting. I knew little about Saouma, though I was aware he was widely regarded as a consummate politician, with a reputation for single-mindedness, totally committed to the institutional interests of FAO. He was said to have a strong personality, was considered unscrupulous by the developed countries and was a controversial figure within the UN system.

After a longish wait, a door opened and Saouma came in to greet me. I found him to be short in stature, beautifully groomed in a superbly tailored suit. He looked much like a Neapolitan businessman, certainly not like a typical agricultural professional, even if he did hold degrees in agricultural chemistry and agronomy and at age 31 had headed up Lebanon's national agricultural research organisation. For many years he had been a delegate to

FAO meetings and joined the agency in 1962. He was elected Director-General in 1975 and when I met him was seeking re-election for a second six-year term to begin in 1982. He was virtually assured of re-election since no other candidates had come forward.

I was immediately charmed. Saouma had a winning smile and his greeting was warm. We quickly reached a high level of rapport in our conversation which lasted over an hour. (We spoke in English, in which he is fluent, though he prefers French, the second language of educated Lebanese). He was a good but not impassive listener. I felt entirely at ease and at the end of the meeting we agreed that our chemistry was positive. Though Saouma's appearance was one of considerable elegance, his personal manner and style was strongly masculine. He gave an impression of intelligence, sincerity and truthfulness, leavened with humour when at his persuasive best. I saw nothing of the insecurity, ruthlessness and self-importance said also to be among his personality traits. His principal deputy at the time, Edward West, once summed him up to me thus, 'Saouma is a superb persuader one-on-one, much less impressive with a group'. He had certainly persuaded me that I could work with him.

The Candidates

Saouma told me there were already three other candidates in the field. The United Kingdom was giving strong support to Ms Joan Anstee, an Assistant Secretary-General in the UN Secretariat in New York. Saouma bluntly ruled out Anstee on account of her sex. (As I learned over the years, the culture of FAO, reflecting the traditionally male profession of most of its staff, was unfriendly to women in senior posts.) I knew Anstee and suspected she had UN Secretary-General Waldheim's personal backing. I was reassured when Saouma added that he had 'eighty per cent' of the say in the appointment, reflecting the relative dominance of FAO as compared with the UN on WFP matters, though not the legal position that gave each an equal say in the choice of Executive Director. Saouma was to make this point several times in the months ahead.

The United States was also fielding a candidate, a senior official in USAID, the United States overseas aid organisation. The United States, as the principal donor to the World Food Programme and the country most responsible for its creation, considered it anomalous that an American had held the post only once and then for a few months only, Saouma said. Though Canada had not yet put forward a candidate officially, it strongly contended that since the previous incumbent's term had been cut short, it was only fair that Canada, the second largest donor to the Programme, should continue to fill the post.

Saouma said flatly that it would not be desirable for the United States to head WFP in which its influence was 'already too strong'. In his view Canada had already had its turn. Referring to the Acting Executive Director and substantive Deputy Executive Director, Bernardo Brito of Brazil, Saouma said he did not wish, nor did he expect, Brito to become a candidate. 'Brito is competent but as yet lacks sufficient maturity,' he commented. 'The way is therefore open if you wish to be a candidate', adding that it would be vital to secure the formal backing of the Australian Government and for it to lobby strongly with governments to seek their support for my appointment. He also warned that Australia, unknown to me, was considering putting forward Patrick Donovan as its candidate. Donovan was Commercial Minister in the Australian Mission to the United Nations in Geneva and a former professor of law specialising in international trade issues.

Saouma told me there was no urgency about announcing a formal Australian candidature. He had no intention of making a decision quickly and he left me with the impression that he preferred to wait until after his re-election in November and that of the UN Secretary-General in December.

As our conversation developed, I felt Saouma was more interested in selling me on the post than in assessing my merits as a candidate. Indeed he told me I was well qualified and tempted me with tales of how I would be feted in every country of the developing world. I left the meeting confident that I was virtually assured of getting the post. That supposition was confirmed when a few days later our Ambassador in Rome met with Saouma. However, much to my surprise, it turned out that obtaining the Australian Government's nomination was an almost insuperable obstacle.

My minister, the Minister for Foreign Affairs, Tony Street, immediately gave his assent. The Minister for Primary Industry, Peter Nixon, whose department had oversight of FAO, was ready to support me. However, the Minister for Trade, Doug Anthony, who was Deputy Prime Minister and leader of the National Party, favoured the candidature of Donovan. There was an impasse.

The stalemate continued through July, August and September 1981. I was very concerned by the delay and felt Australia would lose the post by default. Saouma was pressing me to get Street to inform UN Secretary-General Waldheim as soon as possible of his personal support. He told me Waldheim had earlier agreed with him that an American should not be appointed but he now felt Waldheim, to assure American support for his own re-election, might well yield to American pressure and throw his weight behind their candidate.

The matter was only resolved in late September—that is almost four months after my visit to Rome—when at a cocktail party I ran into Anthony in the company of the Secretary of his Department, Jim Scully. I had had several discussions with Scully and I felt he personally favoured my candidature. At this chance meeting, I reminded both men that a decision was awaited and expressed the hope that Anthony might give me his support. Anthony turned to Scully for advice and Scully simply said, 'I think it's time we put our support behind Jim'. Anthony assented on the spot. The campaign could at last begin.

The Campaign

The Department of Foreign Affairs moved very expeditiously. The FAO Director-General and the UN Secretary-General were officially informed. Instructions were sent to relevant Australian embassies to seek the support of the governments to which they were accredited. Over the whole campaign, I was always appreciative of the high diplomatic professionalism of my colleagues, especially the support given by our Ambassador to Italy, Keith Douglas-Scott.

The US and British candidates were still in the field but neither was attracting support, and the Canadians had weakened their claim. When Saouma suggested that their first choice, a senior official of the Canadian Wheat Board, would not be satisfactory, they had floated the possibility of an alternative, the permanent head of their Department of Agriculture. Canada appeared to be in the situation of having two candidates and leaving it to the Director-General to make his choice. However, in October the Canadians put forward a third name, this time definitively. Dr Paul Gerin La-Joie was a former Quebec politician and President of the Canadian International Development Agency (CIDA), the counterpart of ADAB. He had the strong personal backing of Canadian Prime Minister, Pierre

Trudeau. Gerin La-Joie had impressive personal credentials. As a French Canadian and given Canada's very supportive aid policies towards French-speaking Africa, he was in a good position to get French and African backing. On the other hand, Canada's muddle over nominating its candidate had delayed its campaign. That compensated for the time I had lost in getting the Australian Government's support.

The situation had been vastly complicated by the *de facto* entry of Brito into the fray. A Brazilian diplomat, Brito had been his country's delegate to FAO and the other food agencies and at one time Chairman of the G77. In that role he had developed a very strong rapport with Saouma.

Originally, FAO Directors-General's terms were for four years but after dissatisfaction with a previous incumbent this was changed by the FAO Conference to a single term of six years. Saouma had been elected on that basis in 1976. However, shortly after his election the G77, under Brito's leadership, not only secured the reversal of the earlier decision but made FAO Directors-General eligible for an unlimited number of six-year terms!

Although not a declared candidate Brito did gain support among delegations in Rome, from both developed and developing countries. The donors were impressed by his apparent willingness to 'stand up' to Saouma. The Nordic countries, which had been considering putting forward a candidate of their own, instead came out in support of Brito in October. A senior diplomat in the Swedish Foreign Ministry summed up their attitude in conversation with me, 'You may well be the best qualified candidate but not the most appropriate choice'.

In the light of the reports I was receiving I concluded that Brito was my strongest rival. However, Saouma was dismissive when I mentioned him as a serious possibility. His insouciance puzzled me, since Brito had successfully lobbied the Latin American caucus, who had endorsed him, and he was lobbying other G77 sub-groups.

In December my view was confirmed by the attitude of the US permanent representative to the Rome food agencies, Roger Sorenson. Sorenson argued the WFP was too much under the influence of FAO and Saouma personally. He said this influence extended not only to 'decisions on emergency aid but also to WFP staff appointments and internal WFP decision-making on substantive matters'. This was against developed countries' interests. He contended it was important to separate WFP from FAO and make it more independent, not only in practice but constitutionally. Such a separation,

Sorenson said, would be strongly opposed by Saouma who could always block reform because of his effective control of the G77. While the optimum solution would be to oust Saouma, this was out of the question since he had just been re-elected. The alternative course was to have an Executive Director who was able to compete with Saouma in mobilising G77 support and so have the majority vote necessary to affect constitutional change. The only candidate in the field able to do this was Brito. Therefore, Sorenson argued, the donors should forget their 'selfish and parochial interest' in having one of their own appointed and should instead all get behind Brito and support him in his efforts to 'save WFP'. Sorenson said he was arguing this case with the State Department in Washington and also with delegates of other Western countries. There was considerable evidence that the argument was falling on fertile ground. I knew from the Australian Embassy in Rome that Brito was intimating discreetly that he had shown he had the strength to defend donor interests in WFP.

Sorenson's argument found favour in Washington. The State Department was disposed to withdraw its candidate and support Brito, in exchange for his agreement to fill the Deputy Executive Director position with an American. The State Department argued that the United States would be better off with a developing country because 'the developed countries do not give whole-hearted support to the United States'. Brito, as Acting Executive Director, had been 'far more responsive to US views than the former Canadian Executive Director', our representative was told.

Australia's Alleged Opportunism

The United States was taking a generally negative attitude to my appointment also because of what it and other developed countries regarded as opportunistic Australian policy in FAO and in the CFA to influence Saouma in favour of my candidature. The charges were false. In fact, it was, for me an awkward, coincidence that Australia changed its position in two meetings just preceding the appointment of the Executive Director. Nevertheless, the charges carried credibility, given the pattern of donor opportunism in FAO and elsewhere in the UN system.

At the FAO conference in November 1981, when Saouma was re-elected, Australia broke ranks with the other major contributors by abstaining in the vote to adopt the FAO budget. Beforehand, the principal contributors had linked in an informal association known as the Geneva Group, whose members contributed more than half of the FAO budget. They had agreed to vote against adoption of the budget as a protest against the extraordinarily large increase being proposed by the Director-General. In the FAO, as in other specialised agencies, each state has one vote. Since Saouma was able to command the full support of the G77, it was not possible for developed countries to either block his re-election or to prevent the adoption of the budget. However, they could show their displeasure by casting negative votes. Australia had therefore committed a serious breach of faith in the eyes of the Geneva Group.

I was not even aware of the decision to abstain. I discovered later this had been driven by the Prime Minister's Department, possibly by the Prime Minister himself, for reasons connected with the Commonwealth Heads of Government meeting in Melbourne at that time. Prime Minister Malcolm Fraser was sensitive to African interests and to the importance of improving African agriculture. It was a vote that returned to seriously complicate my re-appointment five years later.

Australia was also under criticism from the United States, and even more strongly from Thailand, after we failed to join them in opposing a WFP development project for Vietnam, which was considered by the CFA at its 12th Session in 1981. No amount of explanation by our Ambassador in Bangkok and by the Department of Foreign Affairs to the Thai Ambassador in Canberra was able to persuade the Thais that the Australian delegation's stand was not intended to be inimical to their interests. As we saw it, projects in multilateral organisations should be judged on technical grounds alone, whereas the objections raised by the United States were obviously political. Our delegation was instructed to abstain on the project if it came to a vote, not to intervene in the debate and generally to take a low profile. This did not help the effort to sway the Thais from their support for Brito to me. Indeed, on the visit to Bangkok referred to in the previous chapter, I sensed the Thai's fear that, as head of WFP, I would change the *status quo* in relation to the Cambodian refugees which, in fact, I had no intention of doing.

US Opposition to my Appointment

The strength of US concern came through clearly in the Acting Secretary of State's reply to our minister's letter seeking support for my candidature. While maintaining their own candidate, the letter argued that, regardless of who ultimately obtained the post, the next incumbent must be prepared to 'strengthen the independence of the WFP from the FAO in order to improve the rational allocation of emergency food aid'. Although Americans who had met and worked with me had a 'high regard for my abilities', the United States would 'prefer to support an Australian for another high post in the United Nations rather than this one'. In what was tantamount to a rebuke, the Acting Secretary of State concluded that 'before launching candidacies, Australia should consult with the United States'.

The minister and Department of Foreign Affairs in Canberra were angered by the State Department's attitude, which they saw as 'naive, unrealistic and inimical to Western interests'. Carried to its logical conclusion, our embassies were informed, the position advocated by Sorenson would mean all UN system organisations ought to be headed either by Americans or developing country nationals. Australia believed that allies of the United States could reasonably expect it to support their nationals for senior positions in the UN system to ensure that overall Western influence was maximised. Our Embassy in Washington was instructed to advise the State Department that my candidature would not have been put forward if our soundings had not made it very clear that none of the other Western candidates, including the American, were likely to find favour with the Director-General of FAO. In our view, the State Department appeared to be influenced more by a desire to outsmart Saouma than by any clearly balanced appreciation of what was in the long-term interests of the United States and its allies. The American attitude softened following that reply; strong representations by our Ambassadors in Washington and to the United Nations in New York; and my personal meeting with the key State Department official, Gordon Streeb.

Meanwhile, Australian embassies around the world worked to gain support for my candidature, with some success. Saouma himself did his part. For example, he called in the Chairman of the G77, a Libyan, a man whom I knew and whom I greatly respected, and asked him to get his government to formally advise him and the Secretary-General of his support for me. This was done. Saouma did the same thing with other G77 representatives seeking his favour, with the same result. Canberra was somewhat bemused to find what it believed to be its own representations having such success with countries like Libya.

The responses of foreign offices to these sorts of representations are not always to be taken at face value. For example, Australia had very good bilateral relations with China and I personally had taken the initiative to extend Australia's overseas aid program to China. None of that counted when it came to the test. The Chinese Foreign Ministry gave us the impression that China would support my appointment. However, Saouma told me the Chinese Ambassador had informed him of China's unequivocal support for Brito. For his part, Saouma simply told the Ambassador that since China was not a member of the CFA, its attitude was immaterial. The Chinese subsequently made it clear they too were indebted to Brito because, under his leadership, WFP had initiated very valuable development projects in China.

The stand taken by France is also of interest. Saouma told me in February 1982 that France was the only country which 'had emphatically' opposed my nomination, the reason being Australia's opposition to the European Community's Common Agricultural Policy. Throughout my tenure of WFP, France was often positively unhelpful to my efforts.

The Final Drama

Nineteen eighty two opened, still with no decision. I telephoned Saouma at the end of 1981 urging him to act; he replied, 'There is no hurry'. I was anxious to get across to him that Brito represented a serious threat but he continued to dismiss this possibility. There was no doubt in my mind that Brito had the support of the developing countries and that most of the donor countries would willingly accept him. Indeed, many preferred him. The general consensus among delegations in Rome was that he was doing a good job. In order to have an opportunity to meet personally with key delegates able to influence their governments I decided to go to Rome for a meeting of the governing council of IFAD, of which I was the Australian alternate Governor. I went on to New York to meet with the new Secretary-General, Javier Pérez de Cuéllar. I had called on his predecessor, Kurt Waldheim, some months earlier. These calls, though essential, were not 'job interviews'.

I found that Brito was indeed playing his cards extremely well. Rather than follow the conventional route of presenting himself as his country's candidate, he had lobbied successfully behind the scenes to receive the support of the G77 in Rome and through the Latin American delegations in New York, the support of the G77 there also. In effect he was seeking to be drafted. He could continue to maintain that he was not an 'official' candidate and thus not directly opposing Saouma's wishes.

By mid-February, Saouma had still not come to a decision. Brito had succeeded in getting the G77 in New York to reaffirm its earlier endorsement of him. The United States had still not withdrawn its candidate even though it was widely agreed he held little chance. I continued to fear that the US might throw its weight behind Brito.

The Canadians were also beginning to nibble at the possibility of having their man appointed to a different post, namely Coordinator of United Nations Disaster Relief (UNDRO). Contests for UN posts often come to resemble 'musical chairs'. If candidates and their governments fear they will not be successful in their first choice they may bargain for a consolation prize. The British candidate, Joan Anstee, was also said to be interested in the UNDRO post. If Canada withdrew from the WFP race, the path for Brito would be even easier.

According to detailed reports in the Rome *International Daily News* by George Weller, a former Pulitzer Prize winning journalist, Saouma had throughout sought to deceive Brito by leaving him with the impression that when the time came there would be little problem in getting the Secretary-General's agreement to Brito in view of his standing with developing countries and the fact that none of the developed country candidates had majority support. Further, according to Weller, Brito was led to believe that after his many years' loyal service, Saouma would never prefer any other candidate.

By mid-February, Weller reported, Pérez de Cuéllar was becoming insistent on the desirability of appointing Brito, who had satisfactorily served as Acting Executive Director for almost 12 months, and that Pérez de Cuéllar and Saouma had 'clashed sharply'. When it was almost too late, Saouma explained to the G77 in Rome why Brito was unworthy of their support.

In a telephone conversation with me on 18 February, Saouma said he would never agree to Brito. Under him, the situation of WFP was 'quite bad'. There was a resource crisis; project approval had been politicised over the deferral by the WFP Secretariat of the previously mentioned Vietnam project; and there had been mishandling of emergency aid requests. What was required, he told me, was a strong Executive Director with the capability of raising funds, in other words someone who fully enjoyed the confidence of the donors. He further said he had absolutely no confidence in Brito, whom he regarded as unreliable. He claimed Brito was always running to him; he had to see him at least once a week. Finally, he could not 'share responsibility for signing the WFP accounts' with him. (That was an ominous justification in the light of my subsequent battle with Saouma over accounts.) I took it that these were the sorts of arguments Saouma had put to the Rome G77 and the Secretary-General.

When what Saouma was saying to the G77 got back to Brito, he decided to pre-empt the Director-General by going direct to the G77 in New York. A biennial pledging conference is held there at which donors announce what they will contribute to WFP over the next two years. Such a conference was scheduled for the last week of February. Brito held a preliminary meeting with donors and G77 representatives in Rome on 22 February, immediately before leaving for New York.

Saouma, by now thoroughly alarmed, exerted pressure. He too had influence within the New York G77 being targeted by Brito. Among Arab states, the Algerian representative was especially influential. The Director-General also had good links with some Latin Americans and influential Asians, particularly India. Through such representatives, Saouma was able to demonstrate to the Secretary-General that support for Brito was far from monolithic among the G77. That was an argument that our Ambassador had also been putting to the Secretary-General, giving him the names of the developing countries who had undertaken to support my candidature. Canada had also vigorously supported its candidate, Prime Minister Trudeau personally intervening on his behalf. By this time neither the American nor the British candidates had any prospect of appointment. The final choice was between Gerin La-Joie, Brito and me. Saouma convinced the Secretary-General to agree to my appointment, which they announced jointly on 24 February 1982. When Brito arrived in New York, he faced a *fait accompli*.

The Decision Made

Saouma rang me at 3.00am Australian time on 25 February to let me know the decision had been taken and an announcement would be made in the next few hours. He also told me he had convened a meeting of the heads of delegation of CFA member countries to inform them of the decision and that the announcement had been 'well received'. All had assured him I would be given their 'full support': so much for the G77's supposed independence of the Director-General. Brito had clearly over-estimated his influence with the G77 in Rome and New York in challenging Saouma. I have little doubt the latter feared that, as Executive Director of WFP, Brito would be a formidable adversary if he subsequently ran for Director-General of FAO.

It had been a long, hard nine months but my hopes had finally been realised. I knew I owed my appointment to Saouma but I also knew he had given me his unqualified backing because it suited his interests to have an Australian. An American would have been Saouma's least preferred choice. Canada was a more important country than Australia and had very good standing with most developing countries and Gerin La-Joie was well known especially in francophone Africa. Like Brito, he had the potential political base from which to successfully contest the Director-Generalship of FAO. For an Australian that would be much more difficult.

POST-APPOINTMENT DONOR ATTITUDES

Donor suspicions of me on account of the Australian Government's actions in FAO and the CFA were strengthened a few days after my appointment had been announced when, at the WFP pledging conference already mentioned, Australia announced a very large increase in its contribution to WFP.

In fact the increased pledge, like our support for the FAO budget, was not connected with my appointment. For more than a year ADAB had been considering the desirability of giving WFP a bigger share of Australia's substantial food aid. Australian delegates at CFA meetings and our representatives in developing countries had been impressed by the way in which the Programme's use of food brought much stronger developmental benefits than had Australian food aid, which placed virtually no conditions on the use by recipient governments of funds generated by the sale of Australian commodities. Further, increased aid through WFP was the most cost-effective way to improve Australia's comparatively poor standing as a donor to United Nations aid programs. From developmental and political perspectives, it made a lot of sense. To this day Australia remains a major donor to WFP.

The decision was made by the minister. While I had signed the recommendation going forward, I sent a separate note making it absolutely clear that I wanted him to consider the recommendation purely on its merits and without regard to my candidature. The desire among governments to obtain UN posts is such that making an increased contribution to the organisation concerned would not be out of the question for some, though it would have been for the Australia of that time given its lack of interest in expanding its influence in the UN system through the appointment of Australians to senior posts

In the discussions leading up to my appointment Director-General Saouma never sought any *quid pro quo* from me personally or from the Australian Government and I had volunteered nothing. The one thing Saouma did ask of me I was unable to get. He wanted Prime Minister Fraser to speak to Canadian Prime Minister Trudeau, who was in Australia to participate in the Commonwealth Heads of Government Meeting, with a view to persuading Canada to withdraw in my favour. As my candidature was not a high priority for the Australian Government, nothing was done, to my considerable disappointment.

My concern that donors expected I would willingly do Saouma's bidding was reinforced by American and Canadian responses to my appointment. The State Department, in discussion with our Embassy, raised the matter of the appointment of my deputy. Delegations, we were told, were concerned that Saouma might himself decide who should be appointed. Accordingly, I 'might like to consider making this appointment in such a way that it was seen to be my choice rather than the Director-General's'. The State Department was politely saying this was the first test of whether I would 'stand up' to Saouma. As will become clear in the next chapter, it was indeed a test.

The Canadians voiced similar concerns, but more tactfully. Our High Commission in Ottawa was told that, while Canada was pleased to see me appointed and would give me their full support, they were concerned the FAO Secretariat 'planned a more interventionist posture vis à vis the Programme'. The Canadians found that 'troubling' as they attached great importance to the WFP's development orientation for which, in their view, a 'reasonable measure of autonomy' was required.

The letter that I sent to our deputy chief in Washington, responding to the concerns of the State Department, shows the attitude I intended to bring to the post:

> As you well know and as you will be able to reassure Streeb, I am my own man. Nevertheless, I have developed a good relationship with Saouma

and I believe that is a pre-requisite for effective work as head of WFP. On the other hand, I have not made, nor has Saouma sought, any understandings on specific points relating to future FAO/WFP working relations. Thus it would be my intention to defer making any decision about who the Deputy Executive Director should be until I have had time enough to get the feel of the organisation and some perception of the qualities I want in a deputy.

Saouma's Vow to Control WFP

Donor fears about the consequences of my appointment for WFP were sharpened by Saouma's truculent remarks to WFP senior staff immediately following Brito's precipitate resignation. He told the meeting he was appointing a senior FAO Assistant Director General, Juan Felipe Yriat, as Acting Executive Director pending my arrival. The normal course would have been to appoint the most senior WFP staff member, Munzer El Midani. To add to the insult, Saouma added that the 'senior staff member of Syrian origin', i.e. El Midani, would not be acceptable as deputy and 'none of you should seek the position'. No foreign travel or home leave should be taken by senior staff until the new deputy was appointed 'after having been chosen by the Executive Director and approved by myself.' The implication was that they had all supported Brito and were not to be trusted. Finally, and from my point of view the most important statement of all, Saouma declared: 'There can be no question of independence for WFP since I have responsibilities in relation to the Programme which I intend to fulfil'. The Director-General's defiant message to them was duly noted by donor governments. It was interpreted, correctly as it turned out, that he intended to further strengthen his grip on WFP.

A CHALLENGE RELISHED

While liking had not diminished, my understanding of Saouma's methods, in particular the way in which he had come to dominate FAO through his manipulation of the G77, had vastly increased. For my part I had done nothing to conceal my character from him. Indeed, I believe he had judged me sufficiently well to realise I was a person of independent judgment. In my many contacts with him, I was straightforward and avoided using flattery. From our second meeting, I made a point of calling him by his first name. At a dinner just after my arrival in Rome, I overheard Yriat suggest to Saouma that I seemed pliable. Saouma replied, 'Don't underestimate him. He is quite strong, enough to stand up to donor pressure'. On one of my visits to Rome in January 1982, I lunched with Saouma's deputy, Edward West, who sought to get across to me that working with his boss was not easy and not to everyone's taste. My response was that my practice was to cooperate. I added that I shared the Australian disposition not to take kindly to being 'pushed around'. Years later, West told me he had advised Saouma not to appoint me.

I would not have sought the post if it did not provide scope for independent management. Early in my campaign I had read the WFP Basic Documents[15] carefully, and was satisfied that the post was not subordinate in the usual sense of that term, rather the powers and responsibilities of the Executive Director were defined formally by governments in resolutions of the UN and FAO, so that in key respects they did not flow from the authority of the Director-General, although he and the Secretary-General retained certain defined powers.

I saw the Executive Directorship as an opportunity to bring the highest standards of competence and integrity of which I was capable to the management of a United Nations agency. I wanted to make WFP an exemplar for international development and humanitarian cooperation.

As the head of a bilateral aid agency which funded UN agencies I was very sensitive to the need to craft the Programme in ways which would strengthen donor financial support, essential if the voluntarily funded World Food Programme was to have the means to serve the needs of developing countries. Equally, I wanted to enhance the multilateral character of the Programme by ensuring that the distribution of its assistance reflected legitimate need and not the politics of donors or the recipient government, though prudence required flexibility in the management of that goal. For instance, it would be necessary, within reasonable limits, to consider carefully the concerns of the United States. The Cold War was still very much in being and I would under no circumstances wish to harm vital Western security interests.

As a civil servant and a diplomat, I had served the government of the day. The policies I was devising and implementing were not necessarily ones with which I personally agreed. As a lateral thinker and decisive person, I knew I would perform better as an overt leader than as an adviser to ministers of uneven capabilities and knowledge. From my experience as a delegate to United Nations organisations I saw strong, good leadership as essential to strengthening the rule of law in international affairs. I knew that the executive heads of UN agencies had, in practice, a great deal more authority than Australian ministers, let alone civil servants. This may seem a large claim. What I mean is that within the ambit of the field for which they have responsibility, there are very few checks and balances on them. The story of how I was appointed is one example. I saw in the Executive Director post, the opportunity to use my talents to the full, something never previously open to me. WFP was to be the summit of my career and not a stepping stone, either to a higher executive post in the United Nations system or elsewhere. I wanted to be free to do what I thought was right.

I hoped, though I was far from confident, that Saouma would share my vision. I saw him as a complex personality of high intelligence and a pragmatist. However, I knew from his reputation there was a risk that he would see my ambition for WFP as a threat. Notwithstanding our liking for one another and my intention to maintain the best possible relationship with him, I expected that differences would occur. I hoped that did not mean our relationship would settle into an adversarial one. I was confident this need not happen. I had no desire to do anything to harm him or FAO and I felt he would see that a better WFP would reflect well on him. In short, I was prepared mentally for conflict but intended to do all I could to prevent its emergence. I therefore left for Rome full of zest and hope, and in no way daunted.

---

15   The resolutions and regulations passed by United Nations and FAO bodies to govern the establishment and operation of the Programme, the most important of which were the General Regulations. Their key provisions are in Appendix I. A full description of the powers of the Executive Director is given in the next chapter.

3

DEVELOPING A REFORM AGENDA

Arriving at WFP, I had to surmount the hurdles associated with politically controversial projects at my first CFA. I encountered the unique bureaucratic culture of a UN system agency; and started to clarify my goals for making WFP a better development and humanitarian agency.

Odette and I arrived in Rome at 5am on a cold and damp April morning after an overnight flight from Bangkok. We were met by the Acting Executive Director, Juan Felipe Yriat, and Bill Barnsdale, my chief of staff or *Chef de Cabinet*, to use UN system jargon.

On the journey from Fiumicino airport into Rome, Yriat, a man in his early sixties, dapper with a good head of white hair, talked non-stop, briefing me on all the complex matters he said were awaiting my decision. I had no intention of giving orders on issues of which I had little understanding and no first-hand knowledge. I replied, 'Please continue exactly as you would if I was not yet here'.

Yriat had been a Uruguayan diplomat and sometime Foreign Minister of that country and an excellent linguist. He was trusted by the Rome representatives of the developed countries and therefore valuable to Saouma, to whom he was intensely loyal. Indeed, I had disconcerted Saouma when I told him of my date of arrival. 'There is no hurry', he said. 'Yriat will take good care of the Programme pending your arrival.'

However, the CFA's thirteenth session was scheduled to begin on 19 April and I had no intention of missing it. Moreover, I preferred personally to fill the void left by Brito. I knew it would be essential to gain as soon as

possible the respect of all my senior staff. That would be no easy task since
I was seen as Saouma's man. The sooner I got to Rome the better, which we
did, only five weeks after the announcement.

COMMITTEE ON FOOD AID POLICIES
AND PROGRAMMES (CFA)

As recommended by the World Food Conference in 1974, the
intergovernmental body overseeing the work of WFP was reconstituted as
the Committee on Food Aid Policies and Programmes (CFA), comprising 15
member states elected by ECOSOC and 15 by the FAO Council, to serve
terms of three years. The functions of the CFA were expanded to include
significant policy roles. It was to provide a forum for 'intergovernmental
consultations on national and international food aid programmes and
policies', formulate 'proposals for the more effective coordination of
multilateral, bilateral and non-governmental food aid programmes,
including emergency food aid' and recommend to governments, through the
World Food Council (WFC), improvements in all aspects of the
international food aid regime. [16]

The CFA was also subjected to an even more complex reporting regime,
without precedent in the UN system. Not only must it report to ECOSOC
and the FAO Council as before, but its policy recommendations had to go
through WFC to which it was also to submit periodic and special reports.

The WFC was created in part because of government dissatisfaction with
FAO, which had failed to anticipate the world food crisis of 1972-1974. The
principal developed countries considered that making world food supplies
more secure was too serious a subject to be left entirely to the world's
agricultural ministers, the FAO's main constituency. The WFC was
supposed to bring together a much broader group of ministerial policy
makers, for example finance and foreign ministers. This was not achieved.
In the event, WFC was captured by agricultural ministers and, after two
decades of wasted effort by an initially strong and imaginative secretariat,
was dissolved in 1996, its functions absorbed by FAO and WFP.

The rise and fall of WFC is an excellent example of the responsibility
national governments must take for the disfunctionality of the UN system.
Governments identified a problem, created a new organisation to solve it,
but left unaltered the powers of the institution at the root of their

dissatisfaction. Indeed, they enlarged its power by establishing a new FAO committee to deal with world food security! Not surprisingly, they then failed to play the role in WFC they had identified for themselves as necessary to improve coordination of policies concerning food production, nutrition, food security and food aid. The outcome, after a deal of wasted expenditure and friction between governments, between ministers and departments involved within governments and between secretariats was that coordination was little changed from 1974.

My First CFA

My first CFA, number 13, was to begin ten days after my arrival. CFA meetings took place twice a year. The sessions were chaired by a delegate from either a developed or developing country in alternate years elected by the CFA. They were held in the 'Green Room' at FAO headquarters. This was a room the size of a medium auditorium with seating for several hundred delegates. The Chairman sat at an elevated podium, along with the Executive Director, the Director-General or his representative, and the representative of the UN Secretary-General. The podium formed the short side of a rectangle, with members seated at a continuous desk on the remaining three sides. There were several parallel rows of delegation places, the length of the sides necessarily increasing in each successive row. This configuration ensured that the proceedings were very formal.[17]

I made a point of always being present throughout each session, out of respect for the delegates and so that I would gain an unfiltered understanding of the proceedings. The Deputy Executive Director sat to my right. Depending on the agenda item the responsible WFP official was on the podium.

On the Chairman's left sat the Committee's Secretary who was responsible for preparation of the agenda, supporting documentation, the record of proceedings and so on. The Secretary was frequently asked by the Chairman for procedural advice. The Executive Director made a formal address at the opening of each session and could intervene on the agenda items as they were considered.

CFA13 began in an unprecedented way. Immediately following the election of office bearers the FAO Director-General administered the oath of office to me. That oath is sworn by all UN officials of whatever rank and amounts to a declaration to serve only the organisation and not the interests of any member state. It is normally administered privately by the chief of personnel of the agency concerned. It is regarded as a routine formality, not always observed with appropriate strictness. It had never before been administered in public for previous Executive Directors. However, I agreed when Saouma told me he would like to do so, even while knowing this action would be seen as symbolic of his authority over me and over the Programme itself.

After giving an opening address, which followed the statements of the Executive Director and the representative of the UN Secretary-General, it was the practice of the Director-General to leave the meeting. However, before Saouma could do so, the representative of Brazil made a pointed intervention. Its purpose was to defend Brito and to criticise the Director-General, not for failing to appoint Brito but to formally object to the 'unjustified and derogatory remarks that had been made about Mr Brito at the meeting on 25 February 1982', presumably the G77 meeting referred to in the previous chapter. The delegate said that his government deplored such comments about an international civil servant 'whose honesty and seriousness in the accomplishment of his duties were recognised by all as exemplary. The fact that another equally worthy candidate had been chosen...should not detract from the merit and dedication of the work of Mr Brito, who enjoyed the fullest confidence of the Brazilian Government' (WFP 1982a).

The delegate then assured the committee that I would enjoy Brazil's full cooperation and added that his Government agreed with 'the choice of Mr Ingram as Executive Director'. Altogether it was a masterful piece of diplomacy but in terms of FAO culture an astonishing piece of *lèse-majesté*.

This was brought home to me later that day when the Secretary to the CFA said to me, 'I presume you want the Brazilian intervention deleted from the summary record of the session'. I replied that the record should always accurately reflect the proceedings and that, accordingly, Brazil's remarks should be reported as given. I was astonished the question had arisen, seeing it as a revelation of a culture quite different from that I had experienced as a delegate in various UN bodies. Clearly, in Rome the secretariat was in charge, not governments.

At this opening session I noted another departure from conventional United Nations practice. This and all future CFA sessions began with the Chairman welcoming the Director-General, 'whose personal interest in the CFA was a source of great encouragement'. It was as if the Director-General was conferring an enormous privilege on governments by his presence.

Similar, often much more fulsome, sentiments were reflected in the opening statements of many delegates from developing countries.

Consideration of development projects

A principal function of each CFA was to consider and approve development projects submitted by the Secretariat. The Executive Director had a limited authority to approve projects between CFA sessions but since most development projects involved multi-year commitments and resource transfers in excess of $10 million it was entirely appropriate that they should be examined and approved by the Programme's governing body. CFA13 approved 21 projects totalling $286 million ranging in value from $2 million to $88 million. One project, for Vietnam, was not approved and another, for Ethiopia, only after great difficulty.

While almost all of WFP's development projects had interesting, often novel, features, my principal concern was necessarily with those that were politically controversial. How these had to be handled gives some insight into the way political considerations influenced decision-making in a supposedly apolitical development/humanitarian UN agency. The situation I found in WFP was not of course unique. While it would be unrealistic to believe that political factors could ever be entirely removed from decision-making about the distribution of aid by UN intergovernmental committees, I concluded that improved WFP project approval procedures might reduce their impact.

To permit detailed consideration of projects a Sub-Committee (SCP) of the CFA was formed. The SCP met while the CFA considered other items on its agenda. Fortuitously, the Vietnam project was the last to be considered. I therefore had time to see how the sub-committee operated and the criteria delegates applied in their critique of our project submissions. It soon became clear that the rigour accorded depended, as might be expected, on the size of the project and on the capacity of the recipient government to implement it, having regard to its level of economic development and the sophistication of its bureaucracy. All projects were designed in cooperation with the recipient and executed by them in accordance with a formal agreement with WFP called 'plan of operations'. Thus, projects for the very poor food deficit countries of Africa south of the Sahara were given less stringent scrutiny than those for Asia, North Africa and the Middle East. Unfortunately, with some very important Asian exceptions, the countries most in need of our assistance were the least able to use it efficiently. This 'aid paradox' applies to all forms of development assistance, not only to food aid.

The Ethiopian Project

However, even in sub-Saharan Africa it was clear that regimes unpopular with the West had to meet tougher scrutiny. At CFA13 the proposal to substantially expand an existing project to rehabilitate degraded forestry, grazing and agricultural land in Ethiopia occasioned much donor criticism. Unfortunately, but not surprisingly, developing country representatives invariably see it as their role to defend the secretariat's proposals and to counter donor objections, with the result that discussion tends to become adversarial instead of a concerted attempt to address weaknesses in the secretariat's proposals. Indeed, on this occasion debate became so bogged down that I was obliged to intervene.

Donor criticism focused on two issues: (i) the size of the project ($86 million) considered disproportionate to overall resources available to the Programme and to existing commitments to Ethiopia; and (ii) the sale of wheat to generate funds for the payment of internal transport costs. Recipient governments were normally obliged to meet these costs from their own resources, but for least developed countries—a category defined in UN resolutions—the CFA authorised payment of a cash subsidy by WFP. Unfortunately, contributions in cash from donors to WFP were always insufficient to allow us to make the cash subsidy without recourse to commodity sales. In this case the Ethiopian Government sold WFP-donated wheat to cover its transport costs. In practice this was the main sort of 'program' food aid delivered by WFP.

I did not know then that, because delegates change frequently, the same issues arise time after time at CFA sessions, eliciting the same replies from the secretariat. On this occasion, as I was to repeat many times in the future, the CFA policy of giving as much aid as possible to the least developed food-deficit countries could only be realised if large projects were developed for the few countries in this category able to utilise efficiently substantial quantities of food. In Africa, Ethiopia was the only populous country that met this criterion. It was obvious, however, that its Marxist leadership and links with the Soviet bloc were the main reasons for criticisms of the size of the project and its high internal transport costs. I gained a foretaste of what was to come in magnified form when the Vietnam project was considered.

The Vietnam Project

This was a food-for-work project aimed at the construction of irrigation works in Tay Ninh Province, in the so-called 'parrots beak' on the border with Cambodia. CFA had twice withheld approval. In its successive revisions to accommodate previous donor objections the secretariat introduced a uniquely onerous arrangement to ensure that the food reached the intended beneficiaries, the unspoken criticism being that otherwise the food would go to Vietnamese troops in Cambodia. There was no doubt that if the project was put to the vote it would gain approval by a comfortable majority but the CFA had a tradition of taking decisions by consensus. The secretariat was under a lot of pressure from the United States and Thailand to withdraw it. Both strongly opposed any development aid to Vietnam. The secretariat also knew that if it did withdraw the project it would be rightly condemned by developing countries for yielding to political pressure. Instead, it had focused on modifying the project to take account of the 'technical problems' raised by the United States and its supporters. In its third manifestation the project had reached a level of technical sophistication and thoroughness well beyond the standards ever previously applied to a WFP project.

Before the CFA met, the US representative, the same Roger Sorenson who had lobbied his government to support Brito's appointment, made an official call on me. Sorenson was not an agriculturist but a State Department diplomat. In my previous extensive experience of dealing with the United States, I had done so as a diplomat representing an American ally. Now I found myself sitting on the other side of the table, holding a weak hand, and realised I was in a very different relationship. This was the first of many encounters with the infamous 'arrogance of power'.

The fact that I was soon to make my first visit as Executive Director to Washington and wanted to make a convincing impression as independent yet sensitive to their concerns, was on my mind when Sorenson arrived. He went immediately to the purpose of his visit, flatly stating: 'How you handle the Vietnam project will be critical in determining our attitude to you over your entire term'. In delivering this threat he scarcely concealed his personal disdain for me, and expectation that, as Saouma's man, I would not withdraw the project, as he was requesting. Indeed, Saouma had strongly warned me not to do so if I wished to have the respect of developing countries. In our early discussions he had shown a worrying antipathy to the United States and it was clear he saw the Vietnam project as a handy way of discomfiting them without having himself to take a public position.

However, the Director-General's situation was quite different from mine as Executive Director of WFP. FAO member states were legally obliged to pay their assessed share of the FAO budget and were always outvoted if that was what the FAO secretariat wanted. To a large extent Saouma could act with impunity so long as he retained developing country support. WFP was entirely dependent on voluntary contributions from governments—and the United States was by far the largest donor. The developing countries were mindful that if resources were to continue, and hopefully increase, the Executive Director must retain donor confidence as well as theirs. They recognised that this was a difficult course to steer.

At CFA13 new objections to the revised project were raised which amounted to nit-picking and which, if applied to other projects, would effectively preclude approval of virtually all projects in all countries. The debate was ritualistic with no delegation's position likely to be influenced by the arguments advanced. The real issue was how to set the project aside, even though a clear majority favoured it, including a number of donor countries. Those donors supporting the project did not want a vote, preferring not to break the precedent that decisions should be taken by consensus; nor did those developing countries which had yielded to diplomatic pressure from Washington wish to be exposed by a formal vote. Since there was nothing remotely approaching a consensus on this occasion the preferred course was to again postpone a final decision. On my advice the Chairman of the SCP, which made its recommendations to the CFA in plenary session, suspended the debate in order to undertake informal consultations with members on a possible solution.

Work in the secretariat was underway on a second project to feed vulnerable groups of mothers and children in Ho Chi Minh City, which was intended for submission at a future CFA. During the week before CFA13—my first full week in the job—I met with a highly respected French nutritionist who had just returned to Rome from Vietnam where he had worked on the design of the new project. He convinced me of the shocking nutritional situation of children in Ho Chi Minh City and of the urgency of

WFP addressing it. This suggested to me a way out of the impasse over the Tay Minh project.

My experience as an Australian delegate to meetings of UN agencies similar to WFP had convinced me that their governing bodies worked more productively when the secretariat involved delegations as partners rather than simply submitted projects for approval on a basis which left little alternative to doing so. I therefore arranged for the nutritionist to address the Committee on the serious nutritional situation in Ho Chi Minh City. This paved the way for delegations to be alerted to our intention to introduce, as soon as possible, a social welfare project to help address the situation and, thereby, to increase the chance of its eventual approval. During the resumed debate on the Tay Ninh project the United States, having expressed its 'unalterable opposition' to that project, which should be 'dropped permanently', indicated that if this were done consideration of a purely nutritional project could be 'considered in a more congenial atmosphere'. I was advised that Vietnam was desperate for WFP to extend aid and would be likely to withdraw the Tay Ninh project if a substitute could be brought forward to the next session. I ascertained that the Ho Chi Minh City project could be speeded up in time for CFA14 which was to meet in October. As a result, during the informal discussions I was able to reassure both supporters and opponents that I was confident of being able to move forward on aid to Vietnam. After a great deal of formal and informal discussion the Chairman was eventually able to read out a formula agreed between him and the most concerned delegations. On the basis that the Executive Director would make certain unspecified 'further studies' of aspects of the project it was agreed to defer consideration of it until a future session (WFP 1982b).

Vietnam withdrew the Tay Ninh project. Instead the humanitarian project was approved at CFA14, though not without extensive debate. On that occasion the issue of whether consensus meant 'unanimity,' as the United States argued, or whether it allowed dissent by a few was blurred. Again, after extensive consultations outside the Committee, the Chairman read out an agreed formula which, after referring to a 'large number' of delegations expressing 'satisfaction' with the project and 'other delegations' their reservations, announced that: 'Taking everything that has been said into account, in particular the humanitarian nature of the project and the close monitoring of it by the Secretariat, I conclude that project Viet Nam 2651 may proceed' (WFP 1983a).

The drama had been intense until the end as shown by the relief and pleasure on the faces of many delegates. The ice was now broken and in due course a series of development projects for Vietnam was approved, though never without difficulty. The Vietnamese were always tough negotiators but, as I found when I visited the country in 1987, they faithfully carried out to the letter the commitments they had entered into. I developed respect, even affection, for the formidable Vietnamese representative, Madame Minh. Other 'socialist' recipients were equally scrupulous, for example Cuba and Nicaragua, more so than most developing countries.

IN WASHINGTON

In view of US satisfaction with the Vietnam outcome, the visit to Washington went off well. The United States consistently made a distinction between economic and social projects in all its involvement with WFP, always more readily accepting, if not endorsing, projects helping mothers and children in countries incurring its political disapproval. However, there was no question of using American food for any of our projects in those countries. The non-fungibility of aid in kind made it easy to do that even if this were not in accord with WFP General Regulation 3 (Appendix I).

The second Reagan administration had only just assumed office. Many of the officials I had come to know during my campaign had been succeeded by new faces. I was particularly disappointed that Elliot Abrams, Assistant Secretary of State for International Organizations, had been transferred to Latin American affairs. He was replaced by a young man in his thirties, Gregory Newell, with no experience of international organisations but encumbered by much prejudice about the United Nations. Newell shared the views of his mentor, Senator Jesse Helms. Unfortunately I was never then, or in subsequent meetings, able to build a comfortable relationship with him.

In Washington I met with a lively group of staff from the offices of Congressional members concerned with the United Nations and food and development issues, arranged through Tekle (Tek) Tomlinson, the UN official in New York, originally from Ethiopia, charged with liaison with WFP. He later transferred to WFP and became our representative at UN headquarters. Tomlinson also brought me into contact with two influential NGOs, Bread for the World and Church World Service, the latter represented by the much respected Larry Minear, with whom I developed an enduring friendship extending into my retirement.

Tomlinson trained as a monk in Ethiopia's ancient Christian Church but became a diplomat. After falling out with Haile Selassie's regime, he obtained refugee status in the United States, where he joined the UN. He was a man of subtle intelligence and distinguished in appearance, with his greying beard looking like what I imagined as a black Old Testament prophet. Tomlinson was highly respected by the secretariat and delegates alike in New York and was completely devoted to WFP and its works. A superb lobbyist for the Programme. He was one of a small band in WFP of the finest people I have had the honour to know and work with.

ELEMENTS OF A REFORM AGENDA

During my first six months I gained a good sense of the concerns of developed and developing countries and of the strengths and limitations of our senior staff. As a result I began to articulate the improvements I considered essential and feasible and which would significantly enhance the Programme's effectiveness. It was an advantage not to be burdened with preconceptions, prejudices or attachment to individual staff. I could think in the detached way that outside management consultants bring to the analysis of organisations they are commissioned to review. I knew I would never again have the same opportunity to see the organisation so objectively.

Altogether, I felt I had joined a competent and deservedly respected agency but one lacking self-confidence and in need of rejuvenation. Because it had been founded on a sound basis under the leadership of its first Executive Director, A H Boerma, subsequently Director-General of FAO, it continued to do good work, but virtually exclusively along the lines laid down in its pilot phase. It was in a deep rut.

At top levels it was also demoralised. Boerma was succeeded by Francisco Aquino who resigned following his defeat by Saouma in the election for FAO Director-General in 1976. For the following six years Saouma had used his powers to discourage strong executive leadership in WFP. He did so 'by keeping senior WFP appointees on an interim basis and by making it clear to them that they owed their appointment directly to him and, therefore, expected their full allegiance in return' (Shaw, 2001 p.212).

It would have been possible for me to keep WFP as I found it, which was what the Director-General expected. That became entirely clear when I moved to make some modest changes. But it would have been entirely out of character for me to coast along and simply preside, so to speak, over WFP rather than striving to improve it. Fortunately, there were dedicated, creative and intelligent staff in WFP who were frustrated by the stagnation and who desired change. I was convinced they would respond to good, strong leadership.

Changing the Culture

I was very disturbed by the stifling bureaucratic culture of WFP, with its pervasive cult of hierarchy and obsequiousness. The Executive Director was treated like a god. If he entered a meeting, even just with two or three senior colleagues, all stood, a practice which I immediately stopped. There was a reluctance to take decisions and virtually everything ended on the desk of the Executive Director. Since almost every decision has political consequences for relations with donor or recipient governments, caution was understandable but was carried to absurd lengths.

It is always difficult for superiors to elicit honest opinions from subordinates. Most prefer to be circumspect until they know what the boss thinks. But I have never found anything to compare with the unwillingness to speak out in WFP. On arrival I met individually with each of my most senior staff to hear their views on what needed to be done to improve WFP's performance. No one offered anything of real value or substance. I had entered a culture of fear, including of me, not least because I was perceived as the D-G's (Director-General's) man. Though UN civil servants have a right of appeal on administrative matters to a tribunal in Geneva, in practice their rights are more circumscribed than those of Australian civil servants. This only increased the fear of Saouma in FAO.[18] I did my best to build a more collegial atmosphere in WFP. Sometimes, especially at the beginning, I probably moved too quickly. For an Australian, I am a very formal person but by Rome standards I may occasionally have been seen as inappropriately informal.

Civil servants are renowned for their love of procedure; in Rome they were obsessed with it. In part this was due to Italian bureaucratic culture introduced through the many Italian clerical officers in FAO, whose work practices WFP had inherited, although I was struck by the excessively rule-bound, old fashioned civil service culture throughout the UN system. It was well short of best practice. This also had to do with the fact that UN system agencies are the most multicultural bodies on the planet. Since there are far fewer shared assumptions about appropriate bureaucratic behaviour and procedures rooted in language and common ideas—taken for granted in national bureaucracies—framing rules to meet every conceivable situation is an understandable way of introducing that commonality. It also leads to strict rule enforcement and may create a timid, conformist, bureaucratic culture.

Furthermore, UN system agencies are modelled after the civil services of the leading Western countries. Coming from a Western country, especially an English speaking one, it is relatively easy to adapt to the UN bureaucratic culture (in practice the working language was English), but for officials from developing countries the learning process is far more difficult and rigid adherence to formal rules may provide a 'safe haven'.

Changing an organisation's culture is the biggest challenge a manager can set himself. I did not decide to achieve this through some grand design. Rather, I focused on securing specific changes that I thought were significant and achievable. The most important was overcoming resistance to the creation of a unified headquarters and field staff.

Reducing the Gulf between Headquarters and Field Staff

On my way to Rome I formed a good impression of our staff in Thailand and during CFA13 I met with and watched the presentations of our officers based in those countries whose projects were under consideration. While of uneven ability, I could see no justification for the snobbery shown toward our field staff by many at headquarters. It was engendered by the fact that the two staffs were distinct and rarely interchanged. That was because WFP followed FAO practice. The latter's headquarters staff was not integrated with its technical assistance experts working in developing countries, many of whom spent most of their working lives with FAO but never served in Rome. FAO had about 4,000 field staff and about the same number in Rome. To the annoyance of developed countries Saouma established, at great expense, posts of FAO representative in most developing countries who, in addition to coordination functions, acted as his personal 'diplomatic' representative with the host government (Abbott 1992, p.11). In key countries these people were often drawn from headquarters professional staff, who otherwise did not serve in developing countries.

By contrast, WFP had many more professionals in the field than at headquarters. The result in both agencies was that most staff responsible for setting policy, designing projects and overseeing their implementation had, more often than not, never lived for any length of time in developing countries. This disjunction was a severe impediment to the good management of our food-aided projects. WFP's mandate was to focus on the poor, which entailed identifying suitable beneficiaries and the most appropriate foods to be supplied to them. This was best done by officers with detailed first-hand knowledge of developing countries.

Our headquarters staff tended to regard themselves as elite development professionals on a par with their World Bank or IFAD colleagues. They saw our field staff as in-country logisticians. It was true that some had been recruited primarily for that purpose, but after twenty years many compared well with their headquarters counterparts. UNDP and UNICEF field staff sometimes dubbed their WFP field colleagues as 'grocers'. A similar superciliousness was common in our headquarters. As I saw it, the identification, design, implementation and evaluation of projects was seamless; similar intellectual and practical abilities were required of all staff. I saw a parallel with the conduct of foreign policy. At one time in the UK and the United States there had been a similar sharp distinction between foreign ministry staff at the capital and diplomats in the field. This distinction had been abandoned after the Second World War and never adopted by new services such as Australia's.

Before taking up my appointment I was asked to record a tape to give staff an idea of the approach I would bring to the work of WFP. In addition to recognising the importance of both the humanitarian and development role the agency played, I made reference to the important role of field staff. This was very well received, a key field officer commenting that my remarks were 'refreshing and encouraging, since it sometimes seems to be forgotten in Rome how much the Programme depends on them for its good name'. Later in the year I saw something of our field work in Bangladesh, Pakistan and the Philippines. I became convinced that the unification of headquarters and field staffs was essential and made it one of my priorities. It was finally achieved four years later, in the face of that same opposition that FAO gave to all my reforms, though resistance from WFP headquarters staff meant the integration was more gradual than I desired and only fully implemented by my successor.

Overcoming Criticism of Food Aid

From the beginning I was worried about the vulnerability of the Programme to some of the criticisms directed against it, for example creating tastes for new foods, production of which was not agronomically suited to the recipient country. Indeed, it was the case that the United States, Canada, Italy and Denmark, to name a few, used WFP to help establish markets for new products. For example, Denmark's provision of its feta cheese for projects in Mediterranean countries assisted market penetration in that region.

I was also concerned about the considerable burden, financial and managerial, sometimes placed on the recipient government in distributing food, which might outweigh the benefit to individuals targeted by our development projects even though our food aid was the only aid likely to reach poor, scattered rural populations. For that reason alone I considered judicious use of program food aid could sometimes be a more appropriate use of food.

It did not take long to get personal exposure to passionate, genuinely felt, criticism of our project aid. Early in June 1982, I addressed the International Federation of Agricultural Producers (IFAP) in London. IFAP was an important lobby group supporting food aid and WFP, the more important because it included developing countries as well as developed. After I had spoken, two female delegates from francophone West Africa strongly criticised our projects in their respective countries as being ill conceived. In West Africa food cropping and marketing were essentially carried on by women, something we had failed to recognise in the project design. The delegates' sincerity left a lasting impression and was a factor in my insisting that the highest priority be given to explicit integration of women's needs and concerns in the design of our development projects. Coming from ADAB I had been sensitised to feminist concerns about Western aid programs. When I arrived in Rome it was apparent this trend had gone unheeded in FAO and WFP.

At the time I joined WFP, Oxfam had just published a damning, polemical, critique of project food aid (Jackson 1982).[19] Knowing how difficult it is to persuade governments to fund overseas aid programs and of the influence the aid NGOs had on their decision making, I was convinced it was essential to improve our project performance in ways which would defuse such criticism.

We also had to find ways to publicise our achievements. When I arrived WFP was doing effectively nothing in the way of public information, though it was paying FAO a large sum to do so on its behalf. Unlike similar agencies, UNICEF for example, WFP was virtually unknown except to recipient governments and food aid specialists in donor agencies. FAO's Information and Press Service, which had no direct knowledge of what WFP did, nor any incentive to publicise our work, did little more than prepare and distribute our press releases.

The Politicisation of Emergency Food Aid

I did not bring the same uneasiness I had had about development food aid to the question of famine relief. George McGovern's original initiative, which set in motion the events leading to WFP's establishment, placed the main emphasis on emergency feeding, though the possible use of food for development was recognised. In the Programme's initial experimental phase this emphasis was reversed, although by1982 emergency aid was taking a significant and increasing proportion of resources pledged to WFP. I knew that some donor governments felt more comfortable with emergency food aid, as did Oxfam and other aid NGOs. This did not mean, however, that emergency work was properly staffed; it was seen as second-best, reflecting the now entrenched 'development' culture in WFP. Overcoming that bias became another of my priorities.

The shift to emergency aid began with the Sahelian drought of 1973-75. Following from experience of relief efforts in that drought the UN General Assembly established in 1975 an International Emergency Food Reserve (IEFR). Pending the creation of a genuine global food reserve of 30 million tons, the General Assembly urged countries in a position to do so to earmark funds and stocks up to 500,000 tons, to be placed at the disposal of WFP as an emergency reserve for responding to food crises in developing countries.

As well as IEFR resources, some $45 million was set aside annually from the Programme's regular resources to fund emergency requests. This was particularly valuable since, if need be, the whole amount could be expended in cash. That was essential if full use was to be made of IEFR contributions from those donors who failed to include sufficient cash with their donation to meet the full costs of transport. For the first six months of 1982, 34 relief operations at a cost of $137,883,900 were approved—not an insignificant sum at the time.

By definition emergencies cannot be predicted, so were not susceptible to advance consideration by the CFA. Instead, a complex system for approval was included in the General Regulations. Regulation 19 set out the procedure as follows:

> Governments desiring food assistance to meet emergency food needs shall present a request to the Director-General of FAO. Such requests shall contain the basic information required about the situation. The Director-General of FAO will request the Executive Director of the Programme to examine it. The Director-General of FAO will decide upon the request, taking into account the recommendation of the Executive Director of the Programme.

It is difficult to overstate how politically important emergency food aid can be to governments of poor, disaster-prone countries. Local food shortages occur frequently. Even two or three millions dollars' worth of assistance can mean a great deal to large numbers of people for whom otherwise their governments could do nothing.

While certain criteria had been laid down for judging requests, FAO had the capacity to stimulate and influence the rationale for these requests, making it very difficult for the Executive Director to recommend a negative response. FAO claimed responsibility for gathering and analysing the relevant data to assess whether a natural disaster justified food assistance; and the WFP Executive Director was unable to make his own assessments. In short the final decision maker, the FAO Director-General, was prosecutor and judge. The division of responsibility between the two organisations lacked substance.

The way the system operated also meant that FAO's Director-General got the credit with the requesting government. Our field staff was incensed by the injustice of this. The resources were WFP's and we, especially our in-country staff, worked exceedingly hard to get food quickly to the victims. Since a stock of WFP food was often already in the country for use in our development projects, it was usually possible to borrow from it and so get some food to victims immediately following the Director-General's approval.

To make sure it got the kudos FAO advised the government of the Director-General's decision before WFP was informed and simultaneously issued a press release, which the local media naturally reported as FAO assistance.

The reader may well ask why WFP in-country staff could not set the matter in proper perspective with the government. In practice this was very difficult. Again, dating from the experimental period, WFP did not have its own representatives but formed part of the UNDP office. WFP senior field officers, however well respected by those with whom they worked, lacked the status to have access at the highest levels of government.

On account of the dual approval process WFP emergency food aid had become a valuable tool for the FAO Director-General to build and maintain his influence with developing countries. Many heads of government of African countries were effectively dictators, with most agricultural ministers having little independent decision-making power, reflecting the low priority given to agriculture. In these circumstances, emergency aid provided the Director General with the access to presidents that technical assistance did not.

I knew I must respond to this politicisation of emergency aid but it was not the only problem. Response times were often far too slow, aid arriving sometimes after the need for food had passed. There was no provision for systematic help to countries with frequent food emergencies to better identify communities in need and improve government capability to distribute food promptly and equitably. Finally, and very importantly, systems were non-existent to identify and prepare development projects which could help to avoid future recourse to emergency food aid.

Improving the Balance of the WFP Workforce

I was impressed by the organisation's logistical skill, that is its ability to mobilise and deliver to beneficiaries the appropriate quantities and mix of foodstuffs required for our development projects and emergency feeding. This area of our secretariat required little improvement beyond straightening out the terrible mess it had got into over the design and introduction of a sophisticated computerised management information system.

Relative to resources and logistics management, project design, emergency needs assessment and evaluation, policy development and general management were understaffed. Naturally, the primary interest of donors was the use in full of their contributions. Better projects came second.

The Programme showed creative skill in its ability to utilise the extraordinarily diverse range of commodities donors insisted on supplying, an important reason for its having prospered. Essential commodities for use in the poorest food deficit countries, and hence the most desirable, were cereals and vegetable oil. Large quantities of wheat were always available but supplies of other cereals, especially rice, white maize—the preferred diet in Latin America and parts of Africa—and coarse grains, such as sorghum, were usually insufficient. On the other hand, there was too much butter oil, milk powder and exotic and expensive foods such as canned fish, meat and cheese and some American specialised processed foods, not to mention dates. To make developmental use of these commodities, which we felt obliged to accept, it was necessary to provide disproportionately high amounts of aid to middle-income countries.

The donors altogether had too much control in this and other ways. In addition to some insisting their food go only to particular countries and projects, all benefited from the fact that surplus food was valued at market prices even though the true financial cost, in terms of commercial sales foregone, was often lower.[20] The result was they were able to claim to be providing a dollar value of aid greater than was the case. The donors had it both ways. They took advantage of the non-fungibility of food when it came to saying where their food would go. On the other hand, when it came to getting credit for their generosity, the donors insisted that aid in kind should be accounted for as if it were fungible cash. With changes in market prices our records had constantly to be adjusted, making accounting for donated food very complex and consuming a disproportionate amount of staff resources. Anomalous though that was I knew to try to change it would be to tilt at windmills.

Following CFA13 my mind began to focus on what concrete steps could be taken to begin to overcome these problems. The biggest lacuna in available skills was sufficient conceptual capacity to draw out the lessons of experience and to encapsulate them in new policies and guidelines. There was only one officer available to write policy papers for submission to the CFA as well as the speeches and statements made by the Executive Director to outside bodies. Perforce, FAO had a major hand in the preparation of policy papers presented to the CFA. If I was to make progress with my reform agenda, it was essential to strengthen the Programme's policy capability. However, before that could be seriously tackled it was even more urgent to strengthen our ability to deal with emergencies and our general administration which was starved of qualified personnel.

---

16 UNGA Resolution 3404 (XXX), November 1975, paragraph 5. Appendix I contains the full operative text.

17 During the eighties FAO re-modelled its other principal committee room re-arranging delegates seating in parallel rows directly facing the elevated podium. This layout implied even more strongly the superior status of chairman and secretariat. Today's WFP Executive Board meets around a circular table at which delegates, chairman and secretariat are also seated.

18 In a fascinating article in the Rome *Daily American* of 5 January 1982 George Weller gives a detailed account of the vendetta against two FAO staff members, Rejanne Pollicino and Raymond Lloyd. Lloyd had resigned from FAO over differences with Saouma. An idealist, he used his private means to advance the cause of FAO reform and women's rights by publishing widely distributed mimeographed analyses often very critical of Saouma. Pollicino, who worked directly for Saouma for many years, was suspected of feeding information to Lloyd. She was suspended on the charge of doing what she used to do for Saouma, namely typing private correspondence, Weller reported.

19 Over twenty years later unease about the uses of food aid for development, including for WFP development projects, continues. As the OECD (2006) concluded: 'Most independent reviews of food-aided development activities range from being guardedly positive to being, on balance, negative. The implication of evidence - based research is that context-specific influences are extremely important, if not dominant, in determining actual outcomes' (p.64). Then as now, however, even though in most circumstances the provision of cash to purchase food in beneficiary countries or in global markets is the most cost- effective means of providing food aid, the reality was and remains that much food aid in kind is additional to other development assistance.

20 Australia was the major exception in this regard, not subsidising wheat production and having to market the whole wheat crop whatever market conditions. As a party to the Food Aid Convention Australia was nevertheless committed to the provision of a specified quantity of food aid annually. (See below Chapter 5).

4

THE CHALLENGE CRYSTALLISES

On FAO resistance to challenges to its de facto control over WFP and on the obstacles placed in the way of my modest effort to strengthen staffing in critical areas; and on the legal opinion obtained from the UN Secretary-General on the powers of the Executive Director.

The principal tools of management in any large civil service organisation are construction of its budget and oversight of expenditure once approved. Each two years the CFA approved WFP's administrative budget. The biennium had just begun, the current budget being approved at CFA12 in October 1981, during the hiatus following the death of my predecessor. It would be eighteen months before I could get authority to establish new staff positions. This was far too long if I were to make the progress I thought essential. With the enthusiastic support of senior staff, including my deputy, at this time still Juan Felipe Yriat, we prepared a supplementary budget arguing for 10 new posts, to be considered by CFA14 at its coming October 1982 session. This was ambitious but I was determined to use my honeymoon period to establish enough credibility among delegations to gain approval.

The risk was mine, or at least so I thought. I also wanted to send a signal–to FAO as well as to WFP and its member governments–that the long leadership hiatus was over. WFP now had a bold, judicious, decision-maker as chief executive, one who could not be relied upon to follow a conservative civil service risk calculus.

FAO ASSERTS ITS 'RIGHTS'

On the day of my arrival Saouma was cooler than in the months beforehand. His manner reinforced the impact of a disturbing letter from him I found awaiting me.

Saouma's three-page letter asserted his prerogatives in relation to WFP. These were based on the narrowest interpretation of the WFP Basic Documents and encapsulated FAO's legal position, one from which it never budged. The letter sharpened my realisation that Saouma saw WFP as FAO's ward. In particular it noted the 'special responsibilities of the Director-General of FAO for WFP', vested under the General Regulations and Additional Financial Procedures of WFP. The most important of these regulations was 27. WFP resources were to be credited to a Trust Fund for which the Director-General was custodian. Our financial operations were to be managed in accordance with FAO Financial Regulations and such Additional Financial Procedures (AFP) as were necessary. In his letter the Director-General further stated: 'I retain authority for submission of the Audited Accounts of the Programme. The certification and report of the External Auditor are submitted to the Director-General of FAO. I thus also retain responsibility for furnishing proof and explanations.'

The letter also contained a threat. In view of the central importance of logistics to WFP operations, commodity purchases and shipping had been overseen by a WFP committee. I was now informed that FAO's Chief of Internal Audit and Inspection would review whether that arrangement should be altered.

The Director-General's interpretation of his rights was based on selected provisions of the Basic Documents, those which supported the *de facto* administrative control exercised by FAO over WFP, a control steadily strengthened by Saouma since becoming Director-General nearly six years before (Shaw2001, pp. 212). It asserted the powers of the Administration and Finance Department of FAO and, in an entirely new practice, the Director-General's authority over the Executive Director's leave.

Provisions in the Basic Documents that ascribed powers to the Executive Director, who was head of the secretariat administering the Programme (GR 14[a] and 14[j]), were ignored. In fact, the Executive Director was responsible for the preparation of projects (GR 16(a)), WFP's raison d'être, for approval by the CFA, the organ responsible for intergovernmental supervision of the Programme (GR 7 and 8); and for the preparation of budgets whose approval constituted authorisation to him to incur expenditure and to make payments (AFP Article XIII and XIV). Moreover, though appointed by the Secretary-General and Director-General for a five-year term there was no provision for his termination.

The Basic Documents did contain provisions limiting the freedom of the Executive Director to administer the WFP and, indeed, for the program's abolition if that was judged desirable. These had been carried over from the experimental period and never revised, though in practice some were ignored. For reasons possibly connected with the ambitions of the first Executive Director who went on to head FAO, the first opportunity to amend the texts in 1965 was missed. The second occasion was when the functions of the CFA were enlarged in accordance with the recommendation of the 1974 World Food Conference. At the time the leadership of WFP was very weak. The Executive Director had acted in the position for over a year but only confirmed in it by Saouma one month before his retirement. The FAO view that it should be responsible for discharging the new function of preparing policy papers, albeit at the financial expense of the Programme as provided for in the Basic Documents GR 14 (h), was accepted by the Executive Director. The result was, as the Director-General said to me, 'WFP is a logistics agency and that should remain its role'.

I replied to Saouma's letter ten days later, in a positive tone of respect. I avoided any direct reference to legalities, although I did imply that the Executive Director's powers were broader than he asserted. In view of the close relationship of WFP and FAO in financial, administrative and personnel matters, I considered it all the more important to 'maintain that close collaboration which I am convinced is essential if we are to achieve our common objectives'. 'With regard to my travel and leave,' I wrote, 'I will of course consult you in advance'.

In short, I avoided confrontation yet still conveyed my view that our relationship was not a simple subordinate/superior one but rather a constitutional one, which ascribed powers to the Executive Director and not only the Director-General, as he was asserting. We were linked, as it were, in marriage, albeit an old-fashioned one with a dominant partner. But that did not mean that the junior partner had no rights and that the senior was entitled to complete dominance.

My *Chef de Cabinet*, Bill Barnsdale, saw my response as reassurance that I would follow my own judgment and could be expected to defend the integrity of WFP. Barnsdale was a former American diplomat who, on retirement from the State Department, had been brought into WFP by my predecessor. He was a complete gentleman with all the patrician virtues common to American diplomats of his generation. Barnsdale was respected by WFP staff and had been close to Brito. Overcoming Barnsdale's suspicion that I might be a Saouma stooge and having his backing helped me establish credibility with staff.

A BUREAUCRATIC MAZE

To get my staffing proposals before governments I would have to consult with the Secretary-General and the Director-General (Appendix I, AFP Article XIII). I discovered that before they even reached the latter they would, by his decision, first be considered by two FAO committees, neither of which included WFP representation, meaning, in effect, they were there to second-guess the proposals of WFP's Executive Director. FAO clearly wanted to keep the Executive Director hemmed in and unable to take significant managerial initiatives that had financial or personnel implications. Its Director-General was willing to make major delegations to senior FAO staff directly subordinate to him, but not to WFP's Executive Director.

Nevertheless, I remained hopeful I could persuade Saouma that when Article XIII of the Additional Financial Procedures said the Executive Director was to submit budget proposals 'in consultation' with the Director-General it should be taken to mean precisely that. I was still under the misapprehension that Saouma, as a person of high pragmatic intelligence to whom I found it easy to relate, would recognise that practices set up for the experimental period should be modified if they burdened efficient management of an agency as large and as permanent as WFP had become.

Moreover, I knew from my previous UN experience that governments had never stood in the way of *de facto* change, for example as had happened with the evolution of UNICEF into an essentially autonomous organisation. As I saw it, the Director-General and I shared the goal of serving the interests of the governments to whom we were answerable and should be able to reach a *modus vivendi*. Yet I was becoming uneasy.

During those first weeks WFP staff also brought to my attention past instances of unwarranted interference by FAO on operational matters. These confirmed that FAO had no interest in seeing WFP, as its founders had, as a distinct entity rather than an integral part of their organisations.

Before submitting my supplementary budget to the FAO committees I decided to consult the FAO Deputy Director-General, my colleague Edward West, whose rank was the same as mine. West received me rather formally. He was tall and heavily built, having at one time held a British amateur heavy-weight boxing championship title. He once told me that he had worked to oppose Saouma's first election and expected to be sacked in consequence but, to his surprise, the latter had turned to him more and more, making him his deputy at the beginning of 1982, shortly before my own appointment. Saouma was dependent on West for the meticulous, uncompromising transformation of his directions into appropriate bureaucratic action. West was the perfect complement to Saouma who was absorbed much of the time with political manipulation.

West spent a few minutes examining our proposals. He told me bluntly they would be unacceptable to Saouma as being 'too ambitious'. A few days later, after examination in more detail, he confirmed his initial reaction. When I saw Saouma about them he was as negative as West had been, totally dismissing the proposals on the grounds that governments would be certain to reject them. I said I would reconsider. I submitted a less ambitious plan, which cut the new staff request to a bare minimum of three professional posts. Saouma rejected the new proposals in their entirety and said FAO would itself amend them. Five days later he presented his changes to me: they provided for only two new professional posts. When I remonstrated with him over this arbitrary action, he said in good humour but with a clear note of menace, 'You are not proposing to fight me are you, because if you are you will regret it.' Though it crossed my mind to say, with a smile, 'I am not one to shirk a challenge', I told him the truth, 'My only desire is to work cooperatively with you to strengthen the Programme'.

WFP had already sent our amended proposal to the Secretary-General, which he subsequently endorsed. However, to maintain good relations with the Director-General I did not contest his revision. Nevertheless, he insisted that the proposal still be considered by his Establishments Sub-Committee and Committee. I was not given the sub-committee's report nor did the full committee discuss our proposals with us. West telephoned to tell me that creation of a program development service, the most important innovation, had been rejected. FAO was cutting back further its own truncated version of my proposals.

Finally, notwithstanding the hoops we had already jumped through, another gauntlet had to be run, namely the FAO Finance Committee. All budgetary proposals had to be considered by this body as well as by the UN General Assembly's Advisory Committee on Administrative and Budgetary Questions (ACABQ) (GR 29).

The FAO Finance Committee had eight members but only two were from developed countries, notwithstanding that the latter overwhelmingly financed the FAO budget. The members were supposedly elected as experts but were usually Rome representatives with little or no experience of budgeting and financial management in international organisations. The committee was wholly dependent on FAO staff for technical guidance. That made me apprehensive. When I was the Australian representative on UNICEF's administration and finance committee, I had been struck by the asymmetry of information as between delegates and secretariat and how delegates were ultimately dependent on the integrity of the secretariat.

Though ultimately endorsing the pared-back proposals, the FAO Finance Committee was gratuitously and unconvincingly negative in its questioning when my associates and I appeared before them. Their message was not only does FAO decide what WFP may present, but FAO also determines what is approved by the committee. There was no remaining doubt in my mind about how weak my hand was.

On the other hand, the ACABQ was a serious body, respected by developed and developing countries. Though developed countries were still in a minority, representatives were conscientious and some were reasonably knowledgeable about the issues. The Chairman was elected by the General Assembly and, most importantly, served by a secretariat independent of the accounts and budget departments of the UN. Through the whole of my time, the Chairman was a highly respected Tanzanian, C S M Mselle, repeatedly re-elected unopposed. Without ACABQ backing for my future budget proposals I would have no hope of making the changes to our secretariat needed to make WFP exemplary within the UN system.

I first appeared before the ACABQ in May 1982 when it was reviewing our audited accounts for the biennium 1980-81. I made a courtesy call on

Mselle beforehand. He was trim, energetic, and rather professorial in appearance, but very much to the point. To my surprise he asked me whether FAO was charging us too much for administrative services. The General Regulations provided, supposedly as a cost-saving measure and to allow easy termination if necessary at the end of the experimental period, that necessary financial and administrative services should be provided, on a reimbursable basis, by FAO staff (GR 14(g)). For technical expertise in the development of projects, the Programme 'should rely to the maximum extent feasible on the existing staff and facilities of FAO, the United Nations and other intergovernmental agencies', with their costs again being reimbursed by the Program (GR 14(h)).

A substantial share of our administrative budget went to pay FAO, ILO, UNESCO, WHO and the United Nations for technical services and, in the case of FAO, administrative support as well. In each case the costs were self-assessed by the agencies. When I met Mselle I had not been briefed on this issue. Mselle put the same question to me in the Committee hearing. I undertook to look into the matter. I left the meeting encouraged that WFP possibly had an influential ally.

A Victory of Sorts

I came before the ACABQ a second time in September for its examination of our supplementary budget, which received its ready approval. In the event, our proposal, as modified by FAO went through at CFA14 without discussion. The fact that our donors had not objected either to the proposals or to the 'unprecedented' step of introducing an 'expansionary' supplementary budget in a time of 'zero budget growth' for UN agencies showed I had already won significant political backing. Nor were the practical consequences insignificant. We were able to upgrade the Emergency Unit to a full Service—an essential reform

The strengthening of our Budget and Administration Branch was valuable also. Insufficient staff to frame establishment proposals on lines insisted upon by FAO had been an enormous handicap. We would now be in a marginally better position to justify the need for appropriately skilled additional staff.

In proposing a supplementary budget, I had been confidently expected to fall flat on my face. The positive outcome was good for staff morale. The FAO/WFO environment was like the world's stock markets, a hotbed of gossip, rumour and tips. Down to the lowest general service officer there was an appreciation that a battle of some sort had gone on with FAO and that WFP had achieved a degree of success.

Winning the Nordics

To ensure CFA support for my supplementary budget, I had worked hard to explain to key delegates my vision for WFP. I attached a lot of importance to the Nordic countries. Each of them was a significant donor; more importantly, they carried great credibility with developing countries as disinterested supporters of the United Nations and committed to developing country aspirations. My predecessors had participated in one-day meetings with the Nordic countries: Sweden, Norway, Finland, Iceland and Denmark. The venue rotated from capital to capital each year. Given they had supported Brito's candidature, it was essential I make a good impression. I wanted them to recognise that I took my duty as an apolitical international civil servant seriously.

The chairman at the 1982 meeting was the redoubtable H J (Kris) Kristensen, long-time permanent secretary of the Danish Ministry of Agriculture and supporter of WFP. I was able to convince him and his colleagues of my bona fides, obtain their support for our supplementary budget and educate them about what I wanted to do to improve the Programme. I was especially pleased that Kristensen fully shared my desire to give WFP a strong, independent policy capability. Thereafter, my relations with the Nordics were always good, although with the inevitable changes in their personnel over ten years I could never afford to take them for granted. I feel a great sense of gratitude for their consistent support. Of all member countries of the United Nations they, more than any others, seek in their foreign policy to act in accordance with the principles of the UN Charter. I was honoured that over time they saw I shared their idealism.

MY SEARCH FOR A DEPUTY

Amidst all this activity, I had still not been able to get the Director-General to accept or reject the person I wished appointed as my deputy. WFP General Regulation 14(e) made the Executive Director responsible 'for the staffing and organization of the Secretariat', but it also provided that 'the selection and appointment of senior officials shall be made in agreement with the Secretary-General of the United Nations and the Director-General of FAO'.

Following CFA13 I had turned my mind to the selection of a deputy. The Director-General and I were at least agreed the person should be from a developing country. Since the choice would almost certainly be made from among delegates and officials of the Rome agencies, none of whom I knew well, I was initially in no hurry. I wanted time to identify a person of high integrity, competence and loyalty. None of the WFP senior staff were suitable. Since no one from FAO approached me, I suspected Saouma wanted the field kept clear for Yriat, whom I asked to stay on as Acting Deputy Executive Director.

Saouma and I discussed the matter in general terms several times but he made no suggestions until one day he asked, 'Have you thought about Gonzalo Bula Hoyos?' Bula Hoyos was Colombia's Ambassador to FAO. He had been in Rome for many years, was clearly intelligent, a brilliant orator, an able parliamentarian alive to all procedural possibilities and able to influence delegates to his point of view. He was also highly emotional and a thorn in the side of developed country delegates. At various times, but not always, he was close to Saouma, whose wife was Colombian. He was said to aspire to a high secretariat post, being bored by his role as a delegate but not wanting to leave Rome. The consensus view was that his skills were much more political than administrative.

Believing that we were having a confidential discussion, I replied that I did not really know him but from what I had heard I was not sure he would be the right person. Saouma did not demur nor did he pursue the matter further with me, but thereafter, for much of my ten years, Bula Hoyos was a dangerous opponent. I often wondered why. Years later he told me that when he had asked Saouma to support his appointment the latter had agreed to propose him to me. After our conversation Saouma told Bula Hoyos I had been unwilling to consider him!

A similar situation developed with the permanent representative of Saudi Arabia, Ambassador A Y Bukhari, who was elected chairman at CFA13. He was seen by delegates as lacking managerial ability. He also was a long-time delegate with influence among Arab delegations. He was close to Saouma. Seeing him in action as Chairman of the CFA, I considered him unsuitable for the post. However, Saudi Arabia had been the most generous of cash donors to the Programme and therefore it was desirable to avoid offending its representative.

One morning Saouma telephoned me. 'You are having a visit from Bukhari', he said. 'He will ask you to consider him as your deputy. We would not want him, would we?' I agreed. Bukhari was making his first official call on me and as Chairman there were many issues to discuss. We talked for an hour but he said nothing about his aspiration. I did not raise the subject. Again much later I learned that Saouma had told him he would recommend him. Bukhari, however, did not think it appropriate to appear to be seeking the post and I saw no advantage in telling him to his face that Saouma had mentioned the matter but neither he nor I regarded him as suitable! As a result Bukhari became almost as much of a thorn as Bula Hoyos.

The previous year Paul Kelloway, a fellow Australian, then with the World Food Council who later joined WFP, arranged a dinner for me to meet the Deputy Executive Director of WFC, Salahuddin Ahmed. Ahmed was likely to run for the leadership of WFC if the then incumbent, Maurice Williams, did not seek a further term. Kelloway hoped I might be helpful in getting Australian support for him. A recommendation from Kelloway, whom I had admired when he worked with me in ADAB, counted for a great deal. He said Ahmed, who had held the top civil service post in Bangladesh and remained in good standing with his government, was an able administrator and also a person of integrity. Ahmed had impressed me at the time of our meeting. I therefore sounded him out about coming to WFP as my deputy. He was interested.

When I told Saouma informally in late May that I was considering Ahmed, his spontaneous reaction was, 'Why didn't I think of him?' Later in the conversation he said, 'I will think over the matter'. Ahmed was well known to Saouma; indeed Ahmed told me he had good relations with him and expected no difficulty in getting his agreement. During the following months, each time I enquired whether he had come to a decision, Saouma put me off. I concluded he did not want me to appoint my own choice, even though he had no substantive objection to Ahmed. By allowing the matter to drag on he hoped Ahmed would lose interest and, perforce, I would decide to make Yriat's tenure permanent.

However, Ahmed maintained his interest, indeed became affronted by Saouma's procrastination. In the end, on the eve of CFA14, faced with strong pressure from delegates, a few of whom I let know of the reason for the delay, Saouma gave way. I immediately got formal approval from New York and was able to announce Ahmed's appointment at the conclusion of the session on 18 October, five months since I had nominated him.

Ahmed proved to be knowledgeable about how the UN system worked, competent as a manager, totally dependable and unfailingly loyal. Over the next ten years I was necessarily away from Rome a great deal. It was enormously reassuring to know I would not be undermined during my absence. I owe him a great debt and we remain good friends.

I experienced similar problems in relation to nearly all future senior appointments. It became clearer and clearer that Saouma's aim was to ensure all my appointees understood that they owed their post at least as much to him as to me. Later, when our relations worsened, the approval process was invariably delayed or otherwise frustrated in order to hamstring my management. Although the Secretary-General invariably accepted the Executive Director's choices, Saouma had increasingly influenced, even dictated, them and had extended the definition of 'senior officials' down to the D1 level, the lowest of the four ranks of political appointees. Under my predecessor he had even interfered on P5 appointments, the top of the career service.

The impasse over the appointment of Ahmed was one of several I encountered even in my first year. On my arrival the sole post nominated by the UN Secretary-General fell vacant. I saw an opportunity to double my policy capability. I chose a US citizen, Charles Paolillo, who had an excellent record with USAID and came strongly recommended by senior US officials. The Secretary-General agreed with my recommendation. However, Assistant Secretary of State Newell regarded Paolillo as a Democrat and tried to block his appointment. Though it was too late for him to do so, he did not forgive me for my choice.

To my surprise, FAO also objected on the grounds that, even though the post was at the Secretary-General's discretion, the Director-General should have been consulted in accordance with General Regulation 14(e). Fortunately, the UN was unmoved by a transparent, but characteristically bold, bluff. I now had two competent policy makers, the other being the Programme's then Senior Economist, John Shaw. (Shaw's title was a misnomer in that there were no other economist posts.) Both were creative and Shaw, who had been with WFP since close to its inception, brought formidable knowledge of its history and the history of food aid.

SEEKING LEGAL CLARIFICATION

The appointment of my deputy and of my supplementary budget were a watershed in my relationship with Saouma. I faced an unyielding and ruthless opponent who would seek to destroy any serious effort to implement my WFP reform agenda. I was determined to go on. But how? My other 'parent', the United Nations, provided the means.

On a visit to New York, I mentioned to the UN/WFP liaison officer my uncertainty about the powers of the Executive Director. Tomlinson suggested it might be possible to get an authoritative interpretation from the United Nations. He arranged for me to meet Emilio Olivares, the Secretary General's closest adviser. At the conclusion of our extensive discussion Olivares recommended I ask the Secretary-General for a legal interpretation of my powers. I took his advice and told Javier Pérez de Cuéllar that the Basic Documents were complex and confusing and I was quite uncertain about the limits of my authority. Pérez de Cuéllar said he had asked the same question when he took over from Waldheim and had obtained an opinion from the UN Legal Counsel. He would ensure that I also got one.

In my meetings with the Director-General on the supplementary budget, I attempted several times to get him to clarify his views about the limits of the Executive Director's authority, particularly in relation to staffing, the issue at the root of our differences over the budget. Saouma would not be drawn, simply repeating that as trustee of the WFP Fund he had ultimate authority in everything. Clearly, if I wanted to get anywhere with him on this critical question I would have to await the legal opinion promised by the Secretary-General.

Obstruction over the supplementary budget was accompanied by withdrawal of previously delegated authority in relation to senior field staff, which had the potential to seriously complicate management of our operations. This was done to show me that FAO could also hamstring day-to-day operations. WFP had no freedom of action except as allowed by FAO.

During this period I went out of my way to comply with Saouma's wishes on matters of personal importance to him, such as providing prompt, positive responses to his requests to provide emergency assistance. Our meetings were amicable. One day, however, Yriat warned me that 'rumour has it that your relations with the Director-General are not going well'. 'Working for him is a source of great satisfaction, but Saouma is an implacable adversary', Yriat warned. I also heard of speculation in FAO about which of our staff was behind my budgetary initiative. The commonest suspect, given FAO's unpopularity with the United States, was the most senior American on our staff, Dick Cashin. Apparently, if I was not FAO's captive I must be someone else's! In fact Cashin did not work on matters concerning WFP's relations with FAO and he and I were never close.

The United Nations Legal Opinion

My relations with the Director-General came to a head immediately following CFA14, when I received the long-awaited legal opinion. This took the form of a memorandum from John Scott, Director, Office of the Legal Counsel, to Olivares under cover of a memorandum to me signed by the Secretary-General and dated 4 October 1982.

I was enormously heartened to learn that my interpretation of the Basic Documents was very much in line with a formal legal reading of them. The conclusion to the opinion read as follows:

The WFP is not an organ solely of either the United Nations or of FAO, but should be and has been considered as a joint organ of both, with the autonomy necessary to preserve its position as such. Therefore the Programme is not subject to the executive head of either of the parent organisations, except to the extent the WFP Basic Documents so provide. Of course, as a practical matter, either such executive head might, on a revocable basis, delegate certain of his joint authority to the other, and the WFP Executive Director might similarly delegate some of his authority to the executive head of the UN or of FAO. But, absent such delegation, the Executive Director has, under the Basic Documents, which were adopted by the competent representative organs...the independent authority assigned to him by these Documents, which should enable him to administer the Programme under his responsibility and under the guidance of CFA.

In relation to staff administration, the opinion said that FAO Staff Regulations and Rules are to be applied '*mutatis mutandis*, for it is the WFP

Executive Director, and not the FAO Director-General who is responsible for decisions in respect of the WFP staff'. Moreover, the Executive Director was not a FAO staff member and the 'Director-General and the Secretary-General do not supervise his work nor does he require their authority to travel or take leave'. I was pleased to note that 'consultation' did not mean 'agreement', as Saouma asserted.

As regards financial management the opinion argued that the relevant provisions were meant to 'assist WFP rather than control it'. Further, it should be noted that the various financial provisions 'relate merely to the mechanical aspects of WFP's financial transactions, i.e. to service operations not affecting the ultimate control over the substance of these transactions, which control is largely assigned to the Executive Director'

An important reason why I had sought the post at WFP was my view that, legally speaking, the head of WFP was more 'independent' than the heads of other UN programmes. The opinion confirmed this:

> The authority of the executive heads of semi-autonomous UN bodies, such as UNICEF and UNFPA, differs from that of the WFP Executive Director, in that the former are in charge of UN subsidiary organs whose staffs (including executive heads) are part of the UN Secretariat.

Thus my predecessors had unnecessarily acquiesced in FAO control over their personnel and financial management of the Programme, control which was stifling progress in the use of food aid for development and emergencies.

The Secretary-General's covering memorandum asked me to give a copy of the opinion to the Director-General, for his information. I would have much preferred, indeed had hoped, that the Secretary-General himself would copy the opinion to Saouma. That he did not suggested he was willing to give me tools to fight the battle but was unwilling to enter into direct combat. That remained the case throughout the struggle.

At CFA14—and at subsequent sessions—the United Nations gave useful, moral support. The Secretary-General is represented at each session of the CFA and a statement is delivered on his behalf. For my second CFA, his statement contained significant references to the United Nations as a 'co-parent' and to the CFA as the Programme's 'governing body' enjoined to give the 'Executive Director the support which he will need to discharge his responsibilities effectively'. To ensure that its meaning was unmistakable, the statement concluded with an unprecedented personal reference: '...I wish to express my personal support for the endeavours of the new Executive Director, Mr James Ingram, whose dedication and experience will, I am sure, be of the greatest assistance in helping the Programme meet these challenging objectives' (WFP, 1982(c), p.40). Coming from a developing country, the Secretary-General was signalling to G77 delegates that I had his support and warranted theirs.

I called on Saouma immediately after CFA14 to give him the opinion and the Secretary-General's memorandum. I wanted him to see that Pérez de Cuéllar had personally signed it and requested I hand it on. I realised this was a momentous step. It would arouse Saouma's outrage and my position as Executive Director might become untenable. Indeed before the meeting I told Odette I could lose my job over this.

Saouma's reaction was as expected: 'It is not for the Secretary-General to instruct me...I am not interested in reading his opinion...I have my own Legal Counsel...I may have to refer this matter to the International Court of Justice...You are an ingrate. I appointed you to this position and went out of my way to get you appointed...I will have to tell outsiders I made a mistake, that you are not a success, in fact you are a *prima donna*...Relations between us will in future be difficult...That will be bad for WFP.' [21]

After half an hour he calmed down, asked me to indicate which were the most important points in the legal opinion. I pointed to the staffing paragraphs. I said that all I was asking was that when FAO administrative staff were providing services to WFP they report to me on such matters. 'It is not my desire to duplicate FAO structures providing financial and personnel services to the Programme,' I said. He replied, 'I will think about the issues'. We parted on cordial terms.

Our next encounter was a week or so later at the autumn meeting of the ACC in New York. Before the afternoon session resumed I saw that Saouma was alone. I walked across the room to exchange pleasantries with him. He responded aggressively and in an accusatory tone: 'The Secretary-General has denied all knowledge of the legal opinion. He is not willing to have a fight with me; all he wants is a quiet life. I am much more important to him than you...You are stupid...I know everything that is going on between you, Olivares and the Secretary-General...All your correspondence is available to me...I am instructing my staff not to cooperate with WFP and I will not receive you again...I have more than five years of my term to go, whereas you have only four and a half...You may well have to leave...before that time...I will take the matter to the FAO Council and ECOSOC'. Several times he said: 'I am elected whereas you are appointed, you are subordinate to me. You went behind my back'. I replied: 'What we have to do is to work out a cooperative relationship and I stand by all I have said previously in this regard', to which statement I received no reply, so ending the exchange. I had cast the die. Unless I capitulated I could expect no quarter.

At dinner that night, Olivares told me that, at a reception that day, Saouma had loudly and publicly attacked him for supposedly conniving with me to get the legal opinion. Olivares was shaken, though unrepentant. He told me that Saouma referred to Pérez de Cuéllar as 'fat belly'. In my experience, Saouma deliberately used an uncouth style to rattle gentlemanly opponents. Olivares speculated it might become necessary to find me another job. He said the High Commissionership for Refugees was coming up and if I was interested I should tell the Secretary-General. That never became necessary. Olivares died unexpectedly the next year and I never again had such a strong champion so close to Pérez de Cuéllar.

The following day I called on the Secretary-General. I said I was 'totally committed to getting on with the Director-General and that, as far as I was concerned, there was nothing personal in our differences, that the donors strongly supported me...and I believed they wished to see the Programme strengthened in the ways I was pursuing.'

Having commented that it was 'completely appropriate for you to have sought and been given a legal opinion on your responsibilities', I was taken aback when he added, apparently having forgotten his memorandum to me, that 'knowing the man' it would have been better not to have given him the opinion. I made no comment. The Secretary-General went on, 'I would like you to be as flexible as possible in your dealings with Mr Saouma, but of course if the situation became impossible then I might well have to intervene, possibly in response to donor representations...Mr Saouma is very clever, but we must be cleverer.' He asked me to keep in touch with him.

The FAO Legal Opinion

FAO eventually produced its own legal interpretation, dated 4 May 1983. It was sent by the FAO Legal Counsel to his UN counterpart. It was never passed to us by FAO nor did the Director-General ever refer to it in conversation with me, though my staff did obtain a copy. The UN and FAO Legal Counsels met several times to attempt to reach a common understanding but were unable to do so.

The FAO interpretation contended that the Secretary-General and the Director-General had not only a right but a duty to give guidance to the Executive Director. The apparent symmetry in their responsibilities was misleading. It was strongly implied, but not quite asserted, that the Director-General's were the greater. The essence of the lengthy FAO opinion was that despite several intergovernmental reviews 'the distribution of responsibilities has remained substantially unchanged, and over the last two decades a body of practice has been developed in the application of the relevant basic texts'. Delegations could be made to the Executive Director and regulatory manuals might be adjusted, but 'only at the discretion of the Director-General'. The internal audit function was specifically identified as one that could not be performed by the Executive Director, given the Director-General's financial responsibilities under the Additional Financial Procedures (Appendix I, GR 28).

These procedures were prepared by the Director-General of FAO, in consultation with the Executive Director, FAO Finance Committee and the ACABQ. They were approved by the CFA and could be amended through the same means as for their establishment. The Additional Financial Procedures were the key to FAO's financial control and could easily have been amended if the Director-General had so wanted. In fact, the practices followed over many years were sacrosanct because they were the practices followed. 'Possession being nine tenths of the law' FAO would not enter into a legal argument with me but would show me at every opportunity that it was in charge.

The FAO legal opinion was probably not prepared for serious discussion with the UN, but for delegates, especially from the G77, to demonstrate that the UN opinion was not the last word. For my part, I had shown the UN legal opinion privately to a few key delegates to protect myself. I knew that FAO was telling delegates that my behaviour was improper and unacceptable and arose from personal vanity. However, I did not circulate the opinion as a document or allude to its provisions in public. UN culture was strongly averse to making public interagency disputes and I could not risk offending the other 'parent'.

INVOLVING THE UNITED NATIONS

Nevertheless, its covert support remained indispensable. A cardinal principal of my strategy was throughout to strengthen the good will of the Secretary-General and his key staff. I gave the same high priority to this as to building support from developed and developing countries. From the beginning I made the deliberate decision to move WFP closer to its 'other parent'. The UN's interest in WFP had languished, which I saw as unfortunate, quite apart from our current difficulties with FAO. It was the UN that provided the framework to avoid duplication of mandates and compartmentalisation of operations, though its performance was weak. I wanted WFP to do all it could to strengthen the UN's system-wide coordination function and to build strong relations with other relevant UN system agencies.

To that end, from the beginning I attended and took a positive part in the meetings of UN Senior Officials, i.e. the heads of organisations other than the specialised agencies, which met periodically under the chairmanship of the Director-General for Development, Jean Ripert. More importantly, I brought WFP into membership of the Joint Consultative Group on Policy (JCGP), a forum of the heads of the development agencies of the UN, namely UNDP, UNICEF and UNFPA, and later IFAD. Its aim was to improve cooperation between these organisations, in part at least as an example to the fractious specialised agencies, especially FAO and UNESCO. I did not consult Saouma. He had no standing in the matter but I knew that if I did he would express opposition. These steps may seem small but it was unprecedented for WFP to move outside the FAO orbit.

YEAR'S END

By the end of my first year it appeared as though a general instruction had gone out from FAO to make life even more difficult for WFP. One action with potentially serious consequences was to oppose the establishment of posts to augment our capacity to provide logistical services to bilateral donors. Some donors occasionally used the Programme to deliver their bilateral aid, this being less costly than doing so themselves. We naturally wanted to provide a satisfactory service, failure to do so not only adversely affecting our relations with them but depriving us of revenue. The posts sought were funded from donor fees and were outside the budget framework. They were not covered by the WFP Basic Documents and should not have been an FAO concern.

It had also become clear that West, who had day-to-day oversight of relations with WFP, was unquestioning in his implementation of Saouma's assumed wishes. My concerns were confirmed when I was given a copy of the confidential report on a meeting between US officials and West that November. It made fascinating, discouraging but not surprising reading, reporting on West's hostility to US interference in FAO matters and his assertion that WFP is 'ours and does what we say'.

Although I faced formidable obstacles, the year ended on a satisfying note. I was now reasonably assured that WFP did make a serious contribution to development as well as to the relief of suffering. The Programme's standing was high with those well acquainted with its work. It was a substantial organisation that genuinely helped developing countries. Its reputation with them was at least as good as any other UN agency and superior to most.

It was clear, however, that field staff morale and hence their performance would be much enhanced if they enjoyed the same status as their peers. This could only be achieved if UNDP Resident Representatives ceased to be the WFP titular representative.

It was also evident that the work of our field staff had little in common with that of technical assistance experts from agencies like FAO. It was preposterous that, 20 years after its formation, the Director-General was perversely increasing FAO control through a narrow, in reality discredited, interpretation of regulations themselves anachronistic, and in need of review.

While all the main donors and some of the developing countries were dissatisfied with that situation they did not know how to change it. Because of the Director-General's effective control over the Rome delegations of developing countries, developed countries brought a defeatist attitude to the possibility of reform being effected through intergovernmental supervisory bodies. There was also incomplete unity among donors. France, Austria and Belgium, all small donors, were sympathetic to Saouma and saw him as serving their interests in FAO. France, the most influential, considered WFP a tool of American foreign and agricultural trade policy, which in no way served France's national interest.

The challenge was formidable. If WFP's potential was to be realised, leadership must rest with the Executive Director. With the legal opinion to hand I remained hopeful that Saouma's pragmatism would assert itself. After all, I had no grand plan in mind. All I wanted was enough freedom, gained by common sense interpretation of the Basic Documents and appropriate delegations, to make the improvements I could see were necessary. So ended a frenetic, exacting, challenging but deeply satisfying 1982. My enthusiasm was undiminished. I relished the task ahead.

---

21 Throughout this narrative, citations of my conversations with Saouma come from records I made of our conversations or from my diary which I began in 1984.

5

A CLASH OF CULTURES

On my efforts to bring greater substance to WFP's policy role; differences over the setting of food aid targets; and FAO's failed attempt to emasculate my first biennial administrative budget.

Today, few recall the bitterness between developed and developing countries in UN organisations in the latter decades of the last century, prior to the end of the Cold War. That division was especially poisonous in Rome. FAO under Saouma was regarded by the G77 as their agency. OECD countries were intensely hostile to him. They saw him as promoting division to maintain his personal power. The controversy surrounding his re-election had not abated. In January 1983 the Rome newspaper, *Daily American*, began a year-long campaign of sustained attack on Saouma's financial management and accountability, culminating in the publication in December that year of a 48-page FAO Dossier, a catalogue of press articles from a variety of sources detailing his and FAO's alleged failings.

WFP was portrayed by FAO as an organisation unduly influenced by developed countries, especially the United States. I was from a developed country; *ergo* I must be a donor tool. Since developing countries had a slight majority among its 30 members, to retain credibility with the CFA, donor support was not enough. I must also convince developing countries I was committed to striking a balance between their interests and those of the donors. The best way to make this clear to all was to continue as I had begun, by bringing forward projects for any deserving country even if they were out of political favour with the United States. This I did. The result was that I always had the positive support of some developing countries and never lost the confidence of the G77 as a whole.

95

Despite their rhetoric, developing countries were realistic enough to recognise that the donors wrote the basic music to which all must dance if contributions to the Programme were not to decline precipitately. For their part the donors, including the United States, at bottom understood the Executive Director must consider both their interests and those of developing countries. With a reasonable amount of political skill it was not that difficult to find an acceptable balance.

In addition, I pursued an increasingly ambitious reform agenda, which was implacably opposed by FAO. The clash between Saouma and me reflected a fundamental difference in the philosophies each of us brought to matters of substance affecting WFP's role and the uses of food aid. And in the atmosphere of the time it was not difficult for FAO to induce key members of the G77 to actively oppose many of my reform initiatives. These were represented as weakening FAO oversight, without which, it was said, WFP would be totally under the thumb of the donors. FAO was able to ensure that, time after time, the FAO Council elected to the CFA sufficient, often the same, developing countries whose Rome representatives were close to the Director-General. Some were from countries with little stake in WFP aid. Often these were FAO's strongest supporters. Some looked for a post in FAO and by all accounts Saouma was masterful at keeping hopes alive over many years. Doubtless some genuinely believed that in supporting FAO positions in the CFA they were acting in the interests of developing countries, many of whom seemed to accept at face value FAO's claim to be the custodian of those interests.

Persuading the developing countries to give me positive support in pursuit of the reforms I wanted was therefore very difficult. Further, as the Director-General became convinced that I was a threat to the interests of FAO as he conceived them he worked actively to discredit me personally with governments and with the UN Secretary-General. This meant that the CFA, ostensibly an intergovernmental technical oversight body concerned with food aid, became a political body where issues were not considered on their merits but in terms of North-South politics, which in Rome turned upon the person of the FAO Director-General. Within the FAO Finance Committee and the FAO Council consideration was even more overtly political. My supporters were fewer and FAO could mobilise more and different critics. Since constitutional reform turned out to be a protracted political process in these three committees it is convenient to structure the narrative around what transpired in them.

FOOD AID POLICY

During 1982 I became more and more convinced that WFP needed to make a serious commitment to food aid policy. FAO had done that many years ago but it had long ceased to give intellectual leadership on food issues generally, which led to the establishment of WFC and IFPRI. As regards food aid specifically, the World Food Conference had conferred the policy role on the CFA. Yet little had been done to give it effect beyond the inclusion of an agenda item for each year's spring session, 'Review of food aid policies and programs', which resulted in a lacklustre debate.

As a first step to bringing substance to the CFA's policy role I proposed it should embark on a systematic overview of the experiences of individual countries, donors and recipients, with food aid. This was greeted warily by some delegates fearful that weaknesses might be revealed with potentially adverse consequences for their governments. Though an obvious and elementary step it showed up the poverty of FAO's claim to be the repository of policy expertise. In the event the experiment was a resounding success. By the end of my second term a book embodying the experiences of eight developing and eight developed countries had been published (Shaw and Clay, 1993).

In 1983, WFP celebrated its twentieth anniversary. It was the custom to mark in some public way the Programme's achievements over the preceding five years. I decided to do so by holding a high-level seminar bringing together academics, food aid practitioners including NGOs, and development and agricultural economists. My idea was to assemble the best available thinking about, and experience of, food aid from both developed and developing countries. I wanted some brainstorming about how WFP might make a greater developmental impact with its projects; and that indeed was what we got. I had informed CFA14 of my intention, including my request that a donor meet the cost of the seminar. Several delegations spoke in support and none objected. However, not entirely to my surprise, I found I had broken open a hornet's nest. Apparently, the discussion in CFA14 had escaped the notice of FAO's top management who, I knew, would not welcome my initiative.

The Director-General contacted Ripert, the UN official of similar rank to himself concerned *inter alia* with WFP. Saouma sought to persuade the United Nations to join him in forbidding the event, unless it became a joint

United Nations/FAO seminar. To delay it and to underline its 'responsibilities' in relation to the Programme, FAO also wanted the seminar to be formally approved by the CFA and then by ECOSOC and the FAO Council! In the end, FAO had to give way, the compromise being for Ripert to advise me in writing that attendance by UN and FAO representatives would show not only their support for WFP but 'reflect their responsibilities in the management of the Programme'.

The Hague seminar exceeded my expectations in terms of the level of representation, the quality of the papers and the accompanying discussion. The proceedings were published (WFP, 1983) and, of course, reported to the CFA in the following year. Nevertheless, the fuss with both FAO and the UN had been time-consuming and distasteful, and a solid indication that FAO, already weakened by the creation of WFC, would do what it could to prevent WFP from moving into food aid policy. Moreover, the UN's unwillingness to firmly reject FAO's bullying was disappointing and a hallmark of the organisation's timidity in giving leadership to the system.

FOOD AID TARGETS

The Director-General and I brought opposing views to the vital matter of how best to maximise donations to the Programme. Each two years the CFA set a target for the quantity of resources of food and cash governments were exhorted to pledge for the next biennium. The amount was recommended to CFA by the Executive Director following its endorsement by the Director-General and the Secretary-General. Obtaining that endorsement was invariably a cause of discord.

An elaborate and expensive pledging procedure had been laid down. Following CFA endorsement the target was considered by the FAO Council and ECOSOC, which invariably supported it. It had then to be approved by the UN General Assembly and the FAO Conference. A special pledging meeting at UN Headquarters in New York was convened by the Secretary-General and the Director-General.

The resources sought were to support the 'regular' activities of the Programme, namely its development projects. Pledges were made in food and cash to cover delivery costs, food purchases, and administrative expenses. From the total pledged, some $45 million was set aside for responding to food emergencies. (Other funds for emergencies were pledged to a separate facility described below.)

CFA15 was to set the target for the 1985-86 biennium. The recommended amount was $1.5 billion. It was approved, as the targets always were, despite the absence of real agreement between recipients and donors, the latter finding it politic to do so despite their reservations. The debate was sterile, with the donors insisting that WFP demonstrate it could effectively use more resources and the recipients ritualistically demanding guaranteed, ever-increasing resources.

Though WFP and FAO always eventually agreed on a target to recommend, in fact we differed strongly over tactics. FAO was stuck in the 'confrontational' mentality of the 1960s and 70s when the developing countries were politically ascendant in UN development assistance agencies. Decolonisation had dramatically increased their votes in the United Nations; the West was concerned to counter the influence of the Soviet bloc in the Third World; and there was general optimism about the value of aid. It was in this atmosphere that the 0.7 per cent of GNP aid target, to which each developed country committed itself, was adopted by the UN General Assembly. By the 1980s times had changed. Developed nations were more and more resistant to expanding the aid activities of UN system agencies, because of dissatisfaction with the benefits of aid and reservations about the cost-effectiveness of assistance through UN system organisations. Targets had virtually ceased to be a useful political device for increasing the quantum of aid as indeed had pledging conferences, originally intended to shame donors to give more than otherwise they would.

Global Food Aid Levels

The World Food Conference had in 1974 set a minimum global food aid target of 10 million tons of cereals, which had occasionally been reached and sometimes exceeded in special circumstances. Nevertheless, FAO wanted a dramatically higher food aid target. Thus, encouraged by FAO, the 1983 Summit of the 101 non-aligned countries advocated a target of 18 million tons.

I approached the matter from a different perspective. The most relevant food aid target had been set outside the United Nations. Flowing from the 'Kennedy Round' of trade negotiations, a Food Aid Convention (FAC) was agreed as a trade-off for a new International Wheat Agreement in 1967. The

Convention provided for a guaranteed minimum of 4.5 million tons of wheat or its equivalent in other cereals or cash. In 1980 the signatories upgraded their commitment to 7.6 million tons. Although wheat-growing countries with large surpluses, in particular the United States, provided more food aid than they were committed to under the Convention, it was clear that only in the most exceptional circumstances of widespread catastrophic famine would food aid exceed 10 million tons.[22]

Secondly, food aid was increasingly being seen as competing with other forms of aid considered to be more valuable development tools by aid agencies and NGOs and sometimes by foreign ministries, which placed a heavy value on aid as a tool of foreign policy. The total quantum of aid, including food aid, was decided in the context of national budgets. How the aid cake was cut up reflected the bargaining power of the proponents of the different forms of aid. I saw food aid's constituency in most donors as having diminishing power in view of the growing criticism of food aid. I considered that over-emphasis on the quantum without regard to effective use was counterproductive. Belabouring donors over their failure to meet targets had little effect on the level of food aid; it did embarrass and annoy them.

The best way of securing more food was to enlarge WFP's share of total food aid, not to harp on the need for ever more food aid. We had to build on WFP's success in the use of food aid for development, through better projects and the more efficient management of resources at our disposal. I also saw it as essential that WFP sell the whole aid community—academics, NGOs and politicians as well as the aid ministries—on the value of our kind of food aid and how it differed from the more controversial bilateral program food aid.

The statistics show how this strategy turned out. Global food aid as a percentage of total Official Development Assistance (ODA) was 11.95 per cent the year before my arrival. It never reached that level again, being in long-term secular decline. Only in years of high humanitarian disaster did it go over 10 per cent. Multilateral food aid in dollar terms (almost all of which was provided through WFP) as a percentage of all food aid fluctuated between approximately one quarter and one fifth. (If data for WFP turnover in tonnage is compared with global food aid, WFP's share is somewhat higher.) Measured in absolute terms, during my 10 years the tonnage handled by WFP more than doubled growing from 1,676,000 tons to

3,861,000 tons (Appendix II). During a period when all aid, not just food aid, was losing favour and UN agencies were handling a diminishing proportion of global aid, WFP's performance was highly creditable. This accomplishment gave the lie to those who argued that my differences with the Director-General somehow harmed the Programme.

Targets for Emergency Aid

Despite the name, the International Emergency Food Reserve (IEFR) was not an actual reserve or stock of food of 500,000 tons; it was an annual target. Donors were asked to announce their contributions to the IEFR one year in advance, but retained complete discretion regarding the release of their pledged amount. They were responsible for meeting the transport costs of their pledged shipments but some, including the United States, did not.[23] In fact the IEFR was only workable through use of the $45 million set aside from the cash resources of the Programme for emergencies. The same procedures that applied to the use of regular emergency resources applied to the IEFR, namely approval by the Director-General on the recommendation of the Executive Director.

As previously explained, the Director-General's emergency approval power was a major source of his support among developing countries. Thus he sought, but failed to get agreement from, governments to make the IEFR into a legally binding convention with resources of two million tons. At every opportunity, he exhorted donors to pledge more, accused them of indifference to needs and bewailed the increasing use of the Reserve to support long-running refugee situations. He gained no political leverage from this use. As I saw it, if donors were convinced by the case we made for each emergency as it arose they would meet all or most of the need, irrespective of the 500,000 tons target. Thus in 1981 they had provided over 600,000 tons. This continues to be the practice, with big fluctuations each year in available resources (OECD 2006, p.19).

DEVELOPMENTS IN RELATIONSHIPS

Following the Director-General's outburst in New York late in the preceding year I did not meet with him again until January 1983. When I did, we had an extended, courteous discussion in which we regained our old rapport. However, he still did not concede that I had legitimate concerns. Before our meeting I had written to him proposing we establish a joint FAO/WFP working party to sort out differences over personnel management. He rejected that because it would 'smack too much of a Lebanon/Israel style confrontation'. What he meant was it would give the impression there was some sort of equality between the two organisations. Instead, he said, 'I am quite prepared to discuss with you outstanding issues over time but not on the basis of systematic review. I am ready to make some concessions, but you must not fuss over minor symbolic matters.'

At a follow-up meeting, which lasted the better part of two hours, Saouma used his considerable charm to induce me to accept a package. He was ready to agree to WFP membership of the various committees concerned with personnel and contracts provided I agreed not to raise any further issues affecting my authority. 'You should not worry about these committees, their views count for nothing, you and I will always be able to agree on what should be done...You will gain much *bella figura* if you accept', he said.

Unless I accepted this package, Saouma would not revert to the *status quo* that had existed before his withdrawal of my delegation to make senior appointments to our overseas posts. That withdrawal had preceded his receipt of the UN legal opinion. If there was now to be cooperation between us, I felt he should, as a sign of goodwill, restore those delegations. While I welcomed his proposal for membership of the committees, the critical issue for me was his agreement that decisions on their recommendations on WFP matters should be the Executive Director's responsibility. Leaving

A meeting of minds?

aside the UN legal opinion, I said it was appropriate for him to delegate personnel and contract decisions to the WFP Executive Director: 'Why do you trust the Executive Director less than your FAO staff to whom you give extensive delegations in such matters?' This question never ever got a reply.

As in New York, Saouma reminded me that my appointment would expire in 1987, adding that the Secretary-General's term expired before mine: 'If our relations are good I would approach the new Secretary-General to get a further term for you', he said.

By the end of April 1983, it was clear that Saouma had no intention of reaching a common understanding of my powers under the Basic Documents, nor to enter into any discussion on the UN Legal Opinion or accede to any significant changes in practice.

FAO's stonewalling made sense politically. West had effectively told me so. 'My discussions with delegations', he said, 'suggested that they do not want to be brought to the point of choosing between WFP and FAO.' When I said that might be unavoidable, he replied, 'Saouma does not care what the CFA decides, since any change in his powers is a matter for the FAO Council and ECOSOC. He is confident governments will support him in those bodies.' 'After all', he continued, 'he was first elected because his predecessor allowed the World Food Council to be set up. He could not turn around and give WFP away also.'

Try as I might, including through many unequivocal public statements, I could never convince Saouma and West that I was not seeking to take WFP away from them and had no intention of seeking any change in WFP's status as a joint UN/FAO body. I expected only reasonable adjustments of practice to enable me to administer WFP more effectively and efficiently. In hindsight, I underestimated the threat I must have seemed. At the time, I expected them to accept that my motives were good. But with FAO trapped in the mentality of competing agencies, it was hardly concerned about the common good of the UN system. As Saouma told WFP staff before I arrived, and West the staff members from the United States Congress, 'WFP is ours'. Change of any kind was ruled out *a priori*. Although Saouma told me not to fuss about 'minor symbols', the symbols of WFP's dependence were of the utmost importance to him.

Failure to Break the Log Jam

To acquiesce in the FAO view of WFP and become totally dependent on the Director-General's goodwill would mean abrogating my responsibilities to governments, the 'owners' of WFP. Moreover, if I gave in I would lose his respect. Saouma respected strength alone.

Acting on a suggestion from Ripert, I addressed a letter to both the Director-General and Secretary-General requesting a joint consultation with the two parent bodies to resolve the fundamental questions of the Executive Director's responsibility and authority. Ripert and Olivares suggested I follow up this request with a more personal letter to Pérez de Cuéllar, in accordance with his invitation to me to approach him if I ever felt the need. I wrote at the end of June in anticipation of seeing Pérez de Cuéllar in Geneva early in July for a meeting of the ACC. I expanded on my earlier arguments. I said that the Programme was unable to carry out its mandate effectively, staff being 'confused as to whom they were ultimately responsible' and that donor concern over the situation would eventually lead to a decline in contributions. The Executive Director must have the administrative authority provided for in the Basic Documents. I explained that with the growth in its role as an investment agency its natural partners in the UN system had expanded to include many agencies besides FAO, which now provided less than half of the outside technical services purchased by WFP. I said I had avoided personal embarrassment to the Director-General by never referring publicly to differences between us, by not discussing the situation collectively, even with senior WFP staff, and by not circulating the legal opinion to WFP staff or quoting from it in memoranda to FAO staff. I also drew attention to unseemly attacks on me by a few delegations from developing countries in the FAO Council.

In Geneva, according to Olivares who was present during their meeting, Saouma said to Pérez de Cuéllar I had insulted him, that he would no longer talk to me, but wanted me to discuss outstanding issues with West. He contended, by now a familiar assertion, that the matters in dispute involved only the role of the Director-General and did not concern the Secretary-General. He claimed to be willing to delegate some authority to me.

Ripert had also initially urged me to meet with West, though after a discussion he had in Belgrade with Saouma he changed his mind, since clearly FAO 'had no proposals to put on the table'. Nevertheless, I invited West to lunch. I had in fact had a long discussion with him a few weeks earlier on a flight back from New York to Rome. Though that conversation and our lunch were helpful in clarifying points of contention in relation to our administrative budget, West was emphatic that he was not authorised to discuss issues outstanding between me and Saouma.

I never received replies from the Director-General or Secretary-General to my letters. There appeared to be no more room to bring about change through appeals to commonsense pragmatism. I had reached a dead end.

AUDIT—A TOOL OF BUREAUCRATIC WARFARE

Soon after my arrival in Rome, in one of our friendly talks, Saouma had said, 'You know if you have a staff member you want to get rid of with the least trouble, use internal audit. Almost every staff member is guilty at some time or other of technical regulatory breaches.' This use of internal audit was facilitated by the incredible detail and complexity of FAO regulations, which made it easy for the unscrupulous manager to use the rules unfairly to discredit staff.

That advice stuck with me, especially when I heard that the internal auditor, K Mehboob, was close to the Director-General and known among staff as 'Saouma's policeman'. After my relations with the Director-General deteriorated, I feared that the weapon would be used against WFP.

Accordingly, when in late 1982 Mehboob sent me his draft audit plan for 1983 I took the opportunity to set some ground rules. I wrote and thanked him for his draft, asked him to let me have a copy of his plan as finally approved and that he let my office know of any subsequent changes. I also requested, in the interests of smooth cooperation, that he channel requests for access through my office or through our administrative department. I wanted to be aware as quickly as possible of any fishing expeditions. Mehboob did not reply. However, five months later I received a blistering memorandum from the Director-General.

I was told that staff of the Internal Auditor had been denied access to the files of our Insurance and Cargo Claims Branch 'in accordance with your instructions and that your interference in the freedom of the Internal Auditors in the performance of their duties is unacceptable'. The memorandum went on to give an exegesis of the WFP Basic Documents along the lines of the FAO Legal Opinion and, citing Financial Rule 202.94, to demand free and unconditional access to WFP documents.

There had been nothing in my instructions, all of which had been copied to Mehboob, which refused access. In my reply to him I expressed surprise that he had not immediately contacted me if he had access problems. I explained that the procedures I had proposed did not derogate from the responsibilities of the Director-General. I did also point out that the audit function necessarily addressed itself to management issues which were the responsibility of the Executive Director, that there was a limit to how much work internal audit could reasonably undertake in WFP and that if the value of the services bought by WFP was to be maximised, there needed to be mutual agreement on priorities. In this regard, I reminded Mehboob, that I had not yet received from him a long overdue report on the contentious issue of freeze dried products, a delicate issue in our relations with Italy.

During the rest of the year I received from Saouma several harshly worded memoranda over internal audit. My arguments were dismissed or ignored. I had no doubt they were written as much to show delegates and, significantly, the external auditor what an unreasonable fellow I was, as to reproach me. FAO's attitude was the more remarkable in that the United Nations Joint Inspection Unit (JIU) had in 1971 recommended that the internal audit function should be transferred to WFP.

External Audit

The United Kingdom's National Audit Office had for many years been FAO's and WFP's External Auditors, the cost of its services being met by WFP. The task was a continuing one so a small team of British auditors was based in Rome. In order to set the highest possible standards of financial accountability, from the beginning I sought a strong relationship with the External Auditor, especially the leader of the Rome team, and readily agreed to the request that his team join the teams evaluating our development projects. I knew that External Audit was unhappy that FAO resisted any attempt at management audits. It also aspired to evaluate some of FAO's field projects, which donors considered were often used as a vehicle to win support from developing countries.

Over the years that relationship proved to be invaluable. For example, when FAO was seeking to cause harm by using its control over contracts to hold up or deny access to outside expert advice, the External Auditor provided (for a fee) specialised personnel to help resolve some of our problems, especially the accounting functions of our poorly designed computerised management information system.

In a previous chapter I told how Mselle, the Chairman of the ACABQ, had drawn my attention to FAO's possible overcharging for the services they provided to the Programme. Out of a total headquarters administrative budget of $56,910,000 some $17,020,000 went to pay for these services, with another $3,600,000 paid for technical services provided by the United Nations, UNESCO, ILO and WHO for development projects in the sectors of their competence. On investigation I discovered how important the issue was. FAO claimed to be subsidising WFP. It was an Alice in Wonderland claim. The supplier was the sole arbiter of what would be supplied and how much he would charge; and the buyer was unable to seek services elsewhere! The Programme had no cheque book and all payments were made through FAO, even though in terms of size of budget, numbers of staff and amount of aid disbursed we were one of the largest UN agencies. That put us in awkward situations as, for example, when FAO denied payment to an outside personnel consultant I had used to help prepare my first budget.

How was I ever to get out of this situation? Mselle had asked whether External Audit had ever examined FAO's costing methodology, implying that I should perhaps raise the matter with them. I therefore sought the advice of the External Auditor's Rome representative, Clive Day, who made a start by investigating the quality of the public information services we bought from FAO.

Shortly afterwards, the Director-General telephoned me to complain that External Audit staff were 'counting press releases' produced for us by FAO at 'your behest'. 'You should know that the External Auditor could act only on FAO's instructions,' he said. Thus FAO was seeking to close off another potential avenue to reform.

Some months later Day let me know that West had met the British Auditor-General in London and demanded Day's recall because of the arrangements he had made with WFP. Day said that Saouma had given him a personal dressing down over these matters. FAO objected to any direct communication between External Audit and WFP. When Day said he was only acting even-handedly, Saouma said he expected him to side with FAO in accordance with the Director-General's responsibility for the WFP accounts. FAO considered it as irrelevant that WFP paid for the external audit but was never consulted on the choice of auditor. Saouma allegedly went on to threaten a transfer of the external audit function from the UK, although this was most unlikely as it was widely known FAO wanted, at all costs, to keep out the very strict national French auditor, *La Cour des Comptes*, preferring the devil it knew. Day reluctantly accepted a transfer to Edinburgh the next year. Despite FAO objections, External Audit continued to deal personally with me and to inform us of its dealings with FAO on all WFP matters. All formal written communications, however, were with FAO alone.

Although not much progress was made on assessing the worth of 'information services', CFA16 (October, 1983) did endorse the need for a quick joint examination by WFP and FAO of the basis for costing FAO's services to the Programme. Continuing FAO bad faith over this was in the end a valuable factor in bringing about the constitutional changes I was seeking.

THE BIENNIAL BUDGET

I presented my first budget for a full biennium, 1985-86, to CFA16. While the 1982 supplementary budget had helped headquarters keep pace with the increasing work load, a substantial increase in staff was essential. Since 1976 new posts at headquarters increased by only 10 per cent despite a 30 per cent increase in the volume of food deliveries and, more tellingly, a 43 per cent rise in commitments to existing and newly approved projects. It had become impossible to design and get approved sufficient new projects in time to use all the food pledged or anticipated.

To my surprise, the Administrative Budget did not cover our field staff or offices. At this time we had 169 professional officers in the field supported by 600 national staff. While both were funded from the budgets of the projects administered by each of our offices, the professional staff was managed under FAO staff rules and regulations whereas the local staffs, many of whom did professional work, came under UNDP's very different rules. Because of the separate financing, field staff was growing more or less sufficiently, though fair grading of field professional posts was being hamstrung by FAO.

Given the constraints imposed on us by the relationship of tutelage insisted upon by FAO I knew I would have to seek fewer posts than really required. Even so, the FAO Establishments Committee only endorsed three of the eighteen new posts I had settled upon. I decided boldness was the only way to get anywhere so I stuck with my plan. This was risky because the CFA was bound to be influenced by the views of the FAO Finance Committee, as well as by those of the ACABQ, from which I expected, and received, endorsement.

Moreover, we had some confidence that under its new Chairman the Finance Committee would be less negative than before. That turned out to be the case. In fact FAO suffered a significant defeat. West tried hard to get the Committee to endorse only nine of the new posts but was unsuccessful. The majority supported our proposals, but some developing countries did not, even though they never ceased to urge increased food aid through WFP!

Ambassador Millicent Fenwick

I was still not confident of CFA approval. After the Finance Committee debacle I expected FAO to do all that it could to retrieve its position. I knew it was making an all-out effort with the United States. The US representative, Roger Sorenson, had been replaced by a Republican political appointee, the late Millicent Fenwick. Ambassador Fenwick had been involved in New Jersey politics since the 1930s and elected to Congress in 1975, but had failed to make the shift to the Senate the previous November. She was a celebrity in the United States, said to be the model for a character in the Garry Trudeau satirical cartoon strip, *Doonesbury*. By this time she was in her seventies. She had been a Vogue model and ran a 40-acre farm by herself during the Depression. She was tall, dressed well, had largely retained her figure and possessed great charm. In her interventions she almost always brought up two of her pet themes: self-composting latrines and the need for delegates to 'listen'. It was impossible to dislike her.

However, it was the Director-General, not I, who won her esteem and confidence. At their first meeting, according to her staff, he showed a video prepared by FAO, of clips of her political career. Thereafter, she received many attentions including flowers on occasions such as her birthday.

I treated her as a fellow professional, receiving her with the same cordiality as any other new Ambassador and briefing her thoroughly on the issues before the Programme. Fenwick was unexpectedly cool. I put this down to the natural reaction of a fair-minded person who was suspicious that Saouma was being demonised. She wanted to make up her own mind. Unfortunately, her admiration for Souma's warmth and misgivings about what she saw as my cold Machiavellianism never completely waned. She answered any criticism of Saouma or defence of me by lumping us together as supposedly possessing 'numbered' Swiss bank accounts!

West also made a good impression on Fenwick. Her deputy, Don Toussaint, a career diplomat who had been my friend and colleague in Jakarta, told us about Fenwick's first meetings at FAO. West set the scene well for the encounter with Saouma, describing him as 'not a diplomat but a man of action and leader of men, quick to react to genuine offence as Ingram had given him'. I was a 'difficult problem', whose appointment West had argued against, but that 'we all must suffer the consequences until his term ends'.

FAO's Tactics

Fenwick was persuaded that my requests for new posts were far too many and unnecessary since 'FAO would always help WFP and could do so more economically than by adding posts to WFP'. She urged Washington to view sympathetically FAO's position. This no doubt appealed to Republican ears. I believe a further influence on Fenwick was her dislike of food aid, which she never failed to see as anything but a handout.

West went to Washington to persuade the State Department to agree to only half the posts I sought, arguing that 'any more would be an affront to Saouma, who would be forced to fight and he would win'.

FAO used different arguments with the developing countries. Having lost the budget battle in the ACABQ and FAO Finance Committee, it argued that the support of donors for my budget showed a double standard. At a time when donors were refusing to give additional resources to most UN system agencies, it was politic to ask why they were willing to make an exception for WFP. The answer, according to FAO, was obvious: WFP was a donor-controlled agency and would do what the donors wanted. Further, the donors wanted to strengthen WFP administratively 'to set in motion its independence from FAO'.

CFA Consideration

Until this session, the CFA plenary had shown little interest in the budget. The Executive Director's proposals went straight to a sub-committee, which effectively met in closed session. FAO could always rely on some very clever parliamentarians from developing countries to represent their views and, if necessary, to stonewall until they got their point of view more than adequately represented. The same situation applied in the 12-member sub-committee constituted for each CFA to draft the committee's report.

I feared that if my proposals followed that route they might well suffer. I felt it imperative to educate the whole CFA about the logic of our proposals and show them the care taken to formulate them. I also wanted to lay on the table some information about the pressures we were under from FAO. I therefore departed from customary practice and personally made our budget case in the full CFA. A few days later, in one of our friendly discussions when I praised Saouma on his political skill, he returned the compliment. 'Anyone who can hold the CFA spellbound for an hour over an administrative budget is politically skilful', he said.

The Committee endorsed my proposals and recorded its appreciation of the excellent management of the Programme. The thoroughness of our preparations had paid off. A palpable surge in morale swept through headquarters. I felt indebted to the team responsible for the budget's preparation under the leadership of Ahmed.

Despite all our difficulties, Saouma and I had maintained a degree of amicability. In mid-November I had my last conversation with him for the year. It turned out to be another of our unproductive marathons. He had asked me to see him and began by attacking me for transferring two of my most senior officers between posts. He said I had acted illegally and improperly in not consulting him beforehand, as provided for in the WFP General Regulations. This was an extraordinary interpretation of the requirement that the 'selection and appointment of senior officials shall be made in agreement with the Secretary-General of the United Nations and the Director-General of FAO.' Until now that provision had applied to staff new to the Programme or to promotions. He said he did not object to the transfer only to my failure to get his approval.

The discussion moved onto familiar ground. Once again I made a plea to define the ground rules between us for administration of the Programme. As before, he passed over this, contending: 'If there is trust then there will be no administrative problems'. 'All you have to do is see me periodically and you will get my agreement to your proposals', he said. I replied that there could be no trust on my part so long as he continued to harass the Programme administratively and politically.

Though the conversation was calm and our tones friendly enough, I again left feeling deeply pessimistic. Saouma was Pope and I was an errant bishop, once his protégé, who must ask for his forgiveness, humbly and contritely. Or, to shift the metaphor, I was a wayward mafiosi who could expect harsh punishment, even execution, unless he kissed the ring of his Don and agreed to behave.

My friend, the late Brazilian Ambassador to FAO, A F M de Freitas, was right when he said that the FAO/WFP relationship was foundering on a 'clash of cultures'. Early in 1983, he said to me: 'It is clear to us that your approach is guided by Western concepts of responsible government and the rule of law, whereas Saouma brings the mentality of the traditional authoritarian ruler still characteristic of the Arab world.'

A week later I left on an extended trip to Brazil, Peru, New Zealand, Japan and India, taking the opportunity to take some home leave in Canberra on the way. I was exhausted and desperately needed a break from the febrile Rome atmosphere.

I had no plan for what to do next, other than somehow build on the esteem in which I was now held by delegations. Most of these accepted that the problems were rooted in WFP's outmoded institutional charter and that personalities were secondary.

There was one encouraging development. The JIU, the only independent investigatory body in the UN system, had decided to do a study of our personnel problems. Its work would eventually lead to the establishment of a Joint UN/FAO taskforce to review aspects of WFP's relationship with the two organisations. The painful process, which extended over nearly two years and led to my first breakthrough, is described in chapter 7. Meanwhile, my efforts to advance my agenda gave rise to an unprecedented confrontation in the CFA, the subject of the following chapter.

---

[22]   For a full account see Hans Singer, John Wood and Tony Jennings, *Food Aid: The Challenge and the Opportunity,* Clarendon Press, Oxford, 1987; and D John Shaw, (2001).

[23]   For a full account of the Reserve see (Shaw, 2001)

6

THE COLLAPSE OF TRUST

Nineteen eighty-four to eighty-five were pivotal years for the reform effort. There were allegations of corruption and attempts to discredit me personally, yet by the end of the period, WFP's standing with the CFA was stronger and FAO's diminished.

I began my diary in 1984 and maintained it until I left WFP in 1992. From this point onwards, it becomes an indispensable source for my narrative, together with official documentation.[24]

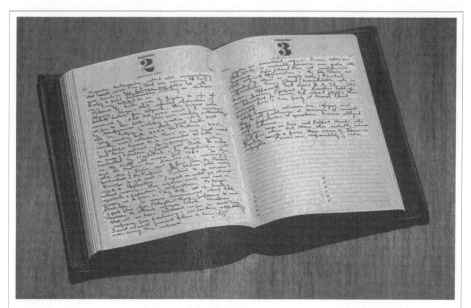

The diary

When I arrived back in Rome, I found little had changed. FAO was still making life difficult. Their strategy appeared to be to wait out my term while obstructing any departures from past administrative practice. My diary describes the situation I found:

Tuesday 17 January 1984

Today's bombshell was a letter from Crowther[25] to Ahmed. FAO is claiming that study of transport ordered by the CFA...requires prior consultation with the Secretary-General and the Director-General. Clearly they want...to insist on the letter of provisions which strengthen their role, while resisting provisions which support the Executive Director. These tactics will eventually make the management of WFP unworkable. Ingram to be blamed? Alternatively it could lead governments to recognise the inevitable: autonomy for WFP.

Thursday 19 January 1984

A story going around F Bldg. Saouma made an inspection a few weeks ago of F Bldg (he did not come to WFP) and came to one office and asked to see the occupant. The secretary said he would be back in a minute. Saouma was apparently not satisfied and said, 'Do you know who I am?' 'No I don't.' 'I am the Director-General', said Saouma. 'Oh, Mr Ingram, please excuse me!' said the secretary.

Tuesday 24 January 1984

An hour and a quarter with Saouma. For the first time (for a long while) no hostility and no menace on his side. Most of the discussion was about my trip, his news and proposed measures about staff discipline (cafeteria, bar, FAO shops)...As he had told FAO staff, there should be more communication and less territorialism. The same should apply to WFP and FAO. Issues dividing us should be settled at a lower level wherever possible—we should only be involved as a last resort. There would be problems but we should make a real attempt on these lines. I agreed. He said that some of his staff (and mine) made things worse out of a sense of over-zealousness.

These assurances were never seriously translated into practice. Saouma hoped, but probably did not expect, that after my absence I would be ready to accept his offer of last year. Equally, I still had faint hopes that he now saw I could not be crushed, that his former tactics were harming his own reputation; and that he would agree to give me the discretion I sought. Instead a scandal over marine insurance and a related, unscrupulous, attempt by FAO to discredit publicly my financial management seriously worsened the relationship.

THE SMELL OF CORRUPTION IN WFP AND FAO

Early in 1984 an extraordinary story of duplicity, corruption and commercial espionage unfolded. It caused a breakdown of trust in my relationship with the Director-General and undermined the latter's credibility with the external auditor and key governments. The full tangled chain of events would best be told as a crime novel but, unlike the sleuth in an Agatha Christie story, I never unmasked the criminals. To this day their identities remain a mystery though I believe that, contrary to my initial fear, the principal culprits were not in WFP.

The scandal precipitated a reckless, but failed, attempt by FAO to discredit publicly my management of the Programme. It also illustrates the legal impediments to the investigation of corruption in UN system agencies arising from their privileged legal status and the diplomatic immunity of their staffs.

The story begins with a request from Karl-Erik Norrman, the Swedish representative on the CFA, for me to meet with the Managing Director of our then marine insurers, the Swedish firm, Hansa Marine Insurance Company Limited. The meeting took place on 9 March 1984. Hansa informed me of an approach to them by a German broker, (hereafter Mr H A— not his real initials) based in Munich, allegedly on behalf of a group of WFP/FAO executive staff, who claimed they were in a position to ensure that the contract would be awarded to Hansa. Mr H A was well informed about WFP insurance matters, I was told. The price of his assistance would be 20 per cent of the annual premium which was of the order of $5 million per annum. The contract was '90 per cent guaranteed to Hansa if they cooperated', he allegedly said. Several meetings took place between Hansa and Mr H A as well as telephone conversations. Threats were uttered in case Hansa agreed to, but later went back on, the deal.

WFP shipped each year more than one million tons of food. On average about 30 ships containing our food were on the high seas at any one time. WFP also chartered ships. Altogether we were big players in marine transport. Our annual expenditure on freight, food purchases and insurance ran to hundreds of millions of dollars. Securing our marine insurance contract was profitable and a source of prestige for the successful company. Equally, it could be a source of corruption for unscrupulous employees. Not surprisingly, therefore, I feared that WFP staff might be working with Mr H A.

WFP had insured through Hansa Marine since 1981, the agreement expiring on 30 April 1984. Our insurance branch decided to go to tender and requested FAO, in December 1983, to send out the tender documents prepared by WFP, as in the past. Contrary to previous practice, the relevant FAO Assistant Director-General insisted FAO sign the invitations to tender. He also insisted on including in the invitees the firm providing health insurance to FAO/WFP staff, even though it was not a marine insurer or broker.

Hansa gave me a written account of all their initial meetings and telephone conversations with Mr H A who, at one point, said he had done 'similar business' before, implying he had been instrumental in obtaining the FAO health insurance contract for the successful firm.[26] Also, unbeknown to WFP, FAO added to the list of invitees a Munich insurance broking firm headed by a brother of Mr H A, who had at one time worked for FAO.

I immediately took three actions. I instructed Mr E Luhe, the head of our transport, insurance and resources division, to undertake an internal investigation to see if he could identify who, if anyone, in WFP was disclosing information to Mr H A, directly or via an intermediary. Fortunately, I had only recently transferred Luhe to that post. Previously, he had no involvement with insurance and was a meticulous administrator who could be relied upon to make a thorough search. Luhe turned up no evidence that WFP staff was acting inappropriately.

Secondly, I informed Saouma personally and in writing of my conversations with Hansa Marine and of my instruction to Luhe. I argued that the affair was a 'criminal matter which should be the subject of a police investigation'. I told him that I understood Mr H A's actions constituted a criminal offence under German law. I suggested it would be appropriate to place all the information at our disposal before the German authorities.

Thirdly, I requested Price Waterhouse Associates (PWA), the international accounting and consulting firm, currently working with the

Programme on another matter (see below), to review our entire insurance relationship with Hansa Marine. PWA had done a review of our insurance operations some years previously and was familiar with our work in all areas of transport and logistics. I took them into my confidence regarding Mr H A's alleged actions and asked them to try to identify whether any of our staff had communicated the information which the latter possessed.

In order to help identify the source of leaks, the Director-General had agreed we would allow the evaluation of the tenders to proceed, while keeping from staff knowledge of the prospective fraud, although we would not let a contract on the basis of those bids. PWA advised that our insurance staff had acted with complete professionalism in their analysis of the bids, had recommended acceptance of the lowest bid and had shown no partiality whatsoever for Hansa, whose bid was the highest of the twelve firms tendering.

Initially, Saouma did not object to Luhe's examination and appointed his internal auditor to undertake a similar investigation in FAO. There was some contact between the two but a couple of weeks after my first meeting with Saouma he made Mehboob responsible for the entire investigation. I pointed out to him that if WFP staff were questioned by Mehboob, an outsider from their perspective, before the evaluation of tenders was complete, any guilty persons would be alerted and the possibility of getting evidence from that process would be compromised. I insisted that investigations within WFP should remain solely with Luhe. In view of our ongoing disagreement about the Executive Director's relationship with internal audit, I feared that FAO might try to put all blame on WFP.

Mr H A continued his contacts with Hansa for some time and initially Hansa kept me informed of what transpired. It became clear that much of the new information he was passing on was accurate but not all. However, some that was accurate was unknown to WFP and could only have originated in FAO.

I kept Norrman informed of developments and confided in the external auditor. I also gave the gist of the story, naming no names, to the UN Legal Counsel, Dr Carl-August Fleischhauer, a German national, who advised how best to proceed with the German government. The ultimate German position was that it was up to either WFP or FAO to lay the evidence before the Bavarian prosecutor, if an investigation was to be undertaken, or to bring the matter to the Italian police. I never felt able to do this, as this would have involved going over Saouma's head on a matter that could ultimately raise legal issues of privileges and immunities for staff, a function for which his responsibility was crystal clear and where I had no standing.

However, despite my repeated urgings, Saouma never went beyond his own internal investigations in respect of which he said nothing to me, even though I was scrupulously forwarding to him all the information we gained as soon as it became available. If, as a result, disciplinary action was taken within FAO, I was never informed. If evidence against WFP staff was uncovered it would certainly have been used against us. It was not.

I learned from Hansa that FAO sent its internal auditor to Stockholm to meet with them. To convince Mehboob of Mr H A's existence, Hansa staff telephoned him in the latter's presence. In the course of the conversation Mr H A claimed his information came through an intermediary and not directly from WFP/FAO staff.

I had not heard from Hansa for months. On the off-chance there might have been further contact with Mr H A, I telephoned on 8 August 1984 and had a very lengthy and revealing conversation. I was told that FAO staff had made a second visit to Stockholm, the main purpose being to request Hansa to arrange a meeting with Mr H A, at which the FAO officials would be present. That meeting took place on 22 May. Mr H A contended that all his information came from anonymous telephone calls. According to Hansa there had been a subsequent meeting(s) between FAO and Mr H A at which the latter passed across to the FAO officials notes of his conversations with his informant. I was told that Hansa concluded that the FAO officials had a 'firm suspicion about the person involved and that he was in FAO rather than WFP'.

There the matter rested as far as I was concerned until October when, at Ambassador Fenwick's request, I met with her and German and Swedish representatives. Apart from the Germans and Swedes, Americans were the only delegates to whom I had given a briefing on the issue, done to protect us in case FAO had misrepresented the circumstances to them. Washington wanted the matter pursued with both organisations, I was told. Fenwick had met earlier with FAO and now echoed their arguments. First she suggested Hansa was at fault, presumably in collusion with Mr H A; then it was WFP, which had prepared the tender specifications. I kept emphasising that from the beginning I had sought a police investigation. Fenwick concluded by saying there was nothing to warrant such an investigation. The German representative explained that attempted fraud was a criminal matter under German law and evidence could be placed before the Bavarian state prosecutor. Asked whether I would do so, I said no. I had completed my investigation in WFP and without more information, there was nothing I could do. Only the FAO Director-General had the legal authority to so act.

I never heard any more about the matter. I found it odd and disturbing that these countries, all of whom had repeatedly expressed the strongest dissatisfaction with the management of FAO and their concern about the many rumours of corruption in the organisation, were unwilling to force the issue. In reality, political considerations were uppermost in their relationships with FAO.

FAO ATTACKS—THE AUDITED ACCOUNTS DEBACLE

Parallel to, but separate from, the affair of Mr H A, our insurers sought to void our current contract with them. When the Managing Director of Hansa called on me on 9 March he showed me a 'letter of avoidance', lodged that day with Luhe, effectively declaring null and void the contract which covered our shipments over the previous three years. Their grounds were that their 1981 tender was based on misleading information provided by WFP about the history of our claims during 1978-79. Hansa said that as a result they had lost money. This was potentially a serious matter which, if substantiated in court, would harm WFP's reputation and be financially costly to us.

Consistent with the Programme's policy of fairness in its dealings with suppliers, I said I would look into the matter. To that end, as mentioned above, I engaged PWA to examine Hansa's allegations. This then provided the cover for their investigation into the possible source within WFP of Mr H A's information. My action satisfied Hansa, which withdrew its letter of avoidance ten days later on 19 March. PWA's investigation showed that the charge was without foundation. The contract was satisfactorily completed and Hansa never took legal action against the Programme.

However, FAO decided to make our alleged failings with respect to this short-lived dispute the centre point of an attack on the competence and probity of my financial management. Saouma accused me of concealing from him Hansa's dispute with us. When FAO learned of the dispute from Hansa, in the course of their investigations of the Mr H A affair, I was accused of agreeing to negotiate a '$10 million claim in preference to taking legal action', the implication being that I was mishandling or covering up a very serious matter about which I should have informed the Director-General as the trustee of the WFP Fund. In fact I had mentioned the matter twice to Saouma and his staff present at our meetings. On one occasion I had addressed my remark directly to the FAO Legal Counsel confident that he at least would understand what a 'letter of avoidance' was, but he afterwards denied that I had. No matter how I explained the true state of affairs, in a dreadful meeting with Saouma and his staff I was repeatedly called a liar.

FAO decided to use the Director-General's formal responsibility for the WFP accounts as the vehicle for attacking my supposed deceit or incompetence in this matter. Each two years the Director-General submitted our accounts of the previous biennium to the external auditor for certification. The accounts for 1982-83 were to be considered in late 1984 by CFA18, after review by the FAO Finance Committee and by the ACABQ, if it so desired. From the CFA they would go to the FAO Council and Conference for final endorsement. Unless the external auditor qualified the accounts their consideration by all these bodies was essentially formal, even ritualistic.

For much of 1984 FAO sought to induce the external auditor to qualify our accounts over the possibility that Hansa might take legal action, in other words to formally state that our accounts did not accurately represent the true financial situation of the Programme. The external auditor was not persuaded. However, FAO took a step intended to achieve the same effect. It attached to the accounts a 'Representation of Financial Statements' signed by the Director-General and the FAO accountant. This statement singled out five 'matters of concern' in respect of which the Director-General stated, 'I am unable to represent the degree to which the account figures affected by these weaknesses present fairly the results of World Food Programme operations...' The five matters were marine insurance, procurement of lyophilised products, shipments in transit, contributions by assisted governments to local operating costs, and demurrage/despatch operations.

With the exception of marine insurance, the matters raised were trivial in the context of WFP's billion-dollar-plus operations. Indeed none of them were 'material' in the accounting sense. The paradox was that if blame was to be laid it was as much the fault of FAO as WFP, because of the past failures of FAO's internal auditor to identify weaknesses in our controls and work with our accountants to remedy them.

On the Hansa matter, FAO's essential charges were that we had arbitrarily terminated Internal Audit's review of insurance and denied it access to documentation related to the dispute. More specifically the 'Director-General, trustee of the WFP funds', was denied 'access to information', a denial which only I could have authorised. 'Such denials', it said, 'were of grave concern'. However, information 'obtained through other sources', that is from Hansa itself, was sufficient to require disclosure of a contingent liability that 'could amount to several millions of dollars'. The Executive Director was engaged in a serious cover-up and the Director-General was justified in his withdrawal of trust. Having embarked on this course FAO would not deviate. By attaching to the accounts its Statement of Representation it strengthened Hansa's claim in the event of litigation. Such behaviour by any trustee, in the face of possible legal action harmful to the financial interests of the beneficiary of the trust, was extraordinary.

FAO took this action notwithstanding PWA's investigation and the advice from our lawyers that Hansa was unlikely to take legal action. Moreover, no mention was made of the parallel issue, namely Mr H A's collusion with staff over the new contract. It was my fear that FAO wanted to put the blame on us for this, which led me to deny their internal auditor access to our insurance files and to our staff.

The external auditor used an unprecedented number of accountants to scrutinise our accounts, the cost of which was borne by WFP. The additional work placed our staff under great stress. For my part, I doubt if a non-accountant head of a UN agency has ever acquired a deeper grounding in the niceties of accounting and audit! FAO several times sent teams of senior officials to London to influence the external auditor. That it would go to such lengths, even after receiving the PWA report and our lawyers' assessment of the worth of the claim, revealed to me and our entire accounting staff, the degree of malice and the absence of trust in our relationship with FAO. The following selections from my diary give some sense of the whole draining, wasteful, expensive and unnecessary process, which extended over six months.

Monday 21 May 1984

> *I asked External Auditor (EA) to call. Day volunteered that Internal Audit's recent activities in relation to WFP amounted to a 'vendetta'...He said they have a low opinion of FAO integrity in relation to issues in dispute. I gave him an account of the H A affair and Hansa's claim against us and also copies of some of the documents. Apparently West has been twice to London and spoke in an imprecise and uncertain way of the WFP 'insurance scandal'.*

Wednesday 1 August 1984

> *Long discussion with...Day (another one who has been eased out at FAO's insistence—promoted to Edinburgh). It would appear that EA has called FAO's bluff and Crowther is rushing to London to find a face-saving formula. I put a lot of pressure on Day (again) for their final comments to address issue of need for WFP to be responsible for its own accounts. Meanwhile Saouma has not passed to WFP for its comments any of External Audit's reports on our development projects.*

My strategy in dealing with External Audit personnel was to conduct our financial affairs beyond reproach, to be completely open in our dealings with them and to persuade them of the moral justice of our cause. On the few occasions I met personally in London with the head of the UK's national audit, I did so alone. WFP's accounting staff was so stretched by the demands the controversy placed on us that I did not feel justified in diverting them from their professional duties.

As I learned, in this and subsequent experiences with the external auditor, his reports on controversial matters were finalised through an extended process of negotiation with the agency being audited. On this and later disputed matters he was in discussion with both FAO and WFP and his successive drafts reflected in some degree the views of the agency he had last spoken to. As a consequence, the finalisation of his reports was a drawn-out, frustrating process. Many times I was convinced I had won my point only to have my hopes dashed when I read the next draft. Because FAO was the client in the legal sense, though all costs were to WFP's account, in the last resort their representations carried more weight than ours, irrespective of the private views of External Audit staff.

Monday 13 August 1984

Day called again. Good news. It appears that our accounts have stood up to intensive scrutiny by 10 auditors plus London's senior staff.[27] *Moreover, it would appear that their attitude has hardened and that they intend to throw the book at FAO, i.e. irrespective of whether FAO retains or withdraws their disclaimer, External Audit will explain circumstances of their intensive investigation. This will 'inevitably put FAO in a bad light'. Moreover, External Audit intends to state that in order to prevent repetition WFP should have Chief Accountant who would advise Executive Director as well as D-G. This could represent a real breakthrough...For the first time (I hope not mistakenly) I see light at the end of the tunnel. When Saouma told me last November that he 'hadn't really started yet' (inter alia he said he would go to the General Assembly to discredit me in the eyes of developing countries), I have expected a major effort to discredit my administration.*

It transpired that Day had misread London's attitude:

Tuesday 28 August 1984

...External Auditor's (draft) report finally received. EA has sold out...Nothing in report to reflect throwing book at FAO, vendetta against WFP, betrayal of trust, etc. Instead, WFP is lectured on issue of access, provision of information, etc. It is a tremendous setback in effort to achieve autonomy and will reinforce the disposition of the timid and weak to leave things as they are and, at worst, will leave the impression with some that in fighting FAO so vigorously I am putting at risk good management of WFP. While some ground may be retrieved it is a bitter situation. Clearly, EA was concerned only about their own reputation. No doubt they feel pleased to have got FAO to abandon its general disclaimer. But the EA's report is damaging and pusillanimous, reflecting nothing of the immense effort to satisfy themselves as to authenticity of accounts. A long talk with Collins (UK Deputy Auditor General) arranged by Day. I told him that their report was most unfair and would be extremely damaging to the Programme, that because of FAO's Letter of Representation any report of the External Auditor was not only an accounting document but also a political one. Collins said that present draft should be seen as a starting point and was somewhat weighted in FAO's favour and that on receipt of our comments a better balance would be possible. He said that paragraph to which

I took most exception would be re-drafted anyway because it had not reflected what was intended, namely the importance of mutual FAO/WFP cooperation. I also told him that our legal advisers had informed us that contingent liability paragraphs were prejudicial and would be seized on by Hansa's legal advisers.

Thursday 30 August 1984

Whole day spent in discussion with EA's Rome staff...While they are clearly sympathetic, will they have any influence with London where summer staff absences and various pressures led to a poorly drafted final report? EA staff complained that they could never match resources applied by FAO. Pity poor WFP.

Wednesday 5 September 1984

In London. External Auditor clearly does not want to get involved in war with FAO, fearing that UK will be replaced by developing country as next auditor. Was therefore unwilling even to say that an unprecedented investigation had been made or to indicate in any way that FAO's allegations as such were ill founded. The most we can expect are comments which to an accountant will make it clear that FAO has behaved foolishly but not say so explicitly.

In the event the external auditor's report was clever. We got what we most needed, namely an unqualified 'Audit Opinion' (WFP 1984(e), p.21), a formal statement signed by the head of the UK's National Audit Office that '...I am of the opinion, as a result of my examination, that the Accounts properly reflect the recorded financial transactions for the financial period...'

On the five areas of supposed deficiency on our part FAO got the searching investigations they wanted. While suggestions for improvement were made in respect of the four minor issues, in relation to insurance FAO got little joy. Because the dispute with Hansa has not been definitively settled there was a clause saying, 'it is prudent for a contingent liability to be disclosed in the Financial Statements' but it was made clear we had acted entirely professionally in our handling of the matter. The reason why I denied access to FAO internal audit, namely the parallel matter of corruption in relation to the new tender and my fear that FAO would seek to place the blame on WFP, was not mentioned. No one, including me, wanted to make the H A affair public.

The FAO Finance Committee had our accounts and the external auditor's report for consideration at its September meeting. The Committee also had the FAO 'Representation of Financial Statements' (WFP 1984 (e), p.23), signed by the Director-General and the Director of Financial Services. In this document FAO tried to do what the external auditor had been unwilling to do in his audit opinion, namely to charge that on the five contested issues the accounts did not represent fairly the financial results of our operations. My diary records what happened:

Thursday 27 September 1984

> *Apparently at yesterday's Joint Finance/Programme Committee Saouma gave a three-hour monologue...and sought to discredit and intimidate the External Auditor and Sault[28] and link them together. At one point he told the assembly, 'especially those of Executive Director's nationality' that he would not make changes voluntarily in WFP texts but only as a result of approval by FAO Council, etc. Lunch with Sault and Gosselin.[29] At least they don't seem to have any doubts about basic soundness of our position and desirability of censuring FAO for its Statement of Representation.*

Monday 1 October 1984

> *Finance Committee: our document [setting out WFP's side of the dispute] not circulated despite Sault's specific request. He got no support from anyone else, although later Angola and Germany made sotto voce noises about 'fairness'. At least we and FAO favoured same strategy i.e. focus questions on External Auditor. Each developing country (except Angola) read out set of questions clearly prepared by FAO. In the event Collin's replies were good. But it will make little difference to the final result which will doubtless be weighted in FAO's favour. When Lincoln[30] spoke he, to some extent, explained away his Statement of Representation.*

Tuesday 2 October 1984

> *As so often happens in Committees, FAO tactics work to WFP's advantage. Thus it was better to speak today rather than yesterday. The so-called contingent liability figured prominently...Usual prejudice and general misbehaviour by Chairman. The External Auditor was good, again clearly telling Lincoln that because a point was not explicitly rejected it did not mean that the External Auditor agreed with it...I doubt that there was anyone in the room who did not feel that FAO should be censured. But that will not happen.*

Wednesday 3 October 1984

> *Another full day of Finance Committee—it was supposed to last one*
> *day...FAO very much on defensive...West made long speech, burden of which*
> *was that WFP was provoking issues to get changes—as if somehow the*
> *Statement of Representation was not aggressive. Atmosphere within the*
> *Committee was not very good mainly because of evident tension between*
> *Chairman, Sault and Gosselin. Generally a day with the gloves only half off*
> *on both sides.*

Friday 5 October 1984

> *Finance Committee finished our report on accounts at 9pm after seven hours.*
> *Ahmed told me that Sault, Gosselin and Sequeira[31] fought well. The result was*
> *not too bad, he said, even if FAO is not censured. At least our point of view is*
> *reasonably reflected. Bukhari [now just the Saudi delegate] and Chairman*
> *were main problems and there were some strong exchanges between West and*
> *Ahmed. That is good because it shows everyone that I am not alone in this.*

Our audited accounts still had to be considered by the ACABQ. In the
event I was pleased by the outcome:

Tuesday 23 October 1984

> *In New York. Very good meeting with Mselle. He said I should not fear that*
> *ACABQ would criticise WFP. I said some positive support would be very*
> *helpful particularly if they came out and said accounting function/audit*
> *should go to WFP. He said they could not go that far.*

Friday 26 October 1984

> *ACABQ report received. It could hardly be better, i.e. quite subtly, but with a*
> *few sharp digs, de facto censures FAO; names D-G as one responsible. We do*
> *not now need to be defensive in any way when Accounts item comes up in CFA.*
> *Indeed it has clarified how I should pitch my opening statement to the CFA.*

CFA18 (November 1984) concluded its examination of our accounts with
the statement that 'having reviewed the matter in all its aspects, the
Committee confirmed its full confidence in the management of WFP, in its
Executive Director and his staff'. FAO was effectively rebuked, the
committee requesting it to circulate, in the 'interest of transparency and

fairness', the ACABQ report and my comments on the Representation, to the FAO Council and Conference. The stakes had been high for WFP. If we had not retained the confidence of the external auditor and the ACABQ the resulting defeat may well have ended my attempts at reform and my personal position may have become untenable.

COMPETING POLICY PAPERS

I have taken the story up to the end of 1984 with our victory on the audited accounts at CFA18. In doing so, I have passed over CFA17 (June 1984), a landmark session, unprecedented in the UN system. The Committee had before it competing policy papers from the secretariats of WFP and FAO. Following my budget success at CFA16 and the steps taken to assert a policy role for WFP in accordance with its mandate, FAO decided to challenge those gains.

First, FAO was signalling its intention to reassert its role as the source of intergovernmental food aid policy by expanding the role of its Committee on World Food Security (CFS). This committee had been created in 1974 by the World Food Conference. Since 'food security' is a rubric that can encompass almost any issue, FAO could claim through it a role in relation to food aid. Its creation was typical of much intergovernmental decision-making. Having decided to set up a new body to coordinate world food issues, namely WFC, the World Food Conference proceeded to make coordination more difficult by expanding the roles of FAO and the CFA. Expansion and duplication of mandates by competing UN agencies was a systemic problem at the time and a source of endless government complaint, notwithstanding that it was the same governments that had created the incoherent intergovernmental structures about which they complained.

Without any consultation with WFP, the Director-General made proposals to the April 1984 session of the CFS. These recommended food aid studies, properly the prerogative of the CFA, and, more importantly, an ambitious program of action which had the potential to make FAO a competitor of WFP in its support of development projects, in emergency food aid and in reviewing world food aid needs and programs. The proposals were an aggressive attempt to take over the CFA's policy role, which I was in the process of reinvigorating, and a threat to WFP as the food aid agency of the UN system. I made a strong intervention in the CFS to argue publicly my case. Fortunately, it turned out that governments were not attracted to giving a substantive, food aid role to the CFS.

Secondly, the Director-General requested me to circulate papers prepared by FAO on three critically important CFA agenda items. The papers were in addition to those written by WFP. Unless we withdrew our papers, delegates would be confronted with competing papers on the items from FAO and WFP. The items were: review of criteria for WFP emergency assistance; review of proposals for improvement of the WFP project cycle; and review of the availability and utilisation of cash resources of the WFP regular program and the IEFR.

WFP tried to resolve this issue before the meeting. We had extensive discussions with FAO about our drafts and made many changes to meet their point of view, to no avail. They were, it seemed, determined to take advantage of a never previously used provision of the CFA's Rules of Procedure (Rule 4), which stated that the Secretary-General and the Director-General 'may formulate for consideration by the Committee any proposals for appropriate action in regard to matters coming before it'.

Past practice had been to circulate all papers in the name of the Executive Director, even if these had been extensively modified by FAO. Quite often WFP did not agree with them, but in a spirit of cooperation to the point of subservience, accepted the revisions as instructions. I considered this behaviour to be contrary to the Basic Documents. I recognised that WFP should consult other UN agencies, in particular FAO, and seek to reach agreement with them; but considered that in the last resort the Executive Director could not present proposals or recommendations to the CFA, with which he did not concur, as if they were his own.

In addition to reversing the erosion of the Executive Director's authority, I also needed to bolster the self-respect of WFP staff, diminished by the weakness of my predecessors. It was risky to take a strong stand on our right to present our own proposals but, if successful, I would make progress toward both goals.

Apart from the question of principle, namely did the WFP secretariat advise the CFA on WFP policy or was that the role of FAO, I felt that FAO expected to swamp us with work in the expectation that our papers would be of poor quality compared with theirs and so show the CFA that they were both the appropriate and indispensable source of policy advice to it.

Whatever else was wrong with the organisation, FAO did produce high-quality policy papers, convincing to most delegates who usually possessed only superficial knowledge of the issues. I had only begun to strengthen WFP's policy capability so the challenge to our small staff was considerable. The burden was all the heavier for me personally because of the insurance scandal and FAO's attempt to discredit me.

Delegations were flummoxed to have rival papers on three very important agenda items. Above all, they did not want to have to choose between WFP and FAO. Immediately before the session the latter increased the drama with another unprecedented step. The Director-General wrote to the Rome Ambassadors to justify his action and explain FAO's position on each of the agenda items. The letter was not copied to me. It was larded with sufficient pejorative adjectives to ring alarm bells among ambassadors. The stage was set for an extraordinarily tense CFA, the drama enticing a full house of observers. Normally meetings of UN committees are pretty boring, even to the participants, and rarely attract outside attention. From CFA17 onwards our meetings attracted capacity crowds.

After extended discussions the CFA decided to consider both sets of papers at this session. In future, it agreed it would be 'preferable' to have only one set of documents presented by the Executive Director, after appropriate consultation in accordance with the Basic Documents (WFP 1984c). Though couched diplomatically, this was a statement of support for WFP.

Criteria for the Provision of Emergency Food Aid

The paper on emergencies criteria was the most contentious, with the stakes the highest for FAO, WFP, donors and recipients. The reader will recall that before I took up my appointment donors had signalled to me their belief that present assessment and approval processes were unsatisfactory and should be reformed. After two years I could see that the system was wasteful and inequitable. This was all the more worrying for me given my view that food aid found its clearest justification in emergency feeding. Emergency food aid was increasingly provided bilaterally but I believed that if donors had greater confidence in our management then more would be channelled through WFP, to the advantage of affected countries since our assistance, for all its faults, was less influenced by political factors.

The CFA's predecessor committee had defined emergencies as follows:
Urgent situations in which there is clear evidence that an event has occurred which causes human suffering or loss of livestock and which the government concerned has not the means to remedy; and it is a demonstrably abnormal event which produces dislocation in the life of a community on an exceptional scale.

The definition was satisfactory in itself but not a very useful guide for assessing need. Moreover, given FAO regarded itself as primarily responsible for needs assessment, WFP did not have the staff or the tools to make a rigorous appraisal of the justification advanced by the requesting government. Drought assessment was the most problematic. The available data was often scanty and largely within FAO's sphere of expertise. Given the Director-General's political approach to drought requests, it was in practice difficult not to make a positive recommendation no matter what we thought about the validity of the request. The only tactic available in such cases was to recommend substantially less food than the government requested.

I wanted to see the development of quantifiable measures for more systematic rationing of available resources. My proposal to the CFA read as follows:
In a situation of scarce multilateral emergency food aid, resources requests from low-income, food deficit countries (as defined for WFP development projects) should be given priority. Requests from other countries should be subject to increasingly stricter standards, depending upon such factors as the level of their income per capita, their foreign exchange reserves, their capacity to borrow from IMF or elsewhere, the proportion of their population affected by the disaster, their commitment to disaster preparedness and prevention and the overall supply of food available to the country.

I had two principal concerns with current practices. First, by responding positively to virtually every request for assistance following a natural disaster we could hinder the goal of national food security. In many situations the provision of emergency food is not necessarily a relevant response. If food is provided for rebuilding of housing destroyed by the earthquake, it should more properly be seen as disaster rehabilitation and a response approved under normal WFP development project procedures. For many countries, destructive tropical storms are normal cyclical phenomena. To provide assistance as a matter of course every time such a phenomenon occurs is, in fact, to create an attitude of dependence on the part of the peoples affected and of their governments. It is therefore necessary to ask the question, 'Is emergency food aid an appropriate response to the disaster?' (WFP, 1984a)

My second concern was WFP's inability to provide emergency food aid for sale, but only as a hand-out to directly affected persons. At the time academic research had demonstrated that famine was often due to market failure. Sufficient food to feed all of the hungry was available but they lacked the means to procure it. Here I was much influenced by the ground-breaking work of Amartya Sen (Sen, 1981), from which I concluded that more flexibility should be introduced into our responses by, for example, authorising the replenishment of buffer stocks to form part of well-managed food security arrangements; or by providing food directly to those governments guaranteeing a minimum food ration within their public distribution systems.

WFP proposed other modifications to the system which, while not directly addressing assessment criteria, could lead to a much more effective and logically coherent response to food emergencies. These included special funding of long-running refugee and internally displaced persons situations.

FAO's paper confined itself exclusively to ways of increasing the quantum of emergency food aid resources and to managerial improvements to WFP's response times. Some good points were made but they were either familiar or impractical, albeit cleverly calculated to appeal to developing countries. Above all FAO avoided any discussion of the allocation of resources, reflecting the assumption that all requests for emergency assistance were equally entitled to a positive response. It turned aside WFP's proposals by claiming that, while attempting to ensure the efficiency of operations, we did not give 'adequate weight to the humanitarian objective of relieving human suffering'. Our attitude was presented as essentially negative and contrasted with FAO's efforts 'to overcome obstacles…and raise the level of resources so that emergency needs are fully and promptly met'. Their crowning rebuke read: 'To deprive the affected people of emergency assistance because of the delays in delivering it, for which they are not at fault, seems hardly justifiable' (WFP, 1984b).

In face of FAO's criticism—Saouma having made it clear to me that WFP should do as FAO dictated—it was pleasing, as I recorded in my diary, to receive endorsement of WFP's thinking:

Tuesday 3 April 1984

A cheering letter today from Pérez de Cuéllar supporting my emergency paper: very positive and cordial. A job like this needs good news occasionally.

I knew I had still to spend much effort at meetings, in corridors and during lunches and dinners explaining WFP's position to delegates:

Friday 11 May 1984

Lunch with Toussaint[32] and Strong:[33] latter endeared himself to me by saying that if I continued as I had been going I would be re-appointed by acclamation. That would be something! I sought to convince them that developing countries were looking to developed countries for a lead, that there could not be more than one person responsible to CFA, which was sovereign, and that Committee should make it clear to FAO that the Executive Director was that person...Much less trouble with Canadians and Australians whom I met later. They agreed that statements should be made early in session saying second papers not wanted in future. In debates on three papers they want us to ignore FAO contributions in our opening statements.

Thursday 17 May 1984

Briefed J Ladan (Nigeria), P S McLean (UK) and Tchicaya[34] (Congo) on CFA. There seems to be some appreciation that dual CFA papers cannot continue...[told] that FAO claimed my presentation of emergencies was not based on any real examination of data. In fact what WFP has succeeded in doing to keep a debased system in bounds is to pare down response to requests. FAO often manipulates the data on which recommendations are made, so that it is impossible not to make a recommendation in favour of the request.

Friday 18 May 1984

A disturbing day. Lunch with Swaminathan.[35] Saouma spoke to him for an hour of his differences with WFP. 'He is clearly obsessed with WFP beyond all else and wishes to drive you out', Swaminathan said.

Wednesday 23 May 1984

Long discussions with Egypt and Brazil and Indian Ambassador over lunch. Indians seem very firm in their support. No one likes double papers but no-one seems to know what to do. Commins[36] said OECD had discussed but as usual little cohesion. Strongest in my support were Australia, Canada, Netherlands, Germany, UK (latter gratifying after my efforts with Minister and McLean). Weakest who spoke were Nordics, led by Sweden, which said as usual, 'these organisations must cooperate'. Worst in this group was Fenwick. Apparently, it was decided that Canada would see if concerted statement with G77 could be arranged against two papers.

CFA17 began on Monday 28 May 1984:

...Big issue is two papers. Lindores made superb speech (as did Powell)[37] telling FAO to get off our back. Enough countries told Saouma no more 2nd papers but there was much confusion of thought about what consultation means and how dissent should be indicated. US have not yet spoken. Fenwick keeps watering down their speech.

Wednesday 30 May 1984

A good day!...I told the CFA what I thought of FAO's cash policy issues paper. In effect, I called FAO's and the Committee's bluff (i.e. the developing members and some of the developed, e. g. France and USA) by saying that WFP was the only food aid agency—as distinct from the many who talked about food aid—that it was a successful institution, that we would decide what improvements to put to the Committee. No doubt FAO will be back tomorrow to deny what I have said and/or the Chairman will give a biased summing up. He refrained from giving it this evening no doubt to allow himself to get instructions.

Thursday 31 May 1984

Not a good day! Discussion on emergencies began. FAO's introduction was very clever and quite conciliatory. The developing countries as usual supported FAO although...had good words also for WFP. No one reads what is written. Everything is interpreted rather than taken at face value...US made a pathetic statement. Everything has depended on Lindores. All along I have doubted whether texts can ever be altered except with acquiescence of Saouma. Governments are simply too disorganised and indifferent to make the effort needed. However, there are signs that Saouma is looking for a compromise.

Friday 1 June 1984

> *A better day! Some more sensible interventions on emergencies from my friends and even the US made a second, more helpful, intervention. I made a good speech at the end which drew a response from West and an intervention from Canada. I cannot help feeling that West's interventions help me a great deal!*

FAO's 'populist' approach was politically more astute than ours. WFP's recommendations for major reform were ambitious and required more time to sell to delegations. Donors reacted negatively to the idea of constrained sales of food. I had underestimated their determination to protect their export markets and their willingness to ignore possible adverse consequences of free distribution of food rations. Furthermore, they had entirely missed the point that the rationing criteria we suggested were the best means open to reduce anomalous responses under the current approval system.

Thus CFA17 requested a future paper on the elaboration of the key concepts in the emergency definition cited above and effectively ignored everything else. To some extent that was my fault. By bringing in issues of fundamental change I had unduly broadened the debate and paved the way for FAO to enlarge it even further. On the other hand, FAO had seriously erred in submitting alternative papers on the project cycle and cash resources. On the former our approach reflected best practice and was fully endorsed by the Committee. Again, on cash resources, our approach was thoroughly professional and FAO's critique was seen as irrelevant.

While the entire session had been acrimonious, with the Chairman, Bulo Huyos, occasionally becoming quite hysterical and launching personal attacks on me, eventually the CFA report supported WFP's approach. I wrote in my diary on Monday 11 June 1984: *What a pleasure to be back in the office after two weeks in that accursed building.*

---

[24] The diary gives a complete record of all my main concerns. However, since this memoir is essentially an account of how I brought about constitutional change in WFP, the diary entries are extracts only.

[25] Dean K Crowther, FAO Assistant Director-General for Administration and Finance.

26 Later that year, on 5 November, the General Service Staff union of FAO issued a bulletin stating 'its absolute dissatisfaction' with the procedures followed by the FAO administration over a new health insurance contract. The union was critical of the existing contract and contended that FAO was not protecting the interests of its staff.

27 In amplification of this point my diary records:
    'Day told me that they had investigated 255 transactions chosen at random in order to be 95 percent sure of accuracy and had set a 0.8 percent error rate as the appropriate level of materiality. For FAO accounts only 110 transactions were analysed!'

28 John Sault, Australian representative on FAO Finance Committee.

29 Pierre Gosselin, Canadian CFA representative.

30 J D Lincoln, Director FAO Financial Services Division and a co-signatory of the Statement of Representation

31 The Angolan representative who had explained at an earlier session he did not want to express any views on grounds that he and others were 'subject to intolerable pressure greater than anything since the Portuguese Secret Police'

32 D R Toussaint, United States Delegation

33 H P Strong, United States Delegation

34 Ambassador J Tchicaya, a leading African delegate, closely associated with FAO and very effective. He was a gentleman of professorial appearance, calm, courteous and dispassionate in making his case, no matter how misleading. I formed a considerable liking for him.

35 Dr M S Swaminathan, a distinguished Indian scientist whom I knew well through my work with the CGIAR, at the time Chairman of the FAO Council.

36 Michael Commins, Australian Delegation

37 Douglas Lindores and John Powell, senior Canadian and Australian delegates, were a formidable team in advancing my reform agenda over several years.

7

THE BERTRAND REPORT

During 1984 and 1985 FAO did all it could to prevent consideration of proposals for reform of personnel management made by JIU Inspector Bertrand; and, having failed in this, to subvert consideration of these by a joint taskforce established by the UN Secretary-General and the FAO Director-General. In part FAO was successful.

In 1983 the United Nations Joint Inspection Unit (JIU) decided to examine the personnel problems we were having with FAO. This turned out to be the critical first step to achieving wide ranging constitutional reform. I played no part in bringing about the inspection and my diary provides no clue as to what prompted the JIU to take action. In retrospect, I presume the existence of our problems was brought informally to the JIU's attention by sympathetic colleagues in the UN secretariat in New York.

The JIU was established by the General Assembly. It was intended as an apolitical, expert body able to undertake broad-ranging management audits that would lead to improved performance by individual agencies and better coordination within the UN system. The 11 inspectors had wide powers and could make on-the-spot enquiries as they saw fit. They were appointed for once-renewable terms of five years and served in a personal capacity. The inspector undertaking our review was Maurice Bertrand of France. He was acknowledged as the most competent and professional in the unit and had spent over a decade focussing on personnel problems of the UN system as well as broader reform issues. His 1969 report on program budgeting led to important system-wide reforms (Williams 1987).

On behalf of the JIU, Bertrand had done a study of WFP in 1970 and had recommended the transfer to the Programme from FAO of certain posts, including all those responsible for internal audit. However, none of his proposals were accepted.

We invited Bertrand to our Hague seminar to familiarise him with the complex intellectual issues affecting food aid. On his own decision he had observed CFA16 (October 1983) and seen for himself how FAO had abused its power to discredit my financial management. Shortly afterwards, I had my first meeting with him on the issues as we saw them. We established a good rapport, which was to endure through the storms ahead.

BERTRAND'S PROPOSALS

Bertrand's report (WFP, 1984a) vindicated all that I had so far done. He placed an interpretation on the Basic Documents that was similar to the United Nations legal opinion but more clear-cut. In his view the intricate overlap of responsibilities between FAO and WFP 'created very serious interpretation and management difficulties', the structure was 'neither rational nor workable' and a 'formula comparable to that of programs such as UNDP, UNICEF or UNHCR' was the 'desirable solution'.

Bertrand's analysis included many specific recommendations that would lead to better management of an agency with our distinct responsibilities. Though he presented alternatives for achieving complete transfer of personnel management to the Executive Director, his preferred means was the amendment of articles 14 (e) and (j) of the General Regulations. That was a bold step. As I wrote in my diary,

> He is a little nervous about proposing an amendment to the General Regulations but, fortunately, is prepared to go ahead. Meanwhile, he will be working on programming, seeing that as the peg for investigating the financial regulations. Bless him!

General Regulation 14(e) provided that the Executive Director should be responsible for the staffing and organisation of the secretariat. However, selection and appointment of senior officials was to be made in agreement with the Secretary-General and the Director-General. As Saouma had shown over the appointments of my deputy and the head of the new emergency service, he could and would use this provision to hobble my management. He had even objected to my transfers of officers between divisions on the grounds that I had not consulted him, even though GR 14(e) made no mention of transfers. With one exception the Secretary-General never questioned my nominations but the Director-General repeatedly did so. Not only were appointments seriously delayed, but the manner in which they were chosen ensured that appointees felt some indebtedness to the Director-General. Despite this, with only very few exceptions, my staff remained loyal to WFP. However, some gave me less than their full support, hedging their bets in case I left or failed to get a second term. I was therefore delighted that Bertrand recommended the abolition of GR 14(e).

The proposed amendment to GR 14(j) was objectively the more important change, Bertrand proposing that it read as follows:

> The Executive Director shall administer the staff of the Programme in accordance with Staff Regulations proposed by him and approved by the CFA. In framing these regulations, the CFA and the Executive Director respectively shall take account of the existing Regulations of FAO but shall adapt them as seems best in their judgment, to meet the needs of WFP. The Executive Director shall promulgate, as necessary, Staff Rules in accordance with the Staff Regulations.

The JIU was responsible to governments, not executive heads of agencies. Accordingly, the Executive Secretary of the JIU forwarded Bertrand's report to me for transmission to the CFA, with copies to the Secretary-General and Director-General. Bertrand wanted his report considered at CFA17 but I convinced him that the agenda was already overloaded with contentious issues. Accordingly, I issued it as an information-only document for CFA17 (May 1984). Knowing of FAO's dislike of his report, Bertrand decided to attend CFA17 as an observer so that he could inform delegations about his proposals.

Friday 27 April 1984

Lunch with Bertrand who telephoned me in the evening after a two-hour meeting with West. As usual I was vilified: all problems are due to me and Bertrand was accused of partisanship…FAO went too far and they have strengthened Bertrand's conviction that he must do more to help us. Dark hints were made to him about a scandal soon to hit WFP, no doubt a reference to insurance.

FAO seized upon distribution of the document to the CFA to stir up a procedural storm in the hope of discrediting the report and aborting future consideration by the CFA. Saouma wrote to the Secretary-General and the Chairman of JIU arguing that the JIU Report had been improperly addressed to me. His letter to the JIU Chairman was characteristically aggressive. JIU's suggestion that its report would be of particular concern to the CFA was dismissed as 'gratuitous'. By its 'intrusion into constitutional and legal issues', the JIU had exceeded its mandate; and the report was 'tainted by lack of the comprehensiveness, objectivity and impartiality', expected of inspectors. The chairman replied temperately to show why these charges were untenable. However, the UN supported FAO. Following a personal appeal to me from Ruedas on behalf of the Secretary-General, I reluctantly agreed not to propose its inclusion in the provisional agenda of CFA18 (November 1984). Fortunately, however, governments took the matter into their own hands at CFA17:

Friday 8 June 1984

> *Not the final day of CFA17 as it turned out. Most of the morning was spent on the agenda for CFA18 with Canada wanting to put [consideration of] the Bertrand report on it. FAO forces tried to prevent this but the Rules of Procedure are clear and finally Canada was successful. The break came with support from Mali and India.*

The CFA decision meant that the UN and FAO were obliged to consider their substantive attitude to Bertrand's proposals. They agreed that Ruedas and West should confer on their response. In informing me of this Ruedas was at pains to say that the UN 'cannot allow any suggestion that the report is some sort of conspiracy against FAO, organised by WFP, JIU, and perhaps UN'. My diary describes the twists and turns that followed:

Thursday 21 June 1984—in New York

> *I asked S-G to try [to] persuade Saouma to go along with [Bertrand's] recommendations. He agreed. In an earlier meeting Ripert said that they would tell Saouma that [Bertrand's proposals] would get through [the CFA] and he would only be doing himself harm by opposing them. I feel he will come to his senses. But Tomlinson thinks not, as does Niazi [UN Internal Auditor], whom I*

lunched with and who will let me have a memorandum to send to Saouma on internal audit function. All here in New York do support me and genuinely try to help within the bounds of their concept of what is good for UN system. But they are typical bureaucrats, seeking to advance deviously and indirectly. More backbone and leadership are required. It is clear that West has deeply offended Pérez de Cuéllar. Latter described him... as 'worse than his master'.

Friday 22 June 1984—in New York

Ruedas telephoned. I was glad to find I had convinced him that Bertrand's view on senior appointments should prevail. Lunch with Fleischhauer [UN Legal Counsellor]. He said that Bertrand's chosen method was marred by complexities of [consequent] amendments to statutes on privileges and immunities... We are currently covered as FAO staff. He said these amendments, although not impossible, would be very difficult to effect. Scenario now seems to be to ask JIU to withdraw its letter to me and to retransmit the report to S-G and D-G.[38] No doubt this will take months. It is going to be an immensely difficult task to get something through and it may take years... I was deeply upset by talk with Fleischhauer. This job is so daunting and the burden seems to get heavier even though I am winning.

Thursday 12 July 1984—in Rome

Ruedas telephoned to say he had met with [FAO]... To his surprise they had accepted that the objective must be to allow the Executive Director to get on with the job without undue interference.

Monday 30 July 1984

As always, the return to office is grim. Greeted by Ruedas' [draft] response to Bertrand. In effect he proposes some experimental delegations to me plus a review of all outstanding problems by UN and FAO. It mainly is appeasement of Saouma (as usual) but I have little option but to go along. Strategy must be to get what we can while leaving door open to further advances. But Ruedas' package gives very little while asserting primacy of FAO and UN in relation to WFP... basically very disheartening.

Tuesday 31 July 1984

Discussed our amendments to Ruedas' paper with him. We worked hard to get something worthwhile and positive for WFP while accepting Ruedas' basic idea. Our aim was to actualise promises in relation to personnel and make these as comprehensive as possible while accepting primacy of UN and FAO in working out solutions to (other) outstanding problems..

Friday 10 August 1984

No word yet from Ruedas. Doubtless as anticipated FAO is stalling and will continue to stall hoping to get through 1985 without any amendments going to FAO Conference.[39] I feel we must try very hard at CFA18 to get JIU recommendations accepted and a study of other outstanding issues [authorised] in time for CFA19...On balance, I feel debate in the open is much more likely to benefit us.

The prevarication on Bertrand's report took place against the backdrop of the UN's financial and political difficulties caused by dissatisfaction of the new Reagan administration and other donors with the management of the UN itself and a number of system agencies, especially UNESCO and FAO. New York did not want a display of disharmony and that meant bowing to FAO's insistence that it was the main partner in the oversight of WFP. Saouma skilfully played on UN sensitivities to delay any resolution of the issues or of acceptable procedures that would enable their resolution. There was no possibility that FAO would agree to WFP's direct involvement as the UN preferred. Matters dragged for months. Occasionally there was a glimmer of light when I thought the UN might make explicit its support for WFP's position, or when governments' impatience with the impasse might provoke action. Then, things would look gloomy again, with only the prospect of another protracted review, by a less than ideal taskforce, of all the same arguments rather than substantive decisions on Bertrand's recommendations and on other contentious issues. That indeed was what emerged at the last minute just in time for CFA18.

Throughout I had sought to shore up the UN's strength of will and to encourage governments to do the same. Of the latter the United States was the key. During the summer and autumn of 1984, Saouma had been dangling my post before the Americans (see below), who seemed tempted. The prospect of having an American executive director of WFP meant that some within the administration wanted the post strengthened. However, if an American was not to be in charge the matter was less urgent. Thus the customary inability of the United States to come quickly to a firm whole-of-government position on any issue prevailed. US failure to articulate clear, timely policies was a perennial problem, not usually due to the inadequacies of particular individuals, but because it was endemic to the system. Too often it meant that the United States was not giving the leadership its power and influence, by virtue of its being WFP's principal donor, warranted. Had it done so a great deal of conflict would have been avoided altogether or cut short.

CFA18 began on 29 October 1984. The committee had before it the Bertrand report, my views thereon and the Joint Comments of the Secretary-General and Director-General (WFP, 1984cde). The latter refrained from any direct commentary on Bertrand's proposals except to state their lack of support for amending the General Regulations. In their view what was called for, 'in the first instance', was:

> for the UN and FAO to carry out a full review of such problems as have arisen, in close consultation with the Executive Director of WFP, through the institution of a joint UN/FAO taskforce reporting to the Secretary-General and the Director-General on the extent to which practical and effective solutions within the framework of the Basic Texts may be devised to resolve such problems.

Reading today the Joint Comments in their entirety it is clear that, although the document is very much a compromise, on balance favourable to FAO's position, it was not a UN sell-out—and did not warrant fully the disappointment shown in my diary. The UN's timidity arose from a strong desire not to wash any dirty laundry in public and certainly not to risk a public fight with the doughty Saouma, who would certainly have threatened to make the issue into a North/South one, both at the 1985 FAO Conference and in the ACC, and even the UN General Assembly.

In the light of my own experience in dealing with Saouma, I remain convinced that, if the United Nations had seized the nettle at that time, FAO's bluff would have been called and thereby years of frustration and rancour avoided. Moreover, a show of strong leadership by the Secretary-General would, I believe, have enhanced the image of the United Nations. I could never understand why New York was so afraid of Saouma. Yes, he had a lot of influence with Ministers of Agriculture but in most developing countries they were not important politically. Recognising this, Saouma had taken advantage of every opportunity to build personal relationships with heads of government, especially in Africa; but even so, his prestige was small measured against the Secretary-General's, if the latter chose to exert it. Unfortunately, during these years, there was an air of defeatism through much of the UN system, particularly in New York, which accounts to some extent for the Secretary-General's excessive caution.

The atmosphere at the opening of CFA18 was electric. The Joint Comments had only been in the hands of delegates for a few days and there was real uncertainty about the outcome. Bula Hoyos was still in the chair, giving FAO the possibility to prevent a consensus. While we had strong support from some OECD countries and the tacit support of some developing ones, the majority preferred not to commit themselves until they saw the shape of the terrain. As usual FAO counted on the skills of supporters like Mexico, Colombia, Saudi Arabia and Congo to influence the G77 in favour of their position and to weaken the resolve of lukewarm developed countries. The following extracts from my diary give some sense of the drama.

Monday 29 October 1984

Fenwick with Bula Hoyos met with Saouma and, out of their meeting, came the idea of a 10-man meeting with Saouma intended somehow to ease the process [of CFA consideration of Bertrand]. Apparently that meeting lasted two-and-a-half hours, Canada walked out and Australia criticised Saouma for his critical remarks about Canada and got an apology! India and Nigeria were good. At end of meeting Saouma apparently agreed to report to CFA19 and also to make delegations to me. Molloy [US] thought Saouma's attitude evolved a lot: 'He is coming to realise, but still fighting within himself, the fact that change has to come'.

Tuesday 30 October 1984

Talking with Anstee it is pretty clear that idea of private meeting with Saouma and key delegations came from Saouma and Bula Hoyos and sold to Fenwick. Saouma complained to Anstee re S-G's message, particularly favourable personal reference to me.[40] The more one considers terms of reference of taskforce, the more heavily slanted they are against us. Interesting reference to confidentiality. Idea will be to stop me leaking or, if I do, to discipline or sack me. Assuming review fails I will have no more options.

Wednesday 31 October 1984

Still have not reached Bertrand item. Lunch with Mexican Minister of Rural Reform. Got across to him, in Lopez-Portillo's[41] presence, that we expected Mexican delegation to behave more responsibly.

Thursday 1 November 1984

Discussion of JIU report began and finally ended at 9pm or so. The beginning was unpleasant with Bula Hoyos slamming down the microphone when I asked for it. FAO had circulated the Terms of Reference [of the taskforce] under its own logo. Ruedas had requested in writing that this not be done. Bertrand prevented from presenting his report despite several requests that he do so. After US got in strong statement of support followed by Italy, Colombia launched into dreadful, insulting tirade. Bula Hoyos behaved most improperly. Loewald [UNESCO] told me afterwards he had never seen anything like it. Lindores said he was embarrassed and ashamed to be in such a circus. Bukhari and Tchicaya took this as an insult, i.e. they were 'animals'...Meeting adjourned in disarray. Afternoon much better. Presumably FAO, realising that it had lost ground, asked its cohorts to behave. By end of evening strong consensus had emerged that taskforce must report to CFA19, that it would consider other matters besides personnel, that some changes could be implemented before taskforce reported and that, if necessary, taskforce should report re possible amendments to Basic Documents. Other side's main concern is to have all changes considered as a package. Bertrand spoke in afternoon and effectively gave lie to Shah's[42] misrepresentations during the morning. Once again standard FAO tactics of 'playing the man' were followed but they did not succeed. There were also many strong references to need to involve ED at all stages, some calling for his full participation. Anstee made suitable noises on this. Anstee told me that she had concluded that taskforce must come up with solutions otherwise she saw no alternative to amending texts.

Thursday 8 November 1984

Miracles never cease. Drafting Committee report adopted by plenary without debate, which gave a nice ending to a difficult session. Report on accounts is good from our point of view. Bertrand less so, with several statements about debate which, in fact, were not made, e.g. statement that a number of delegations were opposed to the taskforce identifying necessary amendments [to the Basic Documents]. We do seem to be developing a momentum and if our coalition can hang together something useful will emerge. But the relationship with FAO will never be pleasant and dirty tricks will always be the norm. All of this would hardly be worthwhile if it were just for WFP but it is about good governance of the UN system and even, beyond that, for good men to oppose tyranny and even evil. Strong words but Ahmed, Barnsdale and Kelloway said so.

Significantly, the CFA decided that the taskforce should address urgently 'all matters in dispute between WFP and FAO, including finance, accounting, auditing, contracts and procurement'. Clearly, FAO had over-reached itself. Thus the strong position taken by the CFA in relation to the Bertrand report owed something to FAO's defeat over its 'Statement of Representation' on our accounts, considered at the same session.

THE JOINT UNITED NATIONS/FAO TASKFORCE

The FAO horse had been brought to water; the problem now was to get it to drink. My diaries for the next six months refer to taskforce issues in nearly fifty per cent of entries, with my emotions on a roller-coaster of optimism and pessimism. As usual there were many other important issues that had to be dealt with, including the African famine.

The saga began at the beginning of January 1985 when Crowther approached Ahmed to see if we could be persuaded to do a deal with FAO prior to the first meeting of the taskforce, with the aim of sidelining the United Nations in accordance with Saouma's frequently iterated view to me that it was none of the UN's business. As Crowther was unwilling to outline the basis of the deal, the possibility died.

The taskforce got underway in late January, with the UN represented by its Under Secretary-General for Administration, Patricio Ruedas, and the FAO by Dean Crowther. WFP was not a member. The process of consultation with us was secured by establishing tri-partite working groups on personnel and finance, all chaired by FAO. Ahmed represented us, assisted by Kelloway and others as necessary.

I was delighted that Ruedas[43] would head the UN team and had come to Rome for the first meeting. I dined with him on 21 January. Afterwards, I commented in my diary:

....He has a strong sense of propriety and...it is counter-productive to talk to him in a conspiratorial sense because it would compromise him in his own eyes as an effective mediator. So, the thrust was to build on the personal relationship of like-minded persons...

That relationship strengthened as time went by. Although I often felt he was yielding too much to FAO, and put considerable pressure on him to change course, I believe Ruedas acted as impartially as possible. He made it clear from the beginning that it was up to WFP to make its case. 'Do not put your proposals in legal terms but on basis of practical solutions', he advised.

FAO was already telling delegates that 'Ruedas is in Ingram's pocket'. This gave me no comfort because I knew that it would only cause Ruedas 'to bend over backwards' to be seen as objective. In his 'bad-mouthing' of Ruedas, Saouma made much of the fact that I appointed the former's daughter to our professional staff. In fact, she applied before the taskforce was decided and Ruedas never made representations on her behalf. She became an outstanding officer. Just as the children of diplomats often become diplomats, so too are the children of its officials attracted to service with the United Nations. To avoid nepotism, at least in my time, they (and the partners of staff members) were not permitted to be recruited to the same agency as their relatives. Ruedas informed the Secretary-General in writing of his daughter's appointment to WFP but he told me that Pérez de Cuéllar did not see that as a reason why he should not represent the United Nations on the taskforce.

Ruedas told me Saouma once came to his office to charge him with partiality and had insisted on a personal meeting with UN representatives on the taskforce working groups to make known to them that bias. On 20 March at a meeting in Rome with representatives of OECD countries, Crowther, according to my diary, reported that

> taskforce negotiations had been very difficult because UN was biased in favour of WFP, having accepted our point of view in its entirety'. To us it seemed exactly the opposite. My diary for 13 March recorded that Ahmed was *not too happy with Ruedas*.

The work of the taskforce came to a head in London in March. My diary takes up the story:

Tuesday 26 March 1985

Ahmed reported. While he and Kelloway seem to feel they have done well I am less happy. Balance is very much in FAO's favour. On finance the result will be a costly and inherently messy relationship in which FAO, by having control of the cheque book, can still frustrate any decision and through audit can still interfere in our work. On personnel, they continue to insist on servicing and have given no ground on senior officials.

Wednesday, 27 March 1985.

Another long talk with Ruedas. [I] intimated that they [i.e. the UN] were much more concerned about Saouma's susceptibilities than about getting a result that was fair to WFP. Suggested that accounts problem could be settled by delegation of powers for preparation of financial statements...I said I wanted an agreed settlement, that appeasement never got anywhere with Saouma, that he had been brought to conference table by UN's strength, that if UN had CFA support it had nothing to lose politically, that for governments the issue was not just about WFP but broader than that. Since I did not wish to leave him with the thought that I did not really care whether or not there was a settlement I made a suggestion in relation to internal audit...

Thursday 28 March 1985

Ruedas telephoned. He told me that UN saw this as two-staged effort and that in second stage some amendment to the texts might be possible. But at this stage they were not prepared to die over the issue of who signed the accounts. He was concerned that I might not regard it as in my interest to have an agreement. I told him 'No', but I could not accept an agreement at any price...explained that, subject to certain changes which I outlined, I could accept formula proposed on accounts. Ruedas was pleased by this—too pleased perhaps. He rang me later to say that he had suggested to Crowther that he and I should get together to see if outstanding differences could not be resolved, which he believed was clearly feasible on the basis of what I had told him. I said this would not work. Crowther was not a plenipotentiary and anything he agreed to could be retracted. But I would have laid my cards on the table. I said I did not trust FAO. Ruedas said they said the same of us which led me to tell Ruedas that...like it or not, the UN was a mediator and...had to bring about an agreement acceptable to both parties. Finally Ruedas got the point.

Wednesday, 10 April 1985

>Asked Ruedas what was happening. UN and FAO disagreed on personnel and audit and perhaps there would have to be a disagreed report on them. He simply did not know. It was evident that UN is standing firm and seeking to call FAO's bluff. Let's hope it works.

Friday 19 April 1985

>My depression was not helped by a telephone call from Ahmed...FAO are simply playing around. As I have always believed, the ultimate outcome will only be known at the last moment, possibly not even this week in Geneva.

The ACC was to meet in Geneva where I hoped for a meeting with the Secretary-General before he met Saouma. That was not to be.

Saturday 20 April 1985

>Ahmed and Kelloway had a long talk with Ruedas who outlined to them points of agreement and disagreement between FAO and UN. We were all very disappointed at the news. WFP internal auditor is subservient to FAO auditor, FAO has too big a say in financial controls, too much say on [personnel] classification, yet has not conceded on personnel servicing. UN and FAO have agreed to no change re senior officials. I telephoned Ruedas and told him that it seemed that once again FAO was getting what it wanted. I was deeply upset and communicated my emotion to him saying among other things that the issue was a moral one and that the UN was sweeping the matter under the carpet, playing for time, etc. I said that neither I nor governments would allow this.

Monday 22 April 1985

>Ruedas briefed S-G on our conversation and latter gave me a sympathetic pat but I have not got the meeting that I sought and which Ruedas considered desirable. Later I met with Ruedas...said he has concentrated on institutional changes and not worried too much about fine points. Overall his approach is probably correct, but life could still be made impossible for WFP.

As I learned a month later from Anstee during CFA19, there was only a very brief meeting between Pérez de Cuéllar and Saouma in Geneva. The taskforce report was finalised through an exchange of telexes. Unfortunately Ruedas was unavailable and in his place Anstee had been the responsible official in New York. She had also been the UN's deputy representative on the taskforce but had no first-hand knowledge of WFP nor a background in UN personnel management. She had been one of my competitors for the Executive Directorship of WFP and continued to cultivate good personal relations with Saouma. Ahmed and Kelloway had commented to me on her weakness in the negotiations.[44]

I did not see the taskforce report until it was formally transmitted to me, after a meeting with Pérez de Cuéllar in New York on 10 May. WFP had had no opportunity to comment formally on the text before its finalisation and distribution to CFA members notwithstanding all the emphasis placed by governments on the importance of full consultation with WFP. This was justified on the grounds that the text was Pérez de Cuéllar's and Saouma's report on the work of the UN/FAO Joint Taskforce on 'WFP Relationship Problems'. I commented in my diary that the delay in finalising the report, and then its release by FAO, was designed to minimise time and opportunity for me to rally governments before the commencement of the CFA on 20 May.

However, I had long concluded that I had no alternative to acceptance of their conclusions. I had told the Secretary-General on 10 May, that while I had not yet received the taskforce report and therefore could not give definitive views, I had misgivings about the failure to transfer services or to make any advance on the senior officials question. I said that I would inform the CFA of my wholehearted willingness to try to make the changes work, while 'in the most diplomatic way' pointing to my reservations on certain points. Pérez de Cuéllar did not demur. Rather, he said, 'Wherever I go I hear a lot about WFP and your management, all of which is good'. He began the meeting by saying that I should not feel I was outnumbered (a good number of his top staff were present), rather that I was with friends. Several times he said that WFP and I had his strong support and his personal sympathy. A few weeks later I got a letter from Pérez de Cuéllar thanking me for my handling of the taskforce and its report.

Government Interventions

During the months the taskforce was working, I had encouraged governments to urge our case on the Secretary-General. In some instances the force and clarity of their representations was complicated by extraneous factors within their governments. My diary entry for 7 December 1984 is illustrative:

Kristensen and Glistrup for lunch...Kristensen said that Nordics were very upset at Saouma's treatment of Norwegian aid minister during FAO Council. Clearly they are depressed by turn of events in Council. So far their will has not wavered—indeed Nordics, he said, had never been so strongly united on a single issue. But they are strongly frustrated. Kristensen said that Saouma should realise that the scene would shift to New York if he did not show more moderation—Kristensen does not like this idea because in Denmark's case it would mean that control would pass to Foreign Ministry. He mentioned ambivalence of certain countries on issue—US, Germany, France in particular, and I gave him my analysis on each from which he did not dissent. Basic support for WFP in USAID and working level of State Department— problem lay in Fenwick's influence on Newell, who was preoccupied with UNESCO and did not want a major fight over FAO on his hands at same time. As for Germany, like US, in that ministries of agriculture and foreign affairs, having got relations back to an even keel with FAO over payment of their contribution, did not want to rock the boat! While [Ministry of] Economic Cooperation was strong in our support its Minister was from same party as Agriculture Minister and he did not want friction with his colleague. As for France, I described my meeting with Rocard, who had said that he had been told that I was seeking to make WFP independent of FAO so that it would 'become a tool of the major wheat exporters, since it would no longer be subject to FAO policy guidance'. When I explained what the issue was really about, Rocard, who said he was no friend of Saouma, expressed his agreement with position I had taken. I said that I believed France could be brought to position of much stronger support through Rocard.

France and FAO

Notwithstanding the dislike for Saouma's methods expressed to me by Rocard and other French ministers, France was essentially undeviating in its policy of support for him. It was hard to believe that this was simply due to Saouma's assiduous cultivation of his close personal links with France as a 'francophone'. France must have judged that the 'national interest' justified that support. What that national interest might be can only be a matter of speculation. French speakers had a strong presence in FAO and France, like the United States, attached importance to the placement of its nationals in key posts in UN agencies. It had been quite successful in the specialised agencies, for example UNESCO and ILO, and apparently saw this as part of its competition with the United States, which held the chief executive posts in the operational agencies UNDP and UNICEF and wished to do the same in WFP, already regarded by France as under 'Anglo-Saxon' control. I went out of my way to convince the French that I was even-handed in my management of WFP and not an American tool. I developed good relationships with the Foreign Ministry, although that was never sufficient to get continuing or consistent support from Paris. More frequently than not, I got opposition.

The United States, Canada and Australia

Canada and Australia were consistently robust in support. Indeed during this CFA they played an influential, even decisive, role. Beforehand, as my diary records, I told them they had three options:

> (i) *to ask the taskforce to look again at certain matters, (ii) to say thanks, but we will work this out ourselves, i.e. by setting up an intergovernmental committee; or (iii) to go along with the solution, to urge its immediate implementation, while requesting the Executive Director to report back on progress, but also give their analysis of ambiguities and defects in the S-G/D-G report.*

In the event they rightly pursued the third option, though with some misgivings, especially on the part of Canada, which would have preferred me to plainly state my dissatisfaction with the taskforce conclusions and recommendations, and even reject them.

Following a good deal of urging from Canada, the United States also gave support. In February 1985, Newell wrote letters to the Secretary-General and Director-General calling for positive action in the taskforce, including, if necessary, amendments to the WFP Basic Documents. Lindores reported to me that Canada told Newell 'support for WFP was an issue of good governance of precisely the same kind that had led the United States to its UNESCO policy'.[46] Other governments making similar representations included the Nordics and the Netherlands.

Lobbying Developing Countries

FAO was lobbying developing countries through its representatives in Rome and through its extensive networks in their home countries. To the limits of our ability WFP was doing the same in Rome but our capacity to lobby in capitals was weak. In our December 1984 newsletter to staff we had informed them of the CFA decision to set up the taskforce and suggested that field staff bring this important development to the attention of governments. I had in mind that there was little reporting to capitals by the Rome representatives of most developing countries and few instructions back to them. They were pretty well free to decide for themselves how best to realise their government's general policies of securing more aid from FAO and WFP and bolstering the Director-General as the supposed guardian of the interests of developing countries.

Following personal representations by Saouma, the Secretary-General wrote to me on 22 March 1985 to rebuke me for the content of the December newsletter. I was told of the 'need, particularly at this stage [in the work of the taskforce], for a quiet and cooperative effort to settle existing problems', which would be 'enhanced by restraint from all concerned in the issuance of public statements'. This did not make sense. The unseemly goings-on at CFA19 had caught the attention of the European press, extensive accounts of the proceedings appearing on two occasions in the *Neue Zuricher Zeitung*; and in any event CFA proceedings were public. To deny our staff an account of what happened would have been absurd and never crossed my mind.

Surprisingly, I received good backing over a riskier step I took. I was particularly concerned at the bias of the chairman of the CFA and asked the UNDP Resident Representative to brief the Colombian Government. This was done, but FAO obtained the record of the discussion. A few days after the Secretary-General's rebuke, Saouma wrote to Ripert, saying he was 'shocked' to learn of the blatant lobbying of the Resident Representative in Bogotá urging Colombia 'to instruct their delegation to the CFA to take positions prejudicial to FAO and in favour of WFP'. FAO said it was concerned that other Resident Representatives were similarly 'misusing' their position and requested that Ripert take action to prevent a recurrence.

Ripert essentially endorsed my view that, acting as our representative, it was appropriate for the UNDP representative to make representations on our instructions, albeit with 'reserve and discretion' in ways which protected the 'common interests' of the UN system.

Saouma replied angrily that Resident Representatives should be instructed not to involve themselves in interorganisational disputes, conveniently ignoring that his own representatives constantly did this on behalf of FAO, not least in relation to the policies and practices of UNDP, which funded many FAO technical assistance projects. He ended by reserving his right to raise the matter in the ACC. He never did, of course, but he calculated the threat would be sufficient to ensure it would be made known to UNDP that it should avoid intrusion into our problems with FAO. In this he was essentially successful. Though some UNDP representatives gave useful, quiet support over the years, they did so entirely at their own discretion and did not report to me if they made representations. On the other hand, some worked against our interests. For example, one was obstructing our work in relation to the ground-breaking use of food aid for the reform of food markets in Senegal. It was also inequitable in as much as other programs comparable to WFP had their own representatives.[47] The UNDP representative was styled 'Resident Coordinator', but his powers of coordination did not mean that the representatives of other agencies were subordinate to him. No agency was more assiduous than FAO in its insistence on its autonomy.

While I thought it absurd that the United Nations did not have a single diplomatic representative, so long as it did not, I decided that WFP must also be represented by its own staff member. I made some progress toward this goal but had to avoid pressing the matter to the point of harming relations with UNDP and the Secretary-General. Much as I sympathised with the frustration of our senior field staff, the issue was of lower priority than freeing WFP from the FAO incubus. I was very pleased when my successor, Catherine Bertini, telephoned me in 1995 to inform me that agreement had been reached to put WFP representatives on the same level as those of other agencies.

THE OUTCOME

I had long accepted that I had no political alternative to gracious acceptance of the taskforce conclusions. In public, I conveyed the impression that we had gained a real victory. Indeed we had, because as I wrote in my diary of 16 May:

while the substance is no better than what we expected (it is nevertheless substantial), somehow the wording is more subtly favourable than I had anticipated.

As the Secretary-General and Director-General said in their letter conveying the taskforce report, the new arrangements brought 'substantial delegation of authority' which would give me 'greater flexibility and authority to manage the Programme than any of your predecessors'. I also wanted to show trust in FAO's good faith in implementing the new arrangements, despite my reservations.[48]

I also made a point of calling on Saouma before CFA19 began. Our meeting on 17 May 1985 was relatively cordial. We both made an effort to resume our good relationship. I summed up in my diary:

Saouma is a very emotional man who is difficult to debate with, shifting ground, logically inconsistent, asserting connections between different events or concepts that don't exist—but all very persuasively put when he wants to. He accused me of seducing him but he came close to seducing me with his proposal to bury the hatchet unconditionally.

Given the clarity of Bertrand's analysis, the cogency of his recommendations and the momentum for change that had developed at the previous CFA, Saouma could feel pleased that so little had had to be given away. Though more than a mouse had been produced, given the cost and time expended, the result was meagre. Ahmed and Kelloway felt that the UN had been far too weak and not a match for FAO in detailed argument. Ruedas, because of his daunting responsibilities, could only give occasional attention to the work of the taskforce and the UN's supporting staff was unable to fill the gap with the same intellectual force.

In any event, by ruling out in advance amending the General Regulations, as recommended by Bertrand, extremely cumbersome arrangements had to be defined for personnel management. In relation to the selection of senior officials, not only was consultation still required for the D1 level and above, but it was asserted, contrary to General Regulation 14(e), that consultation was required for transfers, as well as for appointments and promotions, as stated in the text. I was angry over this but made no reference in my speech and was disappointed that only a few delegates expressed concern at the taskforce failure in this respect. By remaining silent in the CFA I had only myself to blame.

In relation to accounts, a complex division of functions was recommended which made no administrative or financial sense, but was intended to preserve the Director-General's role as trustee of the WFP Fund. That meant he retained the power to sign the WFP accounts and could therefore again harass the Programme.

We were granted our own internal auditor, but while reporting to the Executive Director, he had to submit his program of work to FAO's internal auditor, who would be responsible for oversight of certain accounting functions. As events were to show, FAO had in this decisive area retained its power over the Programme.

A number of other less important functions were transferred to WFP and administrative relationships clarified in useful ways. The most important related to procurement. FAO's regulatory system had seriously impeded the timeliness of our food purchases in the then on-going African famine.

Our supporters in the CFA were alert to these deficiencies which they alluded to in debate. To keep the pressure on FAO, the CFA requested that I report on implementation at the next two sessions of the committee.

Measured handling of the taskforce report strengthened my standing with New York and with the Rome delegations. Tomlinson told me that afterwards the Indian Ambassador was going around saying, 'Ingram is a great man'. That was much needed balm to my ego. It had been an extraordinarily tense six months and I had never been entirely confident I was following the best course. I wondered about my chances of staying on when my term ended in April 1987. In this regard my mood was strongly influenced by Saouma's efforts to hawk my post to the Americans. Even more disturbing was the latter's apparent willingness to consider a deal. This issue, which is revealing of the incoherence of American policy in relation to the United Nations, is the subject of the following chapter.

Implementation of the taskforce conclusions proceeded relatively smoothly. On 9 August 1985, after the CFA, I wrote, *apropos* of WFP staff:

> *Have now got them engaged with the idea of helping to make WFP more efficient through better staff utilisation and job satisfaction. I feel I am starting to get somewhere in improving my organisation…It is such a relief to be free of FAO's harassment, which was carried on unrelentingly for two-and-a-half years.*

My progress report to CFA20 (WFP, 1985a) informed the committee that 'consultation has been carried out in a spirit of harmony' and 'good progress has been made overall'. Of most importance, I was able to show that the new arrangements, once fully implemented, would cost less than before. The debate passed off without incident, with FAO and WFP congratulating one another on our excellent cooperation.

On a visit to the French Alps I had come across a Mount Saouma, and in an effort to improve relations with the Director-General, I had taken some photographs of it and sent them to him under a friendly letter. My diary entry for Monday 30 September 1985, the opening day of CFA20 alludes to this.

> *CFA opened. Saouma not as tense [as at previous sessions] but still tense—as am I. Thanked me for Mt Saouma—he had not heard of it. I had the feeling that he really detests me but, of course, over time relationship may become more acceptable.*

A further opportunity to improve relationships occurred a few days later.

Thursday 3 October 1985

> *Day began with call on Saouma at his request. He wanted to help people forced out of Tripoli (by Israelis) and for me to send El Hage[49] to work out numbers and logistics which might have to be through Syria. In effect, asked a favour and I responded positively and cordially. [He] pointed out that UN staff [had been] withdrawn, that only a Moslem could go—WFP's man in Beirut is Maronite. Thanked me (sotto voce) for promoting him.*

However, differences continued over the issue of senior officers' selection and promotion. As regards promotions, Saouma wanted me to consult him orally in advance of making any recommendation. In that way not only could he influence selection, including putting forward alternatives for promotion, but more easily gain credit with successful promotees.

To counter this I sought his written agreement (and the Secretary-General's) to my choices, in strict accordance with the General Regulations. This procedure made it much harder for him to reject my nominees. If he had acted as a true counsellor I would have had no problem in falling in with his wishes.

Saouma would agree to extend the terms of senior officers only until December 1987, 'so that my successor would be free to make changes'. At this time, notwithstanding our 'good' relations, the Director-General was, behind the scenes, still doing all that he could to ensure I would not get a second term.

My second and final report on taskforce implementation to CFA21 in 1986 advised that this task was now 'virtually complete'. In my statement I said that while there were no differences between us and FAO in regard to the translation into practice of the principles established by the taskforce, the new administrative system still involved 'a complex division of responsibilities,' requiring daily liaison between the two organisations. I was also able to report that all FAO staff to be transferred had moved across and that all agreed functions were now being exercised by the Programme. The new arrangements would mean annual savings of about $500,000 per year. I reserved my right to come back to the CFA if that should become necessary.

Unifying Field and Headquaters staff

The personnel arrangements were indeed a big improvement. They enabled me to create a single WFP professional service, by unifying the previously separate headquarters and field staffs. This allowed policies and instructions to be mediated by knowledge of the political, cultural and economic circumstances of the countries we were assisting. Equally, it gave field staff experience of the constraints set by development theory, the attitudes of donor governments and of the bureaucratic environment in which decision-making occurred, which could only be gained by a stint at headquarters. The development of a rounded, fully effective professional workforce required service in both environments. In practice, however, because staff had been so long entrenched in Rome, implementation was slow and only completed by my successor.

CONCLUSION

So ended the first stage of my effort to reform the management and governance of WFP. I had started by trying to establish a working relationship with FAO that conformed to a common sense reading of the Basic Texts and operated according to the ideals embodied in the UN Charter. It had not occurred to me to seek 'independence' for WFP. I knew Saouma was very pragmatic and assumed we would find reasonable solutions to obvious administrative problems. Indeed that shared pragmatism was an important element in the ease of our early relationship. Unfortunately, as I discovered, his emotional commitment to what he saw as the interests of FAO too often outweighed his pragmatism. That slowly led me to the conclusion that virtually complete *de facto* separation from FAO might be essential to significantly improve WFP.

By mid-1985, however, I still had no plan for making further advances or changes to WFP's Basic Documents. I knew that governments would not be ready for constitutional issues to be re-opened for some time, and then only if they judged this as absolutely necessary. I did know that to build on what I had achieved I must be reappointed for a second term. Since Saouma's own second term would expire only at the end of 1987, while mine finished in April of that year, my chances were probably slender.

---

38   FAO insisted that since the JIU had 'erred' in sending its report to me it must rectify its original error. The new Chairman of the JIU told me he agreed that his predecessor had acted inappropriately in sending the Bertrand report to me as did the Secretary-General. However, since the CFA had decided to consider the report anyway no practical end was served by FAO's insistence on winning its way, except that a rigid insistence on procedure was its principal tactical weapon in its effort to frustrate actions with which it disagreed, i.e. the principle of 'legality' must therefore be inflexibly maintained. Although taskforce implementation was proceeding smoothly, I learnt from Ripert in January 1986, i.e. more that six months later, of UN concern that Saouma still had in mind referring the matter of the Bertrand report to the ACC, since he continued to insist that the JIU had acted improperly. Whatever may have been discussed privately by the Secretary-General with the heads of the 'big four' (the name by which FAO, UNESCO, WHO and ILO were ironically known among staff of the other 20 plus system agencies), the issue was not formally raised in the full ACC.

39   Any textual amendments would have to be endorsed by the FAO Conference which met every two years. Before going to Conference amendments must first be approved by the FAO Council and ECOSOC. If amendments did not reach Conference in 1985 the next opportunity would be in 1987, after I had completed my term. Since the UN General Assembly met yearly timing was less critical for securing its approval of changes in the Basic Documents.

40 Margaret J Anstee, who represented the United Nations at CFA18 and delivered the SG's message. Apart from the congratulatory reference to my performance the message included a favourable mention of Bertrand's work over 16 years. By contrast the Director-General did not refer to Bertrand by name but implied bias on his part.

41 Ambassador J R Lopez-Portillo, said to aspire to succeed Saouma. Certainly, he was very unhelpful to WFP, consistently seeking to win the favour of the Director-General. The Ambassador was a son of the former Mexican President. According to *The Economist* (6 March 2004), the son was referred to by his father as 'the pride of my nepotism'.

42 Vikram Shah, FAO Assistant Director-General

43 At the time Patricio Ruedas was probably the most senior UN official to have risen through the ranks, as did his protégé, Kofi Annan. Of Spanish nationality, Ruedas had a sharp mind, a somewhat quirky sense of humour and was completely dedicated to the interests of the United Nations. As with nearly everyone in New York, he initially suspected I might just be a maverick trouble-maker.

44 Anstee gives her own, misleading account of the work of the taskforce in her memoir (2003).

45 Michel Rocard, Minister of Agriculture 1983–85 and subsequently Prime Minister of France.

46 The United States formally withdrew from UNESCO that year. The United Kingdom followed in December.

47 Indeed, on several visits to developing countries I was amused and disgusted by the sight of multiple diplomatic plated vehicles arriving at a reception each flying the UN flag.

48 According to my diary of 17 May,

in FAO, i.e. among staff, it is said that the taskforce conclusions will last as long as the latest Lebanese peace agreement (an allusion to the ongoing civil war there)!

49 H El Hage, a Lebanese national and senior WFP staff member.

8

APPOINTMENT POLITICS
IN THE UN SYSTEM

My reappointment as Executive Director had to be secured in the face of FAO's total and unwavering opposition and Saouma's effort to gain an unprecedented third term as Director-General of FAO. The United States was also unhelpful. The appointments process is highly political, time-consuming and disruptive to the governance of UN system agencies.

THE BATTLE FOR A SECOND TERM

UN system appointment politics are like politics everywhere, driven by intrigue, ambition and rivalries as much as by differences about policies. Speculation about my future began in 1983 toward the end of my second year in the job. My first term was not to finish until April 1987 and Saouma's not until the end of that year. Even in today's media-driven national politics, speculation about second-term chances and alternative candidates does not usually get under way so early following an election. That it did reflects the interest which had developed in my efforts to transform WFP and Saouma's determination to prevent my reappointment. The first mention in my diary reads:

Friday 3 February 1984

Breakfast with Brad Morse[50]: he lives on cigarettes and black coffee. He said that Fenwick had had the pants charmed off her by Saouma and that he would make this known in the State Department. Morse described Saouma as a bully...and corrupt politician who takes advantage of the civility so important

*to most officials in UN system. He sees Pérez de Cuéllar as wanting a quiet
life, not being an administrator, disliking confrontation. While Pérez said he
would not run again, Morse thought he would be prevailed on to continue.
USA and USSR wanted someone weak. Referred to my own reappointment.
Dismayed that I am up before Saouma's re-election. Added, but you still have
three years!*

Thereafter, references to my reappointment increase rapidly. I frequently
had occasion to recall what Swaminathan said to me in 1984, Saouma 'is
clearly obsessed with WFP beyond all else and wishes to drive you out'.

Saouma Shows His Hand

I did not take much note when one of my American staff told me Saouma
had already advised the United States that he would support an American to
replace me, provided the United States did not put forward a candidate to
succeed the retiring American Executive Director of WFC. On a visit to
New York in June 1984 I learned that the proposal had come through
Fenwick who allegedly said I was not interested in reappointment.
However, it had been rejected. I had reassuring meetings subsequently in
Washington with Peter McPherson, Administrator of USAID, and with
officials of the State and Agriculture Departments. I thought that was the
end of the matter.

As time went by I became convinced that Saouma feared I would myself
run for the FAO Director-Generalship. As head of WFP I would have the
same opportunity as him to travel freely to capitals and to lobby delegates.
The best way, therefore, for him to counter support among delegates for my
reappointment and to protect his own position was to get the United States
to put forward a candidate to replace me.

A Flattering Proposal

To my astonishment early in 1984, just two years into my five-year term,
speculation about my becoming a candidate for the FAO Director-
Generalship did emerge. Olivares told me on 20 March 1984 that, following
my last meeting with him, the Secretary-General commented to him,
'Ingram should succeed Saouma'. Olivares suggested I should get Australian
support to run. I said, 'Too early, I am not interested, I want if possible to
continue with WFP, although Saouma will do everything possible to prevent

it'. He said, 'We will extend you by one year initially, until after the FAO election'. In June, Olivares again encouraged me to seek the FAO post, stressing that it was the turn of the developed countries.

In the months ahead, I was repeatedly asked about my intentions or encouraged to run against Saouma. The Nordics went further, Norway and Denmark urging me in mid-1984 to become a candidate. In doing so they also tested the sincerity of my professed goals for WFP, asking directly would I give WFP its independence if I was FAO Director-General, to which I responded, 'Of course'. Interest among developed countries led Australia to take some informal soundings of the likely level of support for an Ingram candidature. Later that year the senior responsible Australian official asked me whether I intended to become a candidate to which I responded in the negative.

By the end of 1984 several Africans were encouraging me to run, including all my senior African staff members. The African bloc was the biggest in the G77 and the conventional wisdom was that African support was essential for victory against Saouma. The likelihood of African support became clearer when I made an official visit to Egypt in 1985. I took away from my meetings with Egypt's influential Minister of Agriculture, Youssuf Wali, a strong feeling that he would like me to run against Saouma:

Sunday 27 January 1985

At Wali's dinner four other ministers attended which, according to UNDP representative, was best he has seen (for visiting UN agency heads). Wali told me Saouma had suggested to him that he should seek an FAO chairmanship, that as a man of intellect and drive he had a role to play. (Saouma was clearly sounding out whether Wali was interested in running for D-G.) Wali said he was not interested in any international positions and did not attend FAO meetings. He scoffed at idea that FAO assistance was of much value. 'FAO is not a development institution, they do not understand development, the institution is bureaucratic—wrapped up in red tape', he said. He agreed that Saouma must be replaced—said that he should be succeeded by someone from a developed country, cited experience of UNESCO and FAO as compared with WHO and ILO[51] —'better to have in charge the rich than those who want to be rich'. I had said I thought Saouma's successor should come from Africa...He did not agree that developing countries, including Africa, would insist on one of their number.

Although this attention was flattering I felt it would be unwise to turn my sights on the FAO job. WFP's first Executive Director had been elected FAO

Director-General and his successor, Francisco Aquino, had run unsuccessfully against Saouma. If I entered the lists against Saouma so early in my term the charge that my disputes with him over WFP were manufactured to advance my personal ambitions would gain substance. Once I signalled an intention to become a candidate any possibility of a rapprochement with him would be lost and progress toward greater autonomy for WFP would be in abeyance until after the FAO election. If, of course, he won the election my position as WFP Executive Director would become untenable, as it had for Aquino. FAO control of the Programme would be re-asserted and probably strengthened. My goal was to complete what I had set out to do, namely to make WFP an exemplary United Nations organisation.

I did want reappointment. My strategy was simple, namely to go on doing my best to improve WFP and so maintain, and hopefully strengthen, the esteem in which I was now held by developed and developing countries, within and outside the CFA. I considered that no decision would be made until late 1986 at the earliest. I took it for granted I could count on Australian and American support. I turned out to be wrong on both counts.

The Critical Role of the United States

In 1985-86 the key official deciding US policy on my reappointment was Assistant Secretary of State for International Organization Affairs, Gregory Newell, who was very much influenced by fellow Republican, Millicent Fenwick. In February 1985, the Australian Embassy told me of an important meeting between Newell and the Canadians. Reportedly Newell told the Canadians:

Friday 22 February 1985

> ...that he regarded the WFP/FAO dispute as a personality one, that either Ingram or Saouma would have to go, that Saouma would easily be re-elected and that Ingram would therefore have to go, that Ingram, unlike Saouma did not have regard to US interests (Cuba was cited) and that the US would expect to replace Ingram. Apparently this led to a very heated exchange. The Canadians apparently said that the US attitude was inexplicable to them since the issues involved were precisely the same as at stake in relation to UNESCO. Newell was apparently not (previously) aware of the strength of Canadian feeling.

Ottawa and Canberra were both concerned about Washington's attitude. The Canadians let me know that the time had come for me to actively campaign for a second term. They saw my reappointment as a critical issue in the reform of the UN system. Governments must show that they were in charge and that agencies were not the personal fiefdoms of their executive heads. Shortly afterwards, Newell's deputy called on me as my diary records:

Thursday 14 March 1985

Kauzlaric told me that I was doing a good job and WFP was a good organisation, that....there was no deal with Saouma to replace me and that there would be none. However, that did not mean that US might not put forward a candidate of its own. I said that weakened very much what he had said; that three years ago US had analysed that someone who would stand up to Saouma was required; that that diagnosis was still valid; that, while my reappointment would be difficult, the friction likely to be generated over an attempt to replace me would be enormous; that the job could not be done in three years; and that I wished to continue.

Much the same was said on subsequent occasions by different officials in Washington to my colleagues: it was essential that the United States have a top job in Rome—'Nothing to do with Jim Ingram, who is doing a wonderful job'.

I found it hard to believe that the United States would not support me for a second term. Indeed, despite unhappiness about my even-handedness in the provision of assistance to Vietnam and other Marxist/communist states, at the working level of the State Department I consistently enjoyed excellent relations. The same was true of some high officials in the US administration. Paradoxically, two of my strongest supporters were the Cuban exiles, Ambassador José Sorzano, Deputy Chief of Mission at the US mission to the UN in New York and Anthony Gayoso a senior official in Newell's Bureau. My efforts to bring greater autonomy to WFP and improve its overall performance were strongly commended by all.

However, I underestimated the narrowness of the approach of the incumbents (all political appointees) in the position of Assistant Secretary of State for International Organization Affairs in the State Department; and the influence of Fenwick. They did not share my view that building a stronger multilateral system was important in itself and, to that end, the integrity of UN agencies should be respected. Nor did they see the need for policy compromises if the competing interests of other powers were to be given appropriate weight. Moreover, I was not prepared for the extent to which other interest groups in Washington were influential in affecting policies toward the FAO and WFP.

Above all I failed to realise fully how ruthlessly the United States seeks senior posts for itself especially if, as in the case of WFP, it feels entitled to the top post. The executive heads of UN system agencies are key players in directing their work. Where the agency is useful in promoting American interests or conversely capable of damaging them, the United States seeks to play a critical role. That is so even if, by convention, an American does not hold the top post, as is the case with UNHCR. Even US Presidents sometimes intervene, not only in support of their own nationals, but to back non-Americans, as did President Reagan in 1986 when he urged the Secretary-General to appoint a Swiss national, Jean Pierre Hocke, as High Commissioner for Refugees.

During the 1980s WFP remained useful to the United States as an outlet for its surplus foodstuffs. It was also seen as an increasingly important instrument for meeting the food needs of refugees and displaced peoples, notably Cambodians and Afghans, best done under the United Nations banner. In its heyday, USAID led the world in the use of external assistance for economic development, including food aid. Experienced American aid professionals valued WFP's development activities. Politically, however, our development assistance was not seen as very important, except when extended to countries disliked by the United States for foreign policy reasons, for example Cuba, Nicaragua and Vietnam.

Food aid was important in American domestic politics. It enjoyed strong support from the American public for its humanitarian benefits, as well as from the farm lobby in Congress and special interest groups, for example in the shipping and freight forwarding industries.

With these substantial interests it was not surprising that the United States coveted the Executive Directorship. Despite being the biggest contributor to WFP, an American had held that post only once and then for a brief period, first as Acting Executive Director and as titular head for three months prior to retirement. Since my departure in 1992, the subsequent Executive Directors have been Americans.

'Jobs for the boys', was a not unimportant consideration either. United States agencies of government competed for the placement of their officials in UN organisations as a means of rewarding staff. In my experience, American nominees were competent, often very much so. This could not always be said of candidates from other countries. In the case of WFP, three American agencies saw themselves as the most appropriate source of candidates, namely USAID, the Department of Agriculture and, to a lesser extent, the Department of State.

In the light of all these factors, the assumption in Washington was that after a single term I should be succeeded by an American, notwithstanding that I was revitalising WFP administratively and operationally and had removed WFP from under the thumb of Saouma, a goal to which the United States was powerfully attached at the time of my appointment.

Saouma was very much alive to all these factors. Our differences of approach on appointments emerged clearly at a luncheon in Washington in 1984 given by the Secretary of Agriculture to mark the 30th anniversary of PL480. My diary reports the occasion as follows:

Monday 9 July 1984

....*Block's [Secretary of Agriculture] lunch was curious in that he asked everyone around the table to say a few words. Saouma went on about...the number of Americans in his organisation, those to come and how Americans were in charge of (key posts) of finance and administration. I spoke next...an appeal for strong, principled US leadership.*[52] *After the lunch I had a private meeting with Block and his staff. I mentioned WFP/FAO institutional problem, stressing it was not personal. Sympathy seemed to be real and strong...Later met with...staff members of House of Representatives Foreign Relations Committee. They want WFP to dwell more on logistics capabilities in future assessments [of emergency food needs] and also are thinking of ways to help us re Bertrand report.*

It was this sense of shared goals that led me to underestimate the strength of the US temptation to do a deal with Saouma over my post. I knew also that the United States had considered withdrawal from FAO, as well as from UNESCO, because of continuing dissatisfaction with its performance.

The reappointment landscape changed to my benefit later in 1985. In July, Moise Mensah, a native of Benin and a Vice-President of IFAD, announced his candidature for the FAO Director–Generalship.[53] Mensah was a credible candidate, well regarded and decent, though there was doubt that he was sufficiently tough-minded for the job. On the other hand Benin, as one of Africa's smaller countries, lacked influence within Africa, as well as globally. Faced with such a candidate and if the election outcome was uncertain Saouma would find it very difficult not to agree to an extension of my term until the end of 1987, after the FAO election.

Shortly afterwards, Newell was replaced by Alan Keyes, a personable, intelligent and dynamic African-American and very committed Republican.[54] We always had good personal relations but he caused enormous problems over my reappointment, as became clear later.

Edward West retired from FAO and an Irishman, the respected Declan Walton (a WFP foundation staff member) was appointed Deputy Director-General for two years, until the expiry of Saouma's term. That opened the possibility of his post being offered to the Americans by Saouma if re-elected, possibly slaking their thirst for my position.

Another encouraging development was a positive response from the United States to my invitation to submit three names for my consideration to replace the head of our project management division, at the time an American, who had reached retirement age. I took this to mean they had made no definitive decision about seeking the Executive Directorship, since it would not be seen as reasonable were Americans to hold two of WFP's three top posts.

During a visit to Washington in September 1985, acting on the advice of Gayoso, I made my case for reappointment to the Administrator of USAID, Peter McPherson and the Deputy Secretary of Agriculture, Dan Amstutz. Both were highly complimentary about my performance but made no commitments.

However, from a senior official in Agriculture I learnt that Fenwick was still pushing for an American to fill my post and also the name of the official lobbying to fill it, Julia Bloch, a combative Republican appointee in USAID, who had represented the United States at CFA meetings.

In the following months other names were mentioned, including Amstutz himself. I continued to receive reports that the Americans still considered Saouma invincible. On the other hand, Gayoso told me, it was possible that the United States might eventually 'get behind Mensah', even though the information reaching me suggested that Mensah's campaign was struggling with Africans.

By the end of the year all other governments to whom I spoke supported me for another term.

Trouble from Canberra

December brought a bombshell. My successor as head of Australia's overseas aid agency, Bob Dun, who had just visited Washington and Ottawa, called on me. He said the Canadians were very strong in my support and regarded my appointment as a 'foregone conclusion'. However, there were misgivings in Washington. The claim that Australia had put 50 per cent of its food aid through WFP in order to 'buy the job for me' was recalled as was Australia's breach of faith with its allies over the 1981 FAO budget. Further, Dun said, a recent article in the Australian press referring to these matters had aroused the Foreign Minister's interest. According to Dun, the Minister, Bill Hayden, had several times signalled suspicion of WFP's worth, regarding departmental support for it as due to my incumbency rather than any real merit it might have. He had requested a full account of the circumstances of my appointment but was not satisfied and had called for the files which were still with him. As I commented in my diary of 5 December 1985,

> *paradoxically, these "deals" that Australia was supposed to have made were seen at the time as evidence that Saouma would have a compliant Executive Director in Ingram! But US has forgotten that now, remembering it seems, only Australia's alleged unfair tactics in getting the job.*

Hayden refused to endorse my candidature. Nothing would convince him that my job had not been 'bought'. The implication was that I had unscrupulously manipulated the Australian government to serve my personal interests. Further, I had been supported by a Liberal Party government for the WFP post and was a former diplomat. In fact, I never had a connection with any political party and saw myself the quintessential apolitical civil servant. Ironically, because of my good standing with former Labor Prime Minister, Gough Whitlam, I had been tarred a 'Laborite' by the late Sir Keith Waller, Secretary of the Department of Foreign Affairs. The only dealings I had had with Hayden were peripheral, when he was a member of Whitlam's party that visited Ottawa in 1973, while I was High Commissioner there.

As a relatively minor power Australia's interest lies much more than the United States in strengthening the multilateral system, as compared with narrower national goals. That interest can be furthered by Australians occupying key posts. The Nordics, the Netherlands and Canada share that aim, and they are aware that getting one's nationals appointed to senior posts in UN agencies can be an important means of making progress toward it.

Australian ministers lack of interest in the placement of their nationals reflected not so much deliberate policy or the low priority attached to the United Nations as ignorance of the intensity of the political struggle surrounding top appointments. In close campaigns for important posts the personal intervention of ministers can be decisive in bolstering the chances of nominees. The United Nations is an organisation made up of national governments. It is expected that ministers will seek to use their influence with their counterparts to get their candidates elected. There is nothing 'unfair' about the process; it is the process. That is not of course to say that the process should not be improved.

I do not recall in my time any Australian holding a high post in the UN system who owed his position to our government's influence. Like me, their personal efforts were decisive. That was not the case when the UN was in its infancy. Some outstanding Australians had been appointed to the UN and its agencies. At that time Australia, like the Nordics, was genuinely high-minded in its support for the United Nations; indeed that was the cornerstone of the foreign policy of the Labor government which had played a significant role in the writing of the United Nations Charter.

To my surprise, late in January 1986 our Ambassador in Rome telephoned to say that Hayden had decided Australia should seek another term for me and that he and our Ambassador to the United Nations had been instructed to approach Saouma and Pérez de Cuéllar. Their instructions spoke of my outstanding record and dedication to improvement of the UN system as justifications for my reappointment.

My pleasure turned sour when I visited Canberra in March. I discovered that Hayden had given agreement only when officials 'admitted' that the post had been 'bought'[55] and recommended that Australia should drastically reduce the amount of its food aid disbursed through WFP, which in due course was done. This made support for my reappointment perverse. It seemed they wanted to see if I could retain my position with a diminished Australian contribution. Hayden's reluctance became known to the Americans. That was a major factor in the mess that developed.

I accepted that former colleagues had done the best they could to get the

Australian government's support. I sought a meeting with Hayden to explain how WFP used food aid and why, from a development and humanitarian perspective, its impact far exceeded Australia's otherwise unconditional program food aid. A meeting was not granted. Hayden was the only minister from any country unwilling to meet with me. His attitude contrasted unfavourably with other Australian ministers. It was exceedingly odd that the foreign minister of a Labor government took the attitude he did, given Labor's historic support for the United Nations, a policy strengthened by a subsequent Labor minister, Gareth Evans.

The United States Continues its Opposition

Hayden's endorsement had no effect on the attitude of the United States, whose embassy in Canberra was privy to what had gone on. It remained unwilling to support my reappointment or rule out the possibility that it would put forward a candidate. They would not foreclose the option of having an American succeed me unless there was a strong prospect of Saouma being defeated—something they did not expect. The most I could expect was a short extension.

Our Ambassador's argument to Keyes in the State Department was that there was a question of principle involved: by not supporting an incumbent whom the Americans regarded as an 'effective and tough-minded administrator', while dallying with Saouma, they brought into question how serious they were about UN reform. Gayoso was more explicit, as I wrote in my diary:

Thursday 6 March 1986

> *Pressed, he said that US favoured two-year extension (he agreed up until end of 1987 was not enough)...I suspect that pressure for my 'prestigious' job, as Gayoso called it, is strong enough for short extension idea to be basis for compromise between those who insist US must have job and those who recognise that broader US interest requires that I continue.*

In subsequent discussions Keyes made his position clearer. While conceding that the integrity of the UN system was threatened by Saouma and recognising the need for unity with Australia and Canada on the issue of his re-election, Keyes contended that the farm lobby wanted the WFP job for an American. He claimed his hands were tied. However, his 'constituency might be sold on an extension of two years'. In fact this was a bluff. The main obstacle to US agreement was the interest of senior officials in the Department of Agriculture and USAID in securing the post for themselves, not the farm lobby.

By early April, the Australians were able to inform the Secretary-General there was 'overwhelming support for my reappointment'. Furthermore, a second, credible, candidate had entered the lists against Saouma. He was Sartaj Aziz, a Pakistani influential in the creation of the WFC and later minister in his country's government.

Matters came to a head with the United States immediately before CFA21 met in late May 1986. In a meeting between Keyes and our Embassy in early May, Keyes said Saouma, had made a definite offer of my post to the Americans, a 'temptation which was quivering like a jelly on the table'. Saouma's tactics were transparent but could still influence the domestic departments, he claimed. In this situation the best that Keyes could agree to was an extension for me of two years in exchange for Australian support for an American successor and United States willingness to concert with others to deny a third term to Saouma. This amounted to barely concealed blackmail.

I was disappointed by our Embassy's reaction, which took far too much at face value Keyes' claims about the importance of domestic issues. Through Brad Morse's and Tek Tomlinson's contacts in Washington, including with the staff of Congressional committees, we knew that personal ambitions were the dominant factor, including Keyes' own relationships with influential Republicans.

I conveyed my reaction to Canberra as follows:

...Keyes is making the best of what is a weak position and at the same time testing strength of Australia's resolve. He is asking a great deal and giving very little in return. All is coupled with a threat to do a deal with Saouma which runs counter to everything US has been professing it stands for in relation to the United Nations.

The contrast between American rhetoric and reality was nowhere more evident than in Keyes' statement of 12 March 1986 to Joint Sessions of the various Congressional Committees concerned with the UN system. At the time the US was cutting its contributions to voluntary and assessed agencies, WFP being one of the few exceptions. This had caused a serious rift in European relations with the United States. Keyes alluded several times to American attachment to the 'ideals' of the UN and to the need for leadership from executive heads of agencies and the Secretary-General in effecting reforms.

The contradiction between US stated policy toward UN reform and its temporising over opposition to Saouma's re-election was the more pointed in that the Geneva Group, of which the United States was a member, had that year agreed to an Australian proposal to limit heads of agencies to two terms. Australia was actively working to secure unified support from OECD countries for this change, which would mean that Saouma would be ineligible for a third term. However the initial American position, as stated by Keyes, was only that they 'had a general inclination' towards the principle of term limitation. Ambassador Fenwick told Saouma that it did not 'of course' apply to him and that France and Italy were baulking.

When Saouma formally announced his candidature, the Lebanese government actively sought to persuade Australia to agree that, if adopted, the principle should not be applied to current incumbents.

United States Maintains Its Tough Stand

To my disquiet, I learned from American friends that Keyes took his tough line on advice from the US Embassy in Canberra that the Ambassador's representations reflected the views of officials, not ministers, and that Hayden's support was *pro forma*. Therefore, Keyes was running no risk of seriously harming relations with Canberra. This information also explained why our Ambassador in Washington was not pushing my candidature vigorously with Keyes. For the same reason there was no disposition in the Department of Foreign Affairs to have Hayden or Hawke intervene with their American counterparts. I knew that the matter would be quickly resolved to our satisfaction if they did. Because of Hayden's attitude to me I did not feel I could approach him directly. I did not know Hawke personally. I had no option but to rely on my former colleagues in the Department of Foreign Affairs who were reluctant in the extreme to recommend ministerial intervention.

At this point I was deeply pessimistic about the possibility of getting Keyes to change his position. I wanted an early decision, not least so I could get on with my work without this constant distraction. Accordingly, I concluded that an agreement with the Americans on less than a full term might now be unavoidable. I informed Canberra, that if it judged it to be in Australia's interest, I was ready to accept an extension of two years and to stand down in April 1989.

The Department's response was firm. They were not tempted by the deal. The Americans were informed that Australia did not accept any linkage between a further term for Saouma and a second one for Ingram and would 'regard a US move to introduce a US candidate at this stage as most regrettable and untimely'. Keyes was unmoved; he intensified his implied threats. Our reaction, he said, left him in a 'difficult' position. He wanted to 'strengthen the integrity of the UN system' and supported an 'extension' for me; but there were not many outside the State Department who shared his concerns. If we could come to 'some arrangement' he might be able to persuade his colleagues to forego the 'instant gratification' of getting an American in my job. (Gayoso told us there were at least five 'self-proclaimed' candidates seeking support from Senators and Congressmen.) Keyes proposed that the US, Australia and Canada publicly support a full second term, but as part of the deal I would stand down after less than one year for 'personal reasons' and Australia must support the American choice as my successor. Keyes favoured a tripartite approach to Saouma at 'some appropriate' time. Then Keyes would hold Saouma to the commitment he had given him, namely that he, Saouma, would accept my reappointment if there was agreement between our three countries. However, nothing should be done at CFA21, which began the following week, Keyes said.

This was altogether too tough. I therefore informed Canberra that the arrangement proposed by Keyes would inevitably become known and, once it did, would not reflect credit on Australia, the United States or me personally. It should therefore be rejected. Keyes clearly thought he had us on the ropes.

Peter McPherson led the US delegation to CFA 21 and on its eve I had a private meeting with him. I told him categorically that less than two years was not acceptable. I would only go along with such a proposal because I recognised that while the US sat on the fence, the matter would drag on indefinitely and that was counter-productive for the Programme. McPherson sought to justify the US position on the grounds that Congress would not go on supporting WFP unless an American was in the job; and that candidates were already lobbying with congressmen. However, I sensed I had his personal support. His CFA statement was very warm in its praise of my leadership in the African emergency. I was also heartened by the robust attitude of Canada which rejected any idea of a deal. They considered that 'sooner or later the US will have to join in a tri-partite demarche re second term for Executive Director and come out publicly against Saouma'.

Taking the Initiative

Heartened by the strong backing I enjoyed from CFA members, I decided to take the initiative on the basis of the precedent set in UNICEF, whose Executive Director was appointed by the Secretary-General following consultation with its Executive Board. The Board's Chairman conferred with Board members and then reported to the Secretary-General. This method was entirely consistent with the WFP Basic Documents, so could be followed by the CFA Chairman. I started to float the idea:

Wednesday 28 May 1986

Lunch with Lindores. Suggested to him UNICEF precedent. Lindores favoured Bureau[56] carrying on task and will approach Martin. Feels Saouma will put great pressure on Hamdi and agrees that I telephone Wali. Canadians are miffed by what they feel is lack of robustness in Canberra from Foreign Affairs (as distinct from ADAB) in particular rejection of [Canada's] proposal for joint demarche to Secretary-General. But they are as committed as ever to good order and governance and in support of me. Lindores says I must come out ahead whether reappointed or not, since my standing with all governments is so high: believes US cannot get job and cannot afford to do deal with Saouma.

Tuesday 3 June 1986

Hamdi started consultations [on the appointment process] and got favourable response from all, but ten minutes after consulting Cape Verde representative [one of Saouma's strongest supporters] he was summoned to Saouma's office and told to stop. I called on Hamdi but all he conceded was that 'some' objected to his carrying out consultation without authority and that he should not convey results to D-G and S-G. I urged on him his responsibilities as Chairman, that he finish consultations and only then decide exactly what to do.

Wednesday 4 June 1986

Hamdi completed consultations. With Sao Tome absent from session, 22 in favour,

7 pleading lack of instructions, of which three objected to procedure as unconstitutional—USA, France, Cape Verde. Thailand claimed not to have instructions but in fact government supports and Colombia was recorded in negative, though Bula Hoyos subsequently claimed this was a mistake.[57] Tomlinson argued that I should urge Hamdi to prepare his letter to S-G and D-G and then consult on that. Hamdi nervous, but seemingly reassured by his Ambassador.

Thursday 5 June 1986

Hamdi initially attracted to Tomlinson's plan but Martin did not want anything to go in writing. Hamdi decided to make a statement to CFA describing situation objectively, i.e. he had been asked to hold consultations, Bureau agreed, some members expressed concern about procedure, the results were as follows. He showed his draft informally to delegates but Saouma forces intensified their opposition and Hamdi was swayed (I believe) by fear that, because of US opposition, US relations with Egypt would be harmed—doubtless ideas planted by Saouma. Hamdi was ready to give his statement if asked from the floor, but clearly messy situation would result and I asked our friends to desist. Hamdi very pleased by my attitude and session concluded smoothly and in good atmosphere...On balance I think initiative worthwhile. Saouma cannot claim his consultations show different result, Americans are warned of strength of my resolve and of my support and more pressure is put on Saouma.

When Hamdi and I discussed the outcome, which had revealed very strong support for my second term, he was hesitant about taking the initiative in informing the Secretary-General. I therefore brought the result to the Secretary-General's attention through a letter to Patricio Ruedas. We learned through our contacts in FAO that Hamdi's action came as a complete surprise to them; 'a *coup d'état* they called it'.

American Blackmail

Notwithstanding, the strength of my support, Keyes raised the stakes higher. My diary entry for Friday 13 June records that he called in the Australian Ambassador in Washington, and told him the United States put getting the WFP job ahead of any other consideration. They would make a decision on a candidate very soon.

I was disgusted by the whole affair. I prepared a draft letter to the Secretary-General in which I said it would be fitting if a definitive decision about filling my post was deferred until after 'governments have decided on who should hold the posts of Secretary-General of the United Nations and Director-General of FAO'. Meanwhile, I wrote, 'I would understand a decision by them to extend me for one year. If such a decision were to be taken without delay, disruption of WFP's work could be avoided'. Before sending the letter I sought Canberra's reaction.

Tuesday 17 June 1986

To my (pleasant) surprise Canberra does not want my letter sent yet. [General] Walters (US Ambassador to the United Nations and a Cabinet member) is there and they have explained situation to him. He is said to be concerned and will look into matter. They would have been sustained by a tough analysis from Woolcott.[58] Zejjari[59] told me that Huddleston[60] is going around saying that the Australian government does not regard me as a good administrator and support I do have is simply due to lack of alternative candidate! This emphasis on administration makes me wonder whether speculation about Saouma's fear of my running as D-G has some basis. His one claim to the job is his capacity as an administrator. Lindores has apparently reported that...McPherson said he expected US would eventually support me.

Thursday 19 June 1986

Pete Strong[61] told me at some length that...US disagreed with direction I was taking WFP, since they did not want a multilateral competitor in program aid, that I was too independent for their liking....He confirmed US Embassy, Canberra, reported that there was no real steam behind Australian representations and that these, like those of the Canadians, were having no effect (on Keyes). Bridges [US Ambassador, Somalia whom I was considering for senior post] says Keyes not liked in administration (to some extent he was under threat) which may explain his zealous desire to set up WFP post for Amstutz, who is said to be close to White House Chief of Staff, Donald Regan. Spoke with Kerin[62] and Lyng[63] in lobby of FAO. Latter said Amstutz was interested (first admission by US of potential candidate) but was surprised and seemingly concerned at how serious issue had become. Said he would speak to Keyes. So the yo-yo runs.

Saturday 21 June 1986

> Five permanent members of Security Council have approached Pérez de
> Cuéllar asking him to stand again. Prospects seem reasonable but a decision
> will be taken in early October. Clearly, if this happens Pérez will be in a good
> position to press Saouma for a full term for me.

Keyes' duplicity became even clearer in July. An American journalist
friend based in Paris told me that the British journalist, Rosemary Righter,
who subsequently made a name for herself with her incisive critiques of
United Nations specialised agencies (Righter, 1995), had met a week
previously with Keyes. Keyes reportedly told her that the United States
could live with Saouma, provided he could put their man into WFP. I knew
Righter and telephoned her on 15 July. She confirmed the conversation. She
opined that 'Fenwick's support for Saouma and criticisms of me will have
been a contributing factor influencing Keyes'. She described Keyes as 'very
ambitious' and confirmed that Regan backed him also.

Righter's information fitted with advice from another journalist covering
the White House who claimed that, 'Keyes is a loose cannon, feeling his oats
and has good support in White House and Heritage Foundation. Only way
to stop him would be for Australia to approach [Secretary of State] Shultz,
though even that would not be likely to work'. Another source told me,
however, that Whitehead and Shultz were in good standing with Regan and
representations would probably be effective.

Bradford Morse continued to give strong support. He told me on 15 July
1986 that he believed he had convinced the USAID chief, McPherson, of my
'outstanding work' and of the catastrophe that Saouma's re-election would
mean. The American Deputy UN High Commissioner for Refugees was also
very helpful, telling me that he had told McPherson and others of the
'superb cooperation with WFP under my leadership'.

A Change in American Policy

At the end of July the Organization of African Unity had formally endorsed
Mensah as its candidate for FAO, a step which vastly increased his chance
of election. I telephoned Gayoso to give him the news and to follow up on
his suggestion that I make a call on Keyes in early August. He was very
pleased about Mensah and by my information that our Operations Division

would be upgraded to a department at the Assistant Secretary-General/ Director-General level, the same level as my Deputy. I had earlier agreed to continue to fill that post with an American. This upgrading made it even more attractive to them.[64]

A further encouraging piece of information was that the State Department would not put forward a candidate for the WFP Executive Directorship unless the White House, that is Regan, explicitly requested it to do so. Though new names continued to surface the most frequently mentioned remained Amstutz, and his intentions were not really known. The Canadians reported in late June that Keyes appeared to be moving to support my reappointment. The intervention of General Walters may have been helpful. The UN Secretary-General was also preparing to raise the matter with Shultz.

Even at this late stage the Australian Department of Foreign Affairs was unwilling (or afraid) to recommend to Hayden that he raise the issue with Shultz at a meeting they were to have in San Francisco. The most it was prepared to do was to brief him in case Shultz did so. The Department advised Hayden that it did not want to make the issue one of US/Australian bilateral relations. However, Keyes had already done so, when he said that Australia was not 'speaking the language of partnership'. The United States invariably made the appointment of its preferred candidates, whether American or non-American (cf. Hocke), a bilateral issue with states. The fact that we were not ready to do so confirmed once again to the Americans that Australia's support for me was a matter of form. From Keyes' perspective, the United States had nothing to lose by playing hardball with Australia.

Whatever the precise combination of pressures, Keyes at last backed down:

Tuesday 12 August 1986

> *Good meeting and lunch with Keyes. Americans have now decided to go after Saouma. Keyes wants recognition in principle by Australia, Canada and EEC that US has legitimate claim to a top job in Rome. From me, new ADG job for US candidate and my willingness to support that person in event he was proposed as my successor. I readily agreed, pointing out, however, this would not apply if given a 'turkey'. No pressure at all on me to step down early.*

McPherson told me that he believed he played some part in getting the turnaround, helping to establish that it was in the national interest to get

Saouma out. Once Lyng agreed, flatly saying that unless Saouma went FAO would not be any good, the pieces quickly fell into place. 'For unknown reasons many in Agriculture seemed not to be hostile to Saouma', Gayoso said, with his usual irreverent but penetrating humour. 'Altogether a satisfactory day. Now somehow to get Saouma's signature', he concluded.

It was only by the end of September that all loose ends had been tied up and the stage was set for the three governments to jointly inform Saouma of their support for my reappointment for a second term. Australia's one real concession had been to support the accession of my US deputy at the end of my second term, or on my departure. In the event, the highly competent Robert Chase, a former career civil servant with USAID whom I appointed, was not made the candidate of the United States which instead nominated Catherine Bertini, an official from President George Bush's administration. She turned out to be an excellent choice.

The demarche led by Keyes took place on 10 October. The meeting passed off successfully, Saouma insisting, however, that he would 'like to approach the reappointment in his own time and his own way'. There had been much talk that the CFA at its coming session would adopt a resolution requesting the Secretary-General and Director-General to reappoint me. By this time every CFA member, including France and Cape Verde, had told me of their support. Unfortunately, while most had informed the Secretary-General, far fewer had told Saouma, presumably for fear of angering him. Initially, in his meeting with the three emissaries, all of whom came especially from capitals, Saouma contended that only seven or so governments supported me! Saouma claimed inaccurately that a resolution would be 'unlawful' and 'would give Ingram too much power and influence'.

I had myself concluded that a resolution was unnecessary and potentially divisive. Instead WFP was urging delegations to make statements of support at the opening of the CFA. In order to put my relationship with Saouma on the best possible footing prior to the session I called on him:

Friday 17 October 1986

> *Meeting got off to uncertain start…He seemed very concerned that we wanted to take over GIEWS.*[65] *…After satisfying him on this, on my desire to work closely with FAO and have WFP concentrate on essentials of its mandate, tension eased—so much so that he indicated he was not opposed to our having more posts and would not brief delegates to oppose them. I volunteered my willingness*

to see him in future about senior appointments—he spoke of consultation on 'directors', perhaps excluding D1s, and was pleased by my initiative. He recognised that we must respect one another's turf though there were some grey areas such as emergency assessment. He several times spoke of the years we would be working together, that we must avoid self-destructive battles of past. I said I had learned a lot and he conceded that I was like him, i.e. we did not like being pushed around. Told him again that I had fulfilled my ambitions [by attaining the WFP post], and he was very pleased to discover we were nearly same age. He said I had done a great deal to transform WFP. On reappointment he said he would not be back [from New York] until 30 October, would then carry out consultations and make an announcement. I said he was under-estimating the strength of feeling of governments, especially developing countries, including among many of those that supported him as well as me. Many governments supported both of us but they wanted us to cooperate. He said a resolution was bad because of precedent set for other organisations...I said best way to prevent a resolution was to make an announcement on 20 October. All of this led to a bit of shadow play but upshot was that he agreed to make announcement on his return. Subsequently we agreed on 12 noon on 27th and he proposed luncheon for all CFA members and my senior staff. When I left he accompanied me into corridor so that guards could note our cordial exchanges. In effect, the armistice of the taskforce is to be transformed into a peace treaty. Finally he asked me to try to get Australia's support for his election.

Sweet Victory

While my meeting with Saouma was going on, the OECD Group was meeting. John Glistrup[66] reported to me on that meeting, which decided that, as a matter of principle (that governments reserved to themselves the right to determine an appropriate 'consultation' procedure) delegations would state in the CFA their desire to see me reappointed. That would be done at the opening of the session before any other business. By this public action governments were foreclosing any attempt by Saouma to question the extent of support for me. My diary describes how events unfolded:

Monday 20 October 1987

CFA deferred to Saouma's request to speak first: a very ungracious speech;...no reference whatsoever to me personally or to his visit to NY.

Perhaps he never reread his speech after our Friday meeting. OECD hung together and Pascarelli[67] made a stunning statement of support on behalf of all developed countries including many observers: Spain, Ireland, NZ, etc. Then it was in balance on developing side until Kenya joined in. Pakistan led Asian presentation but in the end all four regional groups spoke in favour. Colombia and Argentina spoke but Brazil of all countries failed to do so. Lesotho spoke on behalf of all Africans. Even Saudi Arabia and Hungary eventually spoke in favour. Enormous applause greeted OECD announcement. Chairman's summing-up spoke of unanimous support. Gratifying but embarrassing. Irish representative told me it owed much to Glistrup who stood firm in OECD meeting in face of waverers.

Tuesday 21 October 1986

Walton came to see me. Lunch now set down for Tuesday, but Saouma wants private meeting beforehand with delegation leaders with no announcement to CFA. I insisted on announcement pointing out that more of respective staffs would get message in CFA forum. Walton agreed announcement necessary before CFA report was finalised.

Thursday 23 October 1986

Ruedas has just telephoned to advise that Pérez and Saouma have agreed on text of reappointment announcement. However, as I had warned, Saouma tried for a reduced term but this was rejected by Pérez.

Monday 27 October 1986

Received advanced text of Saouma's address to CFA announcing reappointment and wrote my response. His statement is short but gracious. It is also politically realistic in recognising that the Committee itself has fulfilled the consultation requirement.

Tuesday 28 October 1986

At last! Saouma's speech was well received. In my own I trod a line between graciousness...but not implying gratitude to him personally. I also wanted to state again that cooperation will continue to require mutual respect. Expressions of appreciation on part of all national groups. Lunch went off well and in the end Saouma enjoyed it—his initially rather drawn look being replaced by flush of good colour. We were both very agreeable to one another following the scene of good-fellowship on the podium...After lunch he stood up (saying to me I don't know what I am going to say) and made a good speech whose centrepiece was a Lebanese proverb, the burden of which was that the best way to establish friendship is to first have a good fight. In my reply I took up this theme and also got a good laugh when I said I had learned a lot from him...I wanted to establish to all and to Saouma that there is nothing in my personality or attitude to impede good relations with him and FAO. The reactions were such that I believe I succeeded. However, time will tell. Fenwick never actually congratulated me but she did approve of my lunch address and wrote a nice inscription in my menu. Lunch revealed Fenwick's relationship with Saouma. There was enormous admiration in her voice (sotto voce) when she complimented him on his speech...Saouma is truly incorrigible. He said at lunch that he would be able to help me with my third term!

My re-appointment owed a great deal to my friends in the US administration and to other Americans. I was particularly grateful for Brad Morse's support. I felt he was correct in his view that McPherson had played a major part in getting Keyes reined in. The latter had almost brought shame on the United States but, as fortunately happens so often in relation to American policy, the right decisions are finally taken.

The diplomatic campaign that Australia launched in my support was very professional. I was especially appreciative of the efforts made by my former colleagues in ADAB. They consulted me at every stage. However, as with my first appointment, success owed nothing to the personal intervention of any Australian minister with his foreign counterparts. There is no doubt that a word to the American Secretary of State from Hayden at the outset would have stopped the whole drawn out process of Keyes' attempt to bluff us into demeaning concessions. Such an intervention was thoroughly justified at that time, in view of Saouma's protracted, persistent efforts to inveigle the United States into advancing a candidate and the latter's eagerness to be tempted. Irrespective of Hayden's attitude to me personally, the stakes went beyond my claim for a second term. At issue was the proper governance of the UN system, being undermined by the behaviour of the Director-General of FAO, who was well aware of the weakness of the Reagan administration's professed concern for good governance weighed against bureaucratic divisions and personal ambitions. Australia had shown through its 'terms limitation' initiative in the Geneva Group that good governance was at the heart of its UN policy, but seemingly was unwilling to follow through decisively the logic of that position in its dealings with the US government. Australia seemed to lack a full understanding of how to pull on the many levers of power in Washington in order to bring about a desired result for Australia.

Australia's weakness contrasted unfavourably with Canada's clear-eyed assessment of its interests. It was much readier to stand up to the United States. Without the steadfast support of Canada, Australia's determination to see the matter through would have been weaker, though by overplaying his hand Keyes in the end probably undid himself with Canberra.

THE FAO ELECTION

For me, 1987, the year following my reappointment was a period of great creativity and freedom of action (see the following chapter) in pursuit of my agenda to make WFP the exemplary UN operational agency. Though competition for the election of the FAO Director-General was the main focus for delegations during the year, generating much bitterness, I stayed on the sidelines, putting out of my mind to a large degree the consequences for the WFP/FAO relationship if Saouma was re-elected. Thus my diary says relatively little about the campaign.

However, I did have underlying fears that a new, major crisis in relations would erupt if Saouma gained a third term. Deep down I expected Saouma to win. I also felt grateful for his support for my initial appointment. Throughout my tenure I therefore resisted being the stalking horse for those wanting to get rid of Saouma. My disputes with him were about the proper running of WFP. While my actions in support of WFP had certainly weakened Saouma, that was not their purpose. So in 1987 I was able to speak favourably, and factually, in public about the current good relationship between WFP and FAO.

Australia supports Mensah

When Saouma aked me to help get Australia to support his re-election Canberra had not yet come to a decision. To maintain our good relationship I urged Canberra to make its announcement as late as possible and to avoid actively campaigning against Saouma and lobbying for Mensah. Saouma was counting on the possibility that Australia would run true to form and that ministerial and bureaucratic interests vested in FAO would triumph over those of the minister and Department of Foreign Affairs, as they did with some of the Europeans. His hopes were not entirely unwarranted. The Lebanese Ambassador in Canberra reported to him 'that all except International Organisations in Foreign Affairs gave him a good hearing'. Saouma's hopes reached a peak in February as my diary records:

Friday 27 February 1987

Saouma greeted me with great warmth to tell me of his private meeting with Kerin in which latter intimated that since Australia had invented two-terms ploy to get rid of M'Bow,[68] it would not be bound by it if there was not a good alternative to Saouma. Canadians are pressing Australia to come out for Mensah, citing Saouma's statements that he had Australian support!

Months before, in the FAO Council, Australia, much to my consternation, had caused a furore when it announced that it regarded the two-terms rule as applicable to FAO, hence Saouma's pleasure at what he believed Kerin had said to him. However, at the end of March, Saouma's hopes were effectively finished. I met him at a social function:

Wednesday 25 March 1987

Saouma barely greeted me so I guessed something was wrong. I decided to approach him...When I said I had something to tell him and took him aside the dam burst. With enormous indignation he said Lebanese Ambassador had seen Kerin who had said he did not see how he could support Saouma given his lack of support from other countries! Considered Kerin had deceived him. I said I knew nothing of this, that the decision had not yet been taken, that as previously advised his best course was to stave it off. I said that was what I was trying to do but that Canada was putting on a lot of pressure. He was mollified by this.

As it turned out the decision had been taken and Australia went on to play an active role in the campaign against Saouma's re-election.

The WFP logo

Before the decision was taken I took the opportunity of our good relations to get Saouma's agreement to a distinct logo for WFP.[69] On arrival in Rome

I was surprised to find that the WFP letterhead and CFA documentation showed both the UN and FAO logos. Even the tiniest UN agencies had their own logos which appeared on all publications, letterheads and documents. As with so many things, WFP in this was the exception. Though a small matter in itself, the lack of a logo reinforced the widely held perception that WFP was something less than a full-fledged organisation of the UN system, and instead a branch of FAO; and this contributed to the sense of a blurred identity among staff. I had a logo professionally designed, which was endorsed by senior staff. To set the occasion I invited Saouma to a private luncheon. My diary records our meeting:

Thursday 4 December 1986

> *Successful lunch of nearly three hours. Ushered me into his private lift, out of the building, rode in my car...A little tension at first—he has little small talk which doesn't help. Clearly wants also to put out of his mind our past relationship and simply look ahead. Very critical of West, saw him as cynical and ambitious as well as abrasive and said he had sacked him. Most of discussion was about his re-election. He is clearly worried but fairly confident. Says he wants to be re-elected without bitterness, could withdraw if he judged that not to be the case. I gave him the best advice I could about how to deal with Canberra...; and also sought to explain to him why he has lost support, to think back to how he had behaved ten years ago and seek to recapture it...He listened with enormous seriousness. He gave me all the explanations which he must give to those whose vote he seeks. A pretty convincing performance...sees racism at root of some of hostility to him. Contends that only he can get G77 to accept new reality (of budget reductions and staff cuts)...contends he is not a radical...I feel very pleased to be accepted at last and to be able to help him somewhat. I believe it could last beyond his re-election. Few people with real knowledge would speak to him so candidly. He accepted that I had nothing to gain from my candour. Finally, with some nervousness, I showed him new letterhead. After my long explanation he said: 'What do you want?' I said: 'Your consent to the logo'.[70] He agreed instantly saying, 'We should not let petty things intrude on our relationship'.*

A Revealing Proposal

When Saouma still had hopes of Australian support, he made a surprising and revealing proposal to me at a lunch at his home on 10 February.

The WFP Logo

Speaking of the burden of a third term, he threw out the idea that he would stand down after two years, that meanwhile I should become Deputy Director-General of FAO and that he would support me as his successor. The prospect of his standing down had been mooted and there is no doubt that a Saouma/Ingram ticket would have given his campaign a considerable boost. Indeed Mensah had been criticised by some of his supporters for not strengthening his appeal by announcing a running mate. I was taken aback by his proposal, did not encourage him to elaborate, treating it more or less as a passing thought rather than a considered idea. Neither he nor I ever again referred to the possibility.

From Saouma's perspective once Australia had thrown its weight behind Mensah, I was of much diminished use to him. He also suspected me of working behind the scenes against him. From this point on, until the election in November, I was of value only so long as relations between our two agencies were good since he knew that revived friction with WFP would weaken his electoral chances. His aim was to maintain a superficially good relationship, while making as few further concessions as possible.[71]

It was never easy to stick by my decision not to work actively against Saouma and I was under some pressure to do so from some who had given me strong support when I most needed it. Douglas Lindores, the Canadian delegate who had been so helpful in critical CFA meetings and who was now very active in Canada's campaign to get Mensah elected, was urging me to do what I could to unseat Saouma.

These opposing pressures were on my mind when I was approached by Rosemary Righter, who was consulting on a film about FAO being made by

Thames Television. The film was to focus on Saouma's performance during the Ethiopian famine[72] and was timed to come out close to the election. I agreed to meet Peter Gill, a journalist working on the script. Gill was the author of *A Year in the Death of Africa* (1986), a reasonably balanced account of the famine, which had placed a heavy work burden on WFP. After our meeting I commented in my diary:

Monday 12 October 1987

> *Gill impressed as a serious and open-minded person, and his show will be serious and reasonably fair...(it) can hardly influence the outcome but if Saouma wins, it will mean in the short run that his power is further clipped.*

Subsequently Gill and his TV team waylaid Saouma outside his home, which led Saouma to contest Gill's account of FAO's response to the 1984 famine. Saouma tackled me over my involvement in this and asked for my support in countering Gill. We were able to find a form of words that did not directly address the allegations but simply said the chronology of events did not support them. I doubted that Saouma's suspicions about my role were allayed.

In the event the film was not aired until after the election. I commented in my diary:

> *A real knife job, although none of the facts were wrong...altogether professional and convincing.*

Saouma re-elected

From the sidelines I could see that either the Saouma or Mensah camps had seriously misjudged the extent of the other's support. In the event, Saouma resoundingly defeated Mensah. As Saouma anticipated, the donors had not been united, with division between agriculture ministries that supported him and foreign ministries that did not.

According to my African informants, some 20 African (mainly francophone) representatives, whose governments had pledged support to Mensah, voted for Saouma. The use of a secret ballot meant that irrespective of their instructions delegates could vote otherwise with impunity. By all accounts, FAO staff made extraordinary efforts to influence votes and, according to some, 'money changed hands'. Be that as it may, it seems that Mensah gained no Latin American votes and few from Asia and the Pacific.

Some of Mensah's African supporters felt that the lack of support for him from these regions was due to racism.

Another factor may have been overkill by some Geneva Group members in Mensah's support and against Saouma, to the point of alienating some who were more easily convinced that Mensah was a stooge of the developed countries. I felt that a good candidate from a developed country, with a proven sympathy for third world aspirations, would have had a better chance of success. However, at the time the developed countries considered that their best chance of getting a Director-General to their taste was to encourage the 'right' candidate from a developing country to come forward and to throw their weight behind him. Mensah was seen as that candidate but even many Africans, among others, considered him too lightweight for the job, which may also have been a factor in the result.

My diary entry on the election day summed up my reaction:

9 November 1987

Saouma won by 94 to 59. He made a speech conciliatory in tone but gave no suggestion of any willingness to reform FAO. I went down for McDougall lecture and his report to Conference on work of FAO and was able to congratulate Saouma. He thanked me and said that our cooperation would continue as at present. At least war is not to be declared. Indeed his response was as I expected. How long the mood will last remains, however, to be seen.

10 November 1987

The Mensah debacle is simply a minor example of the disorder of the times: African unreliability, North-South resentments and lack of OECD cohesion. No doubt unavailability of a first-class candidate contributed, as well as Canadian overkill. Zejjari says he was...complimented by de la Taille[73] for having wanted Saouma to win so that I may succeed him!...Difficult night. Over the last year I have not thought much about situation following FAO election. But now the full burden of the past is upon me and hence a degree of weariness in facing future.

50   F Bradford Morse, a former member of the US House of Representatives, and a UN official since 1972. He was appointed Administrator of UNDP in 1976. I knew him from my time as Director of ADAB. He was a person of integrity and drive, representing all that was best in the UN system. His name recurs frequently in these diaries. He died shortly after nominating me for Brown University's Alan Shawn Feinstein World Hunger Award.

51   WHO and ILO were headed by the respected Dr Halfdan Mahler of Denmark and Francis Blanchard of France respectively. I knew Mahler before joining WFP. He was forthright and a voice of reason in ACC meetings.

52   I had made the same point to Timothy Raison the UK Minister for Overseas Development earlier that year: *Called on Raison. He gave a good hearing and seemed well informed on WFP/FAO relations. I urged UK to take role of leadership and that they should not be deterred by their relatively small contribution. If the sickness that afflicts the UN is to be overcome it will require (among other things) sustained attention at a high political level from the countries commanding respect.* (18 April 1984)

53   The fact that Mensah, though from a developing country, was seen as the candidate of the developed countries meant in practice that it was already too late for me to become a candidate, had I decided to take that path.

54   Keyes subsequently twice ran unsuccessfully for election to the United States Senate and was a candidate for the Republican Party's nomination for US President.

55   The actual language used in the submission signed by the Secretary of the Department of Foreign Affairs was: 'I have talked to Dr Dun about your concern that the switch of food aid from bilateral to multilateral mechanisms was associated with Ingram's original appointment. There is no doubt your reading of the situation is the right one. As Dun says, we bought him the job. As a result, the balance of expenditure between multilateral and bilateral food aid is not correct and the share of food grain going to WFP (now 50 per cent) should be reduced.'

56   The Bureau of the CFA consisted of the Chairman (Yusuf Hamdi of Egypt), the First Vice Chairman (R Martin of Belgium), the Second Vice Chairman (W Rahman of Bangladesh) and the Rapporteur(C Sersale of Argentina). Hamdi was competent and charming but cowed by Saouma. Egypt supported my reappointment and I ensured that Hamdi was so informed.

57   I subsequently received a letter from Bula Hoyos to that effect. Some time beforehand he had reversed his earlier hostility to me and was now fulsome in his praise for the Programme and my leadership.

58   R A Woolcott, Australian Ambassador to the United Nations.

59   Mohammed Zejjari was another highly competent WFP staff member of Moroccan nationality who served admirably as my *Chef de Cabinet* for several years.

60   Barbara Huddleston, an American citizen and senior FAO staff member. Fenwick was running the same line.

61   Member of Fenwick's staff and official of USAID.

62   John Kerin, Australian Minister for Primary Industry, and a consistent supporter. His department was responsible also for FAO matters.

63   Richard Lyng, US Secretary of Agriculture

64   Saouma used his power in relation to senior appointments to veto for a year all my efforts to fill this post at the then D2 level. He wanted the current American incumbent, who had reached retirement age, to be extended until the end of my first term. Ultimately, after the CFA had authorised the upgrading of the post and my reappointment had been decided, I was able at last to fill it definitively with an American.

65   FAO's Global Information and Early Warning System, which monitored the emergence of crop failure and other indicators of potential looming food emergencies. It was useful at a macro level but not for the assessment of needs at district and regional level.

66   John Glistrup, Denmark's Rome representative and a tower of support.

67   Ambassador E Pascarelli, Italian representative to FAO and Rome agencies.

68   Amadou-Mahtar M'bow, Director-General UNESCO.

69   Other important matters in respect of which I sought Saouma's agreement during 1987 are referred to in Chapter 11.

70   The logo has since been amended to place it within a laurel wreath as the UN's own logo is placed. I wanted to do this from the beginning but feared that if I did Saouma's jealousy of the United Nations would be aroused and he might object to any change.

71   Chapter 12 explains how superficial was the honeymoon of 1987.

72   To this end, an important sequence in the film was an interview with Stefan di Mistura, a former FAO employee whose principal

function, when he had been close to Saouma, had been to lobby developing countries. At that time, di Mistura appeared to WFP as the quintessential enemy, self-confident, charming, ruthless and very effective in implementing Saouma's instructions. Much to my astonishment, di Mistura approached me in great secrecy in February 1985 to advise that he was resigning from FAO over Saouma's refusal to allow him, at a most critical time, to continue his work in Ethiopia organising a vital air-lift of relief items to famine victims. (At his own request di Mistura had been temporarily assigned to Ethiopia for that purpose.) Di Mistura claimed that Saouma recalled him peremptorily, 'simply to show that he was boss', unable to see that he was motivated by 'a sense of service to developing countries'. I helped Di Mistura to get a post with UNICEF in the Sudan. He had an adventurous temperament and served the United Nations in other dangerous places. I found him to be an invaluable source of accurate information on Saouma's goals and modes of operation.

73　M de La Taille, a senior FAO staff member of French nationality and the FAO liaison officer with WFP for the preparation of our development projects.

9

INTERLUDE:
THE SECOND HONEYMOON

With a lull in the struggle for constitutional reform, in 1987 I was able to devote more time to our emergency operations in Africa and to other significant policy issues: human rights for Cambodian refugees; expansion of cooperation with UNHCR; improved support for long-term displaced people; monetisation of WFP commodities in support of the poor; and improved CFA examination of our proposals for new development projects.

Overall, nineteen eighty-seven was a welcome interlude in my attempt to modernise WFP's constitutional status. From my reappointment in October 1986 cooperation between WFP and FAO was good, as were my personal relations with Saouma. It was common for delegates to refer to the new harmony as our 'second honeymoon'. After all the turmoil and friction of the last years, they were almost as pleased as we were to see the return of peace. I felt liberated:

Friday 3 April 1987

The last working day of my first term. A sense of achievement to have completed it so successfully, notwithstanding Saouma's concerted attempt to have me discredited, sacked or resign. I will hope to end up the second term with the same esteem I now enjoy and with WFP in good shape for my successor: a well-known UN organisation functioning as such agencies should. But, hopefully, without the stress of that first term. I am now a free man, i.e. I can retire at any time of my

choice. But, as Odette realised when the CFA reappointed me, in public office one
is never truly free: there is a moral constraint between you and those who give
you their support. I hope Mensah succeeds because it is evident in FAO that the
old arrogance and aggressive nastiness still flourish.

AFRICAN EMERGENCIES

From the time of my first appointment I had tried hard to stimulate WFP to
a new level of creativity. The difference now was that I could speak out a
little more freely and act a little more boldly. Reading through my diary for
1987 a continuing heavy burden was managing WFP's response to new
crises in Africa. The great drought of 1983–4 had ended but the continent
was beset by new food emergencies set off by armed conflict in
Mozambique, Angola, Sudan and Ethiopia and by drought. That was not
surprising. Over the preceding quarter-century, food production in sub-
Saharan countries had not kept up with population growth, resulting in a
40 per cent shortfall by the mid-eighties (WFP 1988b).

WFP's central role in an improved international emergency effort was
now firmly established. We were responsible for massive internal logistical
operations in Chad, Ethiopia and Sudan. Donor governments, NGOs and
recipient governments were increasingly appreciative of the computerised
information system (INTERFAIS) we had established to provide
comprehensive information on food needs, food deliveries and pledges
which became fully operational in 1987.

INTERFAIS arose out of the work of our Ethiopian taskforce (see below)
whose ambit was later extended to encompass all affected African countries.
Another by-product was the integration of the management of emergency
operations with the management of development projects. That followed a
comprehensive external review of the secretariat by management
consultants, McKinsey and Co. At the time, WFP was the only UN system
agency to take what was seen as a bold, even revolutionary, step of inviting
in external reviewers and, moreover, to share their full report with the
governing body (WFP1986a).

Flowing from the McKinsey review I convened early in 1987 the first ever
meeting that brought together staff from all of our country offices and
headquarters. That it had never been done before reflected the 'them and us'
mentality which I hoped to overcome through the creation of the unified

service. I also continued to meet periodically with all our senior staff in each of the five geographical regions that were the basis of our operations, namely East and West Africa south of the Sahara, North Africa and the Middle East, Asia and Latin America. Travel to the countries we were assisting took up a lot of my time. I needed to see for myself how successful our operations were and build staff morale. A valuable part of these visits was to alert me to problems seen as serious by our field staff which headquarters had dealt with inadequately. Thus I visited West Africa for such a meeting in December 1984 and our missions in Senegal, the Gambia, Mali and Niger, including of course in the last named, Timbuktu. Much otherwise daunting up-country travel had many compensations. I retain enormous respect and affection for the African people. In any one year I usually visited several countries in Africa. For example in 1986/7 I went to Mozambique, Zimbabwe, Lesotho, Ivory Coast and Morocco.

My personal role in Africa's crisis was limited to strategic direction and problem solving. The hands-on work was done by our dedicated staff in Rome and in the affected countries. I use the word 'dedicated' deliberately. I was humbled by that dedication and by the risks to their personal safety that our staff ran. Over the years a significant number lost their lives or were wounded, a trend which has increased through the nineties. Paradoxically it is riskier to work for the UN as a civilian in emergencies sparked by conflict than as a soldier in a UN peace-keeping mission, though that is rarely acknowledged.

In October 1987 Eritreans fighting for independence from Ethiopia attacked one of our food convoys destroying 16 trucks and killing one driver. By this date WFP was managing a massive trucking operation on behalf of the donor community in Ethiopia (see BOX 1). During 1987 we began a convoy system for the transport of food from Kenya into the southern Sudanese provinces, the theatre of the ongoing civil war. We expanded our coastal shipping service in Mozambique and mounted another complex logistical mission to reach refugees and drought victims in landlocked Malawi. Paradoxically in the light of today's desperate food situation in Zimbabwe, during the seventies and eighties that country was the source of much of our food aid. Indeed WFP was Zimbabwe's single biggest customer in many years of those decades.

Our logistical operations in Ethiopia and in Sudan gave rise to many difficult issues over the years between ourselves, donor governments and the governments of the countries whose peoples we were assisting, similar to those associated with the Darfur crisis of 2005. The difference is that today the concept and practice of humanitarian intervention by the international community has developed considerably since the end of the Cold War. Very often it was necessary for me to negotiate directly with the parties, including visits to the countries affected. (For examples see below and Chapter 13.)

Recognition for WFP sometimes came in unusual ways. Thus, we were gratified when the World Bank gave us an untied grant of $5 million to assist our logistical efforts. That was the first time the Bank had done this with any UN agency.

In major complex emergencies many other UN agencies and NGOs become involved with the result that difficult issues of coordination arise. In the nineteen eighties special arrangements were necessary for each emergency. I have been given credit for joining with UNICEF's Executive Director, James Grant, to persuade the Secretary-General in 1984 to bypass the usual bureaucratic processes and establish a special office in Ethiopia for emergency operations that would oversee and coordinate the work of the many organisations concerned with famine relief (Jansson 1987).

The success of that operation under the respected Kurt Jansson[74] led to the establishment in New York of the Office for Emergency Operations in Africa (OEOA) to coordinate the UN system response to the whole African emergency. OEOA was headed by Bradford Morse, the Administrator of UNDP, whose organisation had been less than enthusiastic about the decision to appoint Jansson, arguing it was the function of UNDP's country representatives to coordinate UN system operations. Although food aid was at the heart of the international response and was being coordinated, to everyone's satisfaction, by WFP through INTERFAIS, I made a point of giving unreserved support to OEOA, including by seconding an officer experienced in emergencies and by personally promoting the leadership efforts of Morse and his deputy, Maurice Strong. The OEOA was an advance on previous UN efforts to improve coordination. However, I had reservations about its overall worth.

To quote from my diary for Monday, 26 January 1987:

> *it helped marginally in relation to our coordination effort but we did not do anything we otherwise would not have done; it raised some money for us; it*

gave a good image to UN effort particularly in US for which it took the credit (but nicely). On reflection, it probably helped by being a spur to more intensive WFP activity...

Like every other aid agency, WFP had been slow to recognise the depth of Ethiopia's crisis (Fraser 1998). The reason lay in the fact that every year since 1976, the Relief and Rehabilitation Commission (RRC) in Ethiopia had inflated the figures, reporting that millions of people needed assistance and thereby eroding its credibility with donors. In WFP's case, we had provided food routinely, but in quantities well short of the amount requested. I still remember well my shock when Trevor Page, head of our emergencies service, came to me in May 1984 to describe the truly alarming situation Ethiopia faced. In order to ensure that we acted with appropriate cohesion and urgency I set up a taskforce to meet regularly to monitor our response and report to me on progress.

This experience confirmed my concern that we were unable to assess accurately how much food aid Ethiopia (and others) needed and strengthened my conviction that the system must be reformed.

Page prepared a submission recommending the provision of 26,000 tons of food, which I sent to Saouma early in June. By contrast with his customary practice, Saouma delayed approval for nearly three weeks. The reason for the delay is described by RRC Commissioner, Dawit Wolde Giorgis, in his history of the famine (1989, p 154) and by Peter Gill (1986). Dawit writes that when he called on Saouma to urge immediate approval, 'before I could finish, he [Saouma] cut me off and warned me in a most imperious tone...unless this man (he indicated Tessemma, sitting next to me) were removed from his post...he would not decide anything regarding Ethiopia'. Tessemma was Ethiopia's representative at FAO. Saouma told the Commissioner that he was 'conspiring with the WFP and with other African representatives to defame him'. Once back in Addis, Dawit's superiors decided that Ethiopia could not afford to fight Saouma. Accordingly, Dawit writes, 'I wired Saouma informing him of this decision [to remove Tessemma], and he wired me back the same day approving the emergency allocation'.[75] At WFP we were aware of what was going on. This incident, more than any other, confirmed me in my view that the WFP emergency approval procedures must change.

Box 1: WFP in 1987

❏ For the second consecutive year record quantities of food were shipped: over 2.1 million tons.
❏ Shipments to development projects were also a record: 1.53 million tons.
❏ Food purchases were a record 611,000 tons. Three–quarters were bought from developing countries.
❏ Emergency food deliveries were also a record at almost 900,000 tons.
❏ Some 711,000 tons of food were bought and/or delivered on a fee for service basis for individual donors.
❏ Twenty–one development on–going and completed projects were evaluated to assess their success and articulate lessons for incorporation in the design of new projects.
❏ CFA approved 39 new projects valued at $532 million. Over half were for least developed countries. Regional shares were: Sub–Saharan Africa 37%; Asia & Pacific 33%; Latin America & Caribbean 18%; and North Africa & Near East 13%.
❏ Just over half of new projects were in support of the development of human resources.
❏ Policy principles and operational guidelines to ensure greater and more systematic attention to the role of women were approved by the CFA.

UNBRO—A DIFFICULT DECISION

In 1987 we were still managing the United Nations Border Relief Operation (UNBRO) but I was becoming more and more uneasy about our role and decided that year to relinquish it, though continuing to manage the supply of food to the Kampucheans. I made several visits to the border camps and attended several donor meetings in New York. I came to see that WFP's so-called lead agency role had little substance. We had no say in relation to policy or even operations, other than responsibility for accounting for the resources provided by the donors. Policy was in the hands of the UN Special Representative for Coordinating Kampuchean Humanitarian Assistance and his representative in Bangkok. As with every WFP country operation the UNDP representative was the titular head of UNBRO, although the staff on the ground was WFP staff.

Consistent with my policy of critical review of our performance, begun during the great African drought and used to encapsulate lessons to improve future emergency management (WFP 1986b), in 1986 I commissioned Oxford University's Refugee Studies Programme to evaluate our work. An issue that had been bothering me was the unwillingness of the

Thais to agree to higher education of the Khmer children confined to the border camps. This denial of education compounded the denial of the formal status of refugee and the rights, however slender, conferred by that status. Unfortunately UNHCR, under pressure from Thailand, had been complicit in this situation, so undermining its credibility as an apolitical humanitarian institution.

The evaluation revealed a shocking abuse of human rights. I knew it would be impossible for me to submit such a politically charged document to the CFA on my own authority in view of the fact that responsibility rested with the Secretary-General's Special Representative, not WFP. I therefore sought clarification from the Secretary-General of WFP's responsibilities as 'lead agency'. I was told that New York had neither the time, the inclination nor the intellectual capability to work through the issues. The reality was that, compared with the foreign office of a medium-sized power like Australia, the Secretary-General made do with just a handful of staff and little formal capacity to analyse issues. Policy was made on the run. This suited major governments, who preferred a weak Secretary-General lacking the resources to challenge their appraisals. Accordingly, I passed decision-making to the Special Representative and sought permission to withdraw WFP from its nominal lead role. That was a difficult decision to make. I knew it was likely to be misinterpreted and it was, with me being said to have created a crisis over the evaluation in order to obtain full control of UNBRO! The UN system is highly competitive and all proposals for rationalisation of responsibilities between agencies are thought to be about personal and institutional power. That was a thought far from my mind. WFP lacked the staff with the experience to fulfil such a political role.

COOPERATION WITH UNHCR

The heavy, increasing involvement of WFP in emergency assistance during the eighties reinforced my initial view that WFP's long-term future would depend on it becoming an indispensable actor in the international response to emergencies. As I explain later in this chapter, WFP-style development projects had an uncertain future. On the other hand, the logistical expertise of WFP could become the foundation of an integrated UN logistical capability, replacing the fragmented UN system whereby each agency involved in a disaster response did its own deliveries, including of food in some instances. Bilateral donors recognised our abilities, sometimes using the Programme on a fee-for-service basis to make deliveries on their behalf.

I was especially concerned that donors provided food for refugees through UNHCR and WFP, some mainly or even exclusively through the former. In part this was due to inertia. While criticising the UN system for its poor coordination, donors themselves were unable to overcome their own fragmented policies. The European Commission was a particular offender. Some sense of the complexity of WFP's relationship with the Commission comes through in my diary:

Tuesday 24 February 1987

> *Successful visit to Brussels. We had been urged by Dutch (and Danes) to get closer to Commission and I believe approach I took, namely to concentrate on the development of a cooperative relationship with a fellow food/development agency rather than on their contribution to WFP, paid off. Commissioner Natali agreed to this and certain practical steps to follow. They are very interested in fuller participation in CFA and I said I would explore whether they could be treated as if they were members. Raised issue of their contribution to UNHCR which exceeds theirs to IEFR! While they don't want to be drawn into a WFP/UNHCR conflict they recognise the logic and cost-effectiveness of supply direct to us.*

I made the same argument with other donors, but rather than risking conflict with UNHCR my goal was to win their co-operation. To that end we negotiated a Memorandum of Understanding (MOU) with it in 1985. I developed a strong personal relationship with each High Commissioner. Following a meeting with the then incumbent in June 1987, I commented in my diary: 'They are very pleased that...[WFP] recognises their primary role in food needs assessment, given UNHCR's ultimate responsibility for refugee welfare. In the end I believe we will handle all refugee food aid.' That prediction was realised a few months later:

Thursday 20 August 1986

> *...we have reached agreement [with UNHCR] for WFP to assume responsibility for supplying food in Iran, Pakistan and Somalia. European Community, FRG and Switzerland will transfer their pledges to WFP. This will*

lead to a more efficient operation although no cash gain for WFP. However, I want to consolidate our position as provider of food aid in UN system.

Since those first agreements WFP/UNHCR collaboration has continued and strengthened, the modalities of cooperation being embodied in successive memoranda of understanding.

Protracted Refugee Operations

Strong relations with UNHCR were a prerequisite to a major innovation in the refugee sustenance regime. While not approved until 1989, the issues at stake were of growing concern through 1987, and it was then that I found a solution. Although millions of Afghan refugees stayed in Pakistan for many years, first until the overthrow of the Najibullah regime in 1992 and then of the Taliban in 2001, procedurally, the WFP approval arrangements for sudden emergencies had to be applied. This meant that the Director-General's approval had to be obtained for each tranche of assistance. By 1987 WFP support for the Afghans was in excess of two thirds of resources devoted on average each year to emergency relief. The changes I proposed were approved by CFA27 (May 1989). Their essence was the creation of a new category of assistance, called protracted refugee/displaced person operations (PRO), as a subset of regular resources. Except for operations costing less than $1.5 million, authority for which was delegated to the Executive Director, it was the CFA itself which made decisions on PRO allocations. This, it was hoped, would encourage donors to put more resources through the Programme. It was also decided that $30 million of cash would be available annually from regular resources over and above the pledges by donors to the PRO account. The new arrangements enabled the provision of nutritionally better and more appropriate food baskets and smoother delivery.

Sudden disasters continued to be met from the IEFR, plus $15 million in cash annually from regular resources. Though the changes were resource neutral in their impact on the funding of sudden disasters, they transferred much previous decision-making away from the FAO Director-General and increased the importance of the WFP in the eyes of affected countries, as well as donors. FAO fought against the change but unconvincingly in the eyes of the developing countries, which took into account its statements over many years warning that support for refugees was diminishing the resources available for crop emergencies.

The new arrangements quickly proved their worth. They continue to be used by WFP. They brought immediate benefits for the refugees by facilitating more timely flows of food to them. Moreover, WFP became a full partner with UNHCR in the search for solutions to protracted refugee situations.[76]

During my time the most important were the millions of Afghan refugees on the Pakistan border. I visited Kabul at winter's end in March 1990 with the late Prince Sadruddin Aga Khan, the Secretary-General's envoy on this subject, and the High Commissioner for Refugees, Thorvald Stoltenberg. The communist Najibullah-led government was to collapse in 1992. At the time of our visit, the aim of which was to persuade the government to support our proposals for the return of refugees, Kabul was besieged by the Mujaheddin. Getting into the fog-shrouded airport, surrounded by high mountains, without air traffic control and susceptible to the occasional missile, was hair-raising enough but the atmosphere once there was surreal. There was an eerie quiet in the heavily damaged city, its population nowhere to be seen. Najibullah occupied a tiny office able to be heated in the intense cold. The former head of the dreaded secret police came across as a quiet, deliberately spoken person. Negotiations with his ministers took place in grand rooms in which we all huddled in our overcoats. Our subsequent press conference, accompanied by the noise of the occasional explosion in the distance, was discomfiting. An atmosphere of tragedy enveloped the city. In fact the negotiations, which had been undertaken because of donor pressure, had no prospect of a successful outcome being premature in view of the state of armed conflict between the Mujaheddin and the government.

STRUCTURAL ADJUSTMENT

One important attempt at innovation in my 'year of freedom' was not fully successful. I was unable to get the CFA to see that WFP had the potential, through increased monetisation of commodities, to assist the poorest countries of Africa to ease the burden on their people resulting from structural adjustments to their economies. We had laid the ground for this by winning recognition from the World Bank that WFP had the potential to be a peer and a useful partner in structural adjustment. The issues raised were technically very complex (WFP 1987a,b,c). They were considered by the CFA at its two sessions in 1987. Our papers, prepared in cooperation with the Bank were imaginative and, if implemented, would have enabled WFP to make a more profound contribution to development than did many of our small-scale projects of direct food distribution to beneficiaries in poor, sparsely populated countries. These projects, though directed to laudable social objectives, benefited few and were costly to implement.

Our efforts foundered for reasons unconnected with their merits. The main donors simply did not want a multilateral agency selling food into markets, except under the tightest of conditions which effectively limited the scope to innovate. Dislike of structural adjustment and of the IMF and World Bank coloured the view of developing countries and vocal NGOs. Not fully comprehending the intellectual foundations of the envisaged approach but fearing that they were being hoodwinked, they preferred to see no major change in existing policy. FAO also mounted a whispering campaign that the reforms would make *the WFP Executive Director the most powerful man in UN system*, as I recorded in my diary. I learned the hard way that the path of the radical reformer was as difficult on substance as it was for constitutional change in the UN system. A few extracts from my diary give a sense of the factors at work.

Tuesday 26 May 1987

> *Dinner with Lindores. I became rather annoyed at his putting me in dock by questioning my intentions in regard to structural adjustment and monetisation. He overlooked my having postponed issue for a year at his request, my repeated assurances we were not seeking a fundamental change in WFP and fully recognised that we could not operate in framework other than that established by World Bank...Fortunately, he appeared to accept some role in monetisation for WFP in structural adjustment context. Told him I wanted guidelines to encompass small island countries[77] and support for agricultural research and extension.*

Friday 29 May 1987

> *Intervened dramatically at end of structural adjustment debate to express our disappointment at timidity of donors in appreciating importance of issue for developing countries and...their failure to come to grips with how to use food*

aid to help poor as compensation for burden of structural adjustment. On monetisation guidelines we were criticised for putting them forward, yet in the past we have many times been criticised for being ineffective managers of generated funds. If the guidelines had not been presented now, at the next session we would have been told that we had no guidelines for management of funds. Whole problem is that US, Canada and EC do not bring an open mind to the issue of WFP's involvement, nor do they have any sense of vision in relation to importance of issue. My intervention was deliberately passionate…I wanted the developing countries to know that I felt as strongly about issues of concern to them, i.e. adverse impact on the poor of structural adjustment as I did about my budget, and to destroy any sense they may have that the price of my reappointment was a sell-out to the donors. Whether I succeeded I do not know but I certainly infuriated Lindores, who intervened to take exception to Chairman's summary which he regarded as slanted in direction of WFP's involvement in monetisation in support of structural adjustment. Not really true, but understandable given gulf between his desire for no monetisation and my insistence on some if WFP is to be relevant. This matter will probably be impossible to resolve without some serious friction with US and Canada. I doubt that my intervention will have helped to get a smoothly arrived-at consensus, although I suspect that that is impossible. It is clear from yesterday's debate that I have not succeeded in making CFA a serious forum for developing global policy on food aid. Yet there is no other.

Monday 1 June 1987

There seems to be a real concern among some delegates of developing countries that I am seeking to make WFP like the World Bank with aid subject to conditionality, like Bank structural adjustment lending. In effect, the developing countries and developed will find themselves in agreement, although for different reasons, in denying WFP power to provide general balance-of-payments support to countries embracing comprehensive structural reforms. I have decided report should be drafted innocuously and to say little.

Tuesday 2 June 1987

Was very pleased when Lindores came to say goodbye and told me that he now understood what I was driving at in structural adjustment. Considered Canada could not take initiative on its own but could perhaps do so jointly with others—which, of course, is the point since main food donors must act in concert…Said he saw it as a possible [G7] summit initiative. However, problems exist with developing countries. Nicaragua raised issue with me and I explained that developing countries don't understand the issues and the developed countries oppose our proposal.

Wednesday, 30 September 1987

Meeting with...USAID Acting Head of Food-for-Peace. Intelligent, energetic and well-disposed to WFP. However, I found an extraordinary misreading of our latest monetisation proposals—we are seen as too clever by half! Much of this suspicion goes back to Fenwick (and to Block). Believe I succeeded in stilling their doubts and also at subsequent meetings with Agriculture. Generally, staff in neither organisation dealing with food aid is up to the job.

Thursday 1 October 1987

Called on Jaycox (World Bank Vice President for Africa) at his invitation. They see a necessity of doing more to mitigate impact of structural adjustment on poor and us as very important in this context. Gratified to find [World Bank President] Conable's speech to opening session singles out WFP for cooperation—no other organisation is mentioned in speech!

Our efforts were not entirely wasted. In the UN system it is rare for secretariat proposals to be rejected in total. Thus at its 24th session a few days later the CFA adopted our heavily revised recommendation for changes in monetisation policy. These marginally enhanced our capability to assist targeted groups of the poorest people through the sale of food (WFP 1987d). Face had been saved but in truth I had suffered my only significant set-back in the CFA.

Cooperation with the World Bank (and IFAD and the African Development Bank) did not end. In 1991 we distributed a joint study (World Bank and WFP 1991) on the most appropriate uses of food aid in Africa but it too led to little change. Within the Bank there was at best only half-hearted acceptance of project food aid as a useful form of aid. And I had reached the conclusion that the tremendous ambivalence among governments about WFP's and the CFA's proper roles in relation to household, national and global food security still endured, despite all our efforts to persuade them to the contrary. In my last full address to the CFA, while maintaining an up-beat tone, I spoke more frankly than ever before about the challenges facing WFP in this regard (WFP 1991). In reality I had long decided that WFP's most certain future was to consolidate its position at the centre of the UN system's response to emergencies, which in fact has happened in the years since my departure.

Today WFP's role in development is very much smaller than in my time, when it reached its peak (Appendix II, Table 1). Though we made progress in improving the underlying rationale for our own projects and their evaluation, even in this area we were unable to convince governments that food aid for development needed to be taken as seriously as other aid categories. Despite all the evidence from our evaluations and other studies we had difficulty in convincing governments that food assistance worked best to achieve social rather than economic goals, as for example in school feeding. The justification for food aid as a resource to increase agricultural production was deeply entrenched at the time in the culture of developed and developing countries in Rome, especially the latter. Paradoxically, school feeding is today relatively much more important in the portfolio of WFP's vastly diminished development activities.

I was also unable to fulfil my ambition to make WFP a major actor in the formulation of global food aid policies, for example in multilateral trade negotiations. Consideration of such issues was dispersed through several committees inside and outside the UN system. One reason for this was that I never gained a sufficient number of appropriately qualified staff. In the face of FAO opposition and the climate of the times I had no alternative to focusing my requests for additional budgetary resources on posts for our operations. This meant we had to rely upon the occasional outside consultant to augment our tiny policy group and this was not always successful. For example, my attempt to produce an annual analytical report on food aid and its problems, along the lines of UNICEF's State of the World's Children and UNDP's World Development Report, using a consultant, was a failure.

REFORMING PROJECT APPROVAL PROCEDURES

When Australia came out early in 1987 firmly in support of Mensah to become FAO Director-General warmth quickly drained from the FAO/WFP relationship. FAO's behaviour in regard to two issues suggested that, after re-election, Saouma would resume his implacable opposition to my efforts to further strengthen the Programme. The first was reform of procedures for approval of WFP development projects, which is dealt with in this chapter. The much more important matter, the negotiation of a headquarters agreement with Italy and its provision of a headquarters building for the Programme, is the subject of the following chapter.

When I arrived, the CFA was disappointing as a policy body; and even its consideration of projects was largely ritualistic, although project approval was its most substantive function. The average size of projects was well in excess of $10 million and some were many times larger in very poor countries like Bangladesh and Ethiopia, whose economies and social structures lent themselves to project food aid.

The representatives of developing countries, influenced by the FAO culture of secretariat partiality for their interests, took it as an article of faith that the projects presented by the secretariat should be approved with minimal or, preferably, no change. They were deeply suspicious that 'technical' reservations raised by donor representatives were driven by hidden agendas. Indeed, since the donors, led by the United States, reserved their most cogent analyses of, and questions about, projects for governments close to the 'socialist camp' it was understandable that the developing countries were so suspicious. Moreover, their CFA representatives were usually from their Rome delegations, drawn from agriculture ministries, understandably with little knowledge of, or liking for, food aid. Most received no briefing from their governments and were unequipped to make more than generalised interventions. Even the main donors' questions were usually not very searching and often derived from the reviews of projects undertaken by our own highly professional evaluation service.

In the changed climate of UN reform of the mid-eighties the donors, especially the United States, frequently complained to me about the low level of CFA project examination. Though I shared that concern I was as disappointed by the even lower level of policy consideration and by the inordinate demands placed on our over-extended staff by two relatively long CFA sessions each year, requiring simultaneous meetings of the committee and its sub-committees. Though I had little confidence that useful changes could be agreed in the Roman culture, I decided to take the initiative.

Accordingly, at CFA22 in the autumn of 1986 I informed the CFA that I proposed to seek the advice of eight current and former CFA representatives meeting in their personal capacities, under the chairmanship of the current CFA chairman, Dr Yusuf Hamdi of Egypt, to consider and make recommendations to the CFA on improving its methods of work. We called this the G8.

I did not consult Saouma beforehand because I considered that under the Basic Documents this was a function clearly assigned to the Executive Director. Moreover, it would probably be regarded as an unhelpful precedent by the FAO secretariat which had no desire to weaken its control over FAO deliberative bodies.

In consulting the CFA, I also proposed that the participants be selected by me in conjunction with Yusuf Hamdi rather than by the committee itself. I feared that if the committee was asked to do so, in all probability it would argue interminably about whether there should be such an examination, the terms of reference; how large the group should be, who should be on it; and so on. Quite possibly, nothing would ever be agreed. Procedural discussions are always the liveliest in UN committees, since no expert knowledge is required, everyone has an opinion of equal value and opportunities for mischief abound.

Hamdi and I chose a group comprised of four each of the most influential delegates from developed and developing countries. It held two sessions in 1987 and I submitted its report and recommendations to CFA24 in October of that year. Discussions were constructive and useful, though unduly complex reforms were devised. As I recorded in my diary:

> *a most pleasant and successful experiment which I will seek to apply to other important and potentially contentious issues. However, I remain sceptical that CFA will agree to any change.*

That scepticism turned out to be well founded. The CFA was to meet just before the FAO Conference elected its Director-General. The lobbying of pro- and anti-Saouma factions had not improved the already febrile atmosphere of the house. I was aware that the delegates of Brazil and Saudi Arabia, strong supporters of Saouma, were hostile to the group's proposals. However, I knew also that the Secretary-General, in his message to the CFA, intended to commend my initiative as an example of what should be done in other UN bodies. For his part, the Director-General had sent a cleverly worded endorsement of the proposals as suitable for a 'brief, initial experiment'. We knew FAO lobbyists were arguing my initiative was part of a sinister process to create a precedent for reform of FAO. I took this to mean that, after Saouma's re-election, pressure would quickly mount to discontinue the experiment. My diary continues:

Friday 23 October 1987

Saudi Arabia, Congo and Brazil attacked the proposals, but reasonably temperately. They requested, as expected, that decision be held over until next session. However, after lunch atmosphere deteriorated with particularly scurrilous intervention by India who suggested that I had acted improperly in convening working group, or even addressing the issue at all. I was fed up and for the first time intervened during a debate to give the lie to Indian allegations by showing that the CFA was kept fully informed. This subsequently led to an apology by India and nice statements from Bangladesh, Colombia and Brazil. I had to receive El Salvador President Duarte at 6pm and matter was left over until next week. Not only would it be foolish to push the matter to decision, but I feel the proposals may be dead. I am not sure I really like them: unnecessarily complex in terms of goals actually attainable, as distinct from illusions of some donors.

Tuesday 27 October 1987

Procedures debate concluded fairly smoothly after hard-hitting responses from Hamdi and me. Opposition were fairly gracious, except for India[78] and Argentina which objected to my statement that FAO Legal Committee had no standing. My proposal to return paper with one or two options plus my own recommendation was accepted. I am not too displeased with outcome...As usual US behaved extremely weakly in drafting committee.

I presented my recommendations to CFA25 in June 1988, the year after Saouma's re-election. These were that the projects sub-committee (SCP) would meet immediately before the spring and autumn CFA sessions; and only the spring session would consider policy papers. The latter innovation considerably reduced the burden on our policy people. Substantively, the most important innovation, which proved a great success, was to invite officials responsible for project design and implementation in the recipient country to attend the sub-committee's meetings at the Programme's expense. While these were useful advances, an equally important goal was to establish the conditions that would enable SCP discussions to take place in an atmosphere conducive to a true exchange of views. Under the practice that I inherited the SCP met in a main FAO committee room open to anyone, with never less than about 100 or more delegates, WFP and FAO staff and others observing the proceedings. In such a formal atmosphere delegates' tendency to make declarative speeches was reinforced. Any sort of give and take was impossible. So that a meeting could take place around a table in a more intimate venue it was necessary somehow to limit the numbers present. If that was done it should also be feasible for the SCP to meet elsewhere than at FAO's main headquarters building, preferably at F Building where our offices were located, assuming always that we could create a suitable venue there.

In the event, delegations did agree to limit themselves to two persons present at any one time and to exclude observers unless invited by the SCP itself. However, that result was not achieved without unnecessary fireworks:

Wednesday 1 June 1988

Debate on CFA Methods of Work began. Brazil made a very aggressive statement attacking exclusion of observers and limitation on size of delegations. While in line with his instructions on substance, his pushing to forefront was not. New Pakistani attacked whole concept in detailed speech—hard to believe he wrote it himself. Good support from other delegations but tepid from Madagascar over observers. Ethiopia good. Meeting adjourned after China, which was very forthright in support, spoke. At my reception I blasted Pakistan and tackled Cape Verde, saying I was not going to put up with FAO interference as experienced for last six years. India looked thoughtful and Argentina assured me that their support for Brazil would be low key and pro forma.

Thursday 2 June 1988

When debate resumed next morning it was clear that our pressure had had good effect. India, Cape Verde and Argentina were very circumspect so that Brazil was in fact isolated. Despite all the fuss about observers, only observer to intervene in support of Brazil was Mexico. I gave a generous thank you speech which I learned later was well received and contrasted with Chairman's rather painful summing up. Brazil contested this which only served to underline the extent of his pique. All this going on with Jamaican Prime Minister Seaga on platform waiting to address committee! At Italian reception

Cuban Ambassador told me that Saouma had personally asked him why he did not support Brazil, Mexico, and Costa Rica. He explained that our proposals were in interest of developing countries. Thus, no longer speculation about Saouma's hand in all this. Sweden was clearly told that Saouma did not want any meeting at F Building, which of course is what we will now manage; but first a meeting room.

At building F we had only two small rooms in which to hold staff meetings and nothing remotely big enough to have even an informal meeting with CFA members. However, with the downsizing of FAO staff on account of the austerities being enforced by the developed countries, we had been given additional space in F Building, sufficient to construct a meeting room able to seat about 40 around a long table and to provide the booths needed for simultaneous translation. Behind those at the table was room for one additional member from each delegation and essential secretariat staff. Though very much second best as a conference room it was just big enough to house the SCP and certainly intimate enough to enable discussion instead of speech making. It was not big enough to accommodate observers who, our opponents in the CFA were arguing had the right to observe the SCP. In fact, there were endless UN precedents of meetings being closed to all but invitees. However, it was the only justification open to those trying to block our reform.

As well as hosting the SCP, the room would provide a sorely needed venue to hold informal meetings with delegates to brief them, for example, on issues coming up at CFA meetings or on our work in dealing with ongoing food emergencies. All meeting rooms at FAO headquarters were so wired that proceedings could be listened to by top FAO staff in the privacy of their offices. Since anything I said could be used against me, or against any delegate who departed from the FAO party line, I had made only limited use of FAO rooms for informal meetings. It was simply impossible to hold anything remotely like a genuine exchange of views in them.

Before CFA25 I had informed the Netherlands of my hopes and suggested they might wish to fund the construction of the projected meeting room, which we would call the Boerma Room in honour of the first Executive Director, a Dutch national and Saouma's predecessor as Director-General of FAO.

Even for something as relatively trivial as setting up a small committee room, FAO used every device available to thwart successful completion to the point of providing misleading information to Ambassador Fenwick's successor in order to get him to put pressure on us, which he duly did in a quite ignorant and bullying way.

The Netherlands met the cost and the project was completed literally on the last working day before the Boerma room was to be used for the first SCP meeting. To my intense relief the room was a success and the observers' issue defused itself, as no observers turned up. While physically well short of ideal the room served its purpose. I got the strong impression that developing countries were pleased to be able to hold meetings with WFP away from FAO headquarters. Discussions were always civil and relatively relaxed. All in all we had chalked up a minor but worthwhile reform.

---

[74] Jansson was Head of the UN Relief Operation in Ethiopia from December 1984 to January 1986. He had recently retired from the UN Secretariat which he joined in 1952. He had administered UN programmes in the Lebanon, Pakistan, Nigeria and Kampuchea.

[75] I was pleased to appoint Tessemma to WFP as I did later the Cameroon Representative, Ngongi Namanga, whose recall Saouma also successfully insisted upon. Under my successor, Namanga became WFP's Deputy Executive Director and later the UN representative in the Congo.

[76] WFP's emergence as an important player in support of refugees led Oxford University to invite me to give the third Joyce Pearce Memorial Lecture (Ingram 1989).

[77] Experience with ADAB had made me aware of the development handicaps faced by the island states of the South Pacific. In their circumstances monetisation of our food made more sense than direct distribution.

[78] In March of the following year the Bangladesh Ambassador told me that after the debate Saouma, forgetting the Ambassador was a member of the G8 that had devised the new procedure, said to him, *What a marvellous job India did in opposing Ingram's proposals.*

10

DOES WFP REALLY EXIST?

Parallel to the struggle to reform the WFP constitution was our effort to obtain a separate headquarters for WFP. Member states were in favour and the Italian Government was willing to provide the accommodation, subject to the conclusion of an appropriate headquarters agreement. FAO, which had overcharged us for the accommodation it provided, acted in transparently bad faith over many years of negotiations with Italy and in defiance of the clearly stated views of governments.

The problems created by the absence of a meeting room at our place of business and the effort by FAO to block construction of the Boerma Room underlined for me the need to bring to finality our now ongoing efforts to obtain an independent headquarters for the Programme.

THE RENT SAGA

The WFP General Regulations established the secretariat at 'FAO Headquarters'. When I took up my post in 1982, FAO had expanded beyond the site provided by Italy and was renting premises elsewhere in the city, including 'F Building', located about five kilometres from that original FAO site. The WFP secretariat, along with some FAO staff, was accommodated in F Building. WFP had no entry in the Rome telephone directory, with all telephone calls being routed through the FAO switchboard. Thus it was not unusual for visitors to Rome to have difficulty contacting us. Visitors who did finally getting through to us would ask facetiously, 'Does WFP really exist?'.

The lack of an address and telephone number reinforced the perception that WFP was a division of FAO with no independent identity. That contributed to the low self esteem I had found among staff.

Moreover, our office space was overcrowded. The structure and layout of F Building were inimical to modern management. The eight or so floors occupied by WFP were divided up into small rooms with brick partitions making efficient deployment of staff impossible without expensive alterations. While improving our accommodation was initially not a high priority for me, it became so when we were forced to rent additional space in another commercial building and so split our relatively small secretariat.

As I looked into the history of our accommodation I found that FAO had cheated the Programme of its fair share of the subvention paid by Italy to FAO to compensate for the organisation's expenditure on rental of outside premises. Further, it emerged that FAO was overcharging us for the space we occupied using a formula that was inequitable even if Italy had not been subsidising FAO! In short, we suffered under a double financial disability.

FAO went to extraordinary lengths to deny there was a legitimate issue about property and to block every attempt to resolve it. Dishonesty and intransigence were ultimately their undoing. Though the rent saga was played out over seven years, the end result was that FAO eventually had to negotiate and sign with Italy a headquarters agreement for WFP. This provided the legal underpinning for an entirely separate WFP headquarters building. Today, WFP is accommodated in a splendid building of its own, provided by Italy, fitted out to contemporary standards and with its own spacious chamber for meetings of its governing body.

FAO fought so tenaciously for several reasons. First, the FAO culture was never ever to admit to a mistake, in this case the inflated rent it charged us. More importantly, such an agreement would put a visible seal on the Programme's distinctive identity as a separate organisation with legal capacity to contract, acquire and dispose of property and be a party to judicial proceedings. The fact that the agreement placed the WFP Executive Director on the same level under Italian diplomatic protocol as the heads of FAO and IFAD was also a bitter pill. Such recognition would make it much harder for FAO to maintain its position that the Executive Director must do as the Director-General directed, for example in relation to the FAO accounts. Finally our accommodation at FAO headquarters gave FAO an important tactical advantage. Many of our political difficulties with key delegates from developing countries arose from the fact that the CFA met in FAO committee rooms with the result that the FAO secretariat had easy access to delegates at all times during meetings and could plan their lobbying efforts from the privacy of their offices. This was made all the easier because FAO provided accommodation at its headquarters for the G77, the caucus of developing countries that at this date numbered well in excess of 100 delegations.

The story of how WFP got its own address deserves telling for its own sake and because it shows up acutely the weakness of the checks and balances on the powers of the heads of UN specialised agencies. There is nothing in the present circumstance of the UN system to prevent a repetition of similar abuses of power today.

I knew that governments competed strongly for the honour of hosting headquarters of system agencies. It was quite anomalous that WFP was the exception. Shortly before my appointment I had, as Australian Deputy Governor of IFAD, participated in a vote which confirmed that Rome would remain that organisation's home, despite strong competition from other countries. Even though IFAD was already accommodated in impressive temporary headquarters, to secure a favourable vote the Italian Government had given a firm undertaking to provide IFAD with a purpose-specific permanent building.

With this in mind, I developed strong personal relationships with successive Italian Ambassadors to FAO and the Rome agencies from shortly after my arrival. By early 1984, I had convinced the then Ambassador that WFP should have its own unified accommodation. However, I knew that the process of converting sympathy into a concrete government decision would be difficult. The WFP texts were clear about our location with FAO, which would make it easy for the Italian Finance Ministry to resist entering into what they would probably argue was an expensive and unnecessary commitment.

However, Italian sympathy became more concrete later in 1984 when FAO got into a legal dispute with F Building's owners over withholding of rent, much to the annoyance of the Italians who foresaw the possibility of the eviction of FAO and WFP. They attributed the problem to FAO's *bullying tactics, the same towards us as towards you*, I was told.

Meanwhile, as reported in an earlier chapter, the ACABQ, through its chairman, had drawn my attention to, and subsequently recommended that, the basis used by FAO for costing the services it provided to WFP be examined jointly by the two agencies. This included WFP's rent for its share of F Building. CFA16 in October 1983 endorsed the ACABQ's recommendation and asked that the review be done 'as quickly as possible'. Four CFAs later the committee, impatient at the delay, was emphatic that the matter must be concluded by its next session (WFP 1985b).

Finally, at CFA21, the two secretariats were able to present an agreed paper (WFP 1986c). However, it did not cover the most costly services, which were technical expertise in project formulation and rent. FAO had been uncompromising in insisting on the appropriateness of its methodology for the calculation of these expenses in our administrative budget for 1986-87. In particular, FAO would not agree to adjust the rent we paid to take account of the Italian rental subsidy intended to cover the cost of rented premises! Nevertheless in respect of agreed items there was a saving to the Programme of more than a million dollars per year.

An Interim Solution

On account of Italy's helpfulness, a very satisfactory interim solution to our immediate accommodation and associated financial problems emerged at CFA21. Its Ambassador, E Pascarelli, informed the CFA that Italy would pay our rental costs for 1987 and part of 1986, pending finding an appropriate building or constructing one which might be shared with IFAD. Significantly, he stated that the problems had arisen 'because no formal approach had ever been made to my government to provide accommodation for WFP'. He also said it could be taken for granted that had a request for a separate headquarters been made, Italy would not have treated WFP differently from FAO (WFP 1986c).

The committee took the rare step of adopting a resolution (WFP 1986c) acknowledging Italy's intention to provide a building 'in the context of the Headquarters Agreement with FAO' and urging it to meet future rental costs. FAO sought to obstruct the passage of the resolution:

Wednesday 28 May 1986

> *Fun and games resumed [over taskforce report]...Later worse fuss over headquarters resolution. We knew Saouma had been lobbying against this (injured amour propre or fear of precedent?) and gang of 3*[79] *weighed in. However, our friends rallied and gang of 3 withdrew. Earlier, Gnocchi*[80]

learned that Saouma had sought to get G77 to declare against resolution. Italian Ambassador vigorous in his insistence on need for resolution. US silent throughout until there was unanimity in favour of resolution! A caricature of a great power delegation.

In the light of the Italian offer and to get an agreed final report on the 'basis of costing' issue, we decided not to pursue further with FAO at that time the appropriateness of the methodology they used to calculate our share of rental cost.

THE HEADQUARTERS AGREEMENT

Following my urging that he look into the facts surrounding the Italian subvention, the External Auditor discovered later in 1986 that some $3.8 million had been provided by Italy for the rent of F Building but, unknown to Italy, not used for that purpose. The Italians were angered by FAO's behaviour and, as a result, Italy became more firmly committed to a separate headquarters building and, if necessary, separate headquarters agreement for WFP. To that end, Italy formally advised FAO in April 1987 of its intention to provide us with a headquarters and requested the agreement of both the FAO Director-General and UN Secretary-General to enter into negotiations.

The Director-General readily gave his agreement. However, subsequent developments were to show that, in doing so, he was playing for time, confident that once re-elected he could frustrate the conclusion of any agreement with Italy.

The Secretary-General also agreed to participate in the negotiations and said that he would instruct the UN Legal Adviser to 'take a very positive attitude to the finding of constructive solutions'. He also agreed that John Scott, the author of the UN Legal Opinion on the powers of the Executive Director, should handle the negotiations with Italy on behalf of the UN and FAO but the latter rejected this.

FAO's tactics soon became clear. Rather than directly opposing negotiations it sought to ensure that even if agreement was reached between the United Nations, FAO and the Italian government further hurdles would have to be jumped. At the September 1987 meeting of the FAO Finance Committee, two of FAO's most reliable supporters, the representatives of

Peru and Costa Rica, insisted any agreement would have to be approved by the FAO Legal Committee, another of the bodies effectively controlled by the FAO secretariat.

The negotiations between the three parties proceeded slowly through 1988 but the atmosphere remained positive. To assist the consolidation of our increasingly good relationship with Italy, I invited the Italian Foreign Minister, Guilio Andreotti, to preside over the special meeting we held in May of that year to commemorate the thirtieth anniversary of the Programme's life, to which he gladly agreed.

Monday 30 May 1988

> *Andreotti arrived slightly ahead of schedule. Saouma not too thrusting–for him. Commemorative meeting went entirely as planned. McGovern[81] was a great success–a masterstroke to invite him. Even Sims[82], who had bad-mouthed him, said he had been proud. Andreotti good too, as was S-G's message. Saouma's praise of WFP and me was less than unstinting. Others said his envy very clear. His text was about IEFR and FAC–inappropriate this occasion. [M]y own speech [was] rather bold...Afterwards, several told me that they were inspired, which was what I was aiming for. It was a summation of my WFP/UN philosophy (WFP 1988). Whole day went like clockwork. Lunch passed off smoothly but tour de force was President Cossiga's reception. Italians did us proud. Saouma looked, by all accounts, very uncomfortable...Altogether a most satisfying day which fully realised our objective to involve Italy in our anniversary celebration and show publicly its support for WFP.*

I was, however, concerned that Ripert, the number two official of the United Nations and representing the Secretary-General at the ceremony, had not been given status equal to Saouma's, which would have been in line with UN protocol, because by so doing Italy had minimised the standing of the UN as a co-parent of WFP. While the Secretary-General's message was similar to the statements made on his behalf at each CFA, delivered personally by the number two official of the United Nations, gave it special political weight. I was complimented personally for 'innovations... introduced in the management of the Programme to make it more efficient and more relevant to the future'. WFP's active role in cooperating with sister operational agencies of the JCGP was commended. More importantly the statement stressed the CFA's role as the 'intergovernmental body to govern the Programme', in direct contradiction to the position asserted by FAO. Finally, in a direct slap at FAO's pretensions, the statement spoke of the Programme's 'leadership in the formulation of food aid policies and strategies' (WFP/CFA 1998).

These words had little effect. Shortly afterwards FAO stymied progress toward finalisation of the headquarters agreement. Ahmed, who was observing the negotiations on our behalf, reported in early July that they should be completed by the end of that month. Instead, the exercise was aborted:

Wednesday 27 July 1988

A great blow. Crowther rang Ahmed to say that Saouma has called off Friday's meeting with Italians to put finishing touches to Headquarters Agreement. He vaguely cited Saouma's concern about provisions governing access[83] which he wanted further investigated, but also questioned whether agreement is in accord with WFP's Basic Texts. The agreement would, as drafted by FAO/UN Legal Counsels and Italians, have effectively put WFP on same protocol level as FAO and IFAD. Saouma has clearly just realised this. Not being able to get him by telephone, I sent him a note appealing for reconsideration of his decision. No answer as yet but Valenza [Italian Ambassador to FAO], who went to see Saouma, has apparently accepted meeting is off. Ahmed and I feel this is the watershed and that we must now propose to governments that WFP be removed from FAO control. If they agree, well and good; if not, as Ahmed says, we can call it quits.

Thursday 28 July 1988

Most of the day spent in considering the best tactics for the future. Fleischhauer saw it as no less than a realisation by Saouma that the agreement would give WFP de facto independence. If so, it will be next to impossible to ever get that agreement approved. If it is to be rejected, best would be on grounds of its non-conformity with Basic Texts. I would then seek their amendment. Worst is long-drawn out inconclusive process. Somehow, therefore, pressure must be put on Saouma to show his hand. As usual with FAO, a messy, nasty business. I must leave my successor a satisfactory, clear-cut situation if at all possible or, if I have not succeeded, that it is clear to the world why.

Friday 29 July 1988

> *Wrote to Saouma partly for the record and partly to put pressure on him. I have*
> *requested resumption of formal negotiations by early September. Scott has found*
> *Ferrari-Bravo [Legal Adviser to the Italian Foreign Ministry] extremely angry*
> *about the cancellation. He expressed astonishment at such treatment being*
> *extended to the 'chief legal officer' of an important power by some 'prima donna'.*

THE CONSEQUENCES FOR CONSTITUTIONAL REFORM

In the light of Saouma's action I doubted very much that we would ever get a WFP Headquarters agreement, though provision of a building for WFP by Italy, with an appropriate amendment to the FAO Headquarters agreement, might be possible. It was due to the United Nations Legal Counsel and his representative in the negotiations, John Scott, that we had got so far. Fortunately, the United Nations was not ready to admit defeat. Some technical changes, agreeable to Italy and which went a sufficient way to meet FAO's concerns, enabled negotiations to resume. Nevertheless, by delay and obstruction at every turn, FAO dragged out negotiations and found excuse after excuse to delay signature for another two and one half years!

From this point in mid-1988 onwards, the headquarters struggle went on in parallel with the battle for constitutional change. Indeed, FAO's implacability over the headquarters became itself a factor in achieving institutional independence for the Programme. It generated the same theatre in the CFA, and even more so in the FAO Council, as had the fight over Bertrand's proposals, the audited accounts and other events already described.

The delays in bringing the agreement to finality reflected poorly on FAO. Of critical importance, delegates from developing countries gradually realised that WFP was being treated unfairly and that it was inexcusable for FAO to stand in the way of Italy's provision of suitable accommodation for the Programme. Anyone with a nodding acquaintance with our circumstances in F Building could see its inadequacies. Over time, FAO's intransigence was seen as mean-spirited, a perception reinforced by the UN's positive approach. Thereby, FAO weakened the credibility of its constant iteration that WFP was a tool of the developed countries and that, therefore, Ingram's insistence on constitutional reform must be resisted.

I therefore continue the story of how we finally broke through over the headquarters agreement within the context of the constitutional battle.

79 As noted elsewhere, at each CFA session FAO could count on the support of three or four skilful parliamentary performers which we alluded to in this way. On this occasion the group included the representatives of Colombia and Congo.

80 Maurizio Gnocchi, a senior WFP staff member of Italian nationality.

81 George McGovern, former US Senator and Democrat candidate for President, who played a decisive role in the Kennedy administration in bringing about the creation of WFP.

82 Melvin Sims, leader of the US delegation and a Republican appointee to the Department of Agriculture.

83 Under its agreement with Italy, FAO enjoyed 'extra-territorial' status. In the concluded agreement the WFP Executive Director has sole authority to block or allow access to WFP headquarters, including in particular by Italian state authorities. In short FAO was chagrined that WFP was being given the same 'extra-territoriality' as FAO.

11

HOSTILITIES RESUME

My relations with Saouma broke down early in 1988 and never recovered. By re-asserting control over the Programme and its Executive Director through an extreme legal interpretation of the Basic Documents FAO drove itself into a political corner: by showing itself to be outside the direction of governments in regard to WFP, member states finally realised that the WFP General Regulations were deeply flawed. By mid-1989 a critical point in the struggle to bring autonomy to WFP had been reached, though finality would not come for another two years.

Immediately after Saouma's re-election in November 1987 I left for Australia, Japan and several other countries. I got back early in January 1988 to friction with FAO over WFP assistance to Lebanon.

My philosophy of management in relation to day-to-day business is based on delegation, with the chief executive monitoring the use of that delegation but not interfering in its execution. The WFP/FAO relationship was the exception. I took all decisions in regard thereto and personally wrote most of the many memoranda and letters to the Director-General. That is not to say the help of my closest colleagues was not indispensable. It was.

I was absent from Rome on official WFP business on average once a month over ten years, sometimes for several weeks at a time. I did not seek to manage WFP while on those visits, though I was kept informed of important developments. I had full confidence in my deputy. While I did not always agree with his decisions I considered it far more important to truly delegate and accept the risk of wrong decisions than try to micromanage, especially from a distance. In my view nothing is more destructive of the confidence of subordinates than a boss who only pretends to delegate.

ATTEMPTING CO-EXISTENCE

Ahmed had quite correctly declined FAO's request to subsidise the cost of internal transport for our food assistance to Lebanon, which was classified as 'middle income' and not therefore eligible. He had also communicated his decision direct to the Lebanese minister concerned. That was entirely proper. The FAO Director-General had no role in relation to internal transport but, knowing how important his relationship with the Lebanese Government was to Saouma, I would have thought twice before going direct to the minister.

I planned carefully for this first meeting with Saouma since his re-election. During my absence we both had time to relax and to reflect on the future of our relationship. I confided to my diary:

Friday 15 January 1988
> *Somehow I have to get him to accept need for compromise: underlying threat can only be that war will resume and that we are prepared. However, I dearly hope no new war.*

Wednesday 20 January 1988
> *Meeting with Saouma was as fraught as expected. Atmosphere was cool on my entry and he attacked me over Lebanon (as soon as I mentioned the subject) and the D1s (which I didn't). I was taken aback by this but in retrospect I think in his paranoia he saw me behind Ahmed's decision to reply direct to Lebanese Minister and our refusal to supply ITSH subsidy. Request on D1s was clearly intended as retaliation through reversion to same old bullying tactics. I replied by asking why he was attacking me so: that I had come in the same spirit of cooperation as last year. In the course of this I had occasion to show my teeth (which was good) so that, while all was soon enough straightened out, he can clearly see that if he reverts to his old ways I will fight him just as before. As it turned out discussion was quite useful. I was able to put him in picture on CFA procedures, got his agreement to transfer procurement function to WFP, explained my view on delegation of authority re staff appeals, got his agreement to represent him at next WFP Pledging Conference, and accepted his proposal that list of my D1 appointees be forwarded to his Chef de Cabinet each six months.[84] He undertook to look into other reporting requirements particularly in relation to accounts he said, 'Perhaps either you or both of us should sign'. In return he got my promise to see if we can't help Lebanon draw*

up a nationwide school feeding project for relief purposes and to consider favourably request from Benin for emergency aid (he is concerned that rejection of request would lead to charge of vindictiveness over Mensah). On Lebanon I got it into his head that assistance through WFP was necessarily limited and generally on emergencies that we must be treated as partners.

That discussion cleared the air. I came away hopeful a workable relationship could be maintained. In fact, Saouma was still playing for time. At the FAO Conference he had agreed to the establishment of an intergovernmental committee to review FAO. Donors had forced this. Some had withheld their contributions leaving FAO facing a serious problem of financial liquidity. Until that review was completed to his satisfaction and the organisation's finances were again secured Saouma did not want serious conflict with me.

Disturbing News

A totally unexpected development gave me warning that nothing should be taken at face value. Saouma had still not appointed a successor to Walton as Deputy Director-General. Gossip had it that the post was being hawked to the Dutch and Germans. Both were important contributors and, it seemed, had voted for Saouma. Immediately following my meeting with Saouma, Geoffrey Miller, Secretary of the Australian Department of Primary Industry, telephoned me to say that, in response to an enquiry from Walton asking if he would be interested in the DDG post, he was coming to Rome to meet with Saouma. This was a disturbing development. Saouma had made no mention of it in our meeting. There was no way Australians could both head WFP and hold the FAO deputy post. I speculated in my diary:

Thursday 28 January 1988

...Saouma must be able to conceive of circumstances in which he would appoint an Australian as his Deputy. Could Saouma have got wind of US/Australia negotiations leading up to my re-appointment? Perhaps he assumes I can be successfully pressed to stand aside so US gets WFP, Australia [the] DDG [position]? I can think of no other scenario as plausible as that to explain his behaviour. Ahmed feels that he would not want me running against him for a fourth term, nor elected if he stood down, because of skeletons I could uncover.

Later I learned Saouma had told Keyes' successor as Assistant Secretary of State for International Organization Affairs that my post was available to the Americans if they wanted it and that he would make further delegations to an American Executive Director beyond those he had made to me. I deduced from this offer and other information given to me that Saouma had some inkling of the pressure Keyes had exerted to get Australia to agree to me stepping down after two years.

Indeed, a few days later, my *Chef de Cabinet*, Tun Myat, told me with much agitation that Saouma had talked to the Australian Ambassador about the possibility of my leaving mid-term. Subsequently, Bula Hoyos informed me that Saouma was putting it around that I would be stepping down in mid-term, in the middle of 1989. Of course I denied emphatically there was any deal but the rumour continued to circulate into 1989. It finally died when it was clear I was staying. But the fact that there was uncertainty among delegations and WFP staff for almost a year made my job all the harder.

Throughout this time the DDG post was kept open; indeed it was never filled during Saouma's third term. It stood as continuing bait to influence donors. In relation to Australia, it was intended to soften its approach to FAO reform, ensure timely payment of its contribution to FAO, harm my prospects of getting Canberra's support if I decided to run for the FAO Director-Generalship in 1993[85] and weakened support in Canberra for me and WFP. It was a classic example of the use of human ambition to attain political ends.

An Important Proposal

Early in 1987, before Australia committed itself to Mensah, I made a comprehensive set of proposals to Saouma intended to tidy up the arrangements arising from the taskforce. He agreed not to require consultation with him on D1 appointments, though as mentioned below this was only implemented in full in 1988.

The most important related to the WFP accounts. It was neither accepted nor rejected. I argued that FAO staff in accounts and internal audit, when working on WFP matters, report to Saouma through me. Almost all the work relating to WFP accounts was done by WFP's accounting staff. It could not be otherwise, since a large part of that work related to the translation of donated food quantities into monetary values and their adjustment as laid down in the General Regulations.[86]

My proposal did not exclude the Director-General from turning to outsiders if he wished to double-check the accounts I presented to him. Failure to accept my proposal meant Saouma wished to retain the most important instrument open to him for control over the Programme. Or alternatively, and just as unacceptably, he was implying that he trusted the professional integrity of FAO staff but not WFP.

Some of my closest advisers were disappointed I had not pressed Saouma much harder on reform during the year following my re-appointment, while he was vulnerable. They were convinced Saouma could not afford a return to the conflict preceding my re-appointment and that I therefore had him over the proverbial barrel. The politically astute Zejjari was sure Saouma would make trouble for me after his re-election and that I would never again have the opportunity I had in 1987 to put the seal on WFP's autonomy. They were probably right in their assessment. However, I was revelling in the freedom to act on substantive matters and preferred to believe that if I showed goodwill and refrained from undermining Saouma's campaign my action would be reciprocated. The truth may have lain in Tomlinson's view that, though I was very tough in defence, I lacked the killer instinct.

A Critical Decision

Matters came to a head early in 1988 over finalisation of the 1986-87 biennium accounts. FAO insisted that our internal auditor provide his working papers for review by their auditor. I was unwilling to do this because it would mean abandoning my effort to persuade Saouma to extend to me the same trust he gave FAO staff or, worse still, provide FAO with the means of again pillorying us as it had in its 1984 'Statement of Representation'. As mentioned above, Saouma had never responded to my proposal that he look to me for advice on WFP's accounts.

By keeping discussion at the working level for as long as possible I sought to avoid a head-on confrontation, but to no avail. In accordance with the provisions of the taskforce our auditor submitted a report to FAO on his work in relation to the accounts but Crowther advised Ahmed it was inadequate and he would have to recommend to the Director-General that he not sign the accounts. While I had confidence in our auditor's work, especially in the absence of any criticism from the External Auditor, I was reluctant to force the issue:

Saturday 26 March 1988

> *A disturbed night on account of audit issue. However, we must establish once and for all that FAO role in relation to accounts must be pro forma; otherwise texts must be amended. I will do my best to persuade Saouma...But I shall not shirk the challenge if it comes.*

Ahmed and Crowther continued their dialogue over the next several days. Crowther was always an extraordinarily tenacious advocate of his master's views but finally accepted that we were not giving anything more. I saw Saouma on 31 March and after a long, at times acrimonious, negotiation he agreed that I should sign the accounts on his behalf. Afterwards I commented in my diary:

Thursday 31 March 1988

> *I feel no sense of victory, only flatness and disappointment. He was unwilling to consider my case. Instead, he reiterated the legalistic arguments of his staff...ignoring the fact that I had put my position to him months before. Once again, I explained that WFP staff had, by agreement between the accounting staff of the two organisations, prepared the accounts. This demonstrated that, contrary to the taskforce conclusions, the WFP accounts could in practice only be prepared efficiently and economically by WFP. Thus he could and should look only to me and not to his own staff for information about, and assurances in regard to, them. Finally, when I said flatly that we would provide no more documentation on the work of our internal auditor, he suddenly said, 'I agree, you have won but I don't like your fait accompli, pressure tactics'. Throughout he tried to unsettle me. On entry he greeted me cordially but did not stir from his desk, so after one-and-a-half years of discussion in armchairs across a coffee table, I found myself once again facing the light across his desk.[87] He accused me of being aggressive and tense and contrasted his coolness with my demeanour. The whole thing of course was play-acting...It was clear that, as we had assessed, he knew he could not afford a public battle with me on this issue. Having tested that I did not shirk from such a course, he gave in. He concluded by saying that the issue was a minor one and we should forget it but the behaviour of him and his team showed that it was not minor. We have at last deprived him of the means to harass us as he did in 1984...I am sick of the whole unnecessary need to deal with him in this way and of his inability, even now, to surrender power except under pressure.[88]*

I handed Saouma a letter stating my position. He replied on 7 April, confirming 'that in this instance' he would rely on my certification of the accuracy of the accounts and not require 'strict adherence' to the taskforce provisions. That was a fair statement but, much to my delight, he added a further paragraph: 'I shall further review these matters and give serious consideration to possible additional delegation of authority with respect to oversight and certification of the WFP accounts'. Reading the two paragraphs together it was entirely unconvincing to argue, as FAO later did, that the Director-General was acting under duress.

The Gloves Off

Following suspension of the headquarters negotiations in July, FAO launched a new all-out attempt to use the Director-General's powers in relation to the accounts to discredit me. From this point onwards the gloves were off. Not only was the honeymoon long over but the bride was assaulted and divorce the only option.

On 29 August 1988 Saouma wrote to me, with a copy to the Secretary-General, seeking to place me in the wrong by taking advantage of a request from the External Auditor that he personally sign the usual Statement of Representation in regard to the accounts for the 1986-87 biennium. Saouma declined on the grounds that, because I had been unwilling to provide FAO with full documentation on the work of our internal auditor, and had thereby breached the agreed taskforce provisions, he could not verify that the statements contained in our accounts were correct. 'In the circumstances', he wrote to me, 'having been presented with a *fait accompli*, I have no alternative but to agree that you sign the WFP Letter of Representation and accept the full consequential responsibility'. Somehow FAO had overlooked the Director-General's letter of 7 April which made nonsense of the '*fait accompli*' claim.

The Director-General had decided to go on the attack. This was confirmed in September when he argued with the Secretary-General that a separate WFP headquarters agreement was not acceptable. He also insisted that I submit to him a panel of names, instead of my recommended choice, for 'senior appointments' as had been my practice until then.

From my diary it is clear that I vacillated between a desire to take some definitive action to push forward on constitutional reform and prudent caution not to risk jeopardising my standing with delegations, governments and other key players. My closest associates urged me to make another effort to persuade Saouma to agree to further change. Tun Myat, was very persuasive:

Tuesday 6 August 1988

> *Tun Myat told a story of the Burmese leader Aung Sen. He called on the Governor General to ask for independence. It was refused. He repeated his request more firmly, again it was refused. He then leaned over to the GG, pointing to a pen in his pocket, saying let us assume that this pen is mine, I ask...to have it back but you refuse. At this point Aung Sen leaned forward and ripped the pen from the pocket and said, 'As a result of your refusal to give me my pen not only have you lost it but you now have a torn pocket'. Tun Myat remains convinced that I must ask Saouma for our independence, that he will know that if he refuses it will mean war, that he will not want that and may well agree. He also considers that I am in a very strong position if I use my strength and that Saouma hopes to wait me out by making as few concessions as possible, drawn out for as long as possible. I think that is true.*

Another Attempt At Co-Existence

I agreed to make one further personal attempt to reach agreement with Saouma. If he was reasonable, well and good; if not, I would pursue my reform agenda direct with governments. To this end, Paul Kelloway had prepared an analysis of our problems, the textual changes in the Basic Documents[89] needed to overcome them and ranked from what seemed easiest to secure to the most difficult. I had in mind first proposing to Saouma that he take steps to amend the Additional Financial Procedures. It was these procedures, prepared by the Director-General in consultation with the Executive Director for approval by the CFA, which had been used by FAO to make our lives so difficult over the accounts.

In effect, I wanted the recently obtained delegation in relation to the 1986-87 accounts permanently entrenched. The procedures had been prepared more than twenty years previously and did not reflect changes in administrative and financial practices introduced over the years. Setting aside differences over the FAO-WFP relationship, in relation to financial management there was in any case a strong case to revise the Procedures.

Monday 26 September 1988

> *Made my independence presentation to Saouma. While I got the 'behind the desk' treatment again he was civil throughout–though as usual saying...how I*

broke agreements, had inspired the Thames TV programme against him, and so on. However, it was clear he does not want a sharp break but...will try to keep to the minimum further advances by WFP. While professing willingness to consider changes, his hypocritical responses on particular points show that nothing much can be expected. He is probably relieved that I am seeking changes to Additional Financial Procedures rather than going for the fundamentals. He had Basic Documents with him, well marked with paper clips, and said donors would not want a specialised agency. On the whole I am pleased. I have served notice of my intentions and made a plea for his cooperation.

I gave Saouma my proposals for amending the Additional Financial Procedures a few weeks later but had no response then, or ever, except on a point of procedure. This left me still uncertain as to how to induce governments to put pressure on Saouma to agree to amend the Additional Financial Procedures or to take the initiative in relation to the General Regulations.

FAO MAKES ITS MOVE

As it turned out, Saouma played into my hands when he took an aggressive, public step against me. To our surprise, two days after our meeting of 26 September, FAO informed its Finance Committee of my alleged sins in relation to the finalisation and signature of our 1986-87 accounts. Its purpose was to serve notice that WFP would not be permitted to sign the accounts in future. In effect, FAO expected the Finance Committee to arbitrate compliance with the taskforce provisions in line with its interpretation. The broad aim was to show that I was the aggressor. However, this tactic turned out to be a fatal FAO error, as became clear during the following year.

The committee's action brought a dispiriting sense of *déjà vu*. Many of the same actors as before, namely the representatives of Mexico, Lebanon and Saudi Arabia in the person of Bukhari, who chaired the Finance Committee, were again ready to do FAO's bidding. They were joined by a particularly inflexible representative from Costa Rica, (C Di Mottola Balestra), a long-time resident of Italy, rich businessman and associate of the Director-General. He was ignorant of WFP's work, even of its successful development projects in his own country, of WFP's constitutional status or, indeed, of FAO's. His post as FAO representative, it was said, enabled him to reside permanently in Italy to pursue his business interests. As we subsequently learned from Costa Rican officials, he sent next-to-no reports on his work with FAO nor sought or received instructions from San José, which was reliant upon the FAO representative in that city for advice on developments in FAO. The main point of his interventions in the Finance Committee over the years of his membership was to assert aggressively and insistently that if I maintained my disagreements with the Director-General my only honourable options were to submit or to resign. No other delegates ever publicly put that choice forward and none ever suggested to me in private that I should consider resigning. I would have done so immediately had I lost the confidence of the CFA or if the Secretary-General had joined with the Director-General to request me to leave.

The only new element was the presence for the first time of a US representative. Though hard to believe, the United States, overwhelmingly the major contributor to the FAO budget, for many years had been denied membership of the intergovernmental body with oversight of the organisation's finances. This was due to the controlling influence of the FAO secretariat over who would or would not be elected.[90]

Consistent with the broad US support I enjoyed, I expected that at last our travails in the Finance Committee would be significantly moderated. Instead, the US representative, Ambassador Eckert, turned out to be a 'wild card', siding with the Saudi Chairman and his supporters. Eckert was a Republican who had lost a Congressional seat in New York. He subsequently explained to me that his instructions for the Finance Committee arrived after the event. Once again the United States had shown that its problems with FAO owed much to the poor quality of its Rome political appointees.

Although the External Auditor had not qualified our accounts, he had made some criticisms of our development projects. FAO used those criticisms to create the impression that the External Auditor had somehow done so. We were disappointed the External Auditor was less than robust in his oral presentation at the meetings than the facts, and our cooperation with him, justified. This resulted in the committee's report giving disproportionate attention to our minor shortcomings.

The committee decided that to 'properly exercise' its 'oversight responsibilities' it wished to 'carefully review the...manner in which Member Nations intended the Taskforce Report to be interpreted'. Both organisations were requested to provide 'any and all documentation on this issue as soon as possible' (WFP, 1988b). In other words this session was not the end of the matter. My actions in relation to the provision of our internal audit papers to FAO were to be the subject of an in-depth investigation.

I learned that Saouma was jubilant with that outcome. He was very complimentary to our Ambassador about the role played by the Australian representative, saying, 'I favour him becoming chairman in a year or two'. It was unfortunately the case that sometimes Australian representatives went to extreme lengths to avoid any hint of partiality toward me and the Programme. If only Lebanon's representatives had been similarly motivated! The deeply prejudicial Finance Committee report was considered by the FAO Council:

Wednesday 23 November 1988

After an all-day wait (three days away from real work) our accounts finally reached. What a thoroughly unpleasant occasion but my tactics were vindicated. Overnight I felt that there should be no explicit criticism of Finance Committee—that would be taken by many as lèse-majesté...Led by Mexico (who was speaking regardless of my own intervention) and Lebanon, with a little support from India, a scurrilous attack was made. Interventions by Bukhari and Crowther together promoted FAO case...Bula Hoyos' intervention referred to 'honeymoon' having ended, so enabling me to give a chronology of breakdown. I emphasised my commitment to agreed solution...If anyone is left in any doubt about the existence of a rift, I would be surprised.

I felt satisfied by my intervention and was bolstered by several good statements of support on the headquarters subject, which I had included in my general remarks on the CFA's report to the Council. In particular, very tactfully, Italy avoided blaming FAO for the breakdown in negotiations, making it clear it wanted to see negotiations resume. Their ambassador told me later that, characteristically, Saouma had afterwards strongly attacked him for his intervention!

FAO's purpose in exposing to the Finance Committee its interpretation of why it had been agreed that I should sign the accounts was to serve notice that this would not again be permitted; and so deter an attempt by me to use the same procedure in relation to the 1988-89 biennial accounts. In effect, FAO expected the Finance Committee in due course to arbitrate compliance with the taskforce provisions in line with its interpretation. The broad aim was to 'show' that I was the aggressor. However, this tactic turned out to be a fatal FAO error, as became clear during the following year.

Meanwhile, I was deeply alarmed by informal advice to me from the External Auditor to the effect that our internal audit was not up to scratch. If FAO got wind of that our goose would be truly cooked. However, following a meeting I had with the new head of the UK National Audit Office, John Bourn, his staff withheld formal advice to this effect to give us time to make the necessary improvements. We made a major effort to do so and the External Auditor expressed complete satisfaction with our performance a few months later.

At year's end I was pessimistic about the prospects for constitutional change. My visits to Washington and Ottawa had shown no inclination in either government for further battle with FAO. The Secretary-General was personally committed to bringing a satisfactory outcome over the headquarters agreement and in general was as encouraging as ever. However, I knew that New York would never take the tough action needed to bring change of its own accord, no matter how much it sympathised with us or detested FAO methods. It could be forced to act only under pressure from governments, which in practice meant the United States. Notwithstanding this depressing prognosis, I intensified my efforts in the New Year to convince stakeholders of the need for governments to take decisive action. At the same time I cast about for an appropriate means to inspire them to do so.

Relations With Stakeholders

My survival and later my success owed a great deal to convincing governments, delegates and UN colleagues, especially the close advisers of the Secretary-General, of my dedication to WFP, my professionalism and, above all, my good faith. Since the personalities were always changing, the task was never ending, with every newcomer needing to be wooed to our cause. Indeed the constant flux of officials and ministers involved in the oversight of UN system organisations is a major cause of the dissatisfaction those same governments have with the system

I enjoyed the challenge of using my persuasive talents. That feeling compensated in part for the time it all took. The continuous selling of oneself and one's policies is the everyday art of the successful politician. Reading my diaries, I was reminded of how demanding this politicking was. Every time I had to broach the relationship issue, it was necessary to assess the best approach to take. My diary records a typical meeting with the new German Minister of Cooperation:

Tuesday 17 January 1989

> *Breakfast session with Klein: very dapper and likeable: essentially a PR man according to Kurth[91] but I found him interested in the broadest aid policy issues. As befitting a conservative politician, very concerned whether what we were doing was really of any practical use. Overnight I had decided FAO issue would only be raised at his insistence...He alluded to Saouma once. I said I would follow this up later but never did: time ran out after one and quarter hours. I was not sorry to say nothing because I wanted to leave strong impression of all my strengths and thought better to leave details to bureaucracy. Lunch by Parliamentary State Secretary of Agriculture, von Geldorn. He is said to be open-minded and I took advantage of his request to explain FAO dispute. Schleiffer[92] thought he was very impressed and felt that we had at least neutralised a year of intensive lobbying by FAO.*

Saouma's own actions sometimes helped my relationships. I found this to be so during a visit to Paris early in 1989 when my relations with the French took a favourable turn, in part at least, due to Saouma having presumed too much of his own relationship with them. My Moroccan *Chef de Cabinet*, Mohammed Zejjari, who had excellent contacts, told me the French Foreign Ministry was furious when Saouma insisted on knowing in advance of my visit at what level I would be received. The result was that I had my best ever visit to Paris. I was received by three ministers and a large, formal lunch in my honour was organised. In case this flattery might be lost on me, the key foreign office official told me how rare it was for any UN agency head to be so treated. I felt that one of the French aims was to convince me that their past opposition was not personal.

The French Ambassador in Rome had urged me to give the Minister of Agriculture, Henri Nallet, a full briefing on the relationship with FAO, which I did. Like his predecessor, Michel Rocard, now Prime Minister, he regarded FAO as an organisation 'in crisis' and placed the blame on Saouma. From my visits to Paris it became clearer over time that France's support for Saouma owed little to its Ministers of Agriculture and much to the Foreign Ministry. I found little enthusiasm among the former for FAO or its Director-General's management style; so once again I left speculating as to the overriding *raison d'état* behind France's policy.

This strengthening of relations with France came at an important moment. Ripert had left the UN by this time. France had a lien on the post[93] and its nominee, Antoine Blanca, had been appointed. Blanca was a socialist, son of a Spanish refugee from Franco's Spain and an Arabic speaker. I learned that he was not the Foreign Ministry's choice but owed his appointment to President Mitterand. I feared that Blanca would be pre-disposed in FAO's favour, especially since he was said to see Saouma as a 'son of France'. This made the timing of Blanca's appointment a potentially negative development in terms of resolving our differences with FAO over accounts and audit, for which at least tacit UN support was essential.

My first meeting with Blanca took place in New York some months after the Paris visit and passed off well. I found him down to earth, with no trace of pomposity or self-importance, but lacking in knowledge of the UN system. He brought an initial suspicion of me but eventually became convinced of the rightness of our cause and an ally. He grew in my esteem on account of his decency and I developed a personal liking for him. Years later he and his staff urged on Boutros Boutros-Ghali my appointment to the new post of Humanitarian Coordinator for the UN system, whose establishment coincided with the completion of my term with WFP.

FAO Maintains Pressure

Early in 1989 the Director-General took several aggressive steps. He was now attacking us over my recommended responses to requests for emergency assistance and had gone back on an earlier agreement to transfer procurement in Italy to us, citing various legal technicalities. He was again actively frustrating my senior staff appointments. My nominee for the critical post of Director of Finance and Administration had been rejected after many months on the grounds that at age 37 he was too young for a D2 post. For the first and only time the United Nations, in the person of its Comptroller and Acting Under Secretary-General for Administration, Luis

Maria Gomez, also declined to support my nomination. He was another senior official who knew little of WFP and whom I had to convince of my *bona fides* that year. If there was ever any doubt that the UN system was out of touch with modern management this was a convincing example. However Gomez subsequently proposed an Englishwoman in her early forties whom I found outstanding. I recommended her to Saouma, though I believed she might be too talented to put up with FAO's petty legalisms and harassments and would probably resign after a short stint with us. I was not altogether disappointed, therefore, when she declined my offer. However, after many months a key post was still unfilled.

Saouma was still putting it about that I would be stepping down in mid-term. This created uncertainty among delegates and staff, for example between Ahmed and our Assistant Executive Director responsible for field operations, Robert Chase. Both hoped to succeed me but Chase, an American, realistically had a greater chance. As a successful, former official of USAID, he brought the modern management skills I had been looking for to the revitalisation of our project management. Like Ahmed, he was a person of integrity. I could not afford to have less than a harmonious relationship between them.

By now I had around me some outstanding younger men who were totally committed to what I was trying to achieve for the Programme, especially Tomlinson, Zejjari and Tun Myat, the latter two ultimately filling high posts elsewhere in the UN system. I made a point of searching within the Programme for people to promote into positions where they could help me make the improvements I wanted. In my experience it is risky to choose outsiders to fill high-level posts, though this is sometimes necessary. This is even more so the case in the UN system where governments lay claim to senior posts and to the nomination of candidates to fill them. I found they rarely nominated their top people. Even countries committed to support of the UN sometimes put forward the names of persons who turned out to be less than competent. Any reservations about senior nominees of countries on whose political support I counted had to be raised discreetly with the government or overlooked. This is the case for all agencies but in my case I had the further problem of needing UN and FAO consent to my appointments. It was much easier to get that if my nominees had the strong backing of their governments.

Tomlinson's advice, encouragement and superb lobbying skills remained a great strength. The author of the UN Legal Opinion, John Scott, had now retired and I was able to avail myself of his legal expertise, especially for the headquarters negotiations but also on other legal issues.

I received a great boost early in 1989, when Patricio Ruedas, who had also recently retired, responded without a moment's hesitation to my enquiry whether he would assist my campaign to bring constitutional reform:

Wednesday 22 March 1989

Telephoned Ruedas to ask whether he would represent WFP in further tripartite talks. Also asked if he would come to Rome to review events and see what he could do on our behalf in NY. He readily agreed, though expressing concern that, because he is anathema to Saouma, his leadership might make agreement harder. I was delighted by his spontaneous acceptance; lifted a great weight to know that in NY I will have a credible interlocutor.

Saturday 15 April 1989

Ruedas here: cathartic to pour out the whole story to a peer who can expect to understand fully (or at least better than anyone else) just what the pressures are. Showed him Thames TV film, which stands up well to a second viewing. Saouma is a cool customer.

Monday 17 April 1989

Determined strategy with Ruedas: he is convinced matters will only be resolved intergovernmentally.

The Search For New Tactics

As noted, in the first months of 1989 we had been giving a lot of thought as to how best to energise stakeholders. Initially, I planned to address the reform issue explicitly in my annual report, on which I was required to consult with the Secretary-General and the Director-General before submission to the CFA.[94] To that end we prepared a full review of the relationship issue, detailing the handicaps under which we operated, and justifying the need for further change, including in particular to the Additional Financial Procedures (AFP) in respect of which we proposed to annex our desired changes. This would have been a very bold step. I sent the draft to the Secretary-General to test the water. After a deal of discussion in New York and exchange of correspondence I decided to drop this idea, though New York did not actually forbid such action. In the end it just seemed too rash in the light of the feedback I was getting from governments.

Instead, I accepted Ruedas' offer to approach Mselle with the suggestion that the ACABQ might recommend revision of the AFP. His efforts quickly bore fruit as was clear when I met with the latter in New York:

Tuesday 2 May 1989

> *With Mselle. He accepts control of accounts must pass to WFP but concerned how to bring this about. Does not want ACABQ aligned with WFP (secretariat), Finance Committee with FAO. Feels he can more completely address issue at autumn session when he will review our budget and FAO will also be present. In ACABQ I made our case in low key way. Such questions as were asked revealed sympathy. Met with Pérez de Cuéllar. On FAO he said, 'You know how I feel'. Nevertheless, I appealed to him to resolve matter once and for all. Said he would but expressed distaste at idea of having to deal with Saouma.[95] I said UN should put its position clearly in writing signed by him and that if Saouma telephoned he should simply reiterate that was his position.*

In the event the ACABQ went a little further than I expected, recommending that 'appropriate consultations take place among WFP, FAO and the United Nations and that information be submitted to the Advisory Committee with a view to resolving the outstanding difficulties between WFP and FAO'.

Meanwhile, FAO had made consideration of any revision of the Additional Financial Procedures conditional upon WFP providing all the audit information FAO considered was required under the taskforce provisions. In other words, we must agree that the *status quo ante* would apply to the next biennial accounts before any revision could be considered.

I was not ready to provide the data FAO insisted upon, because I knew that would place us again under the FAO thumb. However, I intended to avoid saying so until that was absolutely necessary, which would not be until early in the following year. There was some discussion between Ahmed and Crowther on clarifying the data to be supplied, but it quickly became clear to us that FAO was doing so only to make more credible an appearance of reasonableness before the Finance Committee which was to meet soon.

Taking The Initiative

For that meeting, for the ACABQ meeting already referred to and for the forthcoming CFA session, we prepared a closely argued, comprehensive briefing document drawing upon the section of my annual report which I had decided to drop. As I saw it, FAO's public criticism of WFP's 1987-88 accounts in the Finance Committee and in the FAO Council had necessarily involved governments in consideration of the relationship. Thus FAO itself had provided the peg, for which I had been long searching, to justify re-opening intergovernmental consideration of the procedures decided upon by the taskforce. The burden of our argument was as follows:

❑   In January 1988, FAO and WFP officials agreed that, since the great mass of accounting data was held in WFP, WFP should prepare the 1986-7 accounts, even though the taskforce arrangements assigned that responsibility to FAO.

❑   On 7 April 1988 the Director-General confirmed in writing his agreement to signature by the Executive Director and waived 'strict adherence' to the taskforce reporting requirements. Of great significance he added that he 'intended to give serious consideration to additional delegation of authority for oversight and certification of the WFP accounts'. This statement gave the lie to the later assertion (19 August 1988) of the Director-General that he had been acting 'under duress' in agreeing to signature by the Executive Director, which presumably the Director-General had overlooked in making his allegation.

❑   The accounting arrangements devised by the taskforce had become outdated when, by agreement, FAO and WFP had each introduced new computerised accountancy systems which reflected the quite different requirements of the two organisations. To attempt to follow the taskforce procedures would have been expensive and consuming of the time of senior accounting staff.

❑   The internal audit reporting requirements involved quite unnecessary duplication of work and meant that the Programme had two external auditors, namely its official one, the UK National Audit Office, and FAO's internal auditor. The relationship between the WFP internal auditor and the Executive Director was necessarily one of confidence and inconsistent with the transmission of these reports to 'another organisation'.

❏   The taskforce procedures were so artificial and complex because the taskforce's terms of reference excluded from consideration any amendments whatsoever to WFP's Basic Documents, including subsidiary documents, such as the Additional Financial Procedures prepared by the FAO Director-General 25 years before. Irrespective of taskforce changes, they were long outdated. It was arguable that those procedures went well beyond the provisions of the General Regulations from which they drew their authority.

❏   The essential change required was to align the formal authority of the Executive Director with the *de facto* situation, whereby he was held responsible by governments for the administration of the Programme including its finances.

THE DRAMA INTENSIFIES

FAO countered with a lengthy document alleging breach of faith on my part, namely that although I had agreed to implement the procedures decided upon by the taskforce, I had wilfully refused to provide the information specified in the procedures. Quite inaccurately, FAO claimed that WFP had been a full party to its deliberations. My diary describes my reaction to the FAO paper:

Friday 5 May 1989

> *Their case is clearly weak...Most revealing statement is that an appointee must do what the appointer requests. Saouma cannot understand a constitutional relationship and therefore cannot abide my insistence on seeing my responsibility to CFA as well as to S-G and D-G. I will doubtless be asked, 'Will you in future supply reports?' Answer must be that in present circumstances this is not an appropriate question. We have compiled and prepared accounts on basis of clear delegation. Yet our position has been misrepresented and extraordinary charges of reprehensible behaviour made. In the process our accounts staff has also been put in wrong. Question should be put to D-G instead. 'Why have you reversed your position of 7/4/88?' Clear that there is an impasse and that taskforce no longer provides adequate basis [for accounts preparation].*

Using these themes I prepared a hard-hitting statement to give in the Finance Committee which met the following week.

Thursday 11 May 1989

> *Fought the great battle (again) in the Finance Committee...I put a lot into this*
> *speech and it certainly had an impact. Crowther looked shocked but managed*
> *to rally to put on a bit of a counterattack. Bukhari as chairman...trying always*
> *to instruct the committee and lead it to support FAO. Only strong support he*
> *got again came from...Costa Rican representative, totally in Saouma's pocket.*
> *Reasonable support [for WFP] from Australia, Africans and US. Coutts[96] acted*
> *pretty skilfully. Brazil, Malaysia and Italy effectively on the fence. But it will*
> *be hard to get something worthwhile into the report. Mussapi[97] shocked by bias.*
> *I have become inured...we did far better than five years ago, a measure of how*
> *far we have come. Bukhari, when challenged, backs off, but one has to be quick.*
> *He tried hard to exclude us from a private session but eventually gave way.*

It took three more days of intensive lobbying by FAO, including Saouma's
personal efforts with key members, to get agreement on the committee's
report. However, the result was a moral victory for us. We were not
criticised in any way. The committee was divided over what should be done
for the future. The majority requested FAO to re-state in writing what
documentation it required for the 1988-89 accounts. A minority called for
a new review 'under the authority of the Secretary-General to consider
future working arrangements for the accounts' (WFP 1989c).

Wednesday 17 May 1989

> *The Finance Committee took the whole day to decide their report...our side*
> *[US, Australia, Cameroon and Ethiopia] stood firm so that at least something*
> *of the actual positions taken in the committee got in. In effect, FAO has taken*
> *a beating in its own committee with a whole week having been spent on the*
> *issue, although of course to the uninitiated the defeat may not seem apparent.*
> *Once report was adopted, Crowther came with a statement he insisted be*
> *included which in effect states that the Director-General can't be forced to do*
> *anything and is answerable only to FAO Council and Conference, i.e. a*
> *raspberry to CFA and S-G (WFP 1989c, p.21). Ahmed sought to make a*
> *counterbalancing statement but Costa Rica argued that it could not be*
> *included. In the end, even Brazil supported its inclusion. FAO's arrogance will*
> *be their undoing.*

Crowther's assertion became the cornerstone of FAO's attempt to block
all further change. Ultimately, it turned out to be a critical strategic

blunder, revealing that governments did not in fact have anything like full control over the Programme, and thus laying down a challenge to them.

When CFA27 (May/June 1989) met a few weeks later, in the debate over the audited accounts FAO asserted more formally the claim that it would not be proper for the CFA to take decisions that would commit the Secretary-General or the Director-General to review or participate in the review of matters which they had decided upon following the taskforce report. Those matters could only be decided upon by the Secretary-General and the Director-General and the competent bodies of United Nations and FAO (WFP 1989c, p.21).[98]

In the event all turned out well from our point of view. The audited accounts were approved unanimously, the ACABQ proposal was 'noted with satisfaction' and the committee decided to resolve the problem of the documentation to be supplied in future by WFP, at its following session when it would have before it the ACABQ's next report; and key delegates insisted that 'sovereign governments could deal with any issue affecting WFP' (WFP 1989c, p.21). I commented in my diary:

Thursday 1 June 1989

> *Degree of support all round very good, although I would have liked to see more interventions urging S-G's involvement and clearer statements on need to amend AFP. However, donors had a common denominator of agreement around ACABQ and it is far better that they proceed on lines thoroughly comfortable to them. Altogether momentum for change has built up much faster than I had expected. No doubt that evident WFP/FAO friction and FAO arrogance has convinced doubters that I am not to blame for situation. Lunch for US representative Christianson. He told me that Saouma had summoned US delegation and given a long diatribe on my sins and had again offered my post, saying in effect he would in return do anything US wanted. I took opportunity to say that as far as Australia was concerned US would succeed me when I left in 92. Christianson clearly satisfied.*

Another FAO Error Of Judgment

The CFA also had before it a related issue, namely our draft financial plan for the coming biennium 1990-91. The Director-General had not been consulted in its preparation which was, according to FAO, a breach of the General Regulations and Additional Financial Procedures.

I had introduced the draft financial plan two years previously as a means of involving the CFA at an earlier stage in the consideration of our administrative budget. Previously, the committee was in the position of either rejecting or approving the budget *in toto*, which was not consistent with my view that the CFA should be much more a true executive board. With a two-stage consideration of our budget, we were able to take full account of the CFA's views before presenting our definitive budget at the following session for approval. The arrangement also deprived FAO of the opportunity to use its Finance Committee to hamstring my efforts to gain the staff needed to implement my reform agenda. The idea had been well received by the CFA and not opposed by FAO during our 1987 'second honeymoon'.

FAO's criticism of the draft was again too extreme. The onslaught was led by FAO's able Vikram Shah, a beautifully spoken, Oxonian style, Indian national of immense courtesy but nevertheless capable of wounding thrusts. Two of my sentences in reply accused Shah of impertinence. FAO took this to be an 'attack on the person and the responsibilities of the Director-General'!

On the substance of the matter, the CFA agreed that I should frame my budget in line with my preliminary proposals, which envisaged the creation of a significant number of new posts. FAO had succeeded only in bringing closer the burial of its ability to obstruct our work.

The draft report contained a paragraph about my 'impertinent' remarks and a second one recording the Director-General's protest. Delegations favoured the paragraph's removal but FAO would not agree. However, Australia, Canada, the Federal Republic of Germany, the United Kingdom and the United States considered their inclusion should not be left unexplained. They requested the relevant passage of the report to be footnoted as follows:

An effort to remove paragraphs 115 and 126 at the request of the Executive Director in the interest of promoting comity between FAO and WFP failed after lengthy debate and after the Director-General's representative opposed any such effort. The debate allowed CFA delegates to greatly enhance our understanding of the genesis of the situation' (WFP 1989c, p.24)[99].

Afterwards I confided in my diary, *altogether one of the best CFAs ever. If momentum can be kept up real change may be possible.*

From this time onwards the tide turned in our favour but with a seemingly endless series of whirlpools and overfalls, threatening to sink the reform barque.

---

84   In fact this was no more than the implementation of an understanding we reached in 1987 before Australia committed itself to Mensah (see below).

85   Saouma did not run a fourth time. There were a number of candidates. An African, Jacques Diouf of Senegal, was successful. Geoffrey Miller was a candidate.

86   GR 3 (b)

87   By this date Saouma had removed the raised platform under his desk and chair which had obliged the subordinate facing him across the desk to look up to him.

88   Any inclination on my part to relent was diminished when I learned that Saouma had dangled before one of my two key American staff the prospect of appointment to represent FAO in Washington when Sorenson retired

89   The WFP Basic Documents consist of the Basic Texts i.e. the foundation resolutions of the UN General Assembly and FAO Conference, the General Regulations, the Additional Financial Procedures and the Rules of Procedure of the CFA (see Appendix I for relevant extracts).

90   On one occasion Australia and Canada were competing for a post on the Committee. Canada had to be taught a lesson so FAO put its weight behind Australia, which was duly elected. Rather naively Canberra congratulated itself on its outstanding success!

91   Eberhard Kurth, a senior official in the Ministry of Cooperation. Throughout my tenure the Germans were knowledgeable and supportive at the bureaucratic level and effective representatives in the CFA.

92   Werner Schleiffer, a staff member of WFP of German nationality.

93   It was the practice in New York for each of the five permanent members of the Security Council to nominate their choice to fill posts *de facto* reserved for them.

94   GR 16(b)

95   A few weeks before in the ACC Saouma made an intemperate attack on Pérez de Cuéllar for having allegedly sat on a report on humanitarian aid for Lebanon for some months, contrasting that with his efforts for other countries. I commented in my diary, *Pérez taken aback and said he would look into this. Noticed Saouma pressing him hard after session.*

96   Douglas Coutts, Australian representative on the FAO Finance Committee

97   Christine Mussapi, my personal secretary through my ten years and a tower of support.

98   In response to his FAO counterpart's request the UN Legal Counsellor gave a more nuanced interpretation:

      I...would rather have stressed that the mandate of the Committee includes providing 'general guidance on the policy, administration and operation of the World Food Programme' and that the Committee could not go further and purport to issue binding directives committing the Director-General of FAO and the Secretary-General of the United Nations (WFP 1989c, p.54).

99   Kenya had inserted an even more pointed footnote.

12

BREAKOUT

Governments, inside and outside the CFA, at last set in motion the reform process. The United Nations was assertive in bringing finality to the headquarters agreement but gave only weak and inconsistent leadership on examining the full range of WFP/FAO relationship issues. The ACABQ instigated a review on audit reports, which contributed to the CFA's decision to establish a sub-committee on the governance of WFP.

So far in this protracted seven-year conflict, WFP had won every battle. Yet we were a long way short of winning the war. Initially, our objectives had been limited to getting FAO to accept that WFP should enjoy the autonomy provided for in the Basic Texts. I had absolutely no thought of 'independence'.

But as often happens in war, objectives change. If in 1988 FAO had not insisted on the provision of the working papers of our internal auditor I would have been content to work within the framework of the changes initiated by the taskforce. However, mindful of Saouma's early advice that internal audit could always be used to bring recalcitrant staff under control, and of his savage use of that power to discredit my administration, I was not prepared to put that weapon in his hands. In consequence my ambition enlarged, first to include amending the anachronistic Additional Financial Procedures and then to include comprehensive changes in the General Regulations. If achieved they, together with a headquarters agreement, would make WFP effectively independent with at least the same capacity as its peers to run its affairs as governments wished, free of harassment and able to use food aid appropriately in the changing global environment. Independence in the sense of making WFP a specialised agency was never on my agenda.

THE UNITED NATIONS TAKE CAUTIOUS ACTION

The United Nations had learned the lesson of CFA27: the time had come for it to take some positive action in line with the wishes of governments. Thus, in the following autumn we got a long-awaited letter from the Secretary-General inviting us to a meeting with the UN and FAO, prior to the ACABQ session. The aim was to resolve differences between us and FAO over the documentation to be provided for certification of our accounts, which issue the CFA had decided to 'resolve' at CFA28, scheduled for November 1989.

The FAO Finance Committee had already met and had been circumspect in its approach, now aware that otherwise there might be too big a gulf between its pro-FAO position and that of the ACABQ. The Committee did endorse FAO's fundamental position that it would not be proper for anyone other than the Director-General to specify what documentation he required from WFP to enable him to certify the WFP accounts. In effect, neither governments, nor the External Auditor nor anyone else could tell the Director-General what he should do in this regard.

To my surprise and disappointment, the United Nations had found common cause with FAO in rejecting my proposal that the title of the agenda item for the coming CFA on the relationship with FAO should reflect the language of the CFA and ACABQ recommendations. Instead, it was entitled: 'Follow-up on issues relating to WFP audited accounts for 1986-87'. This was accurate but did not capture the issues at stake. In my view it was politically foolish to hope to hide what was clearly a political conflict behind bureaucratic terminology. In this respect the United Nations resembles the Vatican in the ubiquitous use of opaque language arising from unwillingness ever to call a 'spade a spade'. I quickly discovered the reason. It seemed that Blanca disapproved of my challenging publicly the taskforce accounting provisions, as I had in our documentation explaining the background to the dispute with FAO over signature of our accounts.

Prior to my arrival in New York for the ACABQ meeting, Ruedas advised me the view in the United Nations was that, strictly legally, I had no grounds for refusing to provide the Director-General with the documentation he requested. In the light of this I agreed that in the tripartite meeting we would agree 'in principle' to do so. However, we would also press for a full review of the WFP Basic Documents. I did so with great reluctance:

Sunday 1 October 1989

...even if Saouma has the right to get audit reports he had shown such malice towards the Programme that a reasonable person would accept the validity of my position. However, as I observed in CFA27, this line of reasoning does not carry weight with continentals. Unfortunately, no one studies facts in detail required. Worst of all is the terrible sense of injustice. One knows how the PLO feels when the 'terrorism' charge is constantly levelled notwithstanding the circumstances. However, I have known since CFA27 that in the end I would have to yield over audit. It seems the time has come; but I also know that change won't be effected without S-G/UN support.

The tripartite meeting never took place. The previous evening, in a private meeting with Blanca, Shah informed him that FAO considered the United Nations had no standing in relation to the WFP accounts, nor would it agree to a tripartite review of the Basic Documents. FAO also put pressure on the United Nations to agree that neither should appear before the ACABQ since it was 'not competent to consider issue'. The United Nations declined to do so. My diary records that, afterwards:

Tuesday 3 October 1989

Saouma telephoned Blanca and said that because of his support for WFP 'you are now my enemy'. He also telephoned S-G to ask him to instruct Blanca to desist from his planned course. Apparently, he told Pérez 'you are either against me or against Blanca'. Same old bullying tactics. Why does S-G take his calls?

I had valuable meetings with the ACABQ Chairman prior to the committee's sessions with us and with FAO as my diary records:

Tuesday 3 October 1989

...Met with Mselle. Found him fairly well informed and sympathetic. Subsequently at lunch with him and Ruedas his only concern is how best to proceed. He is disgusted with S-G's unwillingness to act as head of UN system and not just as FAO co-partner.

Wednesday 4 October 1989

FAO with ACABQ all day: full team of Shah, Crowther and Moore. [Our] contacts say it did not go well. FAO arrogance is now deeply institutionalised.

> *Called on Blanca. Thanked him for UN action, urged their continued involvement. He looked dejected so I sought to reassure him that Saouma, on past performance, could be brought to concede, but government involvement still necessary. The United Nations is with me, though of course still a weak reed. They find it very hard to take a position on the merits of a case and moral leadership is beyond them.*

Thursday 5 October 1989

> *Three-hour session with ACABQ. I was quite exhausted at the end. They focused on 1988-89 accounts. I have had to concede that Saouma has right to ask for reports but questioned prudence, commonsense and good faith of his doing so. Russian suggested I had created this crisis in order to bring about general review. Rejected this, pointing to record. However, all in all I had sense of speaking to sympathetic people who understood difficulty of handing over [internal] audit reports. Quite a few questions reflected misinformation given by FAO previous day. ACABQ continued with FAO that afternoon.*

The ACABQ report was positive:

Friday 27 October 1989

> *Long-awaited ACABQ report arrived. Overall very clever: while not partisan towards WFP pressure is put squarely on FAO. As I expected, critical view is taken of our budget: new impositions are made which are not objectionable in themselves but because of our FAO/UN involvement they add an unacceptable burden. Thoroughness of their views shows up shallowness of Finance Committee, Mselle has also been careful…to deflect any charge of exceeding his functions. However, in criticising our budget he blamed our vacant Division Director post, so throwing up senior appointments problem. While I would have liked an unequivocal statement that time has come to put WFP on same footing as UNDP/UNICEF, I am not surprised that this was not forthcoming in UN environment. Situation is unprecedented and it is not easy to decide how to proceed. On the whole, Mselle has managed to get [us] a very helpful report.*

The ACABQ Recommendation

The report was indeed clever. The ACABQ indirectly took issue with the FAO position on the competence of the CFA. It suggested that the CFA might request the 'external auditor of WFP, who is also the external auditor of FAO...to establish what should reasonably be required for the accounts to be certified'. Since the accounts together with the external auditor's certificate is submitted to the CFA, 'it would seem reasonable to assume that the CFA has the authority to request the external auditor to undertake such studies as it may deem necessary...' (WFP 1989e, p.8)

The ACABQ went much further in relation to the broader problems affecting the Programme. Its recommendation read as follows:

...the ongoing dispute over the WFP accounts is only the latest manifestation of the malaise affecting relations between the two organizations. In the opinion of the Advisory Committee, up to now the Secretariats concerned have not been capable of improving the situation...Member States now need to take steps to ensure optimal use of the resources they are entrusting to these organizations. To this end, the Advisory Committee recommends that the CFA request the Director-General of FAO and the Secretary-General of the United Nations to engage an eminent person or persons to study the UN/FAO/WFP relationships and to make such recommendations as may be deemed necessary. (WFP 1989e, p.9)

The reader will recall that the 'eminent person' idea had been mooted by the United States but dropped when the taskforce was set up. It was resurrected within the UN secretariat to head off the possibility of governments taking the initiative to resolve matters between us and FAO by, for example, amending some of the Basic Documents. Though pleased that the United Nations had taken action, I disliked the 'eminent person' idea since so much would depend on the person selected. Francis Blanchard, the newly retired Director-General of ILO, was the name most frequently mentioned. I did not know Blanchard well though I had seen a lot of him in ACC meetings when he usually made constructive, though often overly nuanced, contributions. He also enjoyed good personal relations with his fellow francophone FAO counterpart.

The UN General Assembly Seized of the Matter

The United Nations took a further helpful step. We knew it had been considering the possibility of the General Assembly adopting a resolution calling on the CFA to give consideration to amending the General Regulations. While I felt governments were not yet ready for this, the possibility of such action in future was opening up.

The ACABQ report went to the General Assembly. It was simply noted 'with appreciation'. That was a small, but symbolically important, step forward. Its political significance was all the greater in that the General Assembly requested the ACABQ's report be placed before the FAO Conference, which was duly done. Although there was no discussion of the report, there was a subtle effect: all was sweetness and light in discussion of WFP items once the General Assembly resolution was passed.

CFA28

Notwithstanding these gains I remained pessimistic in the lead up to CFA28 (December 1989). I gave a lot of thought to the best tactics. I need not have worried. In retrospect there is no doubt that CFA28 was a decisive session. Governments at last began to govern. The debates over three days in December 1989 took a total of 24 hours, the last session concluding only at midnight. The atmosphere was sometimes dramatic but there was also a degree of sobriety among delegations. All had realised at long last that the time for ritualistic play acting had passed.

Although the critical issue at CFA28 was the ACABQ recommendations, the committee first had to approve WFP's administrative budget for the 1990-91 biennium. Debate on that item revealed that FAO was still frustrating the conclusion of a headquarters agreement as well as my problems appointing senior officials. I spoke out on all these matters more candidly and forcefully than ever before. FAO's failings in relation to them undoubtedly contributed to the firmness shown by the CFA when it took up the ACABQ proposals.

The Headquarters Agreement Continued

It will be recalled that in July of the preceding year, 1988, FAO suddenly stopped the final negotiation of a headquarters agreement with Italy. I reported on the negotiations to the FAO Council in November 1988 and was able to get across by implication that FAO was to blame. I was very disappointed that not one delegation took advantage of the lead I had given.

I understood from the Italians that, following pressure from the UN, FAO had proposed changes to the earlier draft. These were acceptable to the Italians. However, it was not until late May 1989 that I saw the correspondence between the UN and FAO, which revealed the obstacles FAO was placing to the conclusion of an agreement.

In July the Italians advised that their financial authorities had determined there was no legal basis for them to meet the costs of our accommodation in F Building without a headquarters agreement. While a serious financial blow, it provided us with the opportunity to bring into the open what FAO was doing to frustrate matters and thereby encourage the CFA to exert political pressure.

During the course of the debate there was an astonishing revelation. WFP had been reimbursing FAO for rent of its premises, even though, since 1971, FAO had been receiving contributions from Italy for that same purpose. FAO was morally in breach of the fiduciary trust toward WFP that it so sanctimoniously invoked at every opportunity in relation to financial management!

It transpired that only in 1985 did Italy formally specify that WFP was included in the scope of the subvention. FAO tried to use this to justify having charged WFP its full share of the commercial rent for F Building prior to that date. However, the Basic Documents specify that WFP is to be accommodated at FAO headquarters. Italy said it had always intended that its additional voluntary contribution to FAO should be used to defray the cost of rent of outside premises. Although the FAO representative sought to blur the issue he did not even attempt to answer the obvious question, why did WFP not get a *pro rata* share of the subvention as it related to rent? It was clear to all that, irrespective of the value of its legal argument, FAO had not acted with due regard to the interests of the Programme. Indeed it may have deliberately taken advantage of its control over the accounts to augment its own revenue at our expense for 14 years.

While this issue was separate from the headquarters agreement, in the minds of delegates there was a practical and a political impact. Signature of a headquarters agreement would automatically mean that Italy met our accommodation and related expenses. That would be the end of the matter. Further, FAO's seeming bad faith over past rent subventions undermined belief in its contention that it had legitimate reasons for delaying negotiations over the headquarters agreement.

Any doubts on this score were put to rest by a devastating Italian intervention at CFA28 giving a detailed chronology of its positive responses to each successive new issue raised by FAO. And, for the first time, the United Nations clearly and publicly distanced itself from FAO and showed its exasperation with the latter's behaviour. Its representative categorically stated that the Director-General of FAO had brought negotiations to a halt and had made proposals to Italy without consulting the United Nations, which 'has been pressing for a speedy resumption of the negotiations and the expeditious conclusion of a headquarters agreement for WFP' (WFP 1989f). Six months previously, Italy had written to FAO to invite it to resume negotiations on all issues still open. No reply was received (WFP 1989g).

I had proposed that the CFA should adopt a resolution to follow up the one it had adopted three and a half years previously on our accommodation. FAO spent a lot of ammunition trying to prevent this, once again arguing that the CFA could not request the Director-General to do anything, since he was not answerable to the CFA but only to the FAO Council and Conference. On this point too the United Nations was helpful, its representative stating clearly that the CFA was entitled to 'seek assistance from the Secretary-General and to address a request to him'.

Although the CFA did not adopt a resolution, it agreed to the action I had sought. It 'appealed' to the Secretary-General and the Director-General to intensify negotiations with Italy, requested me to bring this appeal to the attention of both and to report to the next session on 'progress made on the matter'. This latter request was particularly sweet in that FAO had argued at length that since the Executive Director was subordinate to the Director-General 'it was not envisaged [under the Basic Documents] that he would be reporting on the actions taken by the Director-General and Secretary-General' (WFP 1989h).

The Budget Battle

FAO's tactics of ill-informed, exaggerated criticism of our budget further showed that its interpretations of the Basic Documents seriously impeded efficient management of the Programme. Its attempt to demonstrate it was blameless in respect of the delay of more than one year in filling the post of head of our Management Services Division, to which the ACABQ had referred, was easily ridiculed and revealed an absence of any consistent principles of personnel selection (WFP 1989f).

I reminded the committee that, in the interests of transparency, I had involved them in the formation of WFP's administrative budget and had surrendered to the CFA, without any prompting from it, my authority to incur expenditure without restraint in support of the Programme's field operations (WFF 1989f).

In endorsing the budget, the CFA called for certain of the Additional Financial Procedures to be revised and proposals brought for its consideration to CFA29. Though not connected with the central problem, by requesting these revisions the Committee was setting in motion the possibility of more radical change in the future. The CFA neatly sidestepped any objection from the Director-General by simply calling on the secretariat to take action.

Consideration of the ACABQ Proposals

The critical issue was whether the CFA would act on the ACABQ's recommendation to request the Director-General and the Secretary-General to appoint an eminent person to consider the whole relationship; and, secondly, request the External Auditor to establish what documentation should 'reasonably' be required to be handed over to FAO to enable the Director-General to sign the WFP accounts.

Throughout this extended saga, going back to the 1984 Representation on our accounts, FAO had relied upon accounting jargon to bamboozle delegates into thinking there was something of enormous substance at stake over the issue of signature of the accounts and the distinctions between internal and external audit. Today, following the ENRON and other corporate scandals, there is greater awareness that internal audit is a necessary tool of management, and that external auditors should be the key to ensuring the integrity of accounts, even if, like the now defunct Arthur Anderson firm, they cannot always be fully relied upon to protect the interests of stakeholders. With their technical expertise it was easy for FAO's impressive professionals to give gravity and mystique to matters arcane to almost all delegates. Their success over many years was an outstanding example of the organisation's genius in concealing the Emperor's nakedness.

As I said during the debate, all that certification amounts to is a statement that the accounts being submitted for auditing are the official accounts of WFP. Only the External Auditor can state authoritatively that they correctly record the financial circumstances of the Programme.

Speaking on behalf of the Director-General, Dean Crowther rejected the recommendations of the ACABQ to involve the External Auditor. Furthermore, in denying the existence of any 'malaise' in the WFP/FAO relationship, he tacitly rejected the suggestion that an 'eminent person' be appointed. Specifically asked whether FAO would accept such an appointment, Crowther answered, 'I do not know...the CFA has not yet completed its consideration and until it does the Director-General would not wish to prejudge the issue' (WFP 1989i).

The FAO Legal Counsel was more categorical. He informed the CFA that no request could be binding on the Director-General and that it would be 'legally questionable' for the CFA to make a request direct to the External Auditor. Legally, he contended, requests should be channelled through the FAO Finance Committee. In any case, the request envisaged was not about the scope of the audit but called for an interpretation of the Basic Documents of WFP and the Basic Documents of FAO as they applied to the powers and responsibilities of the Director-General. That was inappropriate, he concluded (WFP 1989i).

The Director-General of FAO was standing pat on the narrowest possible interpretation of his constitutional position, while consistently and flatly rejecting the fact of the WFP Executive Director's constitutional relationship with him.

The United Nations Speaks Out More Plainly

The Representative of the Secretary-General did not comment on the legalities though his intervention was very helpful, concluding '...the United Nations recognised that the development of WFP operations justified a review of the basic arrangements governing its management' (WFP 1989i).

In my own intervention at the end of the debate I hammered home some key points:

❑　The challenge was to come to a mutual understanding of what is reasonable by way of the provision of documents. In defining 'reasonable' regard must be paid to cost: 'present arrangements add hundreds of thousands of dollars to our annual costs'.

❑　Each of the three possibilities for resolving the certification issue had been blocked. The Director-General was unwilling to delegate signature again to the Executive Director as he had done for the 1986-87 accounts. He was also unwilling himself to sign on the advice of the Executive Director, though he signed FAO accounts on the advice of FAO staff. Finally, he was unwilling to advise the CFA on modifications to the Additional Financial Procedures or General Regulations to overcome alleged legal obstacles.

❑   FAO's rigid interpretation of the Additional Financial Procedures in this case was not matched by a similar literalness in relation to other provisions.

❑   When, as in this case, trust between organisations had broken down over accounting procedures there was a need for outside mediation, which could appropriately be provided by the External Auditor.

I referred publicly for the first time to the UN legal opinion which I had obtained from the Secretary-General in 1982. Though delegates were well aware of its contents and of FAO's counter opinion, also provided unofficially to delegates, the deliberative bodies had always acted as if these opinions did not exist. Since the FAO had never sent me its opinion and the United Nations had not resiled from its own, I felt free to act in the light of the latter's interpretation of the powers I had under the WFP Basic Documents. However, I knew that the United Nations would be upset if I officially circulated or formally spoke of the opinion, since their approach was always to maintain publicly the illusion that serious differences did not exist between system agencies. Under no circumstances must dirty linen be publicly washed. It was that policy, exploited by Saouma over seven years, which had inhibited the United Nations from giving the leadership I had been beseeching.

I spoke out now, because FAO was inspiring delegates to publicly argue that I was acting *ultra vires*. I therefore explained the constitutional nature of my relationship with the Director-General and Secretary-General and assured the CFA that all my actions were taken on the basis of the Legal Opinion. I also used the occasion to explicate again the absurdly complicated provisions of the Basic Documents. My relative candour, because it was so unconventional, had the tactical advantage of taking my opponents by surprise.

My concluding intervention, plainly and passionately, urged the CFA to assume its responsibility to govern:

As you must by now be well aware, even though I have been very restrained in bringing my problems to your attention...they go well beyond financial issues. That is the reason why it seems to me absolutely essential that governments assume their responsibilities...after all you created this incredibly complicated set of texts which I have to operate within...One way or another they have to be reviewed and revised. A very good way of beginning...is as the ACABQ has suggested...Simply to go on saying: 'You must all love one another, you must all be nice to one another' is simply a counsel which carries us nowhere. These are your organisations. You claim responsibility for them. You have finally, I have to say to you, to accept your responsibilities (WFP 1989i).

The CFA Seizes the Nettle

The CFA did as the ACABQ had suggested, both on the accounts and the eminent person, with recommendations to be available at its next session. Extracts from my diary give some sense of my fluctuating reactions to the drama:

Wednesday 6 December 1989

Zejjari has obtained a copy of FAO speech for CFA. Absolute stonewalling on ACABQ recommendation (indeed refusal to even deal with eminent person proposal) combined with attacks on me. Perhaps this version will be supplanted by another one. In any event they will clearly try to have their forces fight procedurally...Bula Hoyos has rightly pointed out that Saouma will stall on implementation of ACABQ recommendation. I said that we must give him the opportunity to be reasonable and, if he is not, then consider next step.

Tuesday 12 December 1989

Italy at last made crystalline statement about headquarters which showed where blame lay. Also UN. I was able to play up FAO failure to credit us with any share of Italian subvention. FAO shown up as liars, deliberately delaying agreement. Relationship i.e. accounts, debate overall disappointing. Strong support from most Western countries and some developing but Italy did not speak and some developing were unwilling to take a position. France tried to steer an in-between course. Saudi Arabia, Congo and Brazil (main opposition) joined by India with a damaging statement which must have originated with FAO. So clearly no consensus and problem is how to record decision. Crowther stuck with speech we saw...absolute negativity of Saouma has further angered donors. But I am wondering now whether this will bring benefit to WFP even though US and Canada raised idea of independence. In any event I doubt eminent person idea will get anywhere so issue will be back on next agenda

Wednesday 13 December 1989

Debate on excellent report of rapporteur, with much input by Ruedas, lasted six hours. Not until last 45 minutes was it evident that consensus would be reached. Though opposition (delegates) handled themselves skilfully there was none of the nastiness of yesterday afternoon...For once CFA acted like a mature UN body with serious differences between majority and minority, but resolved without deceit and nastiness so often the case before. Saouma must have decided game was up yesterday afternoon and left his troops free to act simply as representatives. Fact of (UN General Assembly) resolution was undoubtedly important in getting result. FAO's ship is currently dead in the water, badly holed above the waterline. It will be patched up and go on fighting to the end. However, we have won a very important battle but the war is far from over. Revelation of two timing over rent is a godsend. The Custodian has been shown to be acting against his ward: we have now a very powerful case why conflict of interest must be ended.

Thursday 14 December 1989

We are agreed that last night's decision and the statements in the debate concerning the need for fundamental institutional change mark a turning point for WFP. Autonomy can be achieved...but the fight will be hard.

Indeed the fight was hard. Though I never allowed myself to feel confident of the outcome I hoped for, looking back now I see that it was inevitable. It had taken on the colour of a Shakespearean tragedy with FAO unable to vary the tactics that had brought matters to this pass and which would lead to its ultimate defeat. At the time I was always fearful that the slowness of the reform process might mean it would string out beyond my term. I had invested so much in the struggle that I dared not relax. I had to continue to exert maximum pressure and be alert to the unexpected to ensure we did secure WFP's independent future.

Already at CFA28 it was evident that member governments were alive to the possibility that Saouma did not acknowledge his responsibility to them as a policy-making body, which had also to provide oversight of the World Food Programme. Saouma dispelled any uncertainties governments had about him in the lead up to CFA29 (June 1990) by the way in which he responded to the CFA's decisions on the headquarters agreement, on the WFP accounts and on the appointment of an eminent person.

THE HEADQUARTERS AGREEMENT

In order to move matters along quickly, the UN Legal Counsel made a special visit to Rome in February 1990 to discuss with FAO outstanding issues. On arrival, he was told that the Director-General, in view of the 'delicacy of the international legal issues involved', had referred the matter to the FAO Committee on Constitutional and Legal Matters (CCLM), which was to meet in May. The UN Legal Office was further angered when FAO attributed to them support for its submission to the CCLM on the headquarters agreement.

FAO developed a complex set of arguments to delay and complicate finalisation of the headquarters agreement, all of which were cogently refuted by WFP in documentation prepared for the CFA (WFP 1990a). Ultimately, the only significant remaining point was the CCLM'S contention that the agreement would have a 'substantial impact' on WFP relations with the United Nations and FAO and on its legal status and 'that the desirability of effecting such a change would have to be passed upon by the Governing Bodies concerned' (WFP 1990b). To initiate that process we, somewhat cheekily, proposed that the CFA should move to amend General Regulation 7(b) as part of a package of changes I was recommending (see below).

Nor could FAO get around the fact that negotiations with the Italians, begun three years previously, had been conducted according to their draft and authorised on the basis of a CCLM recommendation, itself endorsed by the FAO Council. Both bodies had recognised the urgency of ensuring permanent accommodation for WFP and expressed their appreciation for Italy's generosity.

These transparent delays to the resumption of negotiations meant there had been no substantive progress in the six months since the CFA decision at its previous session. This infuriated most delegates. In view of the immense problems caused in the past due to legal advice at CFA sessions coming only from FAO, the United Nations included a senior legal counsellor in its delegation to CFA29. His intervention included an unequivocal statement that the United Nations saw 'no legal obstacles' to 'expeditious conclusion of a satisfactory agreement', which it did not anticipate would require intervention by the ACABQ or the UN General Assembly (WFP 1990c). This last point showed up the hollowness of the

FAO argument that an agreement would have to be considered by the FAO bodies. This clear statement was among the most pointed snubs delivered to a sister agency by the ultra-circumspect United Nations.

The documentation available to the CFA showed more clearly than ever that, intentionally or not, FAO had short-changed the Programme over rent. The Canadian representative dramatised the financial aspect by tearing up a Canadian five-dollar bill, the approximate cost, minute by minute, to the Programme of rent which had been incurred since the Director-General personally stopped finalisation of the agreement in 1988. To no one's surprise, the CFA concluded unanimously that negotiation of the headquarters agreement should be 'resumed without delay and a satisfactory agreement arrived at expeditiously'. With respect to rent, it agreed to await the findings of the External Auditor (WFP 1990d).

THE EXTERNAL AUDITOR'S REPORT

The headquarters agreement was discussed before the report of the External Auditor. Here too FAO had to resort to excessive legalism. In January 1990 it convened the Finance Committee in special session to consider the request to the External Auditor (EA). FAO contended that only the Finance Committee could request the EA to perform specific examinations and issue separate reports. This was a real snub to the CFA, given all that had transpired at CFA28; and the fact that it is the CFA which has final responsibility for consideration of the EA's reports and meets the costs of his audits. FAO also altered the terms of the CFA request, namely from 'to establish what should reasonably be required for the accounts to be certified' to 'review the matter of the information that the Director-General may reasonably require from WFP in order to be in a position to certify the accounts'. The effect of the change from the general to the more particular was to add to the psychological pressure on the EA to come up with the result FAO, the Programme's 'trustee', wanted.

I invested a lot of hope in the EA's report. In particular I wanted him to state clearly that the complex procedure for accounts certification added little financial protection and was an unjustified burden on the Programme's resources and on its accounting staff. For years I had worked to get across to successive EAs and their staffs that in the interests of good governance they had an obligation to state unequivocally that FAO was not acting reasonably in its use of its financial powers, just as I tried to persuade the Secretary-General to use the prestige of his office to inform governments of the true situation. Though I had convinced both WFP was in the right, neither was prepared to give the leadership necessary to bring an end to a wasteful, anachronistic situation.

I had formed a very high opinion of the new British Auditor General, Sir John Bourn, and was optimistic that at last FAO's bluff would be called. However, the process by which the EA formulated his report filled me with misgiving. Altogether we were presented with five drafts over a period of many months. Time after time we would point out aspects that were inaccurate or required clarification and reach what we thought was a full understanding with our interlocutors. Time after time the following draft presented to us was unsatisfactory, often for new reasons. The EA was engaged in the same exercise with FAO, of course, and was making adjustments to meet their point of view. In effect he was negotiating with each of us, attempting a sort of arbitration before committing himself to a definitive position. On joining WFP, I found that all audit reports are to some extent negotiated, something of which delegates and government officials are not normally aware. However, I had never seen a negotiation as extended and frustrating as this one. My diary contains many references to my exasperation, indeed disillusionment, with the process:

Monday 12 March 1990

Excellent meeting with Bourn and his staff followed by tête à tête lunch. He is really a splendid person and I think thrust of his report will remain satisfactory. Gave him much relevant background information—informed him of the Hansa affair and expressed surprise that to best of my knowledge NAO [National Audit Office] never followed up on all information I gave them. I always wonder whether they had ever insisted upon [getting] FAO's own investigatory report.

Wednesday 21 March 1990

External Auditor's new draft report, while not altering main conclusions, presents them in a context unduly helpful to the whole twisted FAO interpretation.

Friday 23 March 1990

> *After an exhausting morning I believe we got Bristow and Smith (EA staff) to recognise that, though well intentioned, their individual changes add up to a document whose balance is unfavourable to WFP. In the last resort I am more and more convinced that the most important outcome is a clear statement by EA that the current arrangements are anachronistic and absurd. I noted that they have been worried that I will not provide Saouma material he seeks and that they will not be able to complete their audit. They were cheered when I said my concern was to relieve WFP permanently of this incubus and if I could get a clear-cut statement about idiocy of arrangements I will happily send Saouma a truckload of documentation!*

Thursday 19 April 1990

> *My earlier speculations about EA are not, I think, correct. Timidity springs from their view that they are legally answerable to FAO and its bodies, not CFA. Attitude summed up when Press [EA senior staff member] described their report as an 'audit report'! Total failure to realise that they have been asked by governments to arbitrate a situation. On first draft, rejected by Saouma, EA was accused of having acted as an eminent person—precisely what he should have done. I have now come to the conclusion that only course is to propose to CFA that it amend General Regulations. All efforts will have to be now directed to this. No more can be got from accounts issue…We must move on.*

Monday 30 April 1990

> *EA still dithering whether his fifth formal draft is his last. Sent a fairly firm letter to him expressing my misgivings about his approach and urging reversion to some of earlier wordings proposed by his staff and acceptable to WFP.*

The External Auditor's definitive report was received early in May:

Monday 14 May 1990

> *…while the changes favour FAO they don't make much difference in practice. At the same time the covering letter is helpful. Bourn…indeed has a subtle mind; for those equally subtle and intelligent the report is really much more favourable to WFP than FAO. But for the average delegate I think he is too subtle. Overall, his report certainly brings out that the relationship is in a mess… It also has to be said that his solution is not easy to implement. Again*

> *part of his subtlety? That thought has occurred several times but as I told him,*
> *one plain sentence is worth 100 indirect allusions.*

Monday 14 May 1990

> *...Bourn's report and covering memorandum have been classified by FAO as*
> *'Strictly Confidential' which means that it cannot be transmitted to*
> *governments! FAO would not have done this unless they felt that report was*
> *far too favourable to our point of view to be let out. It may be that their main*
> *aim is to suppress it for Finance Committee so that they can extract [from the*
> *Finance Committee] the decision they want.*

Although the External Auditor's report (WFP 1990e) said that the Director-General 'in law' could have any document he asked for, he pointed out in many subtle ways that it would not be reasonable to do so. Again, he said that the Director-General should rely on the Executive Director, rather than on the advice of a FAO official, in signing the accounts. He recognised the critical importance of internal audit reports but considered it 'unusual' for 'such detailed scrutiny to take place twice over', once by the WFP internal auditor and again by FAO's. On this point he added something which we had not thought of, namely that in respect of the accounts relating to the services provided by FAO to WFP, the Director-General could provide a similar assurance to the Executive Director, 'together with any relevant FAO Internal Audit reports'. That statement alone must have led to a fit of apoplexy at FAO. Thus, although the External Auditor made no reference to the rent issue as such, for the well informed it was clear that FAO's secrecy over that matter was a clear example of conflict of interest in its role as WFP trustee.

As I anticipated, in accordance with the 'Strictly Confidential' classification, the FAO Finance Committee was not shown the report but was simply informed that the Director-General would abide by the views expressed concerning the information needed to certify the accounts. So, although the Finance Committee had to be convened to approve a request to the External Auditor, that same Committee could not see the resulting report! Equally, I could not transmit it to delegates until, ten days later, FAO realised its mistake and removed the classification.

I had been awaiting the report before issuing a document to the CFA defining my position in relation to it. On John Scott's advice I expressed disappointment at the External Auditor's decision to follow the narrow terms of reference set by the Finance Committee but, nevertheless, undertook 'to conform to the conclusions' of the report. By doing so I deprived FAO's supporters of any opportunity to evade focussing on steps to a permanent solution to the many problems created by outmoded texts.

The Eminent Person Proposal

I had also decided some time beforehand that I would do what I had long meditated doing, namely formally propose to CFA29 that certain key General Regulations, particularly those relating to financial management, be amended. I presented a document, (WFP 1990f), giving proposed 'essential' changes to the regulations as well as others that were 'desirable'. None of the changes altered in any way WFP's status as a joint programme of the UN and FAO. I recommended that the CFA formally refer the essential changes to ECOSOC and the FAO Council no later than the next CFA session. However, the UN Secretary-General and the FAO Director-General declined to comment on my proposal regarding amendment of the General Regulations, noting that my proposals were 'made without prior consultation with either parent organisation' (WFP 1990g).

Further, the Director-General took advantage of my action to contend that my 'far-reaching proposals' had pre-empted the eminent person proposal. That was an excuse. In reality the Secretary-General and the Director-General were unable to agree. As I commented wryly in my diary early in 1990:

> UN fiddling as usual with pusillanimous draft letter from Pérez to Saouma suggesting Blanchard again for eminent person role. Consultation with us is informal of course. As ever UN, like FAO, condemned to follow same tactical path, i.e. 'appease but never confront'.[100]

Saouma took the position that he could not act before consulting the FAO governing bodies from whom he would seek guidance on the scope and terms of reference of any such review. The matter had therefore been placed on the agenda of the November meeting of the FAO Council. If, as might be expected, the FAO Council considered the matter so important as to require endorsement by the FAO Conference, the earliest the eminent person could be appointed was 1992, when my term would have concluded. In the debate the FAO Legal Counsel informed the CFA that the Director-General 'cannot and will not pre-empt the powers and prerogatives of his Governing Bodies on this matter by presenting...a fait accompli'.

I had an opportunity in Vienna in May to discuss the 'eminent person' issue with the Secretary-General, before the United Nations and FAO had finalised their statement to the CFA:

Thursday 3 May 1990

> *After several postponements finally met S-G...S-G asked what should be done about eminent person. Thereafter frank, even intimate, discussion developed between us culminating in: (1) his intention to see Saouma again to press him to go ahead immediately with eminent person. November, i.e. after FAO Council, is 'too late'; and (2) his request that I put in writing what I had said because 'my staff keep information from me'. His new self-confidence evident and I left feeling that with his personal engagement constitution could be changed. Clearly US/Canadian representations to him have had a powerful effect.*

Since the previous year the United States had become much more committed to constitutional change. That owed something to the good relationship I had established with the new Assistant Secretary of State for International Organization Affairs, John Bolton, with whom I met several times in the lead-up to CFA29. He was responsive to my urging that the United States should put pressure on the Secretary-General and action was duly taken. Bolton also considered that it was time to bring Saouma to heel:

Monday 5 February 1990

> *US will pay in 1990 minimum amount to keep its vote in FAO. But Americans are saying that unless there is a fundamental change (interpreted to mean unless Saouma goes) there is no way that Congress would agree to pay $90m required in 1991—implication being that US will then withdraw.*

Monday 12 February 1990

> *Joslyn[101] says that Washington may decide to withdraw from FAO, 'relations with Saouma are at an extremely low ebb' and asked how that would affect their position with WFP. Told him that legally WFP [was] neither FAO nor UN organ and so long as United States continued in United Nations their role should be unaffected. He said Saouma has reserved 70 secretariat places for USSR: he is wooing them hard which clearly worries US! So much for the end of the 'cold war'.*

Thursday 1 March 1990

Lunch with Jerry Monroe[102] at his request. Purpose as stated was to brief me on US relations with FAO which have certainly reached their lowest ebb. However, his real concern was to ascertain my interest in succeeding Saouma. Initially he sought my reaction to a statement that Saouma would surely run again to ensure that I did not take over FAO! Later he asked straight out whether I was interested. I said no. Tun Myat thought I was...too categorical.

Tuesday 20 March 1990 (in New York)

Pledging conference a bit of a flop from point of view of contributions pledged. In period of tight aid budgets few willing to commit themselves so far ahead. However, very pointed donor statements on FAO relations issue. US particularly trenchant, stating that they are taking up WFP issues with capitals. Apparently US, Canadian and German Ambassadors are also to make strong representations personally to SG...Good statements on relations also by Sweden, Canada, UK, Germany and Australia. Canada disappointed there had not been time to get more to speak in similar vein.

Friday 30 March 1990

Have received copy of forceful US Government instructions to posts re our relations with FAO. US has finally, i.e. after eight years, decided to give unequivocal support to WFP. Danger is that their heavy-handed efforts will be counter-productive.

Tuesday 29 April 1990

US Ambassador Pickering and Bolton have now made representations to S-G re eminent person. As they see it he has the power and moral authority to go ahead himself (i.e. he did not need to have Saouma's concurrence). They seem also to be thinking in terms of a specialised agency, if necessary, i.e. dissolution of WFP and its replacement by a new body.

GOVERNMENTS ASSUME THEIR RESPONSIBILITIES

The eminent person proposal was dead by the time CFA29 began on 4 June 1990, not because I had pre-empted it, but because governments, developing as well as developed, had finally had enough of being told what they could or could not do. They decided at last to take action on their own accord.

The relationship issue was the last substantive item on the agenda to be considered in plenary by the CFA, which meant that informal discussions could accelerate as the session got under way. When the item was reached, representatives of the OECD countries and the G77 informed the committee that there was agreement between them to address the 'issue of the relationship between WFP, the UN and FAO'. After a lengthy debate the CFA resolved to set up a committee of the whole, which would be open to observers, to study and make recommendations on proposals from member states, the Executive Director, Director-General and Secretary-General (WFP 1990h). The committee was to begin work no later than the end of summer and present its recommendations to CFA30. This timetable meant that action to revise the General Regulations could be completed in 1991, when the FAO Conference would hold its next biennial session.

An important factor in bringing about G77 acceptance was the willingness of developed countries to agree to a change in composition of the CFA to give a bigger proportion of seats to developing countries. That was something I had long suggested, knowing the developing countries would have to get a *quid pro quo* if the General Regulations were to be revised. In my discussions over the years with G77 representatives it had become clear they did not think the CFA was representative because of near 50:50 composition and did not, therefore, wish to augment its power.

The G77's other concern reflected FAO's fear that donors would seek to make WFP into a specialised agency. Thus, while stating that it was prepared for the CFA to consider the relationship issue, the G77 representative informed the CFA that 'the institutional framework established at the inception of WFP must be maintained and that the position of FAO as the paramount organisation in the food and agriculture sector must not be jeopardized' (WFP 1990h).

The change in G77 posture was not surprising. WFP staff from developing countries had for some time been reassuring me that developing countries would welcome concrete proposals for institutional change–they were embarrassed by the ever-lasting conflict and the going-in-circles. *Let us hope so*, I commented in my diary.

The CFA decision was unprecedented. Governments seemingly were at long last ready to seek constitutional reform and were themselves taking charge of the process. Extracts from my diary flesh out the official records of CFA29:

Tuesday 22 May 1990

Addressed all P4s and above seeking their support for changes to General Regulations. I was not satisfied with my performance but I gather nevertheless that it was effective. If staff are not on side General Regulations may never be changed. I made it clear there was no turning back and their future depended on success. Zejjari says most are with me.

Thursday 24 May 1990

Addressed G77 CFA members. On advice did not go into detail but justified changes [to General Regulations] at a more abstract level. This approach avoided anything remotely personal, which only promotes G77 division. Mexico felt I should have put forward an ideal scenario (if I had, Saouma would have seized on it as evidence that, as charged, I was ambitious to create specialised agency). Bula struck a discordant note, insinuating that I was representing OECD interests. Saouma has been slowly wooing him back into his camp. I felt the occasion went off exceptionally well. I don't doubt that some useful changes will emerge, the question is how much and how long will it take.

Wednesday 30 May 1990

Our supporters appear to be firm in regarding eminent person idea as dead, but I fully expect UN and FAO to announce they are going ahead. Consensus appears to be in favour of working group to report to CFA30, with the action endorsed by ECOSOC.

Thursday 31 May 1990

Hectic day. UN and FAO have joined in statement which is reasonably factual but reflects differing positions on some issues—fortunately. My failure to consult is noted. Main point is to make no comment on my proposals. Probably Saouma's goal: fearing I might get my proposals through at CFA29 (which in reality would be impossible) he wanted joint statement to prevent this. Otherwise, I don't think it achieves much. But why does UN lend itself to a joint statement? Why cannot it state publicly its private position? Always so weak, always yielding to FAO pressure in the name of I know not what, UN principle?...Good lunch with Nordics who seem fairly robust. Distributed a draft resolution which if nothing else will scare Saouma. Bula Hoyos impressed that I am giving all audit documents to Saouma. His manner suggests that he sees strength on my side. Claims Saouma not lobbying. Cuban representative called. Wants to impress me with their support and constraints they operate under. As he says, WFP aid more important than ever for them.

Friday 1 June 1990

Tomlinson says I should relax and enjoy it. Correct, because I think the tide is with us. But always have the feeling that if I relax my guard I will be overwhelmed. Hysterical memo from Saouma replying to mine forwarding to him all the audit documentation...He had, it is clear, no inkling that I would propose amendments to General Regulations. He lives in his own world and believes that he is the only piece on the board and then is shocked to find the other piece can make an unanticipated move. He had no idea that I would give the [accounts] documents finally. As I hoped, he was planning a big assault over the issue and now finds the ground cut from under his feet. Tomlinson tells an amusing tale of Cameroon Ambassador's conversation with Saouma who...claimed my only goal was third term to which he [Saouma] would never agree...said that I was instrument of industrialised powers and could not be trusted with more power...and that I was already most powerful man in Rome, having stripped him of all but nominal authority re emergencies...His last point led me to give Tomlinson Saouma's letter to Austrians accepting their offer of 5,000 tons for Ethiopia but suggesting it might better go to Lebanon!...Confusing reports about G77 meeting...acceptance that CFA working group must be established but proposal to have it go into next year is still alive; eminent person idea seems dead. Good meeting with donors re emergencies.

Sunday 3 June 1990

Lunch with Cristianson [United States], Lindores [Canada], Fischer [Germany] and Aspinall [Australia]. Lindores very 'bolshie', wants to move to an immediate request to S-G to set up new WFP: could come eventually but not so quickly. Fischer and Cristianson both showed reasonable grasp; now more fully understand what I have been up against. How this will work out I don't know but equally clearly my move, which I have delayed for so long, has been launched at the right moment. Appealed to all to address issue on basis of good governance and not to indulge in threats. Unfortunately that remains disposition of Lindores and Cristianson though I did get across that issue must be handled with great tact. Fischer much more sensitive in this regard. Fischer surprised that Saouma insisted on circulation of our correspondence.[103]

Reason is simple, with his Emperor complex, Saouma is sure that.....all will see my crime of 'lèse-majesté'!

Monday 4 June 1990

For first time Saouma did not attend CFA opening, going to Geneva for UNDP meeting on agency support costs. But doubtless he could have gone in the afternoon. Sign of disengagement as well as avoidance of an unpleasant encounter with me. Last year he could barely bring himself to shake hands. My opening remarks gave little space to relations but the emphasis on governance struck the right note. Saouma's speech (read by Dhutia), though deliberately misleading on three points, to which I replied, was somewhat lower key than I expected. Much confusion over what will happen, though clearly some sort of working group will be created.

Tuesday 5 June 1990[104]

So much has happened that events are already a blur. On rent issue Lindores made a superb speech...Also good US speech and many others, most of which were appropriately strong–except for French. In general debate, PLO delegate requested WFP assistance. I replied publicly, expressing willingness in principle. Thought it an opportunity to underline my political even-handedness. Lebanon also claimed no aid since 1981–they are consistently ungracious as far as WFP is concerned.

Wednesday 6 June 1990

De Medicis [Brazil] as G77 Chairman and Prillevitz [Netherlands] for OECD have worked out a CFA decision to satisfaction of all...Debate was measured given decision already taken, but some excellent statements on our side. Ruedas says that I may have to be drafted for a third term. I rejected this but said I would stop making clear statements of my future intentions. Today's decision is a turning point. At last there is agreement to constitutional change and basic principles could now be established before my term ends. Kelloway feels I have now won the war, though some major battles remain to be fought.

Thursday 7 June 1990

Dreadful final session over adoption of report lasting 8 hours, from 5 pm to 1.00 am. Congo, Colombia with some support from Cuba, successfully filibustered to prevent adoption of passages on 'relationships'.

In fact the imbroglio over the report was of no real significance. Saouma's closest associates among the Rome delegates put on the show to make amends for having given way over substance, but also to serve notice that they were ready for battle on the actual content of change. As always, they enjoyed a bit of fun at the expense of developed countries.

As events were to show, FAO would continue to obfuscate issues hoping still to stall finalisation of reform. However, governments had at last begun to govern, which was what most mattered from my perspective. That they were soon able to agree on long overdue, constitutional reform for WFP established an important precedent for processes of change elsewhere in the UN system.

---

[100] As alternatives to Blanchard we had suggested the former Director-General of WHO, Halfdan Mahler, or Secretary-General of IMO, Chadrika Srivasteva.

[101] David Joslyn, a member of the United States Mission and Chairman of CFA27 and 28.

[102] United States representative to FAO and WFP.

[103] FAO had requested circulation of correspondence between me and Director-General concerning the External Auditor's report on accounts documentation: WFP/CFA: 19/P/7 Add. 3&4.

[104] This and following entries written in retrospect on 10 June 1990.

13

VICTORY AT LAST

Constitutional change and a headquarters agreement with Italy were achieved. With the FAO-WFP relationship clarified, I could push through changes to the way WFP delivered humanitarian aid, including by enabling an emergency response without a request from the affected country; and the creation of a special fund to speed up WFP's emergency food delivery.

Before describing the conclusion to this drawn-out saga, the reader may find it useful to have a brief recapitulation of the inherent disfunction in the structure of WFP that caused me to seek constitutional change:

❏   A governing body unwilling and incapable of discharging the policy role set down in its Basic Documents.

❏   A governing body that would not govern, that is rarely took formal decisions beyond the approval of projects and instead laboured mightily and divisively over the production of a report that supposedly described CFA 'debates' but was never referred to at future sessions.

❏   A governing body most of whose members, whether from developed or developing countries, had no first-hand knowledge of the unique problems involved in using food for economic and social development and unwilling or unable to encourage the secretariat to improve its performance beyond general exhortation.

❏   A 'co-parent', the United Nations, which took only a pro-forma interest and neglected its oversight responsibilities.

❏   A brow-beaten secretariat uncertain of its identity, lacking confidence to make further innovations in the use of food aid or to

273

assume the responsibilities placed upon it by the World Food
Conference in regard to global food aid policy.

❑   Responsibility on the chief executive to raise the food and money
needed to sustain and increase operations and account for their use
but without ultimate financial control, which rested with a 'trustee'
with conflicts of interest.

❑   Responsibility on the chief executive to manage efficiently and
effectively all aspects of operations, though required to use the
services of other organisations (mainly FAO) irrespective of
considerations of cost, timeliness and quality.

❑   Staffing arrangements which had created separate cadres of
headquarters and field staff managed under different sets of rules, that
is FAO rules in Rome and UNDP rules in developing countries.

❑   Extraordinary restraints on the power of the Executive Director
to select and promote staff, especially senior officers.

❑   An organisation whose representative in recipient countries could
not be a staff member of WFP.

❑   An emergency approval system which enabled the head of FAO to
control and take credit for emergency food decision-making but never
blame for unprofessional needs assessment, over which he had control,
or inappropriate or slow responses.

The final stage in the struggle for autonomy was, as always, a drawn-out
process. A working group, known as the Sub-Committee on Governance
(SCG), was constituted as planned but its two sessions were unproductive.
However, at its December 1990 session, the CFA did agree on the substance
of the changes to the Basic Documents and decided to establish a new,
differently constituted SCG to translate the agreed changes into precise
textual amendments.

The CFA held a special session in March 1991 to approve the proposed
changes so that the revised documents could be submitted to United
Nations and FAO bodies for approval in 1991. With the adoption of
identical resolutions late that year by the UN General Assembly and the
FAO Conference the process of institutional change was complete. The
Programme now had similar autonomy to its sister agencies, UNDP, UNHCR
and UNICEF. The headquarters agreement, which defined WFP's identity in

Italy and led in due course to occupation of its own building, was finally signed. As a result, the Programme's public image resembled more closely a specialised agency than did that of its UN peers.

Until CFA30 I had been the driver of change. From then on, the process was led more by governments and their representatives. To some extent I became a bystander. While I had long wanted governments to assume their responsibilities I found it nerve-racking when they did. I had done everything I could to educate governments on the changes they should make but had little confidence they would be able to deal with all the obstacles that would be thrown in their way. For me, therefore, the year following CFA30 was a cliff-hanger, rather like one of those serials I had enjoyed at Saturday movie matinees in the nineteen thirties. Each episode concluded with the good guys facing certain disaster, a disaster from which they somehow always escaped to enable episode to follow episode.

Since one purpose of this book is to give an insight into the parliamentary processes of the UN system I will fill out the bald story with some further extracts from my diary.

THE SUB-COMMITTEE ON GOVERNANCE (SCG)

The SCG was due to meet on 3 September 1990. Beforehand, FAO showed every sign it was not yet ready to give up the fight. The recommendations of the External Auditor in regard to involvement of the Executive Director in the process of signature of the 1988-89 accounts were ignored. A well argued FAO critique of our proposals for change in the General Regulations was prepared and circulated to SCG members and Edward West was brought back from retirement as FAO's representative on the SCG.

The Secretary-General appointed as his representative, Peter Hansen, head of the Transnational Corporations Unit at UN headquarters. Hansen had no prior knowledge of the relationships issue, which may have been a factor in the United Nation's choice. He did have a reputation for integrity, which proved to be well deserved. We quickly formed a good rapport. WFP also had the inestimable assistance of Ruedas and Scott. The principal donors on the SCG were represented by senior officials.

My diary describes what happened at the committee:

Monday 3 September 1990

Atmosphere surprisingly good. Libyan G77 Chairman, as FAO pawn, only seriously disruptive note. He seems to have had sufficient endorsement of his paper [attacking reform] to present it but support for it seems largely formalistic. West sought to answer my opening statement with usual mixture of insinuations, half truths and downright falsehoods. UN statement was good, accepting need for change and enlargement of Executive Director's powers. Very good statement by US [Cristianson]—that while firm in its thrust it was graceful and lacked 'arrogance of power'. Australian statement also went as far as I could reasonably expect. There appears to be a consensus for strengthening powers of CFA and the Executive Director.

Tuesday 4 September 1990

Good atmosphere maintained. West introduced a spoiler's note, with a sarcastic intervention attacking Lindores. Chairman twice pulled him up and he desisted—he got no support...We produced a chairman's summary which he successfully sold more or less intact to a group of key players, though it took several hours. Stage is set for something to emerge but I remain pessimistic...

Wednesday 5 September 1990

Atmosphere seemed less good today, or was it the vapidity and puerility of the debate? Warin [France][105] is a nuisance, making proposals which have a degree of Cartesian logic but politically and practically out of the question. Deregibus [Argentina][106] more and more poisonous. FAO has got at many delegates whose ignorance of WFP and of the UN makes our task seemingly impossible.

The Role of Personalities

That victory in this final year did not come easily owed much to the personalities involved: their strengths and weaknesses, likes and dislikes and ambitions. Reaction to my personality was certainly a factor, with always some delegates never convinced of my *bona fides*. That was the case with Ms Deregibus, an intelligent, competent and hard-working diplomat with a legal background but also, it was said, close to a senior FAO official deeply involved in the constitutional battle. Throughout her time in Rome, Deregibus was unhelpful. Argentina was a small donor of commodities only to the Programme and at this time was not a member of the CFA, so we never had occasion for a personal discussion. However, as was quite often the case, developing countries from Latin America, such as Argentina, Mexico, Brazil and Colombia, with little stake in WFP, were the most obstructive. Argentina had nothing to lose by such action and doubtless saw political value in presenting itself as a fearless champion of the supposed interests of its poorer G77 allies. Although the Cold War had ended, the North-South conflict, entrenched in the UN system for more than thirty years, was not easily let go.

Thursday 6 September 1990 (in Paris)

Ahmed apparently did well [in SCG] clash with West. Though no substantive progress on texts will take place this session, there is disagreement as to whether or not to have an intersessional meeting. According to Cristianson, at a lunch he and Lindores had with West and Shah, latter said Saouma would agree to constitutional changes only after I had left. Surely, given that attitude, a deal can be struck provided it is iron-clad since I intend to leave and will not run for [FAO] D-G.

Friday 7 September 1990 (in Paris)

Blanca had told me that France would not stand in way of textual changes which was confirmed by Quay d'Orsay. Altogether they were sympathetic and responsive when I mentioned some of our problems, for example over Sudan emergency. Saouma must have irritated French very much that they have decided to shift our way.

Monday 10 September 1990

A disappointing and discouraging day. Chairman [Nanjira, Kenya][107] was to have presented his summary but after hours of dithering [back and forth consultation] he had not done so by 4.30 pm when an exasperated SCG demanded to start. Then, in the course of an hour-and-a-half discussion, he yielded to G77 pressure.

Tuesday 11 September 1990

SCP concluded. Good atmosphere restored. Owed something to Tchicaya who countered move by Bula Hoyos to upset matters. Clearer than ever that even extreme G77 don't want an all-out fight at this stage at least on change per se. However, only a small beginning has been made and I still find it difficult to see how agreed texts can ever be produced.

The reason for this pessimism was that the leading delegates from the G77 had ensured that the discussion never moved beyond generalities, not one step having been taken to discuss possible amendments to the General Regulations. Argument went around endlessly in circles. I had no doubt the hope in FAO was that the proponents of change would give up in disgust. At least it had been agreed to hold a second meeting, which was scheduled for 8 October.

During the intervening period we continued our efforts with delegates. I focussed on the various G77 regional sub-groups:

Thursday 20 September 1990

A satisfying meeting with Asian Group–first ever in fact to explain basis of our proposed General Regulations changes. The scales dropped visibly from the eyes of many of them–including India and Pakistan, the two most vocal members of the group. They are bombarded with misinformation from Saouma and FAO: my changes are described as 'extreme'. I was particularly pleased to get across why changes in emergency procedures are necessary–without having to describe FAO sins. Lunch with Ambassadors of Niger, Cameroon and Tanzania. All seem solid.

Friday 28 September 1990

Meeting with African Group. Spoke for an hour to a fascinated audience. For the first time [they gained] some inkling of what are the most important changes and why they are required. Nanjira says Saouma would undoubtedly have been listening in [meeting at FAO in Philippines room] and would have been infuriated especially by my claim that FAO adds no value on emergencies.

Monday 1 October 1990

Meeting with Latins. Chilly to begin with but atmosphere visibly warmed. I left with the feeling we will probably achieve our goals, or at least most of them, but doubtless the road there will be as rough as ever.

The second session of the SCG met from 8-12 October 1990. My diary traversed its progress:

Monday 8 October 1990

SCG resumed to face usual filibuster, though little support given to Saouma's agenda item proposal.

Tuesday 9 October 1990

> *Little progress in SCG. However, Canada is doing its own drafting. This may be the only way, i.e. for a group of sponsors to produce a resolution embodying proposed textual changes.*

Wednesday 10 October 1990

> *I feel the tide has turned and have a sense of the burden lightening. Because of fear of offending Saouma, delegates will not address themselves to a WFP text. Canadians have therefore drafted up a set of changes with many square brackets so that SCG can get down to business. The Canadian 'non-paper' was introduced by Bula Hoyos who has behaved like an angel so far. On Zejjari's advice I spoke today in SCG to answer various queries and to defend some of our proposals. 'Socked it to them', as someone said... opposition seems to be weakening.*

Thursday 11 October 1990

> *My sense of relief, as I have half feared, has turned out to be an illusion. The committee adjourned without taking up the Canadian paper and the G77 announced they would not agree to have discussions on Canadian paper...Aim is to draw matter out endlessly while trying to avoid [blame for] a breakdown, or perchance wear our supporters down to point of accepting unsatisfactory agreement.*

Friday 12 October 1990

> *Last night was apparently disastrous. Many of our developing country supporters recoiled from what they had said yesterday. OECD were shell-shocked following Libyan announcement [not to discuss Canadian paper]. Zejjari came to me with some ideas for a solution on Trust Fund and emergencies which I agreed he could pass to France as his own personal initiative. Meanwhile Canada and Australia are proposing S-G to be in charge of Trust Fund and delegate to ED. Saouma not likely to be entranced by this idea. Zejjari's approach likely to be a more acceptable compromise. A small group met with Chairman to thrash out size of CFA, WFP fund and emergencies...Argentina insisted on limiting ED to two terms and geographical rotation of post. As Tun Myat said, 'Deregibus is out to get you'. No progress made on any issue though at least options were identified.*

When Bula Hoyos sought to introduce the Canadian paper as his own, the Libyan Chairman of the G77 tried to prevent this, but eventually good sense prevailed. As I commented in my diary on the events of 11 October:

> *After usual agonising and unnecessary procedural debate FAO forces routed.*
> *Session ended with apparent breakdown but with onus clearly on FAO forces.*
> *OECD and others jubilant at reversal of tables. Call by Ethiopian and Cuban*
> *Ministers. Cubans told me FAO had really put on tremendous pressure in*
> *name of G77 solidarity to get our supporters to back off. Usual threats that*
> *they will be denounced to their Presidents if they don't toe the line.*

The SCG session ended inconclusively, reporting that it 'was not in a position to make recommendations to the CFA at this stage'. At least, however, serious discussion of possible textual amendments had begun. It was decided to annex amendments proposed by Colombia as the session had not felt able to consider these. Ten days later Canada, which had largely drafted the Colombian paper, advised it had agreed with Colombia to co-sponsor its proposals for consideration by the CFA (WFP 1990i).

The main donors were deeply disturbed at the slow progress and Germany made a formal statement on behalf of thirteen delegations. The crucial passage read:

> ...the principal issues have been known for years and the representatives
> feel it necessary to indicate that time is of the essence and that a serious
> situation will be created if the thirtieth Session of the CFA...fails to take
> significant decisions aimed at solving key outstanding problems. Such a
> failure will inevitably reduce the confidence of the international
> community, including donor states, in the ability of WFP to undertake its
> activities...efficiently and effectively and in the ability of the CFA to
> undertake...intergovernmental supervision of the Programme (WFP
> 1990i p39).

ACABQ PROPOSALS

CFA30 was to meet early in December 1990. In the interval beforehand there were a number of developments which strengthened the prospects for change. I appeared again in November before the ACABQ, which was to consider our audited accounts for 1988/99. I found Mselle as positive as ever about relationships, though searching in his questioning about our accounts.

Mselle gave me no inkling of how his report (WFP 1990j) would deal with relationships beyond a concern, expressed also by Blanca, that the United Nations wanted to avoid a situation where intergovernmental organs in the UN system were at odds with one another. The ACABQ made some very helpful points. It contended that the External Auditor was indeed responsible to the CFA; underlined his endorsement of the high professionalism of our internal audit; urged that, should the CFA make definite recommendations for change, its recommendations be 'specific and clear', to facilitate consideration by UN and FAO bodies. It concluded that, 'Member States now need to take steps to ensure optimal use of the resources they are entrusting to these organizations', i.e. WFP and FAO. By the usual standards of UN-speak, this was remarkably straightforward and a strong endorsement of all that I had been arguing.

In parallel action, donor governments decided that matters would be helped along by a further General Assembly resolution. Consideration was giving to texts of varying strength, but to my relief a procedural resolution was unanimously adopted late in November (see below).

Nevertheless, I continued to find timorousness and uncertainty among governments, due largely to competing bureaucratic interests within them and, often, the absence of a full understanding of the issues. Denmark was an exception. A single ministry, its agriculture department, dominated policy formulation in relation to both WFP and FAO. Its head, H J Christiansen, had been a strong supporter of WFP for many years and often attended sessions of the CFA. Equally he had taken a close interest in FAO and was a long-time critic of Saouma's management. Denmark's representative, John Glistrup, was an official of the agriculture ministry and was an exception among OECD representatives, in that he had been in Rome for many years, so had the depth of parliamentary experience to match key delegates from developing countries long assigned to the Rome agencies.

What worried me most was that the OECD countries representatives in Rome would not be able to overcome their deeply established attitude of defeatism towards FAO:

Tuesday 20 November 1990

> *Long discussion with Glistrup...I emphasised that our side [was] too willing to consider concessions. In fact G77 (as distinct from Saouma) cared only about size and composition of CFA; that, no matter what was agreed with G77 [in CFA], Saouma would seek to undermine it in other fora if he judged he could get away with such action. Accordingly, the main donors should introduce a resolution [in CFA] embodying all changes desired, including size and*

composition of CFA. It would immediately attract support from several developing countries and would be adopted by consensus (with cosmetic changes) if sponsors were resolute. Glistrup concerned about situation arising if UN goes one way and FAO bodies the opposite. I said...Saouma could never be defeated by those unwilling to take risks. His whole strategy and success had been based on willingness to take risks and out-bluff his opponents.

HEADQUARTERS AGREEMENT

Meanwhile, FAO were still attempting to delay finalisation of the headquarters agreement:

Monday 12 November 1990

Saouma on the attack again. I had assumed that he was ready to accept Headquarters Agreement, though stretching out matter for as long as possible. But no, in the worst piece of humbug yet, a document has been introduced putting pressure on [FAO] Council not to endorse agreement. How does one cope with an agency that never plays by the rules and accepts neither consistency of behaviour nor truth?

I lunched the following day with the Italians who agreed the FAO document amounted to an admission that, for over three years, they had been negotiating in bad faith. *I think Italian 'face' is sufficiently involved to get them moving on this,* I wrote in my diary. That turned out to be the case.

Tuesday 27 November 1990

A victory, I think. So many times we have won a battle but Saouma continues to evade the result. But there was clear consensus [in the FAO Council] that Saouma should sign the Headquarters Agreement. At the end FAO Legal Counsel was barely able to speak, whispering into the microphone that he could not say what the D-G would do, even after he had been forced [by Australia] to admit there were no outstanding issues [with Italy]. I had to point out that Legal Counsel was raising...obstacles [extradition and Italian labour laws] on which there had [already] been agreement...I pointed out that Saouma could sign without prejudice to his position on these points, if he wanted to. Italian statement very clear and included passage stating that their subvention had been for rent of Building F.

The sentiments of the committee were so clear that the consistently unhelpful Belgian chairman of the FAO Council had to acknowledge that all who had intervened in the debate had insisted on signature taking place as soon as possible. I wrote in my diary, *We have scored a considerable moral victory on relationships since Saouma's position has not been endorsed and on Headquarters Agreement the emperor has been stripped of his clothes.*

A further encouraging factor was that FAO appeared to be losing control over the G77. The Group had not endorsed the Libyan chairman's[108] last proposals but had produced its own. These, at last, contained a few concrete textual amendments.

CFA30

FAO's Whispering Campaign

I had given a great deal of thought to what I should say in my opening statement to CFA30. The main thrust of FAO's persistent whispering campaign was that I was pressing for change to obtain untrammelled power in my next term. I was said to be the creature of the developed countries and all that stood in the way of their complete takeover of the Programme was its links with FAO, which I was committed to sever. The implication, never explicitly stated, was that the cereals producers would be free to use food aid as they wished, with potentially deleterious political and economic consequences for the developing countries. The irony was that FAO had been a great supporter of food aid while it had control of WFP. As that control slipped so did its enthusiasm for food aid, clearly marked over the years in the speeches of the Director-General in the CFA and elsewhere.

In the eight years of my term, FAO had rarely brought its supposed expertise on the possible adverse effects of food aid to bear on the design of our development projects. In relation to our emergency responses, where potentially deleterious consequences were much more evident, their cautions were even rarer. Indeed, that was one of the main differences in our approaches to the use of emergency food aid, with WFP pushing for assessments of factors such as possible disincentives to local food production. We were mindful of the widespread evidence found by NGOs and academics that in some situations of food shortage free food distribution could do more harm than good. Our evaluations of our emergency responses, an innovation of mine, were revealing further evidence of the importance of understanding their impact. However, Saouma brushed such arguments aside. Several times he said to me, 'The beneficiaries are so poor they must be helped. Technicalities should not stand in the way.' That was the basis of the claim promoted by FAO to the developing countries, that our contest was one between a cold, power-hungry technocrat from the rich world, versus a warm-hearted champion of the poor coming from a developing country.

FAO had constantly and successfully promoted among the G77 the idea that it provided necessary policy guidance to WFP. This had been articulated by Brazil among others the year before at CFA28. At that time, I pointed out that the only reference in the Basic Documents to policy was to the CFA itself, which was charged with evolving and coordinating short-term and long-term food aid policies.[109] That responsibility of the CFA and the role of the WFP secretariat to provide policy recommendations had been settled years beforehand. The CFA could not be instructed except through the oversight bodies of the United Nations and FAO, in particular ECOSOC, which had a coordinating role.

In his opening speech to CFA30 West, on behalf of the Director-General, alluded publicly to some of these claims for the first time. As things stood, he said, the Executive Director already had the authority to make decisions 'involving monetary values of many millions of dollars which far exceeds the authority given to any other leader of an agency in the UN system', including the President of the World Bank. 'It was not a question of freeing the Executive Director from any control, but rather one of who could exercise it between meetings of the CFA.' In relation to emergency food aid, West said, 'questions of some delicacy in intergovernmental relations often arise', a broad hint that the interests of beneficiaries required the guiding hand of the Director-General. It was also essential to ensure that decisions were taken in the light of 'all the considerations that fall under...food security, food situations, nutritional situations and so on', in other words, everything in which FAO had a mandate.

A Personal Decision

The best way to put an end to this insidious nonsense was to remove myself as a factor in the deliberations of the committee. The constant speculation that I sought change in order to enhance my personal power lay behind

Deregibus' proposal to limit the Executive Director to two terms and to require geographical rotation of the post. The developed countries would never accept the rotation provision, which would therefore probably become a serious stumbling block to agreement on major change.

Though, to the concern of many, I had often said privately that I did not wish a third term, there was widespread disbelief. In the Rome climate no-one willingly gave up such a prestigious, and in the views of many, powerful post unless of course he had a better alternative. Moreover, my closest colleagues in WFP wanted me to stay on and may therefore have been less than fully convincing in their denials.

To lay matters to rest, in my opening statement I informed the CFA that I considered the Deregibus proposal 'worthy of the most serious consideration', as I did, and that while thankful to those developing countries in the SCG who had insisted that the proposed change was without prejudice to my continued occupancy, I believed 'there should be no exceptions' and that any change made should apply to me. I went on to say,

> There need be no embarrassment on this score because, as those who know me well are aware, I have never ever had any intention to seek a third term. That remains my position; and to leave no shadow of doubt, let me say that I would not accept a further term if it were offered to me (WFP 1990k).[110]

To hammer home my commitment to the 'two terms' principle and to educate delegates who were on the whole not well informed of developments elsewhere in the UN system, I circulated copies of a just published report on UN reform, in English, French and Spanish (Childers and Urquhart 1990). The authors, widely respected former members of the UN secretariat and UNDP, favoured single terms of seven years that would not be renewable. They rightly considered this to be the most important step readily attainable for reform of the UN system. From my perspective, I said, there was no reason why the CFA should not give a lead to the whole UN system. I partly had in mind that if it did so it would create a precedent for similar action in FAO. The gauntlet was not picked up. The G77 dropped its proposal altogether. I tried very hard to persuade the UK and the Nordics to pursue the matter but they were unwilling. Thus in my final speech to the CFA in December 1991 I spoke of my 'one disappointment', namely the failure to limit the number of terms that could be served. However, the General Regulations have since been amended to limit the WFP Executive Director to two terms. I will have more to say on this issue in the concluding chapter.

Before CFA31 the United States was already confident that I was standing down and their expectation that an American would succeed me was no doubt a positive, even decisive, factor in their commitment to the reforms that I had long sought. Sticking to my decision was essential, though it was not without sorrow. Although I had long decided that my priority was to get for WFP a revised constitutional arrangement that fitted its growth and changing global circumstances, it still caused me some anguish to rule myself out. I loved WFP and would have enjoyed immensely the freedom that the changes brought to my successor. I knew it would be a wrench to finally leave.

My announcement was the political master stroke in bringing about the changes I sought. The atmosphere in the CFA was transformed. Developing countries had become embarrassed by the perpetual turning in circles over reform. My announcement revealed to them that FAO's insinuations were false. They felt free to do what their consciences directed.

The CFA had the SCG's report before it, the most important element of which was the annexed Colombian/Canadian paper. After our opening statements it was clear from the new Iranian Chairman of the G77 that his side was at last ready to move from general discussion to serious negotiations and, to that end, to see a new Working Group established, sufficiently small to make progress. It was made up of five developed countries, namely Australia, Canada, Japan, Norway and the United Kingdom and six developing countries, Bangladesh, Brazil, Mexico, Niger, Pakistan and Zambia. The G77 Chairman attended as an observer. The group worked intensively and successfully under the chairmanship of Ambassador Don Nanjira for 25 hours. My diary records the outcome and my reactions:

Thursday 6 December 1990

> *Negotiating Group finished at 2 am. Final package is very good. I have obtained the essentials of all I sought. G77 met for several hours to decide whether they would accept. Argentina and Congo were main hold-outs. Division remains about how to go ahead. OECD wants to push ahead to draft*

texts. G77 wants a pause—essentially I think from exhaustion at least on part of principal figure, Saleem Khan of Pakistan.

Friday 7 December 1990

The end of the penultimate chapter has been reached. Not only is there agreement on the content of the package but also now on steps to be taken and the timetable [to translate into textual changes in the Basic Texts and General Regulations]. I dare to believe that not only have I won another battle but have clearly won the war though a few more rearguard skirmishes will be fought. I could leave now in good conscience.

The CFA decided that the resumed SCG, which would have the same composition as the Working Group, should meet again in January 1991 for one week to agree on revised texts, discussion to be on the basis of drafts prepared by the United Nations Legal Office, in consultation with FAO and WFP. To ensure that the CFA could endorse revised texts in time for consideration by ECOSOC at its session in the spring of 1991, it was decided to hold, for the first time in the Programme's history, a special CFA session in March. The January SCG moved relatively smoothly to a successful outcome.

Friday 1 February 1991

Another hurdle crossed. SCG has finalised its report. Amended General Regulations are good, though I am disappointed that FAO-inspired amendments defining technical services lay the way open to continuing disputes over responsibilities in relation to needs assessment for emergency victims. Also requirement for consultation re annual report maintained which is quite incongruent with an ED exclusively responsible to governing body. However, these are minor blemishes on a package which UN Legal Office regards as representing a whole order of magnitude shift in status of WFP. Apparently no other precedent exists for change of this size in the UN system—and all done with unprecedented speed. The report is also significant in showing a 'governments take charge' attitude on appointment of ED and future role of Finance Committee. FAO pettiness has been taken care of by a statement of the obvious, that the Executive Director can be removed by the same process he has been appointed. A debt of gratitude is owed to all members of Working

Group...Saouma's only real support came from Khan of Pakistan. Iranian Chairman of G77 is very pleased about outcome, not least because for the first time it has led to G77 harmony and a common position!

This excellent result owed much to the work of the Canadian, Australian and German representatives in the Working Group: Carole Theauvette, Alan Wilkinson and Fritz Fischer. Overall, the US input was helpful and the fact that it stood aside from membership of the Working Group probably contributed to the good atmosphere during the deliberations.

The CFA Completes its Work

My cup was overflowing two days later when the Special Session of the CFA adopted by consensus on 18 March 1991 (WFP 1991a), without prior debate, the agreed changes recommended by the SCG. My sense of satisfaction was all the greater because the headquarters agreement had been signed a few days before. FAO resisted to the end. Even though there was agreement between Italy and FAO on certain interpretative letters affecting the agreement, whose incompletion had been FAO's latest excuse for deferring signature, in order to get pen put to paper I had personally made representations to the Italian Foreign Minister to apply the necessary pressure on FAO. Ironically, after all the fuss over the agreement, Saouma delegated signature to the head of FAO's management department. He declined to attend the luncheon I gave to celebrate the occasion in the FAO restaurant which, I wrote in my diary, ...*turned out to bring a major political benefit. This public occasion will have been the talk of FAO. All will know that FAO have finally conceded and that I have offered olive branch.*

As my diary notes, I gave a strong and conciliatory speech at the conclusion of the Special Session which was strongly applauded. FAO declined to speak but afterwards Edward West graciously offered me his personal congratulations. As a consultant to FAO he could afford to do so. It had become clear over time that most FAO staff charged with fighting Saouma's battle against us found the job distasteful, though I must say they carried out their duties assiduously.

Through this long battle, there was one barometer always reading 'fair' and which buoyed my own feelings. FAO headquarters had many uniformed guards who never failed to greet me with a friendly manner. At the end of those sessions when I felt we had at least held our end up, if not gained a success, I was invariably greeted with the warmest of smiles and greetings radiating good will, though of course nothing was said. In the inbred atmosphere of an international agency it was entirely to be expected that there was intense interest at all levels in the progress of the WFP/FAO relations saga, including among the security staff. It was very reassuring to sense that even among FAO staff I was seen as the 'good guy'.

The UN General Assembly and FAO Conference Deliver

This tale is almost complete. All the CFA recommended changes were passed by ECOSOC and the General Assembly and the corresponding FAO bodies. There are few references in my diary to relationships after the SCG and CFA Special Session completed their work. However, the following extracts complete the record of events:

Wednesday 8 May 1991

> *Tun Myat brought good news. FAO's paper for the Council on changes in General Regulations now received. It constitutes acceptance of changes, which it does not contest—best possible gloss is put upon them. In my own mind the matter is already finished with.*

Thursday 20 June 1991

> *A great day! My best yet in the FAO Council in terms of sobriety and respect for WFP and me personally. Congratulations from my closest colleagues, Tomlinson, Zejjari, Tun Myat and Mussapi and some moving remarks from Namanga Ngongi. John Scott did me a splendid speech, expressing my thoughts in ways which I would not have had the confidence to utter myself...*

Saturday 9 November 1991

> *An historic meeting! I was chatting with Trant[111] on podium prior to opening of FAO Conference. Saouma made a bee-line for me and launched immediately into a discussion about US pressures for Bertini.[112] Cameras clicked, TV cameras focused. After a minute or so he insisted we sit down to continue discussion: 'How old is she? 38, I hear. Would you appoint your daughter? Like a presidential campaign. I have never seen anything like this US pressure involving even Bush...' All this with great cordiality intended to convey*

closeness, even intimacy, between us, to the bystander…As Ngongi said, 'Clear now that Saouma [is] running for re-election; good politics for him to be seen in reconciliation with you'.

THE MAJOR CHANGES

As stated above, the principal concern of the developing countries was to increase their share of seats in an enlarged CFA. It was decided to enlarge the Committee from 30 to 42, with 27 seats reserved for developing countries. That change required the approval of the UN General Assembly and the FAO Conference. Though politically essential at the time to obtain G77 support, the size of the governing body was later reduced to 36 when the CFA was renamed the WFP Executive Board. That arose as a result of a 1993 UN General Assembly decision that all governing bodies of the UN funds and programmes should be 'executive boards' of identical size and composition with similar functions and responsibilities. The change of title brought no significant change in function though it had the advantage of better reflecting the CFA's true role as the intergovernmental body responsible for control and oversight of the work of the Programme. Making that role explicit was the most important constitutional change achieved under my leadership; though it was always implicit in the General Regulations I had inherited. From that flowed what I had also always contended, namely that the Executive Director, who was responsible for the development of policy and management of the Programme, must in the last resort be held accountable by the CFA.

The essentials of the 1991[113] revisions were clear statements that:

❑   The CFA shall 'exercise the responsibility for the intergovernmental supervision of the Programme, including food aid policy, administration, operations, funds and finances'.

❑   The Executive Director 'shall be responsible and accountable for the administration of the Programme'.

❑   The Executive Director has the authority to 'establish special Staff Regulations and Rules' in agreement with the Secretary-General and Director-General.

❑   The Executive Director shall 'represent the Programme and perform such functions as may be conferred on him under agreements with States or intergovernmental organizations', for example under the headquarters agreement with Italy.

❑ The Programme should have legal capacity to contract; acquire property; and be party to judicial proceedings.

❑ The selection and appointment of senior officials above the level of D2 shall be made by the Executive Director in agreement with the Secretary-General and the Director-General.

❑ In relation to the WFP Fund, to which all contributions shall be credited, the CFA 'shall exercise full intergovernmental supervision and scrutiny of all aspects of the Fund'.

❑ The Executive Director shall have 'complete responsibility and shall be accountable to the CFA for the operation and administration of the Fund including the audited accounts'.

❑ The CFA 'shall establish Financial Regulations to govern the management of the Fund proposed by the Executive Director and approved by the CFA after receiving advice from the ACABQ and the FAO Finance Committee'.

Thus, in relation to all the issues which had precipitated the decision of governments to amend the General Regulations, I was vindicated. I had not, however, achieved all the changes that I sought, although the most important of these were subsequently included in a further revision of the General Regulations under my successor and with a new Director-General of FAO (WFP 2000). They related to the provision of technical services and the Executive Director's Annual Report.

Provision of FAO Technical Services and the Annual Report

As the preceding narrative has shown, the process of institutional reform of WFP was partly stimulated when the ACABQ brought to my attention in 1984 the likelihood that FAO was overcharging us for technical services, as indeed it was. More recently FAO's covetousness had been shown up over the improper rent charges levied against us. Accordingly, I had proposed that I have the freedom, consistent with efficiency and economy and subject to CFA approval, to decide from whom I obtained bought-out technical services. The G77 feared this was a cover for 'privatisation' of services, which would likely be bought from private consulting firms. Moreover, there was profound disagreement between UNDP, which funded much of

FAO's technical assistance, and FAO over the latter's charges, with UNDP becoming the executor of some of its own projects. There were therefore reasons for G77 concern. Where they were mistaken was in their failure to realise that the quality of FAO services had diminished over the years to the point where the agency was no longer a best-practice provider.[114] This was well recognised in the agricultural ministries of developing countries but not by individual delegates who hoped for employment with FAO.

The outcome was that in the 1991 revisions the existing provisions about reliance on FAO's technical services were strengthened in regard to areas where FAO was particularly worried, namely its 'global information and early warning systems for the assessment of food situations and needs and project development and evaluation'. The subsequently revised Regulations have dropped these amendments and substituted language that leaves complete discretion to the Executive Director with respect to bought-out services.

The requirement that the Executive Director consult the Secretary-General and the Director-General on his Annual Report to the CFA was retained. That made no sense in the context of an Executive Director responsible to an intergovernmental body charged with oversight of the Programme. Accordingly it was dropped when Bertini further revised the General Regulations.

That these and a few other minor proposed amendments were not accepted reflected, I believe, the strong desire of the G77 to salve the wound they had inflicted on the Director-General's vanity, caused by their courageous decision to accept all the critical changes that FAO had for so long fought against. The G77 also believed that, having conceded on the essential points described, the self respect of the developing countries required that FAO's role be seen to be protected to some extent. FAO was still considered as an agency serving the interests of the developing countries, under assault at the time by the rich countries. Wisely, the developed countries conceded these minor points, which provided the necessary fig leaf that ensured unanimity.

WFP Financial Regulations

To complete the reform process the CFA had to decide on its own Financial Regulations. It was an enormous pleasure to present our proposals to CFA31, my twenty-first and last session in December 1991. However, FAO nastiness was not done with yet. At the opening of the session their Legal

Adviser sought to delete the item from the agenda on the grounds that the UN General Assembly plenary had not yet passed the constitutional reforms resolution. The committee was not deterred and gave provisional approval, conditional on the Assembly's endorsement of the new arrangements, at this stage a pure formality. It further decided that the Financial Regulations would come into effect on 1 January 1992. The United Nations sent legal advice that this was entirely appropriate.

FAO also tried to ensure that the FAO External Auditor should act in that role for WFP. Again, the CFA asserted its power, accepting our proposal that it appoint its own External Auditor. It introduced the very important provision that appointment should be renewable only once. As the financial scandals of the current century have revealed it is too easy for external auditors to get into bed with their clients. As a result, appointment of new auditors after a fixed period is becoming the norm in business. The process of managerial reform was now complete. [115]

Requests for Emergency Assistance

Other than those General Regulations affecting my freedom of administration and responsibility to the CFA, I attached most importance to the provisions for approvals of emergency relief. Though FAO's global information and early warning system for identifying potential crop failure had some value at a macro level it was not backed up by a serious professional system for assessing needs at the level of affected beneficiary. Famine was often due to factors arising from armed conflict as well as natural disaster and crop failure. In certain instances it was not due to an absolute shortage of food but arose from a lack of 'entitlement' to food as defined by Nobel Laureate, Amartya Sen (1981). NGOs had done good work in improving methodologies and I wished to see WFP become the global leader in needs assessment. Our headquarters emergency service, backed up by our field officers, was in a better position than FAO staff to produce realistic assessments of needs at the level of those directly affected.

The reader will recall that the emergency approval process required that governments desiring food assistance should make their request to the Director-General, together with supporting 'basic information'. The Director-General was to request the Executive Director to examine the information and would decide upon it, 'taking into account the recommendation of the Executive Director'. The Executive Director could not test the information, for example by sending an independent mission. He could in practice, therefore, not do much more than consider whether there were resources available to meet the request and if so how much could reasonably be spared to satisfy this particular one. It was understandable that Saouma was well satisfied with a system where FAO got the political credit from governments for the assistance provided but WFP the blame for allocating less than requested.

Accordingly, I proposed an amendment to the relevant General Regulation as follows:

Governments desiring food assistance to meet emergency food needs shall present a request containing the basic information required by the Executive Director. The Executive Director shall examine the request, consulting with other agencies as appropriate, and will decide on it in the light of his assessment and in accordance with guidelines which may be laid down by the Committee (CFA). The Executive Director shall report those decisions to the Committee in such form as it may require.

The SCG decided on the following compromise:

Governments desiring food assistance to meet emergency food needs shall present a request containing the basic information relating thereto to the representative of the Programme in the country concerned..., who shall transmit it to the Executive Director. The Executive Director shall examine the request and, after close consultation with FAO and as required with the United Nations and relevant agencies, decide upon such request up to the level of the authority delegated to him by the Committee to approve development projects. In cases exceeding this level, after due consultation between the Programme, FAO and as required with the United Nations and relevant agencies, approval shall be accorded jointly by the Director-General of FAO and the Executive Director.

Governments were reluctant to abandon the 'two signatures' arrangement because of its supposed protection against abuse. The G77 wanted to maintain the *status quo* and FAO, by its public statements and lobbying, argued that any change was unacceptable. Having regard to all the political balls in play, the SCG's decision resolved most of the problems created by the existing situation. The system, though unnecessarily cumbersome on account of WFP's joint parentage, has worked well in practice with commonsense interpretation.

COMPLEX HUMANITARIAN EMERGENCIES

Quite apart from the issue of approval procedures, the revised General Regulations included a new paragraph which read as follows:

The Programme may also provide humanitarian relief assistance at the request of the Secretary-General of the United Nations. WFP assistance in such exceptional cases should be fully coordinated with the UN system and NGO efforts in the areas concerned.

In the overview of my ten-year stewardship of WFP, which I presented to the CFA in December 1991, I said that I regarded this amendment as 'a most important innovation'. Under the General Regulations we were able to respond only to the requests of governments. That requirement alone made it impossible for WFP to intervene at the most appropriate time in support of all suffering victims of conflict. The basic idea behind the amendment was to find a way around this restriction, which was increasingly inappropriate following the end of the Cold War when national sovereignty was no longer seen as a sufficient reason to deny humanitarian assistance to the victims of internal conflict.

The language of the adopted amendment of the General Regulations was more indirect than I wanted, but my hope was that it would provide the basis for a new dialogue between WFP and the Secretary-General that would help to bring about more consistent and disciplined humanitarian interventions. That in turn would serve to stimulate the development of similar relationships between the Secretary-General and the other humanitarian actors within the system.

The requirement that WFP respond only to requests from states reflected the reality that the United Nations was an organisation of states. In my opinion many of our humanitarian interventions served the political interests of particular states, rather than the community of UN member states. In such cases they should be undertaken by UN agencies only with the direct sanction of the UN Secretary-General, if necessary acting under the authority of the Security Council. Equally, I was convinced that before deciding on coercive measures against states, for example the imposition of sanctions, their likely humanitarian consequences should be assessed and brought formally to the notice of the Security Council (Ingram 1994).

No matter how political our interventions were in practice, never once was I given any advice, let alone direction, from the Secretary-General, even when I sought this, for example, after conflict erupted in the former British Somaliland provinces of Somalia. Our remoteness in Rome from the United Nations may have contributed to this.

I intended that the amendment should work in both directions. It would also be open to the WFP Executive Director to propose to the Secretary-General that he initiate particular actions which might relate to post-conflict situations as well as before, or during, them.

My first-hand encounters with Cambodians on the Thai border, Afghans on the Pakistan border, Eritreans on the Sudanese border and other, less prominent, situations in Africa and Central America, slowly convinced me that the proper role for the United Nations, and hence WFP, had not been thought through. In practice our support for the displaced was a highly political action working to the advantage of one side in a civil war, and to the host country tacitly or openly supporting that side.

Moreover, our interventions substantially furthered the political and strategic interests of the Western powers. It was relatively easy to raise resources from donors for these humanitarian disasters compared with tragedies where the West had no significant political interest. In the latter cases UN system agencies were genuine humanitarian actors, neutral and apolitical. As I saw it (Ingram 1993), there was a fundamental disjuncture in the United Nations between its role as a political organisation and the attempts of its humanitarian agencies, like WFP, UNICEF and UNHCR, to act as if they were politically neutral organisations like the International Committee of the Red Cross (ICRC).

Since the first Gulf War, the unreality of that assumption has become even more evident. More UN humanitarian workers are being killed than UN peacekeepers. Events in Somalia, in Bosnia, in Afghanistan and in Bagdad showed it is illusory to think that in armed conflicts the combatants may not regard the United Nations as being in some degree the instrument of one of the parties involved in the conflict. Nowhere is this more evident that in Iraq today, as the bombing of the United Nations compound in Iraq tragically showed. US policy has compounded the problem in Afghanistan by deliberately blurring the roles of its armed forces and humanitarian agencies which led the apolitical Medecins Sans Frontières (MSF) to withdraw from that country. A former President of ICRC, Cornelio Sommaruga, recently summed up the problem:

> The humanitarian alibi...is when certain states encourage humanitarian organizations, especially those of the UN to act under the protection of peacekeeping troops. In my view, this practice does not help to resolve the political problems nor does it create a humanitarian space in which those with the mandate can reach the victims.[116]

Indeed, the desirability of clarifying and translating into clear guidelines the distinction between UN humanitarian intervention in support of goals set by the United Nations and traditional ICRC or MSF apolitical intervention is still not fully recognised, though there appears to be progress in that direction.[117] That is not surprising in view of the global hegemony of the United States today. While the United States and others prefer to maximise their flexibility to use the United Nations and its agencies to serve their political ends, the ambiguous role of the United Nations will likely continue. Today's only option may continue to be to 'muddle through'.

This is not to say that our 'political' interventions did not also serve genuine humanitarian goals. No matter how politically ambiguous the situation, WFP saved many lives and relieved much human suffering. That was why I had no hesitation in doing all that I could to improve the quality of our interventions and vastly strengthened our relations with UNHCR, the ICRC, UNICEF and others. In other words, though WFP could not always help all, it was still good to relieve the suffering of some.

Moreover, the role of UN humanitarian agencies is unambiguous in relation to natural disasters, for example the great African drought of the early nineteen eighties and subsequent famines in that continent. WFP plays an indispensable role in the global community's response to such events.

The new provision also reflected another strong conviction, formed after my considerable involvement in complex emergencies, that UN interventions in such situations often arose on account of the separate, sometimes competing, initiatives of individual agencies and, of course, NGOs. The result was often chaotic and disorganised.[118] Reductions in human suffering were well short of optimal. More importantly, the intervention could make the political situation that gave rise to the humanitarian disaster more complex. I believed that by involving the Secretary-General from the beginning a pre-requisite for a more coherent international response would be set in place.

Some Personal Experiences

Guiding WFP's response to emergencies absorbed even more of my time in nineteen ninety-one, a year of crisis in the Horn of Africa and of the Kurdish exodus from Iraq following the first Gulf War, than in most years. For the first time the Secretary-General felt free to involve me in humanitarian negotiations on behalf of the United Nations. Until WFP's status was clear, there was no disposition in New York to risk offending Saouma and thereby further complicate UN/FAO relations.

I conducted successful negotiations with the Government of Ethiopia and the Eritrean People's Liberation Front (EPLF), then engaged in civil war, to reopen the EPLF-controlled port of Massawa, in order to enable WFP to deliver food to Asmara besieged at the time by EPLF forces. I found dealing with the future president of Eritrea, Isaias Afwerki, who impressed me as inflexible and authoritarian, very difficult. I was congratulated for my efforts but I knew that my negotiating skills were not the sole or even the main reason for success. Propitious political circumstances and US pressure on both parties were also important factors. In short, I was not seen by either party as a truly apolitical intermediary. I drew the same conclusion from another successful negotiation later in 1991, this time with the government of Sudan.

Following the collapse of the Marxist Ethiopian government, at the request of the Secretary-General I led a mission comprising representatives from the operational agencies (UNICEF, UNHCR, UNDP and WFP) to assess the UN system's appropriate development/humanitarian response to the new political situation, not only in Ethiopia but also in Djibouti, the Sudan and Kenya. Our principal concern was to assess the impact of refugee flows.

The new Ethiopian government owed much of its success to clandestine support from Sudan. Accordingly, it expelled Sudanese refugees in camps near the border. Included among them were adherents of the Sudan People's Liberation Army (SLPA) receiving *de facto* sanctuary in Ethiopia. The SPLA had been fighting for independence for the south from Khartoum for decades. WFP had been involved in providing assistance on behalf of the international community (Operation Lifeline Sudan) to displaced persons in southern Sudan and I had made several visits to that country to help iron out the many problems that arose in our operations, including also in Darfur which suffered severe drought in the nineteen eighties. That province was exceedingly poor and neglected by Khartoum, absorbed as it was in its war with the SPLA.

Addressing in Khartoum the conference that created
'Operation Lifeline Sudan', March 1989

The expellees were facing starvation in Nasir in an area of eastern Sudan close to Ethiopia and difficult to access. To everyone's surprise, we persuaded the hardline government of President El Bashir to allow assistance by airdrop and by river transport up the Nile and its tributaries, something that had been denied by the Sudanese for several years. The primary reason for our success was that the Sudanese government was evenly balanced between those who considered Sudan could not afford to jeopardise IMF financial assistance by launching a military offensive against the returnees and those who favoured a new assault. Our efforts tipped the balance in favour of the former.

It was an exciting, potentially hazardous, experience. We were unwelcome. Our party was travelling in a chartered executive jet, access by commercial airline being suspended. Initially Khartoum agreed to our visit but just before we were due to leave Nairobi the Sudanese requested postponement. I decided to ignore the request. The government was subject to a lot of pressure from the Americans and the British to allow aid to the returnees. My diary records that the

> ...*Sudanese were particularly infuriated by a telephone call from Linda Chalker [UK Minister for Development Cooperation] virtually instructing them to agree to Nasir airlift in abusive language'. As the American Ambassador said to me at a reception the 'only hope rests with Ingram mission', adding that if I did not succeed, I should 'give it to them publicly'.*

The following extract from my diary will give the reader some feel for the atmospherics of this type of negotiation.

Saturday 15 June 1991

> *Decided my tactics must be to seek clear yes-or-no answer re airlift...Discussion with Foreign Minister [Ali Ahmed Sahloul] and Revolutionary Command Council member, Colonel el-Amin Khalifa, not very productive...Meeting with Khalifa in enormous room of Chinese-provided conference centre with Khalifa resplendent in full uniform. I focussed mainly on clearing up his misconceptions and ignorance. Afterwards, we [the members of my mission] consulted and decided I should put privately to [Khalifa] a package offering something for them [airlift to Wau] and full UN supervision...After lunch and much emotional discussion—they feel they have had a raw deal from West and media, with some truth—they accepted airlift from Kenya, provided that two Sudanese Red Crescent officials observe at Nasir and Lokichokio.[119] I regarded this as an advance...After much to and fro, with Abu Oaf[120] playing hard guy, though in his case genuinely meant, deal was struck. Key role played by impressive Finance Minister who is voice of moderation because he knows Sudan cannot afford another financial crisis. Abu Oaf resisted to end...called on influential Vice-President who is Abu Oaf's cousin and source of his power which is clearly considerable, if only because he is only one who seems to have some perspective on totality of emergency operations. He is very bitter about unfair share of aid received by SPLA in south as compared with Government...Abu Oaf warmed up as time went on. Basis of whole thing in many ways was their*

confidence in me which puts special weight on me. Abu Oaf, who is a refined gentleman, said many countries have lost confidence in Pérez de Cuéllar seeing him as tool of US...A fortuitous combination of circumstances contributed to this unexpected result: US threats to go it alone [with an unauthorised airdrop] into Nasir undoubtedly helped. The last thing Sudan wanted was a Kurdish/Iraq style operation. Sudan tactics were diversionary...Its insistence on delaying our visit part of these tactics. UNICEF brought media to Nasir with result the issue got disproportionate attention. Other factors included government's decision...and [WFP deputy representative in Khartoum][121] Da Silva's skill and sensitivity. But my feeling that these so-called humanitarian interventions in conflict situations were only feasible when political conditions are ripe was once again vindicated.

AN IMPROVED IEFR

Apart from constitutional reform and negotiations to secure humanitarian access, my final year was productive in other respects. I was particularly pleased to set the capstone on my transformation of the management of emergency aid. In this narrative I have referred to only one of these innovations, namely the separation of the funding of protracted refugee operations from 'sudden disasters' and the accompanying approval process. In 1991, I was immensely satisfied when I obtained CFA approval for a relatively radical step to substantially improve the flexibility of operation of the IEFR.

It will be recalled that the IEFR had been established following the World Food Conference, as an emergency food 'reserve' of 500,000 tons to be managed by WFP. Its shortcomings had been sharply revealed in the great African drought of the mid-eighties (WFP 1986c), which had led CFA21 (June 1986) to accept our proposal that governments should pledge contributions every year rather than every other year as hitherto (WFP 1986a). However, the fundamental problems remained. The IEFR was in no sense a true reserve, simply a promise to make available at the discretion of the donor a stipulated amount of food to be drawn down in a twelve-month period of the donor's choosing. WFP was good at matching the known foreign policy interest of donors, the foods that they could provide and the dietary patterns of recipients. Indeed, our skill in this respect was one reason why donors often used WFP as their preferred disaster response vehicle. However, it often took weeks, even months, before we could get a response to our requests; and sometimes the donor, after a long delay, decided it did not want to help with that particular disaster. My diary records my chagrin when Australia, after informally consenting to supply food to hurricane-ravaged Western Samoa, months later declined to go ahead. By then it was too late to interest another donor, none of whom had any political interest in that country. This is one example of what was a continuing problem with most donors.

The IEFR had been set up as a facility for an effective, quick response to disasters. That meant food should be borrowed from or bought within the country affected, the region or in global markets. Following that initial response, food supplied by donors would enable beneficiaries to be succoured for as long as necessary. However, our limited cash resources intended for other purposes had increasingly to be used to help pay the cost of transporting donor food to beneficiaries. That meant that there was little cash available for food purchases within the affected country or region to enable the timely distribution of emergency food.

More often than not the first response had perforce to be by borrowing from WFP stocks of food already in the affected country for use on our development projects. Indeed it was WFP's function as an agency to use food for development which had created the infrastructure needed for successful emergency responses. However, borrowing brought a considerable cost by setting back the implementation of development projects. Food was the motivator of action and if delivery was spasmodic and intermittent those in charge as well as the beneficiaries lost the incentive to undertake the associated development activity. For example school feeding, so important as an inducement to parents to send girls to school, failed if it was an on-again off-again activity. In my many visits to our projects I became convinced that timely delivery of food to project beneficiaries was the principal factor deciding project outcomes. Project design was important but not to the same extent. Not surprisingly, donors at CFA meetings loved to dwell on alleged failings in project design turned up by our stringent evaluations of project outcomes. However, they were much less interested in delivery failures where the culpability was mainly theirs.

The reform of this situation was hampered by division between the United States and Canada and other developed countries, in practice the

Europeans and Japan. From the former's perspective, burden sharing was best secured by them supplying most of the food and the latter most of the cash. At the time of the Programme's creation this made some sense but was no longer realistic. The generation of big European food surpluses meant that Europe had become a major source of food aid.

To get over the problem I proposed at CFA30 the creation of a fund within the IEFR of $50 million to be contributed voluntarily over and above commodity pledges and related transport costs. The fund would be replenished each year. The CFA approved a series of related procedural measures but not the creation of the fund. The donors were as usual divided. However, they did respond positively to my offer to refine the proposal through informal contacts with donors and present a reworked proposal to the following CFA. These discussions were fruitful and CFA32 approved the creation of a new fund (WFP 1991b) to enable assured expenditure of 'at least $30 million annually' for the purchase and transport of emergency food aid.[122]

With the passage of this and other measures at my last CFA I had been given a wonderful send-off. During 1991 and 1992 at no time did I ever feel a lame duck. On the contrary it was a period of accomplishment and personal satisfaction.

---

[105] Ambassador J Warin, France's representative to FAO and WFP.

[106] Ms M Deregibus was the Argentine representative at FAO.

[107] The Chairman of the CFA was chairman of the SCG in the person of Kenya's Ambassador to FAO, Don Nanjira. Kenya had been a strong supporter of Mensah and I had excellent relations with the Kenyan government, as I did with most African governments.

[108] The Libyan delegate died in a car crash early in November. He was succeeded by an Iranian whose role was ultimately valuable in getting a successful outcome.

[109] General Regulation 9(a)

[110] CFA:30/INF/7

[111] Executive Director, WFC.

[112] Catherine Bertini, the United States candidate for my post, who was appointed.

113   For the full text of the revisions and accompanying resolutions see
      WFP (1991a).

114   At the individual level FAO included many first-class professionals
      providing technical assistance to developing countries.

115   A few minor changes to tidy up some of the many discrepancies
      between the General Regulations and actual practice that had
      developed over the years were also made.

116   Australian Red Cross, *Action Aboard,* Number 1, 2000.

117   The respected Antonio Donini, most recently coordinator of UN
      humanitarian assistance in Afghanistan, following completion of
      his mission in that country reportedly stated: '...humanitarians
      need to clean up their own camp and define better what
      humanitarian action is about. It's necessary to go back to a more
      "copyrighted" form of humanitarianism in the sense of returning
      to the basic principles that are enshrined in the Geneva
      Conventions and in international humanitarian law'. 'Interview
      with UN Veteran Antonio Donini on Lessons Learned in
      Afghanistan and Elsewhere', in *Briefings,* Winter 2004, Brown
      University, Providence, RI.

118   The situation is apparently no better now than in my time. Jan
      Englund, the UN Under Secretary-General for Humanitarian
      Affairs recently wrote:
          ...we need stronger coordination. Coordination is essential for
          saving lives in a crisis...coordination is not a luxury. It's a necessity.
          Take the tsunami. My office worked with 90 donor nations, 17 UN
          agencies, hundreds of NGOs and scores of private companies. The
          goal: ensure the right aid got to the right people. And by and large
          we succeeded. Given the challenges ahead, however, we must build
          on today's efforts to improve the future (*The Canberra Times,* 17
          December, 2005).

119   The town in Kenya from where the airlift would be mounted. The
      Sudanese wanted to supervise because of their suspicion that arms
      would be shipped as well as food and medicines.

120   Head of the Sudanese Relief Agency.

121   Manuel Aranda da Silva, new WFP deputy representative in
      Khartoum. I met him when he was Minister of Agriculture in
      Mozambique and recruited him to WFP where he has enjoyed a
      successful career. In practice the UN provides a *de facto* refuge for
      some politicians and others escaping dictatorial regimes.

122   Almost fifteen years later the success of WFP's Immediate

Response Account helped to stimulate the creation by the UN of a Central Emergency Response Fund to provide the resources needed to allow humanitarian aid to flow pending specific pledges from donors for new emergencies. However, donor contributions have been disappointing amounting to only one third of the target of $500 million (*The Economist*, 11 March 2006). Likewise, since it establishment, WFP's Immediate Response Account has continued to have great difficulty in reaching its targets. To overcome this problem WFP is experimenting with disaster reinsurance through private firms.

14

LESSONS FROM THE BATTLEFIELD

...all laws and all institutions exist in a kind of limbo, between the ideals they express and the daily transactions among the passions and interests they seek to control. In world affairs...the gulf between the two is wider than within most states.

Stanley Hoffman[123]

Was the struggle worth it? Did the benefits outweigh the costs? Why did the process of reform take so long? Are there lessons to be drawn for the UN system and for other particular agencies?

BENEFITS AND COSTS

During the course of this prolonged struggle I was sometimes asked whether I ever calculated the 'opportunity costs' to the Programme of persisting with my efforts to confront FAO. Might the better course have been appeasement, as followed by my predecessors? Might not a more subtle, patient process of political and personal manipulation on my part have been a more prudent course? The fate of Bernardo Brito, who had sought to out-manoeuvre the Director-General over the Executive Director's appointment, showed how risky such a course would be in the face of an intractable opponent like Saouma. Brito, a former FAO delegate from a developing country, had built a strong constituency among the G77. I had no such constituency. Moreover Saouma's wings had not been clipped by governments or by his colleagues in the United Nations. Early on, when I sought the advice of a highly respected retired Canadian senior official of the United Nations, he commented bleakly, 'The good guys don't always win'. What became clear to me was that the good guys always failed to win by appeasement or political manoeuvres alone. Something more was required. As time went by, knowing Saouma's character and methods, I was sure that only a different course had a chance of success.

With appeasement not an option, the temptation sometimes was to resign. Indeed, several times I did contemplate leaving WFP because of my inability to get either Saouma to change or the United Nations or governments to take a firm stand.

Some delegates worried that my fight was taking up too much of the time of both organisations and harming their performance, especially WFP's as the smaller agency. I accepted that responsible leadership of the Programme required that my conduct should not cause more harm than good. Moreover, I knew if the Programme faltered in any way my position would be at risk, given the hostility I had aroused in FAO. As a result, I was always on my mettle. I was rarely anxious since I was ready to accept dismissal and had no ambition beyond WFP.

Though the struggle with FAO took up a lot of my time and that of two or three of my closest associates, I did my best to insulate staff. For example, my regular weekly meetings with senior officers did not deal with FAO/WFP relationships but focused solely on our substantive work. In the later years, when the progress I had made was evident to all staff, more and more helped informally in all sorts of ways to advance the cause, but not at the expense of their regular work. This is not to say that staff was unaffected. An additional work burden was imposed on accounts and personnel management, and sometimes also on those engaged on the development of new projects. To quote one staff member, who wrote to me:

...as the war developed, daily working relations became more difficult—soon FAO staff was no longer allowed to talk to us, unless authorised by their directors, and some FAO people, who had been good colleagues, began to treat us like they believed Saouma was treating you—with chicanery. Everything that had to go to FAO was first rejected and had to be done again.

For my part, I was so energised as to be able to handle simultaneously two distinct jobs, giving as much time to each as necessary. As the saying goes, 'If you want a job done well, give it to a busy man'. Though FAO pressures may have burdened some staff, my leadership on matters of substance inspired the organisation as a whole to do more.

I do not believe that the course I took had any real cost to WFP. Not once did I seriously doubt that I was doing the right thing. I had stepped onto the treadmill and it would be wrong to get off, if I really put WFP's interests ahead of my own.

On the other hand, my actions did bring substantial benefits to WFP. When I took over the executive directorship in 1982, WFP was in a rut. What it did, it did well enough but it had ceased to innovate and, constrained as it was by FAO's oversight, lacked the will to do so.[124] Immediately before I arrived in Rome Saouma had personally told WFP staff his policy toward the agency would be even more restrictive than under my predecessors. Indeed, as he several times told me, he saw WFP exclusively as a logistics agency to deliver food to FAO-designed development projects and FAO-approved emergency interventions. The cast of his mind was shown by his rejection of my supplementary budget proposals made in my first year. If I had complied with his desires I would not have been able to make any of the changes I made, none of which met with his approval. It was only by acting boldly in the interests of WFP, and thus accepting the risk of confrontation, that reforms were achieved and the essential foundation for subsequent progress laid. This was acknowledged when WFP made me the first recipient of its Food for Life Award in 2000.

Today, WFP is the world's largest humanitarian agency. In 2003 it provided food to 110 million people. The numbers of beneficiaries and the tonnage of food provided are about one third more than at the end of my term, though in some recent years food deliveries have been no higher than during my stewardship (Appendix II, Table 1). The numbers of professional staff since my departure have grown by a factor of four, which is a measure of how FAO control had held back WFP's development. During my ten years, in the face of consistent opposition, professional staff increased by only 50 per cent (Appendix II, Table 2).

A large part of WFP's success is due to the unification of field and headquarters staff, which I initiated and my successor completed. Further, the delegation of management responsibilities to regional field offices, which I had proposed to the CFA but was unable to get approved, in part because of FAO opposition, is in place today. In 1993 WFP staff, not UNDP officials, became the organisation's titular in-country representatives and so the process I started but could not finish, because I had to give priority to changing the relationship with FAO, is now complete.

It is arguable that since Saouma left office within two years of my departure a new Director-General may have conceded willingly to the same changes, without the battle we had waged for so long. Even if that were so, which I think unlikely, I contend that without the head start achieved through reform in 1991, coupled with the other changes I had effected, the Programme could not have responded as successfully to the massive humanitarian challenges of the nineties and beyond. It may well have become largely irrelevant to the major powers, as many UN system agencies did.

Towards the end of the reform battle, the donors were so affronted by Saouma's intransigence that they contemplated replacing WFP with a new specialised global food aid NGO, under my leadership. By that time disenchantment with the UN system had already led to more emergency food aid being channelled through NGOs. While it is too rare an event in the UN system that agencies which have outlived their usefulness are abolished, this may have happened to a WFP compliant to FAO.[125]

The growth and even the survival of WFP would have been impossible without enthusiastic support of most donor countries throughout my tenure. I had made it the foundation of my administration to get and keep donor support. For any UN voluntarily funded programme to flourish that was necessary.

It is now easy to forget how embattled the United Nations was during the years of Reagan, Thatcher and George Bush Senior. Budgetary growth was not just at a standstill; there was great pressure to reduce agencies' expenditure. Yet, through my tenure, WFP's administrative budget kept on growing and new posts were added to our secretariat. Even UNDP, always headed by Americans, suffered serious resource setbacks. WFP was envied for its success in the climate of the times, not only by FAO.

The second element of my strategy was to obtain and keep at least the tacit support of the developing countries. That was achieved by showing political even-handedness in the distribution of our assistance, that is by 'standing up' to the United States and others as I stood up to Saouma. I also showed my independence by speaking out on donor failure to make available on time the commodities they promised and eventually got established the new fund described in the previous chapter. I resisted donor efforts to radically cut back the list of countries eligible for WFP assistance, since for developing countries their cohesion to some extent depended on the possibility of all of them benefiting from our aid. Although my efforts to get approval for more flexibility in the monetisation of commodities were unsuccessful, the fact that I sought this in the face of donor opposition had the merit of further demonstrating to developing countries my good faith and that I was prepared to challenge the donor monopoly over programme food aid.

Throughout, another critical element in my approach was to build close cooperative relationships with our sister organisations and to assist the Director-General for Development to improve interagency collaboration. WFP moved much closer to the United Nations, UNDP, UNICEF, UNFPA and specialised agencies like the ILO, WHO and UNESCO, for example by seeking out more opportunities for collaborative projects. We also strove to build strong relationships with the providers of capital aid, namely IFAD, the African Development Bank and, above all, the World Bank. Paradoxically, we found it easier to develop joint projects with the World Bank, IFAD and bilateral donors than with UNDP and the specialised agencies whose technical assistance programs the latter largely funded. For want of a penny's worth of technical assistance our development projects were often less successful than they could have been, even though WFP's country representative was the UNDP representative, who was also charged with coordination of the work of the specialised agencies in developing countries. That failure is an indictment of the institutional arthritis then, and perhaps still, besetting the UN system.

The most substantive changes were in cooperation with UNHCR and ICRC. With the former we concluded interagency agreements which rationalised what had been, to some extent, a competing relationship in the mobilisation and delivery of food aid to refugees. Instead a rational division of labour was worked out. That rationalisation complemented the new approval process the CFA had endorsed for such assistance.

Overall, however, the results of our efforts to strengthen collaboration were disappointing because of the disfunctionality of the UN system. For example I gave strong support to the creation of a unified development service to take the place of the multiplicity of agency representatives in developing countries, but the UN failed to pursue the idea. By taking these stands, WFP became recognised as a serious player in the UN system, genuinely working to improve interagency collaboration.

WHY DID THE REFORM PROCESS TAKE SO LONG?

The lack of a strong, consistent American policy vastly impeded the speed of my reform effort. As I bemoan so often in my diary, the United States does not see always its own national interest. Many of its officials concerned recognised this and said so explicitly to me. The problem was that while WFP was performing satisfactorily from their point of view, despite harassment by FAO, the United States did not see the issue of reform as urgent. Therefore, it did not rise sufficiently high on the American agenda for a high-level concerted effort to reconcile all the competing interests concerned with WFP and FAO.[126] Once the Americans decided that Saouma had gone too far, once too often thumbing his nose at the CFA, which was, after all, the member governments, their policy came together. That they finally did so only close to the end of my second term, when they expected to see an American placed in my post, was probably a significant factor also.

The story of my appointment and re-appointment is revealing of the enormous importance attached by American administrations to putting their nationals at the top of the UN voluntarily funded operational agencies they regard as important to their national interest. It also shows up the problems that can occur when several US agencies have a stake in an issue and operate without a national position to guide them. In this the United States is no different from most others, with the exception of France (and perhaps the United Kingdom). However, because of the importance and power of the United States its policy incoherence presents serious problems for the management of UN system agencies.

The Role of FAO

The intransigence of the FAO Director-General was clearly the most important single cause for the duration of the reform process. By fighting to the end every change sought, no matter how minor, FAO paid a heavy cost.[127] With flexibility and commonsense on Saouma's part there would never have been any fireworks. His prestige would have risen, his re-election would have been easier and as an institution FAO may have done a little better in getting more funds from donors in the difficult climate of the eighties. However, FAO's initial reaction to my actions, though characteristic of the brutally aggressive style of the organisation at the time, was not substantively at odds with the basic culture of the UN system, a consortium of competing entities dependent on continued funding by governments. They, like the United States, pursued separate strategies formulated without a coherent overarching policy in relation to the system as a whole, or when such a policy nominally existed, without the institutional mechanisms to produce consistency.

For their part developing countries had confused a tactical weapon, solidarity against the developed countries, with a policy. Like some parliamentary oppositions they seemed to feel that every initiative from developed countries must be opposed.

Each entity in the system was created as a result of an explicit intergovernmental decision. And each entity's continued existence, let alone expansion, requires that it maintains the support of the constituency that created it. As the global agenda changes, agencies have to be nimble in maintaining relevance. Survival requires that they move into new activities. Their mandates are necessarily poorly defined because they are the outcome of political bargaining processes. Bargaining continues in subsequent interpretations by secretariats and governing bodies. Inevitably friction also develops between agencies over alleged intrusions onto their claimed 'turf'.

To sit through meeting after meeting of the ACC, of UN 'senior officials', even of the JCGP, was to realise that we were engaged in charades, going through the motions of dialogue which had no outcomes that made for better coordination within the system. ACC meetings were conducted as if they were meetings of sovereign states with little or no sense of collegiality. The only genuinely spirited discussion was about the squeeze placed by the UNDP on its payments to the specialised agencies to compensate them for their overhead costs incurred in the execution of UNDP-funded technical assistance projects; or about which agency should provide the chairman of bodies such as the International Civil Service Commission.[128]

The many cooperative arrangements and initiatives between agencies took place independently of these 'coordination' instruments as, for example, WFP's agreement with UNHCR. Superficial changes in coordinating structures have been made since my time but the underlying reality does not appear to have altered.

Under these conditions, by asserting its dominance over WFP, FAO was acting like any other agency wanting to protect it finances and enhance its power and prestige. That it was able to draw out the struggle for so long was because of its strong, and WFP's, weak constituencies and the failings of the UN Secretary-General.

The WFP and FAO Constituencies

WFP's constituency was spread across several ministries in member states. In developed countries they were the overseas development department, the agriculture ministry and, in some instances, also the trade ministry, and foreign ministries which had oversight of UN system matters. Such a dispersed constituency was inherently weak but, worse still, the constituency was divided within itself.

Aid agencies regarded food aid as inherently second-class assistance. The more food aid the less cash was available to support what were considered better forms of assistance. Only the food aid managers in aid agencies were strongly behind WFP.

Because it was charged against the aid budget at either its world or domestic market price, food aid was attractive to the finance ministries of countries with substantial food surpluses. Such aid was a low opportunity cost to the national budget compared with a similar cash appropriation to the overseas aid budget. Foreign ministries were focused on the big political issues going on in New York.[129] Though they usually claimed a role in coordinating overall policy in relation to UN agencies, they applied few resources to this function. Their main interest in the eighties was in budgetary restraint across the system and 'better coordination' to prevent the waste and overlap for which in fact governments, more than secretariats, were responsible.

Within agricultural departments, with the exception of some of the food surplus countries, there was little support for food aid, which was seen as a necessary evil to support domestic farmers. For an agronomist the Chinese proverb, 'Give a man a fish and you feed him for a day, teach him to fish and you feed him for life', resonated. It also chimed with the self-interest of some who looked for employment with FAO.

Provided WFP was able to use donated food reasonably effectively, all involved were satisfied. Only aid agency personnel concerned with the developmental impact of food aid had a serious interest in WFP's performance and problems. They were mostly mid-level officials and therefore lacked authority in setting the agenda within their organisations, let alone across other concerned departments of government.

Of comparable operational agencies UNHCR and UNICEF, both single issue organisations, had the strongest constituencies and flourished accordingly. UNDP had good support in aid agencies and in foreign ministries but was weakened by the fact that it funded the technical assistance of many specialised agencies who had more focused, self-interested support in often powerful domestic departments with corresponding responsibilities. FAO was pre-eminently in that situation.

The G77

Our constituency among developing countries was very mixed. Where our assistance was a significant component of overall aid receipts the governments concerned were supportive of WFP but this did not automatically translate into support from Rome delegations. Interdepartmental relationships were poorly organised and mechanisms for preparing well thought-out instructions largely non-existent. More often than not delegates were free to act as they wished. Their guiding spirit was the maintenance of G77 solidarity to which most of their governments were strongly committed.

Fortunately, however, time after time at the most critical point in each session what seemed like a miracle to Ahmed and me occurred. Always, when we seemed about to be defeated, one or two delegates from developing countries stood aside from their colleagues. Thus, try as it might, FAO never succeeded in the CFA in turning my differences with the Director-General into a struggle between rich and poor countries. In FAO bodies, particularly the Finance Committee, that was not the case. However, those bodies were never ready to censure me, as Saouma would have liked, because I did have donor support and was managing the Programme broadly to the satisfaction of developing countries.

A factor handicapping my reform effort was the professional orientation of Rome delegates. As agriculturalists, delegates from developing countries were ashamed of their countries' dependence on food aid, primarily necessary because of their government's failure to increase domestic food production sufficiently, and for which some bore part of the responsibility. Through the 1980s, dependence on food imports, especially in Africa, was growing. Accordingly, as delegates saw it, no matter how limited the possibility of doing so effectively, WFP food aid was best used to increase agricultural production, an FAO responsibility. In fact, the food aid WFP used to promote social goals through income transfer was more efficient than when used to support most agricultural production projects, not least because FAO, other donors and the governments of developing governments failed to commit the complementary resources needed to make such projects work. That they were complicit reflected their ambivalence about the worth of food aid and the general incoherence of the bilateral/multilateral aid regime.

Saouma (1993) has claimed that FAO's role to further the interests of the majority, i.e. the developing countries, was thrust on the organisation on account of the absence of the Soviet Union from membership: 'Thus it was that FAO, spared by East-West conflict, became the theatre for numerous confrontations between the North and the South'. Through that conflict, there emerged from the G77 'a definite will to modify along more human lines, the quantitative model of development which had hitherto prevailed...' Presumably this is a reference to the New International Economic Order (NIEO) debate in the United Nations, which preoccupied vocal spokespersons of the G77 under strong Marxist influence during this last decade of the Cold War. However, in Rome delegates were mainly agricultural technicians, more pragmatic than ideological as compared with their diplomatic peers in New York. Certainly in the CFA, there was no indication that the developing countries wished us to follow a different model of development, although their lack of support for my proposals on program aid could be construed as such. However, I do not believe that overall our approach to development was a factor in impeding my reform effort; rather the reverse. With their rigid mindset about increased agricultural production as the primary goal of food aid they and FAO were much more conservative than the WFP secretariat in seeking to change the conditions that gave rise to poverty in developing countries. WFP was more intellectually flexible and 'politically progressive' than FAO. In the Rome climate that was not grasped by most G77 delegates.

Instead, developing countries were suspicious that my emphasis on improving WFP's efficiency and effectiveness was camouflage for increasing donor influence. This was not surprising given that developed countries were trying to take control in the UN and in those specialised agencies they considered were too much under the influence of developing countries.

For developed countries food aid had the potential to destroy their export markets. To ensure that our assistance did not do this, our projects were 'cleared' by FAO's Committee on Surplus Disposals. It was for reasons such as these that WFP was placed in Rome as a ward of FAO. What was overlooked was that food aid as used by WFP could promote other developmental goals. That was why the United Nations was WFP's other 'parent'. Unfortunately, over the years the UN lost interest in its ward, notwithstanding its mandate to oversee the system's developmental responsibilities.

In these circumstances the pursuit of my reform agenda would have been impossible unless in their hearts delegates from developing countries knew I was nobody's tool. Over time, it became clear that I was motivated by a profound concern for the better use of food aid to promote development, overcome poverty and relieve death and suffering in food emergencies. My visits to the field, which I always found uplifting, strengthened my conviction that we were reaching the poor and delivering real benefits to them, more so perhaps than other UN system development agencies. This sounds partisan but with first-hand experience of bilateral aid delivery in Indonesia and the Philippines, seven years as head of Australia's aid agency and ten years with WFP I have seen a vast number of aid projects–bilateral, multilateral, and NGO–whose positive impact was negligible.

FAO's influence with the G77 was helped by its exploitation of the self-interest of delegates,[130] especially the desire of many to obtain posts in the secretariat. Delegates had to earn these posts through unwavering support over many years and were expected to act as FAO directed on the substance of issues as well as procedurally. Rebellious delegates were reported to their governments who, in some instances, were successfully pressed by the Director-General to re-assign them, examples of which were given in a previous chapter.

Proceedings in the CFA, in its drafting committee, in the FAO Finance Committee and Council were unprecedented. Though usually polite enough, compared with say the Australian Parliament, a few of FAO's supporters resorted to the most cynical use of procedure, filibustering, bluff and transparently misleading interventions. Though there was a small 'cast of stars', FAO also had a troupe of less adroit players who could be drawn on as necessary. Most of the delegates were in the chorus and simply followed the broad party line.

FAO staff, actively and blatantly, sought to influence the outcome of committee deliberations, by passing written suggestions and instructions to their supporters, for example in the sub-committee established to draft the CFA's report on its proceedings. The sub-committee's sessions went on for many hours over several days and long into the night. *De facto* the debate in the CFA was often effectively reopened in the drafting committee to ensure that much more weight was given to minority positions favoured by FAO than reflected in the original debate and, if necessary, the chairman's summing up. The proceedings verged on the childish, with extended debates over trivial points, used tactically as part of the process of wearing down the proponents of accuracy of reporting. Too often they were successful. In the larger scheme of things that probably did not matter but it was disheartening for our staff at the time.

In New York it was inconceivable that the UN Secretary-General's staff would act similarly against UNICEF or UNDP, which were subsidiary bodies of the United Nations. FAO was unconcerned about the harm it did its 'child', as delegates liked to describe the relationship, in pursuit of its overriding objective to maintain *de facto* ownership of WFP. Overall, the proceedings were travesties of good governance. If we had been in New York the press would have reported what was going on and it would eventually have stopped. But Rome is not New York and FAO is not the United Nations.

While the average level of delegates from developed countries was reasonably good, though in my experience nowhere near as high as at the United Nations in New York during my postings, they tended to be outshone by a small number of FAO's stars from developing countries. The latter also had the advantage of usually being posted to Rome for many years so they knew well all the parliamentary tricks, whereas most developed representatives were assigned for a few years only. Though developed country delegations for CFA and FAO meetings were reinforced from capitals, many understandably disliked Rome's particular culture of multilateral diplomacy. However, as pressure for institutional reform mounted, key developed delegations sent some very skilled delegates to CFA meetings.

I do not want the conclusion drawn that FAO was responsible for all the trouble-making that went on in the CFA and its sub-committees. Some of the more talented developing country delegates enjoyed a 'bit of fun' at the expense of the major industrialised countries, as a reaction against the latter's lectures and perhaps, too, as a way of asserting that, though they were people of colour from aid dependent, poor countries, they were just as able as the representatives of the Western countries. Moreover, the Cold War was still a factor and though the Soviet Union was not represented in FAO, some of the mischief making was probably inspired by the NIEO debates in New York.

Moreover, though successful as 'spoilers' and hence impeding my efforts, collectively FAO's acolytes always stopped well short of playing the role of 'wreckers'. They did not want to harm WFP, only stop or delay my reform efforts. That perhaps was the measure of their political sophistication.

Unquestionably, as a result of the long dominance of the developing countries in FAO, encouraged by the secretariat, the developed countries brought a defeatist mentality to achieving any reform in FAO through parliamentary processes. Unfortunately that mood carried over to the CFA, even though developed countries held 13 of its 30 seats.

The Complexity of the Basic Documents

The complexity of the foundation WFP documents was systematically used by FAO to obfuscate understanding by delegations of the issues at stake. With the turnover of delegates and the lack of high-level administrative experience among many of them, it was a difficult, never-ending, task to explain why the texts presented serious problems for effective, efficient management.

Like all UN system foundation texts, the documents owed their complexity to a series of political compromises between the interests of powerful states, regional groupings and secretariats. The WFP texts were unusually complex because they also had to reconcile the interests of two distinct organisations and did so by creating a condominium which, however, was made quasi independent! At the time there was no confidence that a UN system food aid agency was more than experimental. When, *de facto*, it became permanent the texts were not sufficiently amended to reflect the new status. That need not have mattered if the FAO had shown the same flexibility as the UN had in relation to the evolution of the wards for which it had sole responsibility. Changes in practice were accepted without necessarily amending texts. Indeed, as one academic observer recently wrote, 'In fact, the UN's very adaptability has lessened incentives–at least for the most influential Member States–for seeking major institutional reforms. It appears that the founders…wanted it this way' (Luck 2004).

As well, getting governments to agree to significant modifications to texts is harder to achieve than the initial agreement, because of the strength of interests benefiting from the *status quo* and the often inherent complexity of the issues which emerges more fully over time. The difficulty of finding a common denominator of agreement is not therefore surprising, nor is the likelihood that the new arrangements will themselves soon require modification. An example is the laborious process over many years of UNDRO reform that led to that organisation's abolition and the creation of the new post of Humanitarian Coordinator, which in turn has proven to be less than satisfactory, as I predicted (Ingram 1993a).

The United Nations Role

The United Nations bears much responsibility for the years taken to resolve WFP/FAO issues. It knew what was going on, was appalled, yet dithered for years. Sufficient change could have been achieved during my first term if the leads given by the Bertrand Report and the ACABQ had been seized upon by the Secretary-General. In saying this I do not mean to belittle the help that was given during my first term. I always had at least the tacit backing of New York. The provision of the UN Legal Opinion was of immense help, as were the messages of the Secretary-General's personal support read at each CFA by his representative. Certainly, given the looseness of the UN system, had WFP not been a joint UN/FAO organisation no Secretary-General would have considered he had the constitutional basis to play any role.

Pérez de Cuéllar was not by temperament given to bold leadership. At a dinner at No 10 Downing Street for the heads of the system's agencies, Mrs Thatcher made this point, tellingly and tactfully. In her toast of welcome to Pérez de Cuéllar she said, 'I understand that as Chairman of the ACC your position is not unlike mine'. After a slight pause, she added her punch line:

'As far as I am concerned I favour more *primus* and less *pares*.' The implication was unmistakable.

The UN secretariat and the secretariats of some other agencies were through the nineteen eighties demoralised by the relative loss of confidence in them among the major powers, especially the United States. The latter tended to blame their weak influence and the relative dominance of developing countries, aided and abetted by the Soviet Union, as due to the weak or compliant leadership of the Secretary-General and other agencies' heads. The US approach to improving performance was to use the power of the purse. This did not work in the case of UNESCO and FAO.

At times the prospect of insolvency loomed. ACC meetings gave a lot of attention to the financial crisis. There was a great deal of hand-wringing but no action. Once, after a particularly depressing presentation by the Secretary-General, the Director-General of ITU[131] (another Australian) made a sincere and passionate intervention, 'We all stand behind you. Tell us how we can help. Some of us could join you in a delegation to President Reagan to persuade him to relax American financial pressure.' This seemed to me a useful suggestion and I awaited the Secretary-General's response with some expectation. To my surprise, he did not respond directly saying only, 'Some of you are looking for leadership from me. I am not a leader. I did not seek this chair, it comes with my post. I would just as soon see one of you take my place.' While on this occasion I think Pérez de Cuéllar was wrong, he cannot be blamed if he thought this was just another example of ACC play acting.

In the atmosphere of the eighties my problems were a long way from the top of the UN's priorities. Indeed, I found a lot of ignorance in New York of our work. Thus when the secretariat produced overview papers of UN accomplishments it quite frequently failed to even list WFP. This reflected the mind-set in New York which had long seen WFP as an exclusive FAO responsibility. This was all the more regrettable, given the Programme's concrete achievements in fighting hunger.

By inclination, and in line with the reactions of many of his closest advisers, the Secretary-General's underlying rationale for continuing equivocation combined with silent support was fear that an image of disunity would further weaken the UN's standing. Saouma exploited this by threatening at various times to bring the issue of WFP's relationship with FAO to the UN General

Assembly, to ECOSOC or to the ACC. The sub-text was that in so doing he would make it an issue of North-South relations. This was probably bluff and in my view should have been called but, in the climate of the times, it is understandable that Pérez de Cuéllar considered confrontation with Saouma carried risks to the system that he could not afford to run.

THE LESSONS

The unwillingness of the Secretary-General to act decisively as head of the UN system is at the heart of the lessons to be drawn from the WFP experience. Though a negative lesson, it is important because it reveals the fundamental flaw at the heart of the UN system, namely that it lacks substance to the point of existing in name only. It is at best the institutionalisation on paper of the noble goal of a coherent institutional structure to address world problems, at worst an actual hindrance to attainment of that goal.

Although no other UN agency has faced the same combination of factors, WFP's experience was not atypical. The role of personalities, the power and ambitions of agency heads, the political divisions within governments and governing bodies, the ultra-bureaucratic culture of secretariats, are all characteristics of system agencies and long identified (Pitt 1984). They have been so from the beginning. They remain so today. Moreover the structure of the system is antithetical to strong leadership. Neither the Secretary-General nor the ACC had legal power to direct FAO or any other specialised agency to do anything against the will of its executive head, who was answerable only to the organisation's governing body. The Secretary-General had moral authority but chose not to exert it. I have explained why his caution was understandable given the difficulties facing the UN through the 1980s. However, to some extent at least, the cause also lies in the fact that UN system agencies are organisations of sovereign states and exist to serve the interests of states. In short, they are political bodies. Even the secretariats of quite minor units under the direct authority of the Secretary-General rarely received directions from him. The reason was that each owed its existence to interest groups within national governments. So long as enough of those interest groups continued to support the entity, out of conviction for the worth of its work for their state interests and/or the self-interest of the civil servants responsible for its oversight (e.g. the opportunity to attend conferences or get jobs with its secretariat) any intervention by a secretary-general had little prospect of success and could have adverse political consequences. It is risky for secretaries-general to try to do what governments cannot do. Only a secretary-general with exceptional leadership talents would try.

To carry the argument a stage further, there are simply too many agencies for any government to keep under consistent purview.[132] Inevitably, therefore, the UN system became highly decentralised and lacking in coherent direction. It was also inevitable that ECOSOC would fail at the intergovernmental level to bring cohesion, for the same reason, namely the existence of so many agencies and the difficulty of establishing coordinated government policies cutting across many national ministries. That is a difficult enough task for domestic policy making. Only major issues of peace and security are important enough to rise to the top of the agendas of national governments; so to in the UN system, where secretaries-general make these their primary concern.

Governments rarely recognise that they bear most of the blame for duplication, although agencies are also blameworthy, which is all that governments want to see. This was apparent in the joint meetings I attended of the ACC and the intergovernmental committee of the UN General Assembly with oversight of system programme coordination, and in ECOSOC. It was a 'dialogue of the deaf': government representatives and agency heads were not listening to one another.

The issue is as old as the United Nations. At its fourth session in 1949, the UN General Assembly adopted resolution 310(IV), entitled 'The problem of the proliferation and overlapping of the programmes of the United Nations and of the specialised agencies'. This has been the subject of countless reports and resolutions since then but all attempts to overcome the problem have been disappointing. In 1977 the General Assembly created the post of Director-General for Development to ensure 'effective leadership' over the components of the system, 'exercise overall coordination within the system in order to ensure a multidisciplinary approach to the problems of development on a system-wide basis', and '...efficient management of all activities in the economic and social fields financed by the regular budget or by extra budgetary resources'.[133] That post was abolished by Secretary-General Boutros Boutros-Ghali on taking office in 1992, but a position of Deputy Secretary-General was created in

1996, inter alia to achieve coherence in the economic and social development fields. However, that office has no more power in relation to the system than did its predecessor. To be effective a system coordinator needs some powers of direction or coercion; but none has ever been given such authority. At best he is a facilitator or mediator able to call and chair meetings, assemble data and otherwise seek to promote cooperation between agencies.

The same problem exists at the state level as the unhappy history of the WFC shows. Governments established a new intergovernmental committee to systematise consideration of international agriculture issues, set up a first-class secretariat to support it, but gave WFC no power of direction. Inevitably, the separate agencies ignored its precepts, never doing anything they judged to be contrary to their interest. Governments when wearing their WFC membership hats were no more able than secretariats to 'coordinate'.

The developed countries that pay most of system organisations' budgets understand the problem. They blame political irresponsibility on the part of governments who pay only a nominal share of budgets and on secretariats. The Geneva Group had its origins in this view. At the end of the nineteen eighties United States Assistant Secretary of State Bolton (1989) came up with the concept of the 'Unitary UN'. 'The lack of effective central control in the UN system', he said, 'increases the need for...member governments to guide our participation in the different UN agencies with an eye on the overall system'. For the reasons I have given that idea inevitably foundered and, equally inevitably, it continues to re-surface.[134]

Although the possibility of effective leadership at system level is not realistic, I am convinced that good, strong leadership at the level of agency heads is attainable and is the key to stronger cooperation at the agency level and, if accompanied by a few critical steps, could revitalise the economic and social work of the system.

My experience in the system suggests that the central point is to focus on ways to narrow down what the system tries to do and in the process create a leaner, less diffuse structure. The political imperatives that underlie the system have led to the creation of over forty distinct organisations reporting to ECOSOC. This does not include sessional and standing committees and expert ad hoc bodies the number of which varies over time. The core of the system's problem lies in the desire to encompass, no matter how superficially, the whole corpus of issues that can be said to have some effect beyond a single state. It is in large measure tokenism at its worst, since many of these entities have no discernable impact.[135]

Four strategies which, if progressively implemented, could bring about a materially leaner, more effective system involve:

1. Recognising explicitly that the goal of the UN economic and social system should be to build global legal or quasi-legal regimes to better regulate state relations in a globalised world (FAO's best work has followed this path) and pruning the present structure by closing down agencies that do not make a direct contribution to that goal.

2. Streamlining the research done by the present myriad of agencies to ensure it is relevant to the goal and delegating much of this work to bodies outside the UN system which can be governed, as the CGIAR international agricultural research institutes are, by respected expert peers. To the extent necessary, some UN research institutes may be spun off from the system and their governance changed in line with the CGIAR model.

3. Ensuring remaining institutions, including the current specialised agencies, concentrate on the formulation and negotiation of appropriate international conventions or other regimes. To the extent that they provided technical assistance it would be directed toward enabling poor countries to give effect to regimes and conventions.

4. Creating a new specialised agency to consolidate the humanitarian assistance functions of existing organisations (Ingram 1993b).

With fewer, more practically focused governing bodies, it might be expected that the quality of representation on them would be improved and governments would be in a better position to develop more consistent oversight of the system as a whole. Thereby the current vicious circle, by which government interest in the UN system declines because of the ineffectualness of the system and ineffectualness grows with the decline of good governmental oversight, could become a virtuous one.

THE LESSON OF LEADERSHIP

The fact that WFP autonomy was achieved through intergovernmental action, despite its seeming impossibility, is an important lesson in itself. No matter how daunting the task and formidable the obstacles, reform is possible. Secondly, reform was achieved through an evolutionary process not on the basis of a comprehensive blueprint for change. The third lesson is that reform is most likely to be successful if the focus is on component organisations not the whole system at once. The outline for reform suggested in the preceding paragraphs is consistent with such an approach.

The critical ingredient in the success of the reform process was leadership. In my experience a moment usually comes when the leader must speak candidly and fearlessly to stakeholders about the problems faced and the solutions required. However, transparency and boldness are uncharacteristic of the UN system. I broke with strong precedent when I exposed in the CFA and in FAO bodies, with judicious candour, some of the harassment we were subjected to by FAO. I am convinced that if I had not done so, I would have failed to obtain wide understanding in governments of the issues and the steps needed to resolve them.

United Nations' discretion resembles that of the Vatican. Both speak cautiously and obliquely, out of a profound culture of institutional protection. Their intention is not to conceal scandal but stems from fear that openness will be used irresponsibly against them. The UN is wise to be circumspect in what it says publicly, as I was in my administration of WFP. However, circumspection can easily become an unvarying reaction and lead to a culture of concealment and timidity. Unless a chief executive is ready to speak out fearlessly, but temperately, on critical issues he may do his organisation a serious disservice. If obliqueness and evasion become the norm neither the long term institutional interest of the United Nations nor the common good of the international community are well served. If the organisation is losing credibility no amount of concealment will help to change that situation, as is shown by FAO's experience.

The Power of Secretariats

The distinctive political nature of UN system agencies requires that their chief executives are the drivers of their reform. Without leadership they stagnate. Governments must be led to assume their responsibilities to govern. No single government, including the United States, can do this. Developed and developing countries each have vested interests in the *status quo*. More often than not governing bodies fudge issues, make generalised 'motherhood' pronouncements instead of giving concrete, practical directions or weakly go along with secretariat proposals, after cursory examination. On the other hand, it is rare for secretariat proposals to be rejected in their entirety, although several sessions may be necessary for them to gain acceptance and they may be substantially amended, as my structural adjustment proposals were.

When complex issues of substance are addressed, the documents defining the issues and recommending particular courses of action emanate from secretariats, though of course they reflect any prior views of their governing bodies. The preparation by secretariats of policy papers is a principal source of their power. That is why FAO fought so hard to retain its oversight of WFP policy documentation submitted to the CFA.

The ability of secretariats to set the agenda for the sessions of governing bodies is also a way of controlling what governing bodies consider. The WFP Basic Documents gave the Secretary-General and the Director-General the power to propose agenda items and scrutinise the Executive Director's suggested agendas before passing them to the CFA for approval. As my narrative has shown, the Director-General used that power to frustrate my reform efforts.

While it is essential with weak governing bodies for secretariats to lead, through agenda setting and the formation of policy proposals, it is easy for them to slip from leadership to control and to convince themselves that what is good for them is good for those they serve. Carried to the extreme, this can lead secretariats to politicise issues, dangle jobs and allocate aid as a tool of influence over governments and individuals within them.

An important reason for the undue reliance of delegations on secretariats is the proliferation of UN economic and social agencies and units in the United Nations proper. With so many entities available governmental expertise is very thinly spread. Even the United States, which follows the work of agencies more closely than any other government, applies inadequate resources to their supervision. Staff with oversight of WFP came from several agencies and turned over frequently. The result was that the United States had a surprisingly weak institutional memory of the history of issues arising in the CFA, weaker for example than Canada's.

Comparatively speaking, the power of secretariats lies somewhere between that of parliamentary governments, as in the United Kingdom, and Presidents of the United States. There is in practice a separation of powers, as in the United States, but the ability of UN oversight bodies to successfully initiate significant action is weaker than that of Congress. However, the British Prime Minister has more power than the heads of UN agencies to set the agenda and decide the details of policy. To apply this analogy to my circumstances, I was throughout my ten years in the position of a President or Prime Minister whose party never has clear control of Congress or Parliament. By contrast, the Director-General always had control of FAO bodies.

Countervailing Powers of Governments

Faced with their relative weakness of control, governments turned to other measures to ensure their influence. Thus, voluntarily funded agencies like WFP, over which financial control could be retained, were preferred by the United States and other donors, to the specialised agencies where their influence was weakened by the 'one country, one vote' decision-making system. Accordingly, the former continued to prosper, though none as strongly as WFP, when the rich countries tried to cut back on the budgets of the UN and specialised agencies.

States also attached importance to the placement of their nationals in both categories of agencies. They gleaned, partially and not always accurately, much of their knowledge of WFP's inner workings from their nationals. I have told the story of my appointment and reappointment because it shows just how much importance the United States attaches to the placement of its nationals in key posts. I was replaced by an American, who in turn has been succeeded by another American. At the time of my departure, the United States headed three of the four main voluntarily funded agencies. Since then it has surrendered control of UNDP to a non-American.

The pressure on agency heads by some governments for the placement of their nationals is sometimes very strong. There is also pressure for their promotion, irrespective of merit. Once I was astonished when Algeria pressed crudely for the appointment of an official, who had no relevant qualifications, to a top post, simply on the grounds that WFP at the time had no Algerians in its secretariat. The Italians also pressed the claims of individuals in inappropriate ways. Concern for the greater good of WFP caused me to sometimes yield to such pressures.

Another unfortunate practice is for developed countries to subsidise the emoluments of their nationals or seek the placement of some in particular high level posts for periods of several years without cost to the agency concerned. I was never willing to agree to requests to place nominees funded by governments in WFP posts. [136]

From my experience I am convinced that the concept of an apolitical career civil service with staff appointments and promotions managed on merit principles is a foundation for a UN system which respects itself and retains the respect of governments. A grave responsibility of the heads of agencies is to strengthen practice in this regard. Its importance was recognised from the beginning but has never been realised.[137] Dag Hammarskjöld's poignant remark in 1953, quoted by Brian Urquhart (1990), sadly remains applicable:

> Sometimes, when I look ahead, the problems raised by our need to develop a truly international and independent secretariat seem to me beyond human capacity. But I know that this is not so...We are in the fortunate position of pioneers.

Leadership Qualities

If leadership necessarily comes from the heads of economic and social agencies, are there particular requirements for leadership in the UN system? Political leaders everywhere need a vision, the ability to inspire voters with their vision and to accept compromise in its pursuit. The same abilities are also essential for good leadership in the UN system but the need for statesmanship is greater if the system is to prosper. The executive heads of system agencies should ideally also be managerial leaders. An immense literature exists on this topic. Suffice it to say that I incline to the school that management is an art which can only be partly learned, though leadership techniques can be improved through experience and appropriate instruction.[138]

All major UN agencies are political institutions not expert bodies, though some of their off-shoots may have attributes of the latter. Their important decisions bring benefits and costs in varying degree to member states. The differing interests of rich and poor nations are at the root of political division in UN development and humanitarian agencies. Good leadership requires that agency heads always act to reconcile interests. In so acting I sometimes displeased the United States, one reason why it temporised in its support for my re-appointment.

If it had not been for FAO's malign influence over the G77 I have no doubt that my scope for independent action would have been greater. Thus the views I gave in 1988 to the Rome Chapter of the Society for International Development are still applicable. Having identified cancellation and restructuring of debt and improved market access for the agricultural and industrial products of developing countries as the two issues most important of resolution, I went on to say:

> In these, as in all matters affecting our interdependent world, there is a need for a steady and deliberate effort to promote a harmonisation of interests of industrialised and developing countries. This calls for leadership of a kind which the founders of the United Nations envisaged. However, I would have to say that the UN is not very well placed to assume it. One reason is that until quite recently...when developing countries were able to set the agenda in the UN, I believe that UN secretariats did not do enough to ensure a degree of balance as regards the legitimate concerns of the industrialised countries. Now that circumstances have altered and the industrialised countries are more assertive in pursuit of their interests, there is a danger that UN secretariats may go too far in the other direction...We must not allow...our agencies, which embody the concerns of all sovereign states, to be used to serve the interests of one group only. Leadership requires that our essential integrity is recognised by all parties concerned. Difficult though it may be, the UN must be responsive to changing circumstances but at the same time be seen as consistent in respecting the views of all and balancing their interests in pursuit of a more orderly world economy conducive to equitable economic growth for rich and poor countries alike.

To effect major change in WFP in the face of FAO's obstruction I had to lead by building a basis of support that cut across 'parties', developed and developing countries alike. I did so by respecting the interests of both. They saw that within the political reality of an agency wholly funded by voluntary contributions, overwhelmingly from rich countries, I strove to satisfy all.

The United States at times considered that I denied it the influence over

WFP to which its dominant contributor status entitled it and which it has secured since my departure. While I was always sensitive to its demands and recognised that constitutional change would not be obtained in the face of its opposition my experience demonstrates that there is more scope for positive leadership in the UN system than academic analysts may appreciate.[139]

Finding Good Leaders

If the wise leadership of the 'philosopher king' should become the aim in the UN system what can be done to help achieve it? Urquhart and Childers (1990) have said many perceptive things on this subject and have offered comprehensive proposals to improve selection of the UN Secretary-General, the heads of the specialised agencies and of the various programs and funds. I do not intend to repeat them here. Instead I will single out a few for which this case study provides clear support. Their study is a generalised one which out of discretion does not name names or give specific examples.

Limited Terms

The single most important attainable change is to set limits on the terms of executive heads. Its simplicity and ease of comprehension should enhance the prospect of its adoption. I agree in principle with Urquhart/Childers that, rather than allowing two terms, agency and program heads should be limited to single terms of seven years. No matter how successful an executive head has been, he will have achieved most of what he is capable in this time. However, the politics of re-appointment is such that a strict limit of two terms, preferably each of four years' duration, is probably the most that is realistically attainable.

Some progress has been made in this regard. For example, WFP's Executive Director was limited to two terms in 1993. FAO followed in 2003, although the incumbent Director-General, already in his second term of six years, was exempted and was re-elected for a third term, despite reported criticisms of his performance by some governments.[140]

The difficulty of achieving strict adherence to the two-terms limitation has again been revealed by the process of re-appointment in 2005 of the International Atomic Energy Agency Director-General for a third term. The United States sought to use the two-terms rule to block his re-appointment, but other governments saw this as a rationalisation for a politically motivated policy. Accordingly, though the two-terms rule may be valued in theory, governments want to preserve their flexibility.

Rotation of nationals

It should be a requirement that immediate successors always come from countries different from their predecessor's. Earlier in the history of the UN system it was understandable, if undesirable, that the President of the World Bank and the executive heads of some of the operational agencies should always be US nationals. However, in this globalised, post-colonial world such an arrangement is anachronistic.

Recruitment

Difficult though these limited reforms are to achieve across the system, the identification and selection of suitable candidates for chief executive posts is much more challenging. Whether heads are appointed or elected, some machinery should exist to identify qualified candidates, including internal candidates, and there should be some formal procedure for the involvement of governing bodies, including various possibilities canvassed by Urquhart/Childers.[141] However, one of their proposals is impracticable, namely to forbid campaigning by candidates. Incumbents would still be able to campaign in all sorts of informal ways as could outsiders with the right connections and backing from their governments, as in fact I did in relation to my initial appointment.

Urquhart/Childers rightly point to a 'cascading' effect flowing from the appointment of better leaders, by which they mean that the quality of lower-level appointees will thereby be enhanced. My experience in relation to senior appointments is relevant. From the time of my appointment, my greatest frustrations arose from the obstacles placed by governments and the FAO Director-General in my way in the selection of well qualified senior personnel. It is hard enough under the best of circumstances to make good personnel choices. To the extent that the 'cascading effect' comes to operate, the best future leaders of agencies may well be more likely to come from within them or from other agencies of the system as happens within national civil services like Australia's. A less politicised, more cohesive, international civil service with a stronger *esprit de corps* could be the result.

Other steps to reduce politicisation of the international civil service should be taken, including strengthened systems of recruitment through competitive examination at entry level.

Improving Accountability

Finally, a word about strengthening accountability of agencies: above all the role of external audit should be as strong, expert and independent as possible. As my account shows, even auditors as professional as the UK's were influenced at least to some extent by their desire to retain the valuable contract awarded by FAO. Confining the auditor's role to traditional accounts auditing, unaccompanied by broader investigative powers into financial corruption, leaves a serious gap in oversight. Again some progress has been made by, for example, putting limits on the duration of appointments and a requirement for a periodical change of auditors. Also, some agencies have followed the example of the WFP, which in 1997 established an independent office to oversee internal management. The General Assembly, in its resolution of 13 September 2005 (paragraph 164) has made useful suggestions in this regard. It has strengthened the UN's Office of Internal Oversight Service and requested the Secretary-General to commission an independent external evaluation of the UN systems auditing and oversight systems.

The marine insurance affair in WFP revealed to me a potentially serious gap in UN system agencies' accountability arising from their diplomatic immunity. Who does investigate, judge and punish criminal actions committed within agencies?[142] During my time in the system a major tax fraud going back many years and adversely affecting the revenue of the UN and the United States government became widely reported in the US press. It involved a substantial number of staff and many millions of dollars. A few staff were initially dismissed but thereafter 'amnesties' appeared to be the main outcome. Corrupt employees may be dismissed but criminal charges seem rarely to be brought. Like some churches in relation to child abuse, the UN system seems to prefer to conceal from public gaze crimes which would otherwise be criminally prosecuted.[142]

The roles of the ACABQ, the UN system budget and expenditure watchdog, and of the FAO intergovernmental committee with apparent oversight of FAO's budgets and financial management, have a critical place in this narrative. The former did excellent work due to its independent chairman, who was supported by a professional secretariat. The FAO Finance Committee was a caricature of a serious oversight body. It remains essential to improve the quality of supervision by such committees. At a minimum, some test of professional suitability of appointees is necessary as is the availability of independent advice to the committees beyond that provided by the secretariats being examined.

The role of JIU Inspector Bertrand showed how important—indeed essential–it is to have an independent management review capability within the system. The designated organisation should be given a significant budget and its staff professionally recruited from within and outside national governments and the UN system. Supervision should be by a small committee of genuine peers appointed by the General Assembly.

CONCLUSION

Even this modest list of recommendations will be difficult to effect across the system. The more practical course is to work institution by institution. On the whole, as my account of the effort to reform WFP suggests, governments bear more of the responsibility for the disfunctionality of the UN system's economic and social work than do agency heads. Indeed governments have a far better international civil service than their own behaviour, so often hypocritical, deceitful, even quixotic, deserves. Serious, sustained reform requires governments to face their own failures as well as ensuring better leadership by executive heads of agencies. However, governments are unlikely to reform without the leadership and vision that can come only from the executive heads of the system. Until both happen, real change will not occur and dissatisfaction with the UN and the UN system will continue.

---

[123] 'America Goes Backward', *The New York Review of Books,* Vol. L, No. 10 (2003)

[124] Not one of the directors, despite my asking each privately, made any suggestions for possible improvements.

[125] Two agencies which were eventually abolished were UNDRO and WFC.

[126] At times the United States and others saw my conflict with Saouma as helpful to their struggle to undermine him. Sometimes I even feared that they preferred to see it continue rather than be resolved. Privately, as my diaries show, I consistently regarded it

as being a conflict over principles of good governance. I always represented it as such in my discussions with governments.

127 That the FAO culture had become inimical to the best interests of the agency is shown by the experience of another international organisation linked to it. The International Board for Plant Genetic Resources was founded in 1974. It was located at FAO headquarters and was serviced by the latter. It developed a fraught, acrimonious relationship with FAO. In 1992, the Board was separated from the FAO, re-established as the International Plant Genetic Resources Institute and shifted out of Rome.

128 This is not a criticism of my former colleagues, most of whom were hard-working, competent officials with a commitment to the ideals underlying the UN. Only a few deserved the title, 'Lords of Poverty', a label applied in a brilliant, polemical account of the UN system of the nineteen eighties (Hancock 1989).

129 The United Nations itself during this period was rent by conflict between Western countries and the G77 over the power of the majority to pass resolutions intended to pressure the former to change policies, for example in relation to Palestinian aspirations or the ordering of the global economic system. The rich countries felt their control over vital national interests was being threatened. At a more abstract level the basis of friction between the two groups has been described as due to 'significant tension in the system between the diplomatic and political approaches, the latter emphasising voting as the means of decision making, whereas the former emphasises the autonomy of sovereign states' (Finklestein). In the CFA this difference was reflected in the insistence of the developed countries that decision making should be on the basis of consensus whereas the G77 asserted the appropriateness of majority decision making. The compromise was to avoid decision over whether consensus meant unanimity, as the United States argued, or to insist on voting. In practice it was tacitly agreed that consensus meant something like 'substantial majority'.

130 For an overview of this and other aspects of the source of the FAO Director-General's power and an overall assessment of the work of FAO and the other Rome agencies, namely WFP, IFAD and WFC, see Talbot (1987and 2000).

131 The malaise affecting much of the system did not extend to the smaller, more technical agencies like ITU, ICAO, UPU and IMCO.

132 To give one example from the area of humanitarian relief, the JIU recommended in 1990 that no less than eleven distinct system entities, in addition to UNHCR, should be members of a working

group to examine the relatively straightforward issue of systematising data that would give early warning of possible refugee flows.

133 General Assembly Resolution 32/197.

134 At its 2005 session the General Assembly had before it comprehensive proposals (A/59/2005) from the Secretary-General for reform of the UN which were based upon the recommendations of an expert panel he had established. Paragraph 168 of the General Assembly's resolution of 13 September 2005, headed 'System-wide coherence' *inter alia* called for the implementation of the following:

> Coordinating our representation on the governing boards for the various development and humanitarian agencies so as to ensure that they pursue a coherent policy in assigning mandates and allocating resources throughout the system.

This reads like the same pious hopes uttered so often in the past but that have failed to bear fruit.

135 The General Assembly(A/59/2005) decided on 13 September 2005 on some steps that should improve the operation of the UN's work in areas of development and human rights, such as the review of mandates older than five years and a possible 'one-time staff buy-out to improve personnel structure and quality'(paragraph 163). While it appears that at least to some extent operations within the system as a whole will be included in the prospective reviews, the resolution unfortunately makes little more than time-worn suggestions in relation to the work of ECOSOC itself (paragraph155).

136 I do not refer here to the Junior Professional Officer scheme which provided a valuable means for identifying potential permanent appointees at the starting grade.

137 The General Assembly's 2005 decision (A/59/2005) alludes to the need for an apolitical civil service but offers no proposals on how to achieve that goal. The emphasis is on greater efficiency and the establishment of a system-wide code of ethics.

138 In its Survey of Corporate Leadership in the issue of 25 October 2003, *The Economist* identified 'ten commandments' for successful leaders of public companies, which I believe are applicable also to leadership in the UN system, as follows: a sound ethical compass; the ability to take unpleasant decisions; clarity and focus; ambition; effective communication skills; the ability to judge people; a knack for developing talent; emotional self-confidence adaptability; charm.

139 For example Haas (p. 71), has summed up UN system executive leadership as follows:

> A modest and self-effacing style of leadership is the predominant pattern. It is determined by the dominant coalition of states...if the organisation is ruled by a single hegemonic state, then the executive head is merely the agent of that state, thus making independent leadership impossible.

In the light of my experience such a depressing conclusion is far too categorical. On the whole my colleagues had strong personalities and some, in the difficult circumstances of the eighties, did their best to reconcile interests as I sought to do.

140 *The Economist*, December, 2005.

141 Some agencies, for example UNHCR, have introduced more transparent processes.

142 Presumably, were a UN system staff member enjoying diplomatic immunity to commit a serious crime outside his organisation's premises, established practice would enable immunity to be waived and the suspect tried in the courts of the host country.

143 Despite the extraordinary scale and cost of the Volcker investigation into the Iraq Oil for Food scheme there appears to have been few prosecutions or resignations. Corruption may have been deeper in the Security Council, governments and private firms than among UN staff.

EPILOGUE

A HEART WARMING TRIBUTE

My story is complete. It is December 1991. CFA32 is holding a special session to thank me for my leadership. My diary gives a brief account:

Friday 7 December 1991

> *Very pleased and touched by the special CFA testimonial session which lasted three hours. Especially moved by Peter McCawley's statement (he came especially for the occasion) indicating Australia's and especially AIDAB's pride in me. It brought tears to my eyes. At the end a standing ovation of several minutes. Most of the speeches were very good—some the best I have heard in the Green Room, the scene of so much drama and so many victories. Shah on behalf of Saouma made an enigmatic speech that seemed to imply criticism more than praise. Peter Hansen came especially from NY and gave a very warm tribute. The day I came, i.e. 4/4/1982, I told Saouma that I would make my mark on WFP...clearly I have. Ahmed moved by my response, in which I called him the 'perfect model of an Islamic gentleman'.*

In many ways the statement that satisfied me most on that occasion was by the Cuban representative, Mr E Melendez Bachs, the Minister President of the State Committee for Economic Cooperation. He travelled to Rome especially for the meeting and made a generous, extended intervention describing in some detail my support for Cuba. Though I saw nothing exceptional in what I had done for that country, having treated its requests for assistance on their merits, it was clear that my even-handedness and the open mind I had shown on my visit there had won Cuba's respect. Nearly ten years later, when WFP made me the first recipient of its Food for Life Award, the then Cuban Ambassador in Rome wrote a very warm letter of congratulations. My support for Cuba was still remembered with appreciation, he wrote

During my term with WFP I made extended visits to several communist or quasi-communist developing countries, Cuba, Nicaragua, Ethiopia, South Yemen, Vietnam and China. In all I formed a favourable impression of leading technocrats like Melendez Bachs, whose dedication, integrity and competence came across more strongly than many of their counterparts in other developing countries. Yet I sensed a touch of sadness, even tragedy, in some of those with whom I developed a more personal relationship: the inner psyche of good people whom circumstances had placed on the wrong side of history, perhaps. Like is attracted to like, and as a serious person I was attracted to the seriousness I found among these men.

I had the same gratitude and respect from developing and developed countries. The most senior US delegate to attend CFA sessions, Andrew Natsios, now head of USAID, stayed for the special session which took place two days after the formal business of CFA32 had finished. He gave a brief but moving tribute to my leadership and management skills, my independence and character. The following year I received a formal, handsomely mounted Certificate of Appreciation signed by the US Secretaries of State and Agriculture and the Administrator of the Agency for International Development for my 'leadership in the struggle against world hunger'. At times in this account I have been very critical of the United States but I always admired the vigour, idealism and generosity of spirit exemplified in the work of the many dedicated public servants I interacted with over these ten years.

A few weeks beforehand, I had been thrilled by the announcement that I had been chosen to receive the Alan Shawn Feinstein World Hunger award, conferred at Brown University, Rhode Island the following year by the late Audrey Hepburn, for my personal leadership of WFP. The Award and associated prize was given annually at the time to provide 'public recognition for extraordinary efforts or contributions to the reduction of hunger in the world and its prevention in the future'. As I commented in my diary:

> It does mean a lot for WFP, and with the General Regulations amendments, puts the 'seal of international approval' on [WFP]'. Snobbery is such a powerful sentiment that (lacking such seals) WFP has laboured under many handicaps.

Audrey Hepburn conferring the World Hunger Award.

Some would see that as my most important achievement. I had converted not only the reality, but the image, of WFP from a seeming minor player on the international aid scene, purveyor of second-rate assistance into a key UN agency widely applauded for its humanitarian and developmental work.

My response at the end of the special 'tribute' session sums up how I felt:[144]

...it hasn't been particularly easy, but I must say I leave with a great sense of accomplishment...it's the process that counts for me as much as the result...I believe very strongly that...while we seek for compromises...a compromise has to be rooted in more than just striking some sort of mean, it has to be founded in some sense of ethical values. So, I've tried...to be guided by....some sense of principle in seeking to do what I did...Now, while I leave with a certain sense of release and of course with a great deal of sadness, I leave with no regrets at all. It has been...an absolutely fantastic experience to have been head of the World Food Programme. A fantastic experience because, rhetoric aside, the World Food Programme does do a great deal of good, and in this imperfect world there are not that many fallible human institutions that manage to do a great deal of good. The other reason why it's been a fantastic experience...is because it's really the culmination of my diplomatic career...The role of the United Nations is to manage interdependence, and if you believe in the primacy of peace...and you also recognise that justice is a condition of peace, you have to want to work...if you're a diplomat in the United Nations. On RAI Uno [the main Italian TV network] they carry the maxims of La Rochefoucauld...One reads: 'Nothing is so contagious as an example. We never do great good or great evil without bringing about more of the same on the part of others.' I leave hoping that I have done some good, that I've influenced others in that direction, but my greatest hope, indeed expectation, is that the new CFA will set an example of enlightened governance to the whole United Nations system.

Mohammed Zejjari, Tun Myat, James and Odette Ingram,
Salahuddin Ahmed, Tekle Tomlinson

---

[144] Document CFA: 32/13, pp 114-115.

APPENDIX I:

EXTRACTS FROM THE WFP BASIC DOCUMENTS

BASIC TEXTS

EXTRACT FROM UN GENERAL ASSEMBLY RESOLUTION 3404 (XXX) ADOPTED 28 NOVEMBER 1975

The General Assembly

Recalling its resolution 3348 of 17 December 1974 in which it endorsed the resolutions of the World Food Conference,

Considering that in paragraph 6 of resolution xxii of 16 November 1974 the World Food Conference recommended that the United Nations/FAO Intergovernmental Committee of the World Food Programme should be reconstituted, so as to enable it to help to evolve and co-ordinate short-term and longer-term food aid policies recommended by the Conference,

1. Decides that the United Nations/FAO Intergovernmental Committee of the World Food Programme shall be reconstituted as the Committee on Food Aid Policies and Programmes, which shall comprise thirty States Members of the United Nations or Members of the Food and Agriculture Organization of the United Nations, fifteen of these Members to be elected by the Economic and Social Council and fifteen by the Council of the Food and Agriculture Organization of the United Nations, it being understood that outgoing members shall be eligible for re-election;...

343

4. Requests the Economic and Social Council and the Council of the Food and Agriculture Organization of the United Nations, when they elect members of the Committee on Food Aid Policies and Programmes, to take into account the need for the balanced representation of economically developed and developing countries and other relevant factors, such as the representation of potential participating countries, both con-tributing and recipient, equitable geographical distribution and the representation of both developed and developing countries having commercial interests in international trade in foodstuffs, especially those highly dependent on such trade;

5. Further decides that, in addition to discharging the functions hitherto exercised by the Intergovernmental Committee, the Committee on Food Aid Policies and Programmes shall help to evolve and co-ordinate short-term and longer-term food aid policies recommended by the World Food Conference and shall, in particular:

(a) Provide general guidance on the policy, administration and operation of the World Food Programme;

(b) Provide a forum for intergovernmental consultations on national and international food aid programmes and policies;

(c) Review periodically general trends in food aid requirements and availabilities;

(d) Recommend to governments, through the World Food Council, improvements in food aid policies and programmes on such matters as programme priorities, commodity composition of food aid and other related subjects;

(e) Formulate proposals for the more effective co-ordination of multilateral, bilateral and non-governmental food aid programmes, including emergency food aid;

(f) Review periodically the implementation of the recommendations made by the World Food Conference on food aid policies;

6. Decides also that the Committee on Food Aid Policies and Programmes shall report annually to the Economic and Social Council and the Council of the Food and Agriculture Organization of the United Nations, which, in considering the reports of the Committee, shall take into account the responsibilities of the World Food Council, and that the Committee shall submit periodic and special reports to the World Food Council;

8. Further resolves that the Committee on Food Aid Policies and

Programmes shall be serviced by the Executive Director of the World Food Programme, acting in consultation with the Secretary-General of the United Nations and the Director-General of the Food and Agriculture Organization of the United Nations, and that in this respect the Executive Director shall be guided by the relevant provisions of the General Regulations of the World Food Programme and in particular shall continue to rely to the maximum extent possible on the technical services of the United Nations and its subsidiary bodies, the Food and Agriculture Organization of the United Nations and other organizations of the United Nations system, without any duplication of such services;

EXTRACTS FROM WFP GENERAL REGULATIONS

2. Having regard to the functions of the United Nations in the general field of economic and social development, and the special responsibilities of FAO in securing improvements in nutrition and in the efficiency of food production and distribution, the Programme is undertaken jointly by the United Nations and FAO in cooperation with other interested United Nations agencies and appropriate intergovernmental bodies.

3 (a) (ii) Countries participating in the international emergency reserve should, pending the establishment of a world food grain reserve, indicate to the Programme, over and above their regular pledges to the Programme, availabilities of primarily food grains or of cash con-tributions which might be called upon for emergency food aid purposes, in accordance with United Nations General Assembly Resolution 3362 (S-vii). Developing countries not in a position to make contributions in cash or in kind to the reserve should, where possible, indicate their willingness to make interest-free loans of commodities to be used by the Programme.

3. (a) (iii) Appropriate commodities and acceptable services shall be determined from time to time by discussions between contributors and the Executive Director in the light of operational needs.

(b) Commodity pledges may be made either in monetary terms or in terms of fixed physical quantities of specified commodities. In the latter case, a nominal value will be placed on the commodity pledge by the Executive Director at the time of pledging, based on world market prices or the nearest approximation to the world market prices at the time. This nominal value will be adjusted at the time of each delivery of a commodity to conform to the world market price, or the nearest approximation to the world market price, at the time. All commodities delivered to the Programme will be valued at world market prices, or the nearest approximation to world market prices, at the time of delivery. Contributions of acceptable services shall be valued either at world market prices, or the nearest approximation to the world market prices, or, where a service is of a local character, at the price contracted for by the Executive Director.

4. (b) meeting emergency food needs; and

(c) promoting world food security in accordance with the recommendations made to it by the United Nations and the FAO.

5. (a) For meeting emergency food needs, a portion of the resources of the Programme shall be reserved each year for use by the Director-General of FAO. The amounts to be reserved shall be determined by the Committee on Food Aid Policies and Programmes from time to time in accordance with changing circumstances. In cases of special needs, the Committee may, at the request of the Executive Director, in consultation with the Director-General of FAO, allocate further amounts for use by the Director-General to meet emergency food needs. Any unused balance of the emergency allocation shall return to the general resources of the Programme at the end of each year.

(b) The Programme shall, within the framework of emergency assistance cooperation in the United Nations system and in accordance with appropriate recommendations of the United Nations and FAO, seek to ensure coordination of emergency food assistance.

7. The organs of the World Food Programme shall be:

(a) a Committee on Food Aid Policies and Programmes (hereinafter referred to as 'the Committee') jointly established by the United Nations and FAO and composed of 30 States Members of the United Nations or Member Nations of FAO;

(b) a Secretariat located at FAO Headquarters in Rome and reporting to both the Secretary-General of the United Nations and the Director-General of FAO.

8. Intergovernmental supervision of the Programme shall be exercised by the Committee.

9. (a) The Committee shall help evolve and coordinate short-term and

longer-term food aid policies recommended by the World Food Conference. It shall, in particular:

(i) provide general guidance on the policy, administration and operation of the World Food Programme;

(ii) provide a forum for intergovernmental consultations on national and international food aid programmes and policies;

(iii) review periodically general trends in food aid requirements and food aid availabilities;

(iv) recommend to governments, through the World Food Council, improvements in food aid policies and programmes on such matters as programme priorities, commodity composition of food aid and other related subjects;

(v) formulate proposals for more effective coordination of multilateral, bilateral and non-governmental food aid programmes, including emergency food aid;

(vi) review periodically the implementation of the recommendations made by the World Food Conference on food aid policies.

9. (b) With regard to the operation of the Programme, the Committee shall examine and approve projects submitted to it by the Executive Director. In respect of the approval of projects, however, it may delegate to the Executive Director such authority as it may specify. It shall examine and approve the administrative and project budgets of the Programme. It shall review the administration and execution of approved projects and other activities of the Programme.

10. The Committee shall report annually to the Economic and Social Council and the Council of the Food and Agriculture Organization. It shall also submit periodic and special reports to the World Food Council.

13. The Committee shall ensure, in the programmes under its supervision, that:

 (a) In accordance with the FAO Principles of Surplus Disposal and with the consultative procedures established by the Committee on Commodity Problems (CCP), and in conformity with the United Nations General Assembly resolution 1496 (xv), particularly paragraph 9, commercial markets and normal and developing trade are neither interfered with nor disrupted.

(b) The agricultural economy in recipient countries is adequately safeguarded with respect both to its domestic markets and the effective development of food production.

(c) Due consideration is given to safeguarding normal commercial practices in respect of acceptable services.

14. (a) The Programme shall be administered by a Secretariat, headed by an Executive Director.

(b) The Executive Director shall be appointed, for a term of five years, by the Secretary-General of the United Nations and the Director-General of FAO after consultation with the Committee.

(c) The Executive Director shall be responsible for servicing the Committee.

(d) The Executive Director shall operate through three divisions, subject to such modifications as may from time to time be approved by the Committee.

(e) The Executive Director shall be responsible for the staffing and organization of the Secretariat. The selection and appointment of senior officials shall be made in agreement with the Secretary-General of the United Nations and the Director-General of FAO.

(f) Every effort shall be made to keep the cost of management and administration of the Programme to a minimum consistent with the maintenance of efficiency.

(g) General financial and administrative services shall be provided on a reimbursable basis through the regular FAO Administration Department, and to this end the Executive Director shall rely to the fullest extent possible on the existing staff and facilities of FAO, within the context of sub-paragraph (f) above.

(h) For other services the Programme shall rely to the maximum extent feasible on the existing staff and facilities of FAO, the United Nations and other intergovernmental agencies within the context of sub-paragraph (f) above. The additional cost involved shall be reimbursed from the Programme's resources.

(i) The representative of the Programme in each recipient country shall be the Resident Representative of the United Nations Development Programme or the Regional Representative of the United Nations Development Programme, as the case may be. The Programme field staff stationed in a recipient country shall form part of his office.

(j) The Executive Director shall administer the staff of the Programme in accordance with FAO Staff Regulations and Rules and such special rules proposed by the Executive Director as may be approved by the Secretary-General of the United Nations and the Director-General of FAO.

15. All States Members of the United Nations or Members or Associate Members of any specialized agency or of the IAEA shall be eligible to submit requests for consideration by the Programme.

16. (a) The Executive Director shall be responsible for assuring that projects to be implemented are sound, carefully planned and directed toward valid objectives, for assuring the mobilization of the necessary technical and administrative skills, and for assessing the ability of recipient countries to carry out the projects. He shall be responsible for assuring supply of commodities and acceptable services as agreed. However, he has the responsibility to seek, in consultation with the recipient government, correction of any inadequacies in project operation, and may withdraw assistance in the event essential corrections are not made.

18. (a) Governments desiring to establish food aid programmes or projects assisted by the Programme shall present their requests in the form indicated by the Executive Director. Prior to the submission of the project application, the knowledge, skills and experience of locally available technicians, including those of the United Nations, FAO, the Programme and other United Nations organizations, should be drawn on to the extent feasible and necessary for the purpose of assuring maximum refinement and improvement in the project plans at the earliest possible stage, particularly with reference to the administrative and technical aspects thereof. Requests shall normally be presented through the UNDP Resident Rep-resentatives, who shall keep the FAO Country Representatives and, as appropriate, the representatives of other United Nations agencies fully informed...

(c) The Executive Director shall, upon receipt of requests, proceed to appraise them, and, in doing so, consult with and seek advice and cooperation from the United Nations, FAO and other interested and cooperating international agencies and bodies according to their respective fields of competence.

19. Governments desiring food assistance to meet emergency food needs shall present a request to the Director-General of FAO. Such requests should contain the basic information required about the situation. The Director-General of FAO will request the Executive Director of the Programme to examine it. The Director-General of FAO will decide upon the request, taking into account the recommendation of the Executive Director of the Programme.

21. Upon approval of an emergency operation by the Director-General of

FAO, an agreement, which may be in the form of an exchange of letters, shall be concluded forthwith between the Executive Director and the recipient government.

23...(b) The recipient government shall report as may be provided for in the agreement between the Executive Director and the government on the progress of distribution of WFP commodities.

(c) As agreements are carried into effect, recipient governments shall give full cooperation so as to enable authorized personnel of the Programme to observe operations from tune to time, to ascertain their effects, and to carry out evaluations of the results. The Executive Director shall submit reports to the CFA on emergency operations.

24. In the assessment of prospective economic and social development projects, and in their implementation and subsequent evaluation, full consideration shall be given to the prospective and actual effect of the project upon local food production, including possible ways and means of increasing such production, and upon the markets for agricultural products produced in the country.

25. Adequate consideration shall also be given to safeguarding commercial markets and the normal and developing trade of exporting countries in accordance with the FAO Principles of Surplus Disposal, as well as safeguarding normal commercial practices in respect of acceptable services used by the Programme.

26. As a means of safeguarding commercial markets, the Executive Director shall comply with the following requirements:

(a) At an early stage in the preparation of a project which may be of such significance as to threaten to interfere with or disrupt commercial markets or normal and developing trade, he shall consult with the countries likely to be affected.

(b) He shall also inform the chairman of the Consultative Sub-Committee on Surplus Disposal of the FAO Committee on Commodity Problems of such preparations.

(c) If questions concerning any proposed project are raised before the Consultative Sub-Committee, its views should be promptly reported to the Executive Director, who shall take them into account before proceeding with the project.

(d) To facilitate the consideration of policies within the field of surplus disposal, he shall make available to the Consultative Sub-Committee documents relevant to these subjects prepared by the Programme.

27. The Director-General of FAO shall establish a Trust Fund under Financial Regulation 6.7 of FAO, to which all contributions to the Programme shall be credited and from which the cost of administration and operation of the Programme shall be met.

28. The financial operations of the Programme shall be carried out insofar as possible under the existing Financial Regulations of FAO. The Director-General of FAO, in consultation with the Executive Director, the FAO Finance Committee and the United Nations Advisory Committee on Administrative and Budgetary Questions (ACABQ), shall develop, for the approval of the Committee, such additional financial procedures as are necessary to meet the special needs for the administration of the Programme.

29. The biennial budget of the Programme shall be reviewed by the FAO Finance Committee and by the ACABQ, and submitted together with their reports to the Committee for approval. Supplementary budget estimates may, in exceptional circumstances, be prepared and reviewed to the extent feasible under the same procedure before submission to the Committee for approval. The financial reports of the Programme shall be submitted to the FAO Finance Committee and to the ACABQ. After review by the FAO Finance Committee and by the ACABQ, if the latter so desires, they shall be submitted with any comments which these committees might wish to make to the Committee for approval.

30. The Executive Director may undertake, in consultation with the Secretary-General of the United Nations and the Director-General of FAO, studies of problems related to the effective operations of the Programme and such other functions as may be given to it.

31. The Executive Director, in consultation with the Secretary-General of the United Nations and the Director-General of FAO, shall arrange for expert studies to be undertaken, as needed, to aid in the consideration of the future development of multilateral food programmes. In developing these studies, he shall arrange for as much as possible of the investigations to be made as part of the regular staff activities of FAO and the United Nations, and of other interested and competent intergovernmental organizations.

EXTRACTS FROM WFP
ADDITIONAL FINANCIAL PROCEDURES

Article I

The financial procedures of the World Food Programme (hereinafter referred to as 'the Programme') being partly covered by the provisions of the General Regulations of the Programme and of the Financial Regulations of FAO, the present Additional Financial Procedures are primarily intended to supplement, and should be read in conjunction with, these provisions. Any amendments or additions thereto shall be developed and adopted in accordance with the procedure set forth in General Regulation 28.

Article II

The Trust Fund referred to in General Regulation 27 shall be called the World Food Programme Fund (hereinafter referred to as 'the Programme Fund') and shall be administered in accordance with the Financial Regulations of FAO as supplemented by the present Additional Financial Procedures.

Article V

1. The value of all pledges made and all contributions received shall be credited to accounts established under the Programme Fund.

2. The Executive Director may accept cash from outside sources to meet expenses connected with the Programme-assisted projects. Such monies will be credited to sub-Trust Funds of the Programme established for the purpose. Unless otherwise provided for by the Committee on Food Aid Policies and Programmes (hereinafter referred to as 'the Committee') such sub-Trust Funds shall be subject to the provisions of FAO Financial Regulation 6.7.

Article VII

The Director-General of FAO shall act as custodian of the funds in the Programme Fund and he or any official designated by him shall determine the bank or banks in which such funds shall be kept.

Article XIII

1. The Executive Director, in consultation with the Secretary-General of the United Nations and the Director-General of FAO, shall prepare budgets for:

(a) technical advisory, administrative and servicing costs;

(b) projects and emergency operations.

Article XIV

1. The project budgets approved by the Committee shall constitute authorizations to the Executive Director to incur obligations and make payments for the periods of the respective projects.

2. The budgets established by the Executive Director for projects approved under his delegated authority shall constitute authorization to incur obligations and make payments within the limits established under Article XIII. 5.

Article XVI

The Director-General of FAO shall be responsible:

(a) for recording the pledges;

(b) for the maintenance of such accounts, ledgers and cash books as are necessary to record:

(i) the receipt of all cash income of the Programme;

(ii) the expenditure incurred on behalf of the Programme;

(iii) the receipt of commodities;

(iv) the movement and disposition of commodities;

(v) the utilization of services;

(c) for the maintenance of a file of documents supporting the entries in the accounts, reflecting commodity transactions and the utilization of services.

Article XVIII

Financial reports

The Director-General of FAO shall prepare the following:

(a) Monthly:

(i) contributions pledged and received;

(ii) expenditure related to budgets.

(b) Periodically:

a statement of the financial position of the Programme, including particulars of pledges and contributions received, expen-diture, investments and any other relevant data for the information of the Committee, of the FAO Finance Committee and of ACABQ of the current financial status of the Programme Fund;

(c) Annually:

an annual statement of accounts of the Programme and such other supporting statements as may be required by the Committee.

Article XIX

The provisions of FAO Financial Regulation X shall be applicable, mutatis mutandis, to all transactions of the Programme.

Article XX

1. The annual accounts of the Programme shall be submitted to the External Auditor of FAO.

2. The annual accounts together with the external auditor's certificate and report shall be submitted to the Committee after review by the FAO Finance Committee and the ACABQ if the latter so desires.

APPENDIX II:

STATISTICS

Table 1: WFP Food Assistance by Category 1982 – 2004
(Shipments and Local Purchases - thousand tons)

Year	Projects (Development)	Emergencies (Sudden)	Emergencies (Protracted)[1]	Total	%Emergencies Sudden and Protracted
1982	1,110	566		1,676	33.77
1987	1,555	606		2,159	28.06
1992	1,395	1,275	1,191	3,861	63.84
1997	1,022	1,126	637	2,786	63.20
2002	586	2,319	922	3,827	84.68
2003	521	4,031	1,374	5,926	91.20
2004	557	1,772	1,220	3,549	84.30

Note:
There are significant fluctuations from year to year in deliveries by category and in toto. However, the long-term trends of declining development assistance and increasing emergency assistance are well reflected in the data.

Source: WFP

[1]. This category of 'emergency assistance' was not in use in 1982 and 1987, at that time being subsumed within the general 'emergencies' category, which covered assistance to all short and long-term emergency operations. For a full explanation see above pages 145-146.

Table 2: WFP Staff
(*Holding Contracts of one year or longer*)

Year	Professional[1]	High Level[2]	General Service[3]	Total[4]
1983[5]	312	5	755	1,072
1987	356	6	1,029	1,391
1991	461	9	1,072	1,550
1998	1,022	11	1,083	2,116
2002	1,250	27	1,407	2,684
2004	1,626	39	1,589	3,254

Source: WFP

[1.] Professionals: grades P1 to D1, including Junior Professional Officers, UN Volunteers and National Professionals, i.e. professional staff from the country in which they are employed.

[2.] Grades D2 and above.

[3.] Clerical and other support staff.

[4.] This total of 'permanent' staff gives a somewhat misleading impression of the scale of WFP's operation. In any one year the organisation employs, in addition, on contracts of varying duration, for example for distributing food to disaster victims, several thousand professional and other staff, including consultants. Some 6,898 and 7,652 were so employed in 2002 and 2004 respectively.

[5.] For 1983 the figures are for established posts, not for staff actually employed.

APPENDIX III:
THE UNITED NATIONS SYSTEM

(As of 1994).

ECONOMIC AND SOCIAL COUNCIL

SPECIALISED AGENCIES
ILO
International Labour Organization
FAO
Food and Agriculture Organization of
the United Nations
UNESCO
United Nations Educational, Scientific
and Cultural Organization
WHO
World Health Organization
IBRD
World Bank
IMF
International Monetary Fund
ICAO
International Civil Aviation
Organization
UPU
Universal Postal Union
ITU
International Telecommunications
Union
WMO
World Meteorological Organization
IMO
International Maritime Organization
WIPO
World International Property
Organization
IFAD
International Fund for Agricultural
Development
UNIDO
United Nations Industrial Development
Organization
GATT
General Agreement on Tariffs and Trade
(Later replaced by WTO, World Trade
Organization)

WFP
World Food Programme
ITC
International Trade Centre
UNCTAD/GATT

**FUNCTIONAL
COMMISSIONS**
Commission for Social
Development
Commission on Human
Rights
Commission on Narcotic
Drugs
Commission on the Status of
Women
Population Commission
Statistical Commission
REGIONAL COMMISSIONS
Economic Commission of
Africa (ECA)
Economic Commission of
Europe (ECE)
Economic Commisssion for
Latin America and the
Caribbean (ECLAC)
Economic and Social
Commission for Asia and the
Pacific (ESCAP)
Economic and Social
Commission for Western
Asia (ESCWA)
**SESSIONAL STANDING
COMMITTEES
EXPERT, AD HOC AND
RELATED BODIES**

INSTRAW
International Research and
Training Institute for the
Advancement of Women
UNCHS
United Nations Centre for
Human Settlements
(Habitat)
UNDP
United Nations
Environment Programme
UNFPA
United Nations Population
Fund
UNCHR
Office of the United
Nations High
Commissioner of Refugees
UNICEF
United Nations Children's
Fund
UNIFEM
United Nations
Development Fund for
Women
UNITAR
United Nations Institute
for Training and Research
UNU
United Nations University
WFC
World Food Council
UNDCP
United Nations
International Drug Control
Programme

REFERENCES

Books and Articles

Abbott, John (1992), *Politics and Poverty: A Critique of the Food and Agriculture Organization of the United Nations,* London and New York: Routledge.

Anstee, Margaret Joan (2003), *Never Learn to Type,* Chichester, UK: John Wiley and Sons.

Bolton, John R (1989), 'The Concept of the "Unitary UN"', *Current Policy,* 1191, July 1989: United States Department of State.

Charlton, Mark W (1992), 'Innovation and inter-organizational politics: the case of the World Food Programme', *International Journal,* XLVII (Summer), Canadian Institute of International Affairs, Toronto, Canada.

Childers, Erskine with Urquhart, Brian (1990), 'A World in Need of Leadership: Tomorrow's United Nations', *Development Dialogue* 1990: 1–2, Uppsala, Sweden: Dag Hammarskjöld Foundation.

Childers, Erskine with Urquhart, Brian (1994), *Renewing the United Nations System,* Uppsala, Sweden: Dag Hammarskjöld Foundation.

FAO (1954), *Disposal of Agricultural Surpluses. Principles Recommended by the FAO.* Rome, Italy: FAO.

FAO (1961), 'Expanded Program of Surplus Food Utilization, Report by the Expert Group to the Director-General of FAO, in *Development through Food: A Strategy for Surplus Food Utilisation,* FFHC Basic Study No.2. Rome, Italy: FAO.

FAO (1985), *Food Aid for Development,* Three Studies by Gerda Blau, Mordecai Ezekiel and BR Sen, Rome: FAO.

Fraser, Colin (1988), *Lifelines: For Africa Still in Peril and Distress,* London: Hutchinson.

Finklestein, Lawrence S (1988), 'The Politics of Value Allocation in the UN

System', in Finklestein (ed), *Politics in the United Nations System*, Durham, US: Duke University Press.

Gaitung, Johan (1986), 'A Typology of United Nations Organisations', in Pitt and Weiss.

Gaitung, Johan (1986), 'On the Anthropology of the United Nations System', in Pitt and Weiss.

Gill, Peter (1986), *A Year in the Death of Africa: Politics, Bureaucracy and the Famine*, London: Collins.

Giorgis, Dawit Wolde (1989), *Red Tears: War, Famine and Revolution in Ethiopia,* Trenton New Jersey: The Red Sea Press, Inc.

Haas, Ernst B (1990), *When Knowledge is Power: Three Models of Change in International Organizations*, Berkley, Los Angeles and Oxford: University of California Press.

Hancock, Graham (1989), *Lords of Poverty: The Power, Prestige and Corruption of the International Aid Business,* New York: The Atlantic Monthly Press.

Hayden, Bill (1996), *Hayden: An Autobiography*, Sydney: Angus and Robertson.

Hossain, Mahabub and Akhash, M Mokaddem (1993), *Public Rural Works for Relief and Development: A Review of the Bangladesh Experience.* Working Papers on Food Subsidies Number 7, Washington DC: IFPRI.

Ingram, James (1989), 'Sustaining Refugees' Human Dignity: International Responsibility and Practical Reality, *Journal of Refugee Studies*, 2 (3), pp. 329-339 and pp. 354-358, Oxford University Press, Oxford.

Ingram, James C (1993a), 'The Future Architecture for Humanitarian Assistance' in Weiss, Thomas G. and Minear, Larry (eds), *Humanitarianism Across Borders: Sustaining Civilians in Times of War*, Boulder, Colorado: Lynne Rienner.

Ingram, James C. (1993b), 'The Politics of Human Suffering', *The National Interest,* Spring 1993, Washington D.C.

Ingram, James (1994), 'The International Response to Humanitarian Emergencies' in Clements, Kevin and Ward, Robin (eds), *Building International Community*, St Leonards, NSW: Allen and Unwin.

Jackson, Tony with Eade, Deborah (1982), *Against the Grain*, Oxford, UK: OXFAM.

Jansson, Kurt, Michael Harris and Angela Penrose (1987), *The Ethiopian Famine*, London and New Jersey: Zed Books.

Luck, Edward C (2004), *UN Reform: A Cause in Search of a Constituency*, Paper prepared for US State Department and National Intelligence Council.

Mintzberg, Henry, (1980), *The Nature of Managerial Work*, New Jersey: Prentice-Hall.

OECD (2006), 'The Development Effectiveness of Food Aid: Does Tying Matter?' *The Development Dimension*, Paris: OECD.

Pitt, David and Weiss, Thomas G (eds) (1986), *The Nature of United Nations Bureaucracies*, Boulder, Colorado: Westview.

Pitt, David (1986), 'Power in the UN Superbureaucracy: A Modern Byzantium?' in Pitt and Weiss (1986).

Righter, Rosemary (1995), *Utopia Lost: The United Nations and World Order*, New York: The Twentieth Century Fund.

Saouma, Edouard (1993), *FAO in the Front Line of Development*, Rome: FAO.

Sen, Amartya (1981), Poverty and Famines: *An Essay on Entitlement and Deprivation*, Oxford, UK: Clarendon Press.

Shaw, D. John, (2001), *The UN World Food Programme and the Development of Food Aid*, Basingstoke, UK and New York, US: Palgrave Macmillan.

Shaw, John & Clay, Edward (1993), *World Food Aid: Experiences of Recipients and Donors*, London and Portsmouth: James Currey and Heinemann.

Singer, Hans, Wood, John and Jennings, Tony (1987), *Food Aid, the challenge and the opportunity*, Oxford, UK: Clarendon Press.

Talbot, Ross B and Moyer, H. Wayne (1987), 'Who Governs the Rome Food Agencies', *Food Policy*, November, 1987, London: Butterworth &Co.

Talbot, Ross B (1990), *The Four World Food Agencies in Rome*, Ames, USA: Iowa State University Press.

Urquhart, Brian and Childers, Erskine (1996), *A World in Need of Leadership: Tomorrow's United Nations*, second edition, Uppsala, Sweden: Dag Hammarskjöld Foundation.

Urquhart, Brian (1990), 'The United Nations and its Discontents', *New York Review of Books*, March 15, 1990, New York.

Williams, Douglas (1987), *The Specialized Agencies and the United Nations: The System in Crisis*, London: C. Hurst & Company.

Wit, Lawrence and Eicher, Carl (1964), *The Effects of United States Agricultural Surplus Disposal Programs on Recipient Countries*, Michigan State University.

WFP and Government of the Netherlands (1983), *Report of Food Aid Seminar, The Hague 3-5 October 1983*, Rome: WFP and Government of the

Netherlands.

World Bank and World Food Programme (1991), *Food Aid in Africa: An Agenda for the 1990s*, Washington, D.C. and Rome.

WFP DOCUMENTS (ROME: WFP)

(1982a) WFP/CFA: SR 1. Summary record of first session of CFA 13.

(1982b) WFP/CFA: 13/20. Report of the CFA on its 13th session, April 1982.

(1982c) WFP/CFA: 14/18. Report of the CFA on its 14th session, October, 1982.

(1983) WFP/CFA: Report of the CFA on its 16th session, October, 1983(1984a) WFP/CFA: 17/9 Add.1. Emergency Operations: Guidelines and Criteria for Emergency Food Aid.

(1984b) WFP/CFA: /17/9 Add.1, Supp.1. Emergency Operations: FAO paper.

(1984c) WFP/CFA: 18/4 Report on WFP personnel problems by the United Nations Joint Inspection Unit.

(1984d) WFP/CFA 18/4 Add.1   ditto.

(1984e) WFP/CFA 18/4 Add 2   ditto.

(1985a) WFP/CFA: 19/8, Review of UN/FAO Joint Taskforce Report.

(1985a) WFP/CFA: 19/9, Report on the Review of basis of costing of services provided by FAO and other specialised agencies.

(1985b) WFP/CFA: 20/20, Report of the CFA on its 20th session, October 1985.

(1986a) WFP/CFA: 21/24, Report of the CFA on its 21st session, May 1986.

(1986b) WFP/CFA: 22/5, Report on WFP management review.

(1986c) WFP/CFA: 22/7, 22/7 Add/1 and Add.2, Evaluation of emergency operations: lessons from the African food crisis.

(1987a)WFP/CFA: 23/5, Review of food aid policies and programmes.

(1987b)WFP/CFA: 23/5 Add.1, Roles of food aid in structural and sector adjustment.

(1987c)WFP/CFA: 23/5 Add.2, The management of funds generated by food-assisted projects.

(1987d) WFP/CFA: 24/5, Monetization of food aid.

(1988a) WFP/CFA: 25/18, Report of the 25th session of the CFA, June 1988, p 54-57.

(1989a) WFP/CFA: 27/7, Review of protracted emergency operations for refugees and displaced persons.

(1989b) WFP/CFA: 27/8 Add.1, Briefing Document in respect of WFP audited accounts for 1986-87.

(1989c) WFP/CFA: 27/8/INF 1, Comments of the FAO Finance Committee (May 1989).

(1989d) WFP/CFA: 27/16, Report of the 27th session of the CFA May/June 1989.

(1989e) WFP/CFA: 28/2 Add.2, Administrative budget estimates for 1990-91: Comments of the ACABQ – October 1989.

(1989f) WFP/CFA: 28/PV/2, Verbatim Record of the Second Session.

(1989g) WFP/CFA: 28/PV/3, Verbatim Record of the Third Session.

(1989h) WFP/CFA: 28/8, Report of the 28th session of the CFA, December 1989.

(1989i) WFP/CFA: 28/PV/4, Verbatim record of the Fourth Session.

(1990a) WFP/CFA: 29/P/6, Status of the WFP Headquarters Agreement.

(1990b) WFP/CFA: 29/P/6 Add. 2, Report of the 54th Session of the FAO Committee on Constitutional and Legal Matters.

(1990c) WFP/CFA: 29/SR/4, Final Summary Record of the Fourth Session.

(1990d) WFP/CFA: 29/13, Report of the CFA on its 29th Session.

(1990e) WFP/CFA: 29/P/7 Add.2, Report by the External Auditor.

(1990f) WFP/CFA: 29/P/7, WFP and FAO relationship issues.

(1990g) WFP/CFA: 29/P/7 Add.5, Joint Statement of the Secretary-General and the Director-General of FAO.

(1990h) WFP/CFA: 29/13, Report of the 29th session of the CFA, June 1990.

(1990i) WFP/CFA: 29/3, Report of the Sub-committee of the Whole on the Governance of WFP.

(1990j) WFP/CFA: 30/INF/3.Comments of the ACABQ on the Financial Report and Statements of WFP for 1998-89, and related matters.

(1990k) WFP/CFA: 30/INF/7, Statement by the Executive Director.

(1991a) WFP/CFA: Report of the First Special Session of the CFA.

(1991b) WFP/CFA: 32/13, Report of the CFA on its 32nd session, December 1991.

(2000) WFP: General Regulations, General Rules, Financial Regulations, Rules of Procedure of Executive Board.

INDEX

Made in the USA
Lexington, KY
03 September 2010